FROM SWEDEN TO AMERICA

From Sweden to America

A History of the Migration

Editors: Harald Runblom and
Hans Norman

A Collective Work of
The Uppsala Migration Research Project

UNIVERSITY OF MINNESOTA PRESS,
MINNEAPOLIS

ACTA UNIVERSITATIS UPSALIENSIS,
UNIVERSITY OF UPPSALA

1976

Studia Historica Upsaliensia, 74
ISSN 0081-6531

Published in Sweden, Norway, Denmark, Finland, and Iceland by
Acta Universitatis Upsaliensis and distributed through
Almqvist & Wiksell International,
Stockholm, Sweden

Published in all other countries except Canada by
University of Minnesota Press,
Minneapolis, USA

Published in Canada by
Burns and MacEachern Limited,
Don Mills, Ontario

ISBN 91-554-0355-7 (AUU)

ISBN 0-8166-0776-1 (UMP)

Library of Congress Catalog Card Number 76-1541

Jacket and Hardcoverdesign Per-Ivar Glaser

Printed in Sweden by
ALMQVIST & WIKSELL Uppsala 1976

Contents

Acknowledgements

The research on mass overseas migration from Sweden which is presented in this book has been performed by a large number of students and scholars within the framework of the research project "Sweden and America after 1860" at the Department of History, Uppsala University. A list of the project members is presented in Appendix 3.

In preparing this book the authors have received a great deal of assistance from many persons. We should like to extend special thanks to Kermit Westerberg, who has translated the major part of the manuscript and to Tua Öhvall, who has done important complementary work with the English text. Margaretha Eriksson has drawn most of the maps, graphs and other illustrations. David Gaunt, Kenneth Lockridge, and John Rogers have checked parts of the manuscript and John Rogers has prepared the General Index.

We are indebted to The Population Association of America for permission to reproduce Everett S. Lee's model on migration factors, published in *Demography,* Vol. 3, 1966, and to Methuen & Co., Ltd. for their willingness to let us incorporate a diagram from Brinley Thomas' book *Migration and Urban Development* (1972). We are also grateful to Prentice-Hall, Inc., who has allowed us to use a diagram from J. A. Estey's *Business Cycles* (1956), and to Princeton University Press for permission to publish a figure by Alan Pred in *The New Urban History* (1975). We finally thank Robert Ostergren, University of Minnesota for the permission to publish two maps (Diagram 2:6 and 2:7); Thorvald Moe, Oslo, who kindly consented to the printing of Diagram 2: 11; and Rolf Adamson, Stockholm University, whose scheme of theoretical analysis is presented on page 63.

Uppsala, January 1976

Introduction

Some more general observations about migration research might be appropriate. The study of migration can be seen as a specialty in its own right where migrational phenomena are isolated and their timing, structure and effects on society and individuals are investigated, and where a comparative point of view is desirable.

Soon the migration scholar will realize that geographic mobility is by no means typical only for an industrial society. Even the old agricultural community was often characterized by an extensive population mobility. That North America had a more mobile population than other continents has been proven to be a myth. Our Scandinavian experience, for example, shows that many areas of Northern Europe had a very high general mobility already at the beginning of the 19th century.

Migration research can also be practiced in its connection with the study of social and economic development. That is to say, we choose the migration variable as an indicator of change. This is natural especially when we deal with external migration, which is the main field of this book. This angle of approach can give new and stimulating insights and perspectives.

Different types of geographic mobility can be discerned. The most important dividing line may be found between voluntary and forced migrations, although this line is not always very easily defined. Our studies have mainly been oriented towards voluntary migrations. This does not mean, however, that we look upon voluntary migrations as more important than population turnover as a consequence of slavery, and political and religious persecutions.

The opportunities for conducting emigration research have differed very much. In many countries there has even been a strong resistance to touch this area of study. That is the reason why the considerable exodus from the East European countries hardly has been systematically investigated at all.

Another general difficulty has been the poor source coverage of most migration movements. The calculations of emigration streams must often be performed with indirect and very unreliable methods. The work with the fairly complete Swedish source material has provided us with inspiration since it enables us to place the external migrations in their proper context of internal and general population mobility.

In this context it must be stressed that most migration research reveals the strong common patterns and consistency of population turnover. Therefore it must be possible to make use of many of our findings, especially those regarding the mechanisms of industrialization and urbanization in other countries with similar experiences and a similar economic development.

1. A Brief History of a Research Project

By Harald Runblom

This book deals with Swedish mass emigration to America from the mid-nineteenth century to 1930. The results presented here have been, for the most part, the work of students and doctoral candidates at the Department of History at Uppsala University. For a number of years now there has existed a research project with the offical name "Sweden and America after 1860: Emigration, Remigration, Social and Political Debate". Unofficially this project has also been called the "Migration Research Project", a fact which clearly indicates that migration has taken a central position in the research.

The Scholarly Situation

The mass emigration to America must be regarded as one of the most profound European experiences of the nineteenth century. Sweden had three and a half million inhabitants in the middle of the century. During a period not much longer than a man's lifetime more than one million Swedes emigrated. It is therefore surprising that few Swedes had studied this emigration before the 1960s. Two major exceptions which provide an important factual base for anyone studying emigration from Sweden are, however, worth mentioning: 1) the work of the prominent statistician Gustav Sundbärg and his assistents collected in an official report of the Commission on Emigration published during the first years of this century, and 2) the geographer Helge Nelson's comprehensive work published in 1943, *The Swedes and the Swedish Settlements in North America.*

Interest in mass emigration has been earlier and much greater in America than in Europe, and the view of the transatlantic migration has been influenced mainly by the receiving countries. Swedish immigrants have, like other ethnic groups, shown a great interest in investigating their immigration and settlement in America. This is illustrated by the long list of books and other printed matter from the Augustana Historical Society and the stream of publications on Swedish immigrants from all over the

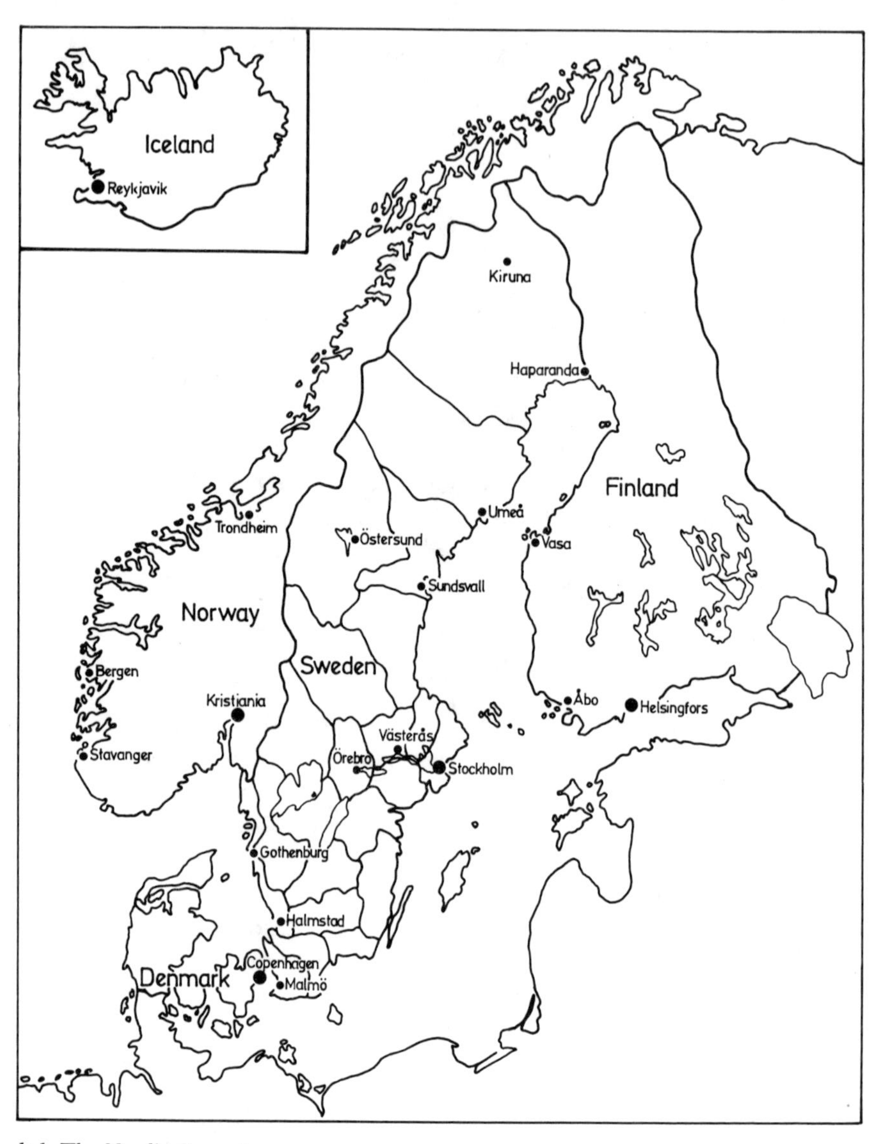

1: 1. The Nordic Countries.

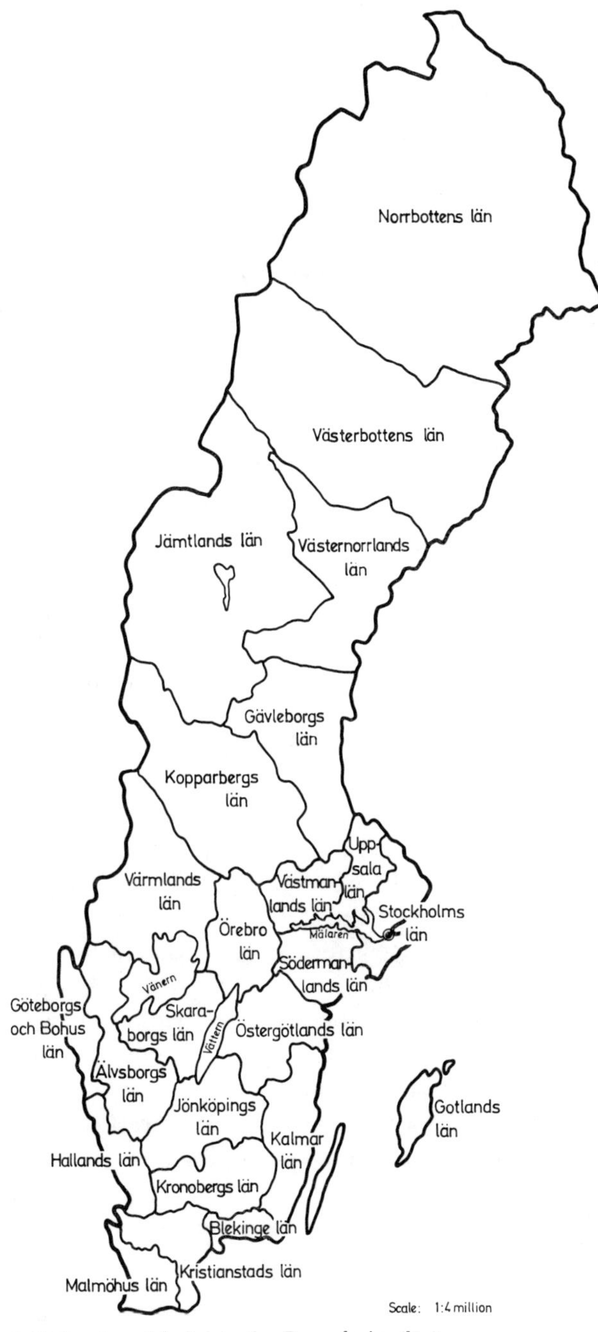

1: 2. Sweden. Administrative Boundaries (*län*).

United States. These publications are typical of the literature written about immigrant groups in America. Interest is often focused on the own nationality, while comparisons between different immigrant groups are almost non-existent. This literature was often a part of the immigrant groups' identification process. There has been a tendency to portray one's own countrymen as good and successful Americans.

The strong interest in emigration research in Sweden since the beginning of the 1960s is not an isolated national phenomenon but rather a part of a general trend in European historiography. The changing status of international emigration research in the period from just before the start of our project (1962) to the present is reflected in the reports given to the International Conferences of the Historical Sciences in Stockholm in 1960, and in San Francisco in 1975. At the Stockholm Conference Frank Thistlethwaite challenged the European historians to direct their efforts to a scientific field that had originated with social scientists rather than historians. Thistlethwaite pointed out that the European background of mass emigration had been largely ignored and suggested that the transoceanic movements ought to be seen in a broad social and economic context. He especially stressed the importance of internal migrations as well as labor and seasonal movements both within Europe and between Europe and other continents. The nature of emigration could not be revealed except through studies of its relationship with the industrial and demographic "revolutions".[1]

Fifteen years after the Stockholm Conference it is evident that European scholars have studied mass emigration from many different angles. At the San Francisco Conference, in a point-by-point discussion of Thistlethwaite's proposals, Sune Åkerman stressed the shift of emphasis from the receiving to the delivering countries. A new approach to social history has also established new and more subtle theoretical frameworks for these studies.[2] This is also reflected in the re-interpretation of Brinley Thomas' theory of the interplay of migration and capital flows in the transatlantic economy as presented in Chapter 2 of this volume.

During the last decade a significant amount of emigration research has been done in a number of European countries as exemplified in a series of sub-reports to the San Francisco Conference.[3] The present situation is characterized by a wealth of new data about the background of emigration

[1] F. Thistlethwaite (1960).
[2] S. Åkerman (1975), pp. 15 ff.

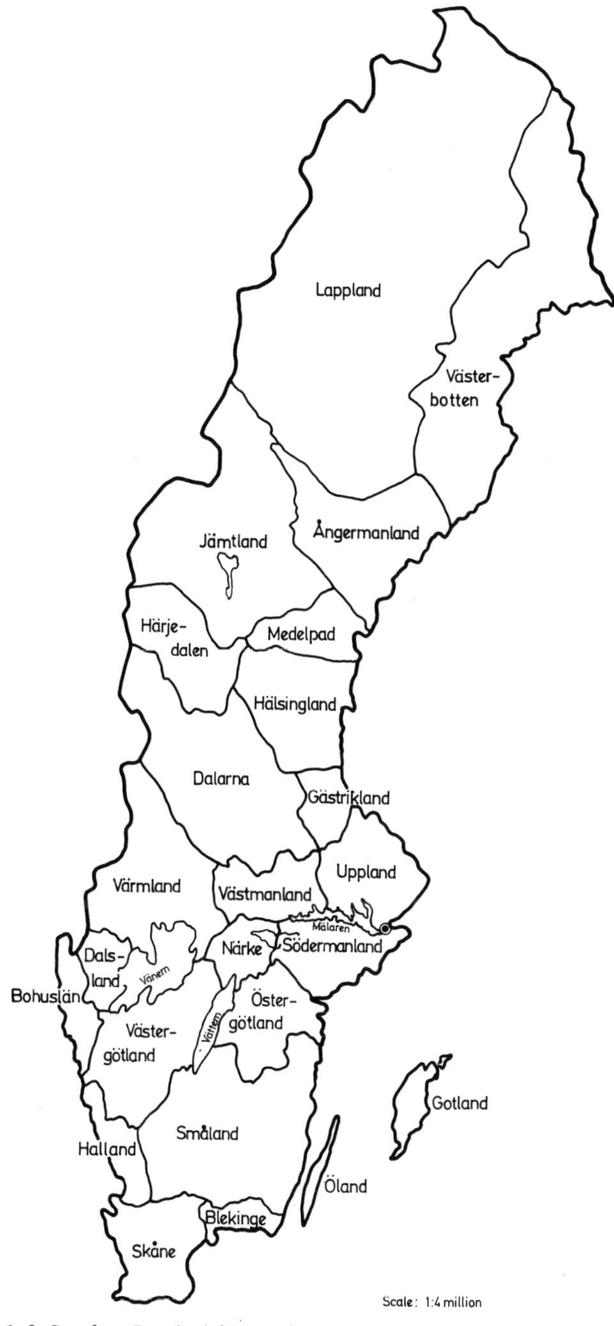

1: 3. Sweden. Provincial Boundaries (*landskap*).

in various countries, and there is now a growing demand for coordination through comparative studies and overall interpretations. This is not the place for an evaluation of individual contributions to migration research, but special mention should be made of the new interest in ethnicity among social scientists and historians in the United States and Canada during the last decade, an interest which has created a new basis for the study of cultural interaction between immigrants' new environment and the countries of their origin.[4]

The Work within the Uppsala Group

The decade of the 1960s and the early years of the 1970s, through the founding of project groups, brought about new possibilities and new contours to Swedish historical research. Some mention of the team-work of the Uppsala Group is here in order. More than thirty scholars on the graduate (licentiate and Ph.D.) level have been attached to the project. Judged by Swedish standards this is a large group.[5] In rough outline the studies can be attributed to the following main fields:

1. Collection and analysis of demographic sources.
2. Local studies treating the background, the structure and the course of emigration.
3. Activities of steamship companies and emigrant agencies. Spread of information and propaganda.
4. Process of innovation.
5. Debate on emigration and emigration policy.
6. Internal migration, seasonal migrations and inter-Nordic labor mobility.
7. Interplay between urban and industrial centers and their rural surroundings.
8. Migration and social mobility.
9. Remigration.
10. Colonization, demographic patterns and the assimilation of immigrants in America.
11. Migration of students and scholars.
12. Swedish relations to Latin America, Ethiopia and China.

[3] G. Dupeux (1975) and appendices.
[4] For a review of trends in immigration studies see R. J. Vecoli (1972).
[5] A list of the members in Appendix 3.

As can be seen from this survey the planning of the work has been flexible. The focus has moved from studies dealing predominantly with external movements to internal and seasonal migrations and finally to social and demographic structures in general, especially the history of the family. Most of our research has been presented in the form of doctoral dissertations. This means that our cooperation has had two goals, to do research in our special field and for most members of the group also to obtain a Ph.D.-exam. The cohesion of our special type of team-work has been based upon seminars, tutoring and a common longterm planning of the research.

During the years of our research activities we have been able to create a net-work of contacts both with other university disciplines and with international scholars. These contacts have taken different forms. We have had the opportunity to arrange courses and conferences and to welcome visiting scholars who have stayed for a longer or shorter time in our workshop. At the same time we have had the privilege to present our own results for an international audience. For us the establishment of a Nordic cooperation has also been valuable. Within the frame of this cooperation we have been able to start a new journal, American Studies in Scandinavia, edited in Uppsala 1968–73, which has published articles from Nordic emigration research as well as other material from the American studies field in general.

Another instance of Nordic cooperation has been the research project "Nordic Emigration" which among other things is preparing a Nordic emigration atlas. Some maps from this atlas have been published in this book. In the same vein we have tried to reach the many dedicated local historians of the mass emigration. To some extent this contact has been established through three special institutions, *Emigrantinstitutet* (The Emigrant Institute) in Växjö, *Emigrantregistret* (The Emigrant Register of Värmland) in Karlstad and *The American-Swedish Institute,* Minneapolis, USA.

We have received strong financial backing from different foundations. An initial important grant was given to us by the *American Council of Learned Societies* (1962–1968). *Statens Humanistiska Forskningsråd* (The Swedish Humanistic Research Council) has subsidized our project in a generous manner during the period 1964–1976. From 1968–1975 we have also had a substantial support from *Riksbankens Jubileumsfond* (The Bank of Sweden Tercentenary Foundation) which enabled us to expand our activities a great deal.

A most important aspect of project research is to find suitable localities. Thanks to *Uppsala Universitet* (the University of Uppsala) this problem has been solved in a very satisfactory manner. Finally we must mention the support given by *Arbetsmarknadsstyrelsen* (The Swedish Labor Market Board) in the collection and processing of research material concerning Swedish migration.

2. Theories and Methods of Migration Research

By Sune Åkerman

a. Introduction

Migration research, like research in general, can be of a deductive or inductive character. Both approaches are represented to a great extent within the extensive migration research pursued within different university disciplines. The work performed by the Uppsala Group in this field is characterized by a broad empirical study of external population exchange in its connection with other migrational movements. We have tried to avoid research traditions and methods within any one single discipline. Since interest has been focused mainly on mass emigration to North America, the task will turn out to be of a historical character with its possibilities and its limitations. At the same time it must be emphasized that there have been attempts to link up with studies concerning the important and much discussed migration problems of our time. This aim has had its consequences for the choice of methods, which often diverge from the usual historical ones.

The work and planning of the Uppsala Group can be regarded as an explorative research. Gradually, by raising and investigating various partial issues of the large mass emigration complex we have tried to create a sort of overall view of the mechanisms of the external migrations. This strategy is reflected in the outline of this chapter, which intends to give a survey of structural observations and various possibilities for combining them.[1] Finally, an attempt to build a more coherent model will be pre-

[1] In this delineation, *structure* will be used as a key concept. This term is ambiguous, however, and different meanings can be attached to it. This is of course confusing. On the first level it stands for *distribution,* cf. demographers' concept of *age structure.* Even if we intend to show something more complicated it is often the average position of only a few variables which constitutes the structure. As Dennis L. Meadows et al. (1973) pointed out, it is, however, the interplay between the variables which is most important. This has also been stressed by German scholars (G. Mackenroth 1955 and H. Linde 1959). They have suggested a new concept "Generative Strukturen". Thereby they introduce a new dimension: In contrast to a population of animals, a human demographic and social structure is able to react upon itself

sented. One main theme which emerges is the accentuation of the behavioral aspects of migration. The conception of the human being as *homo economicus* is thereby questioned at the same time as great areas of economic research concerning migration form a basis for an attempt to suggest a new model.

In its original shape this chapter also included three comprehensive parts: *Searching for Structure, Spatial Aspects of Migrational Movements* and *The Adaptation Process.* These themes were intended to emphasize how important it is to search for patterns by special empirical investigations in order to reach new levels of generalization and more theoretical insights. This research strategy was most clearly reflected in Searching for Structure.

Spatial Aspects was intended to stress the importance of cartographic analyses which are indispensable for this type of research. This delineation was based on a series of maps and other graphical illustrations.

The part devoted to The Adaptation Process was at the same time an attempt to survey the vast literature which has been produced in this field during the post-war period. It goes without saying that the assimilation problem is one of the most central for the migrants and that this book could have dealt with this issue more thoroughly.[2]

The other two themes have only been touched upon since they have been covered in other chapters as well where there also are some further examples of the development of methods. There has also been some consideration of space and this version is predominantly an attempt to isolate certain theoretical aspects.

in a deliberate way. My own use of the concept is very close to Linde's (1959) but does not resemble the more metaphysic meaning of the word that can be found within the "structural school" of Claude Lévi Strauss and others.

It is astonishing to realize that the great system builders of the 19th century have shown so little interest in the migrational phenomenon. That is the reason why we have difficulty in finding starting-points in their works for our theoretical approaches when we more directly study the development and conditions of population mobility. This is almost a paradox in the case of Karl Marx who was so profoundly interested in the relation between city and countryside. As always, there is of course an indirect impact from these grand attempts to interpret the structural changes of different societies. Among the generalizers, only T. Parsons and E. G. Ravenstein will appear in the following, although I do not wholeheartedly agree with their scholarly orientation.

[2] From slightly differing points of view the Adaptation Process has been treated by Tedebrand, Norman, and Carlsson in Chapters 8 and 9.

b. On the Definition of Migration

It is necessary to comment on the special terminology that is developed by migrational researchers. To begin with there is a main difference between *external and internal* migration. External migration implies both *emigration* and *immigration*. By definition these migrants cross a national border. *Transocean* migration which is also called *intercontinental* is a special type of this external migration. One and the same migrational stream can be called emigration or immigration depending on whether it is seen from the point of view of the *delivering* or *receiving* country. Immigration is often equivalent with *re-migration*. There is no special term for external re-migration. Consequently this word can be used both about re-migration from, e.g., North and South America to former delivering countries in Europe and the counterstream which always occurs in connection with extensive migration from the countryside to urban areas when former migrants return to agricultural areas. When this re-migration is not directed to the migrants' birthplaces or parishes of earlier settlement but to neighboring areas we talk about a *boomerang* migration. Movements which advance step by step from small places to more densely populated and urbanized districts are called *migration by stages*. If such a general migrational movement does not occur in a series of moves by the *same individual* this phenomenon is called *chain migration*. The occurrence and extent of these different migrations has an obvious theoretical implication.

Concerning internal migration the words emigration and immigration are replaced by *out-migration* and *in-migration*. These movements are then qualified in different ways. It is for example important to tell whether people moved from a lower level of industrialization and urbanization to a higher one. This is designated *progressive* migration. The reverse is called *regressive*. When moves are performed on the same level it is called *interchange or circular migration* and it implies no considerable changes, either for the individual or for the delivering or receiving areas. It is also possible to link up with scientific terminology and compare it to *steady-state movements*.

When migration is connected with structural changes and re-allocation of population it is called *effective*. This phenomenon seems to be related to the distance which is covered. Hence *long distance migrations* often gain considerable *net effects*. *Short distance migration* can also be effective, though the distance factor generally implies that re-migration will decrease with increasing distance. The distance factor has been pointed out as most

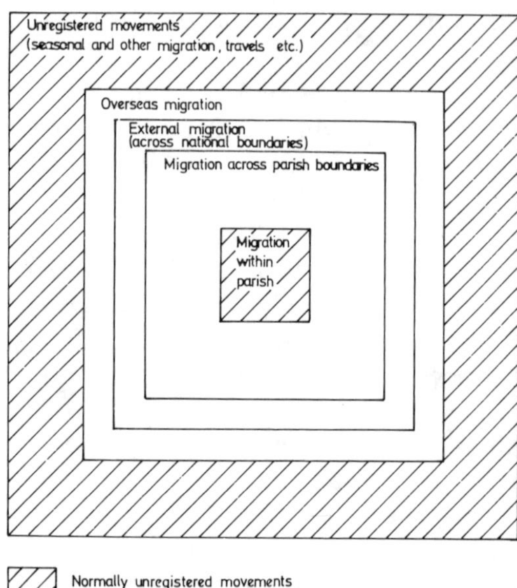

2:1. Different Levels of Population Mobility.

important and this requires a further specification. Migration can be stratified into short distance movements within a zone with a radius of 10–20 km, an intermediate distance zone within 50 km and a long distance zone farther than 50 km. These limits are of course operational and have no deeper significance for our interpretations. *Figure 2:1* is an attempt to illustrate the total population movement. It can be seen that short distance movements are to a great extent performed within the lowest administrative unit that is covered by statistics. This is called *local* or *intra-parish* migration. Since these movements are poorly covered in the empirical material it is a difficult item to treat; if these administrative units are quite large or of various sizes a considerable part of the total migration eludes scholarly analysis.

Seasonal or *labor migrations* could last from a couple of weeks up to half a year or more. They were influenced by conditions of harvest, lumbering in the wintertime and brick production or construction works in the summertime etc. Obviously these movements which were of a great importance in the agrarian society as well as during the first stages of industrialization have been only sporadically covered by our source material. They are normally not defined as migration but this must not conceal that they are related to migration in general. This might be reversed; there are considerable "migrations" which rather should be equated with seasonal movements. Improved communications have created the possibility of migration and re-migration within a calendar day. So-called *commuters* who travel from their place of living to their work are by no means a new phenomenon but can first be traced to the urbanization of the late 1800s. This interesting field is hard to treat in historical source material. The same can also be said about *job mobility,* i.e. the shift of work places or work position which might or might not cause geographical mobility.

There are good reasons to add to this process of defining migration a more thorough commentary:

1. By means of classification or typologization we can fix the content of a "migration" and thereby interpret its significance and function. This method has been recommended by W. Petersen, among others, in the Encyclopedia of Social Sciences. It is obvious, for example, that it can be both necessary and effective to isolate "military mobility" (movements by military conscripts) from other types of migration. Such mobility is, of course, steered by other forces than those affecting labor market mobility. Consequently, it not only claims an entirely unique pattern but also requires its own set of explanations.

Petersen is highly consistent in applying his classification and thereby rejects the significant overlapping which appears to exist between different types of "migrations". Consequently, he questions the fact that certain general features can be traced and attributed to migration. It is difficult to accept this fundamental idea of cognitive theory. For this reason I have chosen to work with "population mobility" as the overarching concept and to make distinctions between different geographical movements on practical grounds, since the interpretation of migrational development has also to be made on the basis of contextual analysis. Therefore, it is essential to observe the interplay between different migrational movements.

One can add to this the fact that French research has experimented with Petersen's line of argumentation. J.-P. Poussou, for example, has worked with a definition of seasonal migrations, temporary migrations, and "military mobility" under the larger concept of "migration". The danger with this method emerges very clearly in Poussou's case when he also classifies "*glissement*" (migration by stages) as one type of migration, and movements from the countryside to the cities and other economic centers as another type.[3] We obtain a confusion of criteria which can only destroy our at-

[3] J. P. Poussou (1970) esp. p. 22.

tempts to gain clarity in this definition problem. It is altogether obvious that these two types of mobility cannot easily be distinguished from one another on either practical or theoretical grounds.

However, the arbitrariness in these definitions is not the end of the matter. Poussou also isolates *brassage* or micro-mobility from migration. The idea here is apparently that *brassage* does not lead to any "systematic changes in terms of the migrant individuals". This aspect does not lack significance, but then neither seasonal migrations nor temporary migrations can be classified as migration.

2. In our studies we frequently aim to encompass social and economic changes in connection with geographical mobility. Like Poussou, we can use this aspect of total mobility in order to isolate systematic changes from movements which do not lead to any changes whatsoever. The sociologist J. J. Mangalam has been most consistent in recommending such a distinction. To illustrate his viewpoint he refers to the pendulum movements of university teachers across the American continent, as an example of mobility which ought not to be classified as migration. The situation is entirely different when a farmer in-migrates to a city: there the process of adjustment expresses itself in a change of social system, a change of occupation, etc. Yet it is also apparent that obtaining this degree of distinction in consequences can tend to be impractical as well as troublesome in terms of a historical material.[4]

3. Another important dimension is *voluntary–involuntary* migration. Here our interest is focused on the *motives* which can have effectivized the decision to migrate. On the whole, we seem to be working primarily with voluntary movements, but it is not difficult to find migrations which have an involuntary character. Examples of this include movements by political refugees, which in certain periods have proved to be highly extensive. Mention can also be made of religiously motivated migrations which frequently took the form of involuntary movement.

Yet even less dramatic forms of geographic mobility can, at least on a theoretical level, be classified as voluntary–involuntary. By way of example we can take mobility which coincided with conditions on the labor market. One can theorize that migrations during favorable business cycles ought to be a more direct consequence of voluntary changes of employment, inasmuch as the choice of employment broadens. On the other hand, unfavorable business cycles force many persons to leave their jobs as a result

[4] J. J. Mangalam (1968).

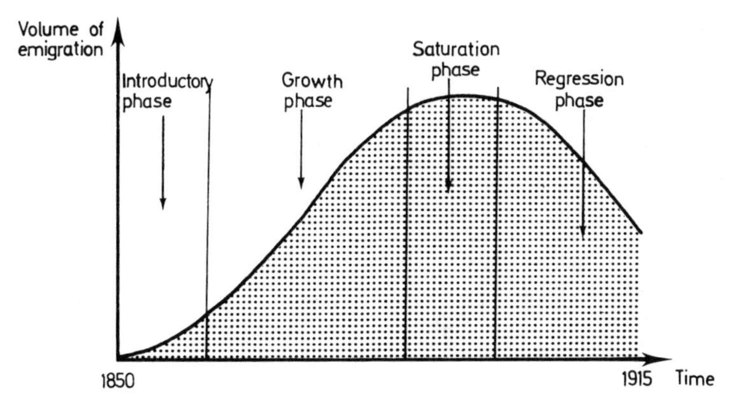

2:2. A Theoretical Growth Process.

of lay-offs and dismissals. American labor economists and their Scandinavian colleagues have obtained research results which indicate that this is an important aspect of the definition problem.[5] Obviously, it is difficult to treat this aspect in terms of remote historical periods, but it still warrants pertinent consideration.

c. Searching for Sequences

It is quite necessary for all historians to consider the time dimension. Many researchers, especially those who are interested in social and economic change have tried to systematize their observations in the form of phase developments.[6] It has been natural for the historically inclined migration scholars to link up with this tradition.

Emigration as a Process of Growth

The development of mass emigration from Sweden to North America, analyzed in detail in Chapter 5, can be portrayed tentatively by way of a growth curve. Research has frequently used such a construction to describe so-called innovation processes. In Figure 2: 2 the growth curve has been adjusted in line with the time axis in order to illustrate emigration

[5] B. Rundblad (1962).

[6] E. Tuma (1961) gives a survey of the approach of different scholars to this problem. Introduction, pp. 18–43.

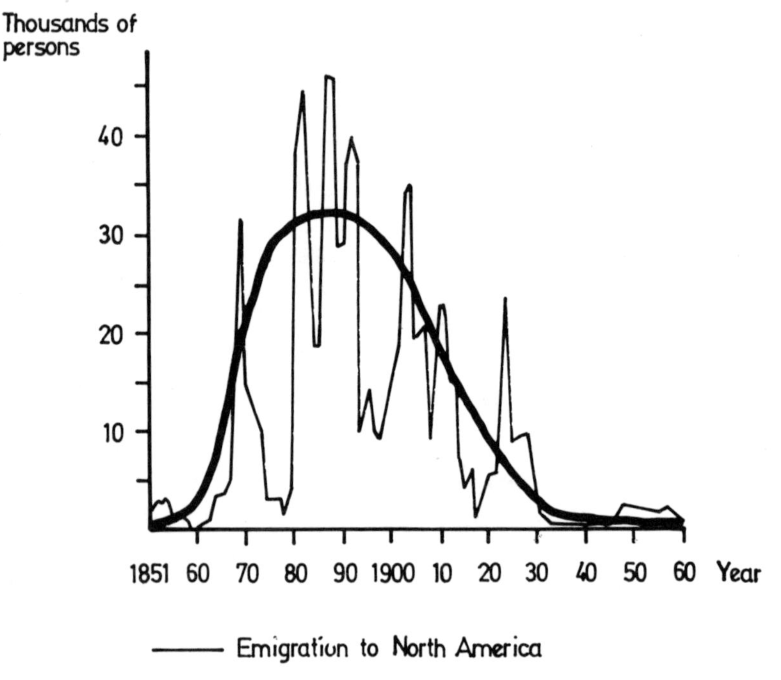

2: 3. Registered Swedish Emigration 1851–1960 Compared with an Approximate Growth Curve.

from Sweden. Emigration from other European countries had a different timing: in other words, their growth curves may have a reciprocal phase-shift relationship.

As shown in Figure 2: 3 we can theorize that an introductory phase with only a few scattered acceptances is followed by a strong growth phase which, of course, can vary in relation to external circumstances. This leads to a saturation phase, after which the growth curve declines during a longer or shorter period of time.

This represents the normal growth process. However, we can also theorize a renewed upsurge of emigration where the curve takes the form of a double S.

The regressive phase can also take a steep or more moderate angle of inclination. If we test this hypothesis and observe Swedish mass emigration as a growth process we find that the annual emigration rates in the official statistics approximate a growth curve. The sharp notch in this curve may largely be due to external factors which have disturbed the self-generating effect of emigration. Such factors include the American Civil War, World War I, and special constellations of trade and business cycles. Hence economic prosperity in the country of emigration may coincide with a severe recession in the country of immigration. At a later stage in this discussion I will return to the dramatic oscillations in the growth curve and advance other possible explanations for this phenomenon.

Is it possible to relate this construct to the well-known oscillation caused by demographic echo-effects? As was the case in Sweden during the 1850s, these effects arise as a result of unusually high birth rates over several years' time, which subsequently reproduce themselves and exert extra pressure on the labor market around the period 1875–1880. It should be possible for us to amalgamate these two perspectives without disarranging the empirical data. This would provide a welcome opportunity for tracing *a combined effect,* which can conceivably help to explain the dramatic fluctuations of the emigration curves.

Emigration as an Innovation Process

Studies of the innovation process have been successfully conducted for the purpose of delineating the way in which a rural population began to use certain tools and machines or the way in which an urban population accepted certain articles of consumption.[7] Research has frequently had the ambition of analyzing a simple consumer pattern and capturing changes in basic value judgements which may be reflected in this type of behavior. However, it encounters greater difficulties in studying the emergence of changes in a political, religious, or cultural value system. A moment's hindsight tells us that the introduction of a new and different migrational behavior in a geographical region may give rise to a diffusion process which has more in common with the complicated changes in value structures.

We often take for granted that an innovation is something which affects a population from the outside and receives gradual acceptance by larger sections of this population. However, this does not always have to be the case. It is also possible that the innovation arises within a given population and subsequently spreads to others. Research in this field has focused interest on the innovation phenomenon *per se* and on the chronological dimension in a study population. It is essential that we delineate the

[7] P. Lazarsfeld (1972).

changes in a study population which can either facilitate the spread of an external innovation or serve as the breeding ground for an internal innovation. As we will see, these distinctions are important for our theoretical considerations.

A further distinction must be made at this point. Although a growth curve can enable us to capture all processes of diffusion, we must not draw the conclusion that every growth process is obviously related to diffusion *per se.* This is true at least in our type of research, if we theorize that diffusion must have a geographic and social dimension. I will return to this topic in another context. Here I will simply make an attempt to combine several basic ideas from innovation research with a wide range of observations which seem to disclose that streams of migration contain a strong self-generative element.

The structuralization of a growth process into different phases remains a rather arbitrary procedure. This is especially true of the lines drawn between different phases. At the same time, however, we must be allowed to draw operational boundaries which are of pedagogical and analytical value. On the other hand, we must avoid being influenced by our own phase creations and refrain from reading into them more than what is allowed by our empirical observations.[8]

Introductory Phase

Theoretically speaking, an initial growth phase can develop over a relatively long period of time. External factors as well as basic structural features in a population which has been exposed to an innovation can delay or accelerate this growth. It should be pointed out here that situations which do not lead to a rise of innovation acceptance are equally worth the interest and attention of research.

In this discussion I will take a critical attitude toward energetic efforts made by certain sectors of research to explain migration as a chance phenomenon.[9] If this line of reasoning has any relevance at all, it is with regard to the initial growth phase. It cannot be denied that the early acceptances of a migration offer have a somewhat haphazard nature. At the same time, however, the acceptances which assume decisive im-

[8] Limits between phases are thoroughly treated by E. M. Rogers (1971).

[9] See for example N. W. Henry, R. McGinnis, and H. W. Tegtmeyer (1971). Cf. also the so-called Monte Carlo model presented by T. Hägerstrand (1953).

portance for the subsequent process cannot merely be described in terms of a stochastic process. In discussing the spread of information, researchers have succeeded to some degree in isolating certain persons acting as opinion or information agents. Thus a two-step spread of news and knowledge can be discerned.[10] We have reason to expect that this particular group of individuals plays an active role in the initial phase of mass emigration.

We should also be able to trace an opinion-making group of this type in Sweden during the 1840s and 1850s particularly in the urban environment. In view of the international character of this innovation, the major port cities of Gothenburg, Stockholm, and Gävle occupy central interest with their transoceanic contacts and possible groups of opinion makers. Other port cities, particularly those with intra-European contacts, as well as major inland centers, also played a role in this context. However, this emphasis on the importance of the urban environment for the spread of information must not override our previous observations regarding the contact sphere in rural areas. The prominent, internal exchange of population as early as the mid-1800s must be regarded as an indication that the rural environment had its own agents of opinion and that strong possibilities for a relatively rapid spread of information existed at least on the regional level.

Growth Phase

This next phase implies a definite upswing in the curve. Stray instances of emigration, such as scattered groups of individuals who gathered around a leading figure characterized as an agent of opinion, now take the form of a more even stream of migrants. While the initial phase was represented by ten, twenty, or a hundred or somewhat more emigrants every month, the growth phase sees movements by thousands of persons in one or two weeks.

However, this does not mean to say that this stage of emigration structurally matched the general population turnover in the country of origin. We can expect a rather strong selectivity both in terms of individuals and geographical regions. The rural population should emerge as a stronger element here but only in those areas which had close contacts with

[10] This observation or the so-called two-step hypothesis is especially associated with the American sociologist P. Lazarsfeld and his studies on distribution of new tools and machinery within selected rural areas in the US.

the special types of urban environments mentioned above. The impulses to emigrate can be expected to have a response among sectors of the population which have slightly above-average positions on the social scale. In the countryside this would essentially apply to homestead owners; in cities, artisans and similar groups. We can also expect to see a tendency toward group emigration in this phase, as reinforced by transport factors and the entire context of emigration. Such movement might conceivably take different forms, not only in terms of families and immediate neighbors but also more organized contingents. In view of transport factors and conditions in the receiving country, it is also likely that men dominate this movement to a certain extent. In the opening stages of the growth phase cities should play a somewhat larger role than rural areas with regard to emigrant recruitment.[11]

We can weigh the issue of dividing the growth phase into an early and a late period. It could then be said that emigration becomes a genuine mass phenomenon in the latter stage of growth. As far as structure is concerned, emigration should have increasing similarities to total internal migration. Although there is no substantial difference between this stage of growth and the saturation phase, we can still expect to see a play of dynamics which may be most obvious in the regional spread of emigration. If our theoretical premises are correct, this late period of growth must see a constant change in the regional pattern of emigration, whereby new areas are caught up in this movement. Strong territorial gains ought to be made even in this late stage of growth.

Saturation Phase

During the saturation phase Swedish emigration is represented by movements of hundreds of thousands of persons over such short time intervals as five-year periods. We can assume that mass emigration structure at this point matches that of internal population turnover. Then, the following features should emerge: lowered average ages among emigrants; a more even distribution between men and women, which perhaps also leads to a certain overrepresentation by women; reduced emigration by families and large groups; and perhaps a lack of distinct selectivity among emigrants in terms of occupational skills and personal characteristics. Moreover, the regional spread of movement should by then have reached its maximum extent.

[11] Changes of migrational composition over time are discussed more closely in Chapter 5.

Regression Phase

It is natural that research on the innovation process focuses central interest on the initial phases of development. However, the regression phase also warrants attention as a valuable illustration of the entire process. Like the initial phases, it is to some extent dependent upon the play of external factors. If, as in the case of Sweden, we can work with a diminishing economic gap between the delivering and receiving country, then emigration must assume more of the character of labor market mobility. Factors which conceivably promoted this tendency are the rapid development of the transport sector and the gradual rise of general levels of information. Our knowledge of migrant labor movements would lead us to the theoretical observation that the proportion of male emigrants increases to a substantial degree and that the average emigrant age is presumably reduced somewhat further. Female emigration should not only take the traditional form of family movements and represent such limited labor market sectors as domestic help but also include industrial labor. As far as the regional distribution is concerned, it is reasonable to theorize a contraction of the recruitment. In other words, the central traditional emigration districts should remain, whereas more peripheral areas should rapidly cease to recruit any emigrants at all. This phase should also see the cessation of recruitment from the lower middle-class bracket which figured in an early stage of emigration and perhaps continued during peak years of movement.

It must be emphasized again that this combined innovation and growth model of emigration provides a simplified picture of the conceivable development. It can serve, however, as a supplement to other general model constructions which I will discuss later on.[12] At the same time, I readily admit that the inner logic in this model can be questioned in certain respects. It can also be said that specifications excluded for reasons of space are needed here and that situational aspects can probably be introduced in several contexts. As far as the latter are concerned, however, it should be remembered that this model attempts to develop a system approach. The nucleus of our thesis is the self-generative effect of migration. This is an empirical observation which has been made in a number of contexts, and it will serve as one of the connecting thoughts in this book.

[12] A fairly successful attempt to test the fundamental features of this model is performed by A. Wirén (1975), who presents the development in a southern Swedish region (Blekinge) with stress laid on the initial phases. Compare also B. Kronborg and T. Nilsson (1975).

The Self-Generating Effect

There seems to be some uncertainty as to the definition and interpretation of the self-generating effect. Moreover, critics maintain that it is an assumption in the above model and that we have failed to define the explanatory capacity of self-acceleration. It is held that this model can only be tested on a micro-level. Such criticism probably stems from the argument that the self-generating effect occurs only through personal contacts and that research must therefore focus on the individual in order to determine how these contacts influenced the entire process.[13]

The latter is based on a misconception, for it is possible to make observations on an aggregate level as well. Even a rather cursory analysis of the cartographical material in Chapter 5 demonstrates this. The impression left by these maps is that districts which recruited emigrants at an early stage retained this pattern later on. What we can observe here is an important dimension of all migrational sequences, namely a *consistency of the direction and goal of migration.* Prior studies have observed this in the context of internal population turnover. Mass emigration reveals similar features. In other words, the key to understanding this consistency is the self-generating effect of migration. It alone can explain why a certain area, which in other respects does not differ from neighboring regions, continually sends a disproportionately large number of migrants to a specific destination. The spontaneous element in these migration sequences is not to be exaggerated, however. The emigration to North America appears to have been influenced by the transport organization and emigrant agencies. So we must be open to the possibility of external impact on the course of movement. We will deal with this topic at a later stage of discussion.[14]

d. The Confrontation between Model and Empirical Data

In effect, it appears reasonable to regard the course of mass emigration as a growth process and to assign major importance to this self-generating mechanism. Moreover, we have been able to isolate this effect from other factors with the use of a multi-variate analysis. This research will be

[13] B. Odén in *Beretning* (1971).

[14] See below, Chapter 7.

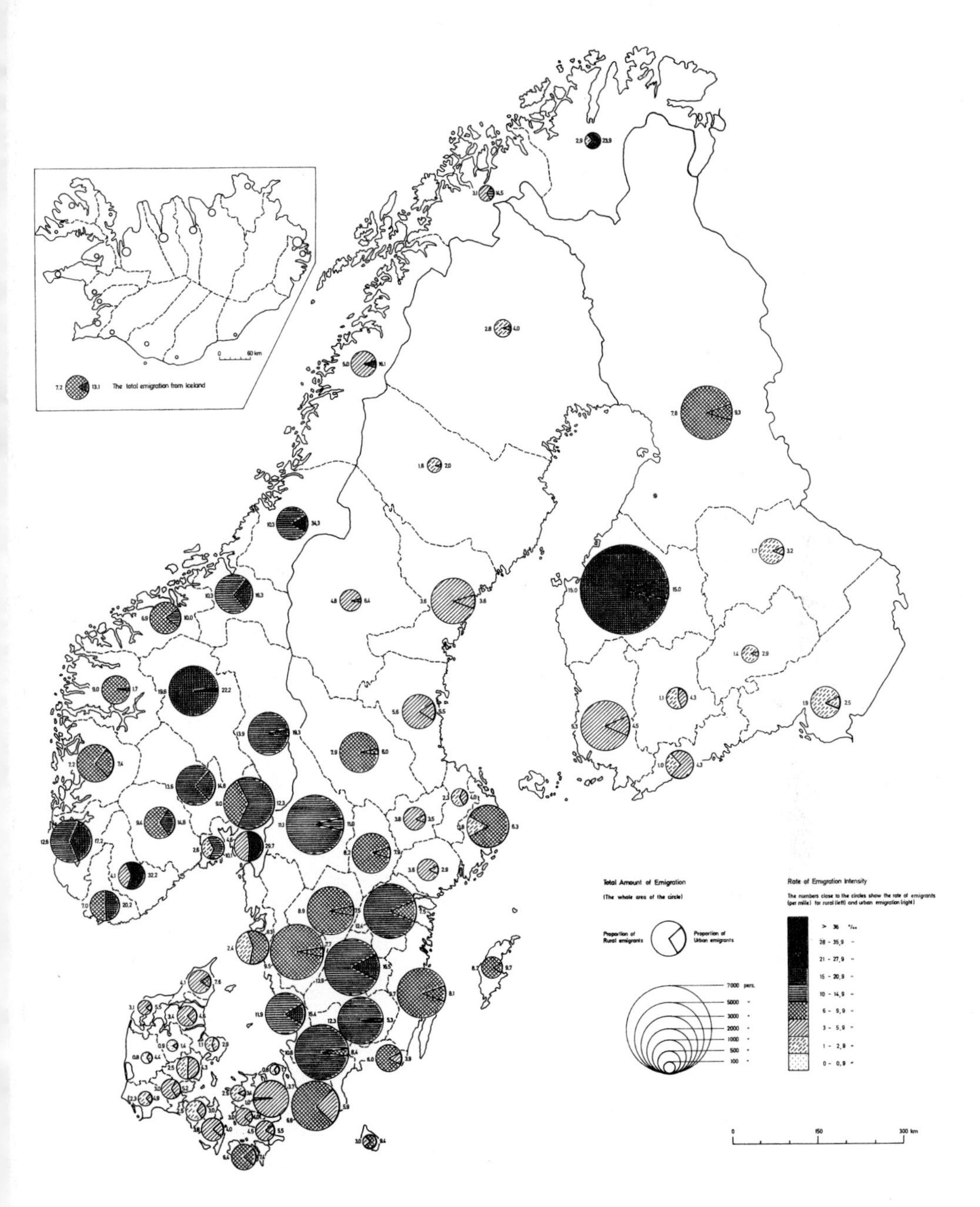

2:4. The Peak Years of Urban and Rural Emigration.
Source A Nordic Emigration Atlas under Preparation by a Group of Scholars in the Research Project "Nordic Emigration".

presented in a later section.[15] But how does the diffusion effect enter into the picture here?

To begin with, Figure 2:4 can shed light on the role of cities in the mass emigration from the Nordic countries. Generally speaking they seem to have had the predicted key position in the information and communication system. A rapid growth of the inclination to emigrate can be registered. This map illustrates only the culmination period of the mass emigration in each country (the 1880s in all countries except Finland where the period 1900–1909 has been chosen). The frequency rates show that the emigration was stronger and in many cases much stronger in the urban than in the rural areas. Mapping of an earlier period would have given the same result. The interplay between urban and rural emigration, however, has been much more complicated than Figure 2:4 seems to imply.

The next stage of our analysis will be to study another set of maps produced in the *Nordic Emigration Atlas*. They show the timing, intensity and spread of the mass emigration in five-year periods from 1865–1914. The importance of a comparative method of analysis is clearly illustrated.[16]

The maps show that mass emigration began at different points in time in the five countries. It appears as if the development at the end of the 1860s had reached the growth phase in Norway and, to a lesser degree, in Sweden. On the other hand, Danish emigration had only reached the initial phase of growth, whereas emigration from Finland and Iceland had not even developed to that point. It must be emphasized that the legends of our maps were drawn in order to carefully register this important initial phase of growth.

These maps only cover emigration by the rural population. Yet they deal with a majority of emigrants since the economies of these countries still had a strong agrarian character at the turn of the century 1900. At the same time there is reason for us to return to urban emigration later on. As mentioned above, emigration from the Nordic countries represented three different stages of development during the last five years of the 1860s. It is valuable for us that two countries, Finland and Iceland, illustrate a *tabula*

[15] See below, Chapter 6.

[16] It seems to be of special interest to compare the pattern of emigration diffusion in the German-speaking part of the European continent with the Nordic one. W. Köllman and P. Marschalck (1974), pp. 509ff. (Cf. also the map material in J. Puskas (1975) p. 35 with its strong ethnic implications.) Such a comparison reveals the importance of *inheritance laws* to emigration in certain areas of Europe. W. Conze (1948–1951).

rasa at this point. In their case and, to a certain degree, in the case of Denmark we can follow the development from the very beginning.[17]

Finland can serve as an illustrative example. An analysis of the initial phase shows that our growth model alone does not sufficiently explain the development. The possible sphere of contacts between different sectors of the population should single out southern and southwestern Finland, and especially the coastal areas near the two largest cities of Helsinki and Turku, as conceivable centers for the spread of emigration behavior. At the same time we should expect that this behavior reached the eastern and northern sections of the country at a relatively late date. Moreover, we can assume an intermediate position for the northern coastline along the Gulf of Bothnia and, in particular, for the province of Österbotten which had long-standing contacts with Sweden. To our surprise, we find that some northern and eastern regions were the first to be affected by emigration. This occurred at the same time as the first emigration from some small areas along the Österbotten coastline while nothing has apparently happened in southern and southwestern Finland. It is also striking that the Åland Islands, which by tradition served as a bridge between the Stockholm area in Sweden and southwestern Finland, are unaffected by emigration at this stage.

We did not expect the Finnish emigration to reach the proportions of its maximum extension during such a short period as a decade. Moreover, this 10–15 year period coincides with the very low frequency of Scandinavian emigration during the 1870s. At the same time we seem to face an even more rapid and dramatic initial phase on Iceland. Unfortunately, Icelandic emigration is less well studied than movement from the rest of Scandinavia, and we can so far only speculate on the actual course of development.[18] However, it is likely that Icelandic emigration was strongly affected by the transport organization and that its dramatic development

[17] G. F. Pyle (1972) has performed an analysis of another historical diffusion process (epidemics). His results conform more to the hypothetical outline.

[18] Research is proceeding, however, within the framework of the Nordic Emigration Project at the Dept. of History in Reykjavik. Iceland raises the whole issue of emigration from other islands and archipelagos. Research has observed that emigration gradually assumed a high level of intensity on Åland as well as two other larger islands in the Baltic, the Swedish Öland and the Danish Bornholm. On the other hand, scholars have failed to note that emigration appears to have reached these islands and the Swedish Gotland at a comparatively late date but that it spread throughout the districts at a very rapid pace. This represents an interesting parallel to Iceland.

was due to a combination of factors: (*a*) the recruitment activities of the transport sector; (*b*) severe setbacks for the Icelandic economy; and (*c*) the normal self-generating effects, which can have a special impact on an island population.

It is evident, at least with respect to Scandinavia, that the diffusion of information among rural areas in pre-industrial society traveled much faster than we imagined. We also indicated earlier that internal migration, labor migration, travels, etc., seem to have been rather extensive in these countries. Yet the two-step hypothesis may still prove correct, even though cities played a less dominant role in the initial phase than was anticipated. Studies on emigration structure confirm the fact that our presumed group of leaders and opinion-makers was active in this context.[19] On the other hand, our maps do not provide documentation of the role played by cities in Sweden or Norway. Instead of acting as centers for the stimulation of emigration, large cities such as Stockholm, Gothenburg, Kristiania (Oslo) seem to have been surrounded by districts of low emigration. In order to understand this observation we must have access to different and more detailed evidence.[20]

However, in the case of Finland we can also trace an influence from several ports in Österbotten at an early stage of emigration. A closer analysis of this region confirms the fact that our prior assumptions were not quite incorrect. A relatively satisfactory explanation can be offered for the somewhat unexpected spread of emigration in northern Finland. Here we can see the value of enlarging our angle of perspective to several countries at the same time. It is obvious that Finnish emigration was influenced by an early and substantial stream of movement from neighboring regions in northern Norway as well as by early emigration among the Finnish-speaking people on the other side of the Torne River, which marks the boundary between Finland and Sweden. We can assume that the same applied to early emigration by the Swedish-speaking population from Österbotten, which had close contacts with Swedish emigrant districts on the other side of the Gulf of Bothnia.[21]

At least in the case of Denmark and Sweden it is also largely possible to trace the start of emigration in central districts and its spread to more peripheral regions. In Denmark, for example, emigration began on the

[19] N. Runeby (1969).
[20] E. De Geer (1959).
[21] This problem is being studied by E. De Geer and H. Wester of the Uppsala Group.

eastern central islands and subsequently spread to Jutland in the west.[22] Likewise, emigration from Northern Sweden began rather late and did not culminate until after 1900, i.e. at the same time as emigration from Finland, which consistently lagged one phase behind developments in Sweden. However, these rough descriptions of the spread of Swedish and Danish emigration are not quite satisfactory. As shown by the maps, emigration began at an early stage on northern Jutland and in the southern provinces of Norrland. This may be related to the position of Gävle as an emigrant port in this area of Sweden, and in such a case our original prognosis would be confirmed. However, it may also be due to an early influence from the Norwegian port of Trondheim, which was most important for emigrants from Northern Sweden. Certain instances of early emigration along the northern Swedish coast have their explanation in the special transport system and dominant information channels of the region.[23]

We have established that the dispersion process can be localized to a short time period and that, as a result, the growth phase did not generally lead to any marked changes in the extent and character of the recruitment fields. In this respect the growth phase was not as dramatic as we had expected. On the other hand, it is clear that strongly decreasing emigration rates led to a geographic narrowing of the recruitment fields, whereby regions of high emigration in previous decades were the only ones to recruit emigrants during trough years. This observation emerges even more clearly if we use annual emigration rates instead of five-year average figures. Moreover, attention is called to the self-generating effect. It is somewhat paradoxical that the regressive phases of emigration leave the most dynamic impression in this respect.

However, these remarks do not necessarily apply to the social dimension of emigration, which is more difficult to grasp. Critics have argued that external circumstances can have a strong impact on the social and demographic structure. It can be added that a historian who has access to empirical data can be tempted to project this evidence into his model construction from the very beginning. Hence, if the model is substantiated by the data this circular method of testing can hardly be considered

[22] The regional as well as other aspects on the Danish emigration are thoroughly dealt with by K. Hvidt (1971).

[23] The transport systems and the routes of emigration are commented upon in Chapter 7.

acceptable.[24] I do not claim that my attempt lacks such features. However, the gap between theoretical assumptions and empiricism is large enough. I hope, for the model not to be labelled a rationalization.[25]

Swedish emigration definitely reflects the assumed transition from marked family and group emigration to movements by single individuals. It also shows that a male dominance in the early phase evened out toward the saturation phase, whereafter it emerges again in amplified form. Consequently, we can observe a constant rejuvenation of the emigration population, especially among the adults. Our assumption that emigration must have been more socially selective in an early phase of growth than during the culmination period is largely confirmed. This also has significance for our understanding of the interplay between internal and external migration. However, all of these observations are not as uniform, and the change is not as consistent, as our model would imply. Different regions in the same country, for example, can represent different phases of growth and thereby complicate our interpretation of aggregated statistics. More importantly, emigration to cities and industrial areas in North America seems to have had a comparatively high proportion of unmarried males in the initial phase of movement. This fact emerges clearly if we compare our Swedish material with Finnish emigration, which made its first major advances as late as in the 1880s. A prominent share of emigrants in this phase went to mining areas and industrial regions of the Middle West.[26] We have called such a sequence the "Ljusne Model" (Figure 2: 5).

This systematization of migration sequences and demographic changes is related to the *receiving area*. In my own tentative model I underplayed the conditions in these areas for a specific reason. It seems to be a reasonable assumption that when presented with rich preferences a given emigrant population purposely selects destination areas. A case in point is just the emigration to North America. But it appears that these destinations can have a different impact on the structure of emigrant populations

[24] Interpretation problems of this type have been dealt with in an amusing and alarming way by T. D. Hackett Fischer and A. J. Köbben.

[25] It seems to me that a more important objection is to be found in the fact that, in a study covering several decades, we must consider not only one population but many. The difference between the population of a nation and that of a parish is here only a matter of size. The great turnover of individuals found in some Swedish parishes can thus be projected on a nation-wide level. This complication is probably valid for all studies of growth covering a longer period.

[26] Finnish emigration is thoroughly surveyed by R. Kero (1974).

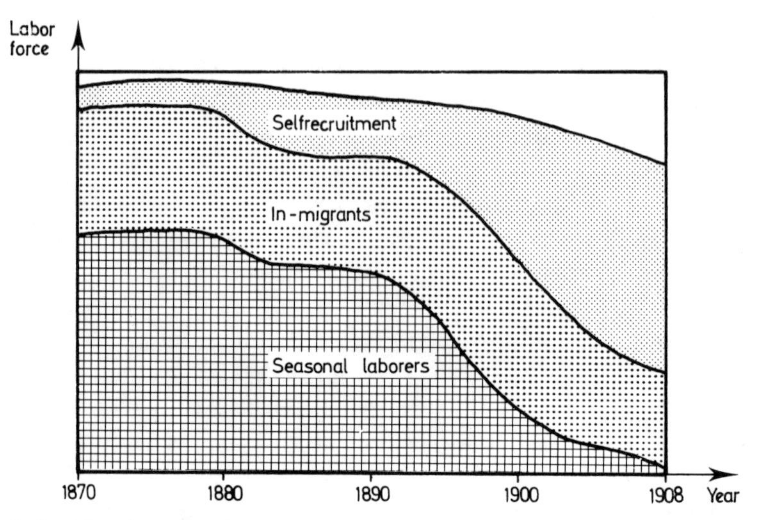

2:5. "The Ljusne Model". Phases of Labor Recruitment in a Sawmill District 1870–1908. *Source* B. Rondahl (1972), p. 264.

in a way which I did not foresee in the model. *Hence, even if our assumed growth process seems to operate we might consider whether there are two relatively different structural sequences at work here.* One of these sequences concerns settlement and colonization on the North American continent, while the other refers to the process of industrialization and urbanization. Several of our studies show that urban emigration takes another form from that proposed in our rough nationwide scheme (see below).[27]

e. Other Empirical Starting-Points

Before proceeding with our discussion about possible theoretical angles of approach I will stress a few basic patterns. This strategic information treats the connection between delivering and receiving areas of migration, the potential inclination to migrate, and the complicated interplay between different population mobilities.

The Radii of External Migrations

This discussion brings us to the nucleus of these *phase-shift* constructions. Migrations can be regarded as a stream of movement which flows from a

[27] Commentaries on this subject are made by B. Kronborg and T. Nilsson (1975).

well defined delivering area to a corresponding receiving area. Above I have merely stated this to be the case, but the matter must, of course, be studied empirically. It is not enough to make a superficial analysis of the passenger lists and observe a large number of *radii* between delivering districts in Europe and receiving areas in North America. What is decisive for results on an aggregate level is the relationship between this type of channelled migrational movement and instances of scattered movement. I can illustrate this with reference to a couple of maps (Figures 2:6 and 2:7) drawn up by the American scholar Robert Ostergren.[28]

By relying on the membership records of the Augustana Lutheran Church, to which most of the Swedes belonged in his Minnesota study areas, Ostergren has made a fairly complete reconstruction of birth fields in Sweden for a number of American congregations. Two of these birth fields are shown on the above maps. The Chisago Lake congregation (Figure 2: 7) clearly reflects the axis-migration we discussed earlier. It is no coincidence that this congregation consisted largely of farmers, since the tendency for concentrated settlement by emigrants from the same district in Europe appears to have been prominent in these settlement areas.[29] In the case of Chisago Lake, most immigrants came from a very limited area in southern Sweden. There are also indications of concentrated emigration from some other provinces. Moreover, a rather large number of individual emigrants are scattered throughout Southern and Central Sweden. In fact, there are examples of rural congregations in Minnesota which have an even stronger birth field concentration. Although birth fields can only approximate the parishes of emigration they probably provide satisfactory indications, especially for agrarian emigrants. Migrations within the agricultural sector of the Swedish population were very frequent, but the majority of these movements took place over short distances. Therefore, our access to additional information would not drastically change the inner field for Chisago Lake on the map nor would it alter the general scope of distribution.[30]

The Rush City congregation (Figure 2:6) poses a sharp contrast to Chisago Lake. The birth field here is distributed throughout Southern and Central Sweden, and it is difficult to find real concentrations. Although the

[28] R. Ostergren (1972).
[29] The situation of this current research area with its mosaic of various ethnic groups and nationalities is also studied by J. G. Rice (1973). See also the standard study by M. Curti (1959).
[30] Compare Chapter 9.

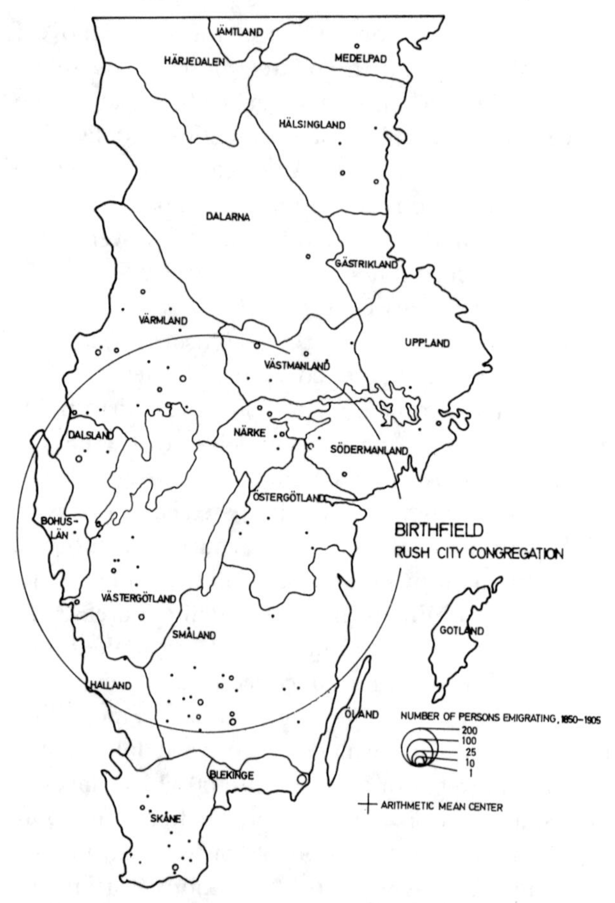

2:6. Birth Field. Rush City Congregation, Minnesota.
Source Parish Registers of Catechetical Examination of the Augustana Church; R. Ostergren (1972), p. 43.

embryo of a concentration possibly emerges in southwestern Småland, the rest of the distribution appears to be almost haphazard. It is possible, but far from certain, that the immigrant population in this small urban center, more so than that in Chisago Lake, had already in-migrated to cities and industrial areas in Sweden prior to emigration. In such a case our maps may have missed some strong instances of concentrated emigration, but this is not very likely.

We may find these maps accurate enough to designate the Chisago Lake and Rush City congregations as two typical cases of mass emigrant re-

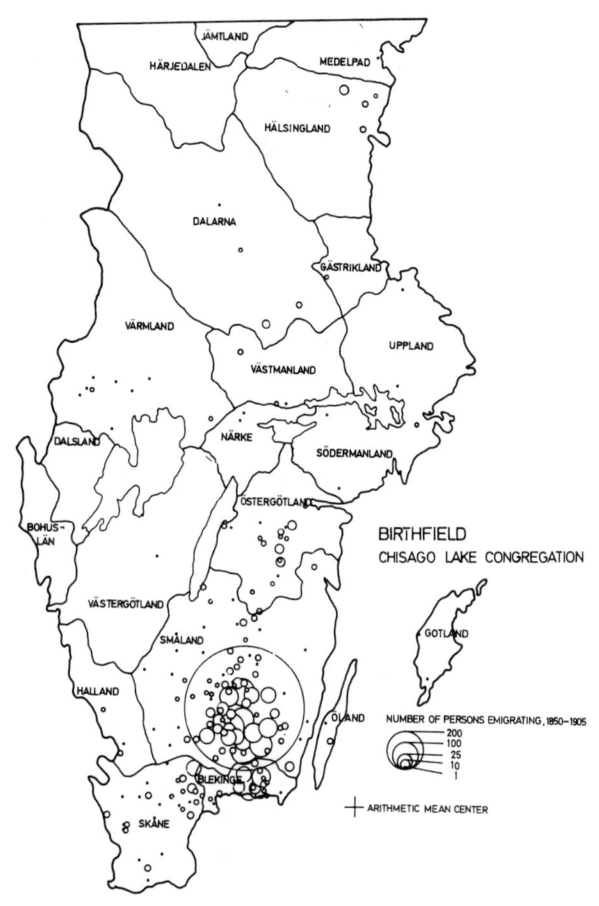

2: 7. Birth Field. Chisago Lake Congregation, Minnesota.
Source Parish Registers of Catechetical Examination of the Augustana Church; R. Ostergren (1972), p. 38.

cruitment. As such, they have important implications which can facilitate our understanding of the mechanism of mass emigration. Although we cannot use the birth fields to draw far-reaching conclusions about conditions at the actual moment of emigration, we can establish the following: the scattered birth field of the Rush City congregation would theoretically represent the normal pattern for immigrants with a weaker tendency for ethnic separatism in the receiving country. Rush City also illustrates that a congregation based upon ethnic affiliation sometimes drew its membership from scattered regions in the country of emigration. The strength of these ethnic ties is more apparent in congregations like Chisago Lake. We might speak in terms of a higher level of *ethnic density*. It must be remembered that these fundamental features of emigration to America, however striking and colorful, were and still remain an integral part of population mobility in Europe and in other countries and continents as well.

The relationship between scattered migrants and concentrated movements by individuals from a distinct emigrant district to a specific destination has been singled out as key information in our analysis.[31] Our basic purpose has been to reconstruct connections and transitions between the different phases of migratory movements. In reality, we have found it difficult to capture the relationship between scattered migrants and migrant groups which might be regarded as essential to the development of mass movement. In our studies we rarely have access to longitudinal information of one area of destination, even throughout a five-year period. In most cases we are forced to rely on *cross-sectional data,* such as censuses, which are imperfect in terms of time and space dimensions. Although naturalization papers can provide more relevant information, they do present us with problems concerning omissions.[32]

The distinction between scattered and other types of migrants is brought to the fore when an individual migrant from a large city actually represents a different emigrational context from the expected pattern. If, for example, this individual has in-migrated to an urban environment from a particular rural district it is important for us to know whether members of his family, relatives, or neighbors have already emigrated to North

[31] Very interesting observations concerning the interaction between the structure of settlement and social organization in the delivering countries and the behaviors and adjustment of immigrants in the receiving countries are presented by C. A. Price (1963*a*). Compare especially his map material with that of the *Nordic Emigration Atlas* (1976).

[32] This problem of losses is discussed by C. A. Price (1963*a*, 1963*b*). The passenger lists of emigrant ports form a fairly complete source, but they contain weaknesses; in a rather large number of cases these lists only record ports of debarkation in North America as opposed to intended areas of settlement. Moreover, we still run into difficulties in establishing scattered migration. A stream or chain of migration was frequently initiated by movements of a few individuals. In order to distinguish these individual migrants from real scattered migrants we must follow the development of thousands of small streams over a series of years. According to our definition a migrant stream can also include subsequences of movement which are often related to kinship. During the course of mass emigration, and in movements from the countryside to the cities, it was common for one family member to move ahead of time, only to be joined later on by relatives. By focusing on this micro-level we can not only trace the components of a growth curve but also demarcate the intensive oscillations of mass emigration.

America. In such a case it is likely that the individual moved on a first-stage basis to an area where his relatives had settled earlier.[33]

We have found that the studied development corresponds in some respects to our growth model. However, divergencies have also been observed on certain points. Moreover, as is so often the case in dealing with empirical data, the realities turn out to be so complex that they are difficult to fit into an overarching explanatory model. Nevertheless, our attempt to systematize emigration sequences may be instructive. The Australian sociologist, Charles Price, has reinforced our thinking in this respect. He has concentrated on chain migrations related to immigrant countries, and it is interesting that he too has confronted problems in linking sequences in the delivering and receiving countries.[34]

Potential Migration

From a theoretical standpoint we ought to reconsider the rapidity with which mass emigration spread throughout Europe. Large segments of the population which did not emigrate must have been aware of this new migration alternative. It would be most valuable if we could determine the share of the total population during different phases of mass emigration which weighed the prospect of emigration without coming to a definite decision. How, then, would a curve of inclination behave compared with the curve of emigration? Questions of this nature are seldom raised in migration literature, presumably because of difficulties which seem to deter measurement of something so transient as the inclination to migrate.

However, it is clear that the rapid growth of mass emigration ultimately reflected an extensive readiness to migrate. Recent Dutch interview studies indicate that the inclination to migrate frequently exceeds very much the level of actual movement.[35] If we can project the same for emigration to North America we might conclude that the emigration of nearly 500 000 Swedes out of a population of 4 million in roughly one decade must have been due to a profound mood of departure among a majority of the Swedish population.[36]

[33] Compare J. Moore (1938) and F. Nilsson (1970).
[34] C. A. Price (1963*a*).
[35] S. E. Ellemers (1964). For a general discussion about potential mobility see H. Tetzschner et al. (1974), pp. 108 ff.
[36] See Chapter 7.

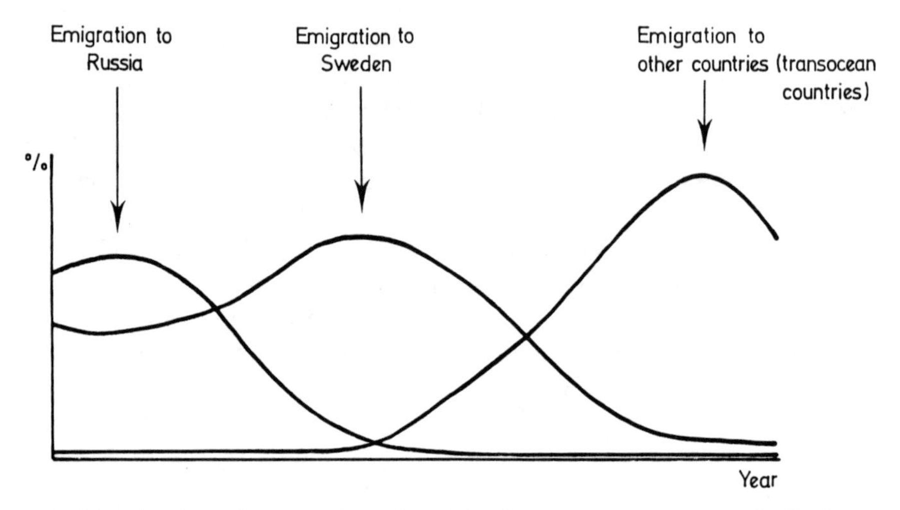

2:8. Migrational Development of Vasa län, Finland 1860–1910. Percentage Distribution.
Source Registered Passports from Vasa län, Finland; E. De Geer and H. Wester (1975), p. 51.

Fortunately, we can make an estimate of the extent of potential migration in our historical perspective by turning to the contents of a Swedish emigrant agent archives discovered almost intact in the late 1950s. The source series in this collection covers the most important emigration period, namely 1878–1911, and includes correspondence between the agency and prospective customers. These letters number in the tens of thousands and give an idea of the proportion of letter-writers who were seriously interested in emigrating compared with those who expressed a desire to emigrate and also actually implemented their decisions. In analyzing this information we have disregarded simple requests for advertising brochures, posters, and the like. Approximately 25 per cent of those who seriously weighed the prospect of emigration did pursue their plans. Many of the others who never emigrated even stated a date for departure. These estimates apply to the 1880s and indicate that there was a strong feeling of unrest among the population at that time.

The Interplay of Migrational Movements

I have emphasized above that emigration ought not to be studied separately from other types of population mobility. This can be illustrated by a study of an area in the Finnish province of Österbotten, which figured in our map analysis. As shown in Figure 2:8, this study area was characterized by substantial population mobility and initially saw a period of extensive labor migrations to St. Petersburg. At that time Finland was a grand duchy of Imperial Russia. During the mid-1800s a certain amount of labor migrations and emigration developed which were particularly directed to the Swedish sawmill districts across the Gulf of Bothnia. These movements appear to have culminated in the 1880s when labor migration to St. Petersburg had almost entirely halted. At the same time, emigration to America made strong advances in the area and eventually reached a peak during the first decade of the 1900s, when emigration to Sweden sharply diminished.[37]

In this Finnish example we can capture some of the complex patterns of population turnover discussed by Frank Thistlethwaite in his report to the XIth International Congress of Historical Sciences in 1960.[38] In other words, the relatively dramatic sequence in Österbotten is not unique to the area but can be found elsewhere as well. Human populations have apparently satisfied their migrational needs in different ways from one period to the next, and these successive streams of movement reveal a rather logical rhythm.

f. Other Attempts at Model-Building

Compared with most work in the social sciences, research into migration has made good progress in formulating major and all-encompassing, explanatory models, and in the following paragraphs I will analyze some of them.

The very fact, however, that this special research field is situated between several disciplines has been regarded as an obstacle to rapid development on the theoretical level. Hence it has been pointed out that statisticians have long occupied a dominant position among those who have expressed an interest in the area of migration. The obstacle, then, would seem to stem from the fact that the latter often lack an in-depth knowledge of research in the social sciences as well as of history. There is a good deal to be said for statements of this kind. However, there are grounds for emphasizing that the theoretical debate has still been waged on a rather successful level of interchange in recent years.[39]

[37] E. De Geer and H. Wester (1975).

[38] F. Thistlethwaite (1960).

[39] General aspects on model building closely related to my own approach can be found in C. Erickson (1975).

A Demographic and General Approach

The American scholar, Everett S. Lee, seems to be the first demographer since the end of World War II who has ventured to experiment with a major explanatory model, one which also follows Ravenstein's well-known line of development.[40] Lee has pointed out four groups of factors which appear to influence the migration process. These are:

1. factors connected with the area of origin
2. factors connected with the receiving area
3. intervening obstacles
4. personal factors

This rather self-evident statement can serve as a frame of reference for research, and it can steer its direction toward interesting areas of study. Lee presents a series of hypotheses regarding the volume of migration under variable conditions.

There are a number of important factors here in addition to economic development. One of these is the degree of complexity in a region's economic structure. Another is the structure of the population which affects migration. Lee also asserts that, barring any obstacles, a stream of migrational movement should be expected to accelerate in an almost mechanical manner over the course of time (compare observations made above). Migrational streams tend to follow definite channels, and every such stream is paralleled by another in the opposite direction. Migration is also dependent upon the presence of *intervening obstacles*.[41]

The effectiveness of a migrational stream depends upon whether the *minus factors* are predominant in a delivering area and whether the intervening obstacles are strong at the time of out-migration. During periods of favorable economic conditions we can also expect "more effective

[40] E. S. Lee (1969), earlier published in Demography 1966. Cf. E. G. Ravenstein (1885, 1889).
[41] Since Lee wrote his article, geographers not in the least, have been more observant of the obstacles to migration, especially those which have formed *barriers.* These barriers can be of a political, cultural, ethnic, economic, psychological or social nature. It is also obvious that where a complete freedom to move in different directions has been at hand the migration tradition and the migration pattern in practice almost can serve as barriers to movements in certain directions. Compare the so-called *rural-industrial barrier* which is especially dealt with by the Uppsala Group (B. Rondahl 1972 and S. Åkerman 1972*a*). It may be added that intervening opportunities might moderate the inclination to migrate between two areas. This almost self-evident condition which influence the migration distance, has even been characterized as a "Theory". The observation was presented in a systematic way by S. A. Stouffer (1940).

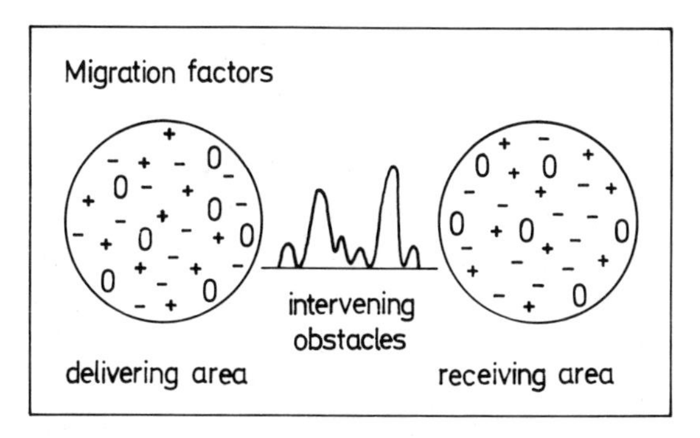

2:9. The Migration Model of Everett S. Lee.
Source E. S. Lee (1969), p. 286.

streams of movement".[42] Finally, says Lee, it is worth emphasizing that in several respects an emigrant population appears to occupy an intermediate position between the populations of the delivering and receiving areas.[43]

Although Lee's article generally refers to research findings obtained from various fields, we must recognize the fact that his construction is generally based on deductive arguments. Their value can only be tested by means of empirical studies. Lee pays very little attention to the problem of testing his model. At this point we can assert that some of his hypotheses cannot be verified on the basis of current Scandinavian migration research.

Economic and Geographic Approaches

It is impossible and hardly necessary in this context to discuss the preliminary stages of the building of models in economic migration research. It may suffice to call attention to the fact that economists for a long time concentrated on deciding whether *push* or *pull factors* have been the most decisive for the timing of emigration. This has been a popular research field ever since Jerome's investigations in the 1920s. To an outsider the

[42] Lee gives the concepts of minus and plus factors a very general definition. The connection between economic trends and the net effects of the migrational streams seems to be more complicated than Lee has observed. Both this and the general level of migration are thoroughly discussed by R. Heberle (1955).
[43] Note that our results above diverge from Lee's postulates which are inconsistent to the type of a U-shaped selection of the migrants, which we have found in a couple of our studies. (S. Åkerman et al., 1974).

fascination of this problem might seem hard to understand, since it is fairly obvious that this is no question of either/or, but a complicated interaction between factors both in the delivering and in the receiving countries. Those more advanced models which will be treated in the following conform to such considerations. It is important, however, to emphasize that even these models are based on the fundamental idea that there is an imbalance between different regions which tends to be equalized by migration. This assumption should be questioned, however. So far no one has been able to prove that the economic, demographic, social, and ethnic system of migration ever has attained an equilibrium or ever endeavoured such a state. On the contrary, dynamics and imbalance are characteristics of the structure of the industrial society as well as of migrational movements.

When discussing different migrational structures the results reached by the Myrdal Group in the 1930s must also be commented upon.[44] It must be pointed out that this research was organized by means of a coherent but rather simple model. By classifying small administrative units according to their industrialization and urbanization level (and growth in this respect) they expected to find a systematic re-allocation of the population as a consequence of a rather complicated migrational pattern. They also expected economic changes to influence the structure, level and effects of migration in a crucial way. As a whole the hypotheses of this research program were verified even if the analyses of short-term economic trends and internal migration gave some surprising results. It is remarkable how close the basic thoughts of the Myrdal Group are to *the central place theory,* which was formulated much later.[45] This is shown by Allan Pred's model (Figure 2: 10).

A Myrdal-type pattern can be seen in our own results covering the migration in and out of the city of Västerås. Figure 2:11 is a condensed representation of the total registered population movement of the city of Västerås 1895–1930 (27 000 inhabitants in 1920). The only exception is the internal migration within the city, which, however, has a rather restricted area.

[44] D. S. Thomas (1936).

[45] Cf. G. A. Carrothers (1956). Walter Christaller has been of special importance for the development of this specialty. To a certain degree the recently introduced systems analysis can be considered a development of the central place theory and other similar attempts. A. Mabogunje (1972) has suggested such a systems analysis approach for the rural–urban migration. His frame of reference has been the recent African experience.

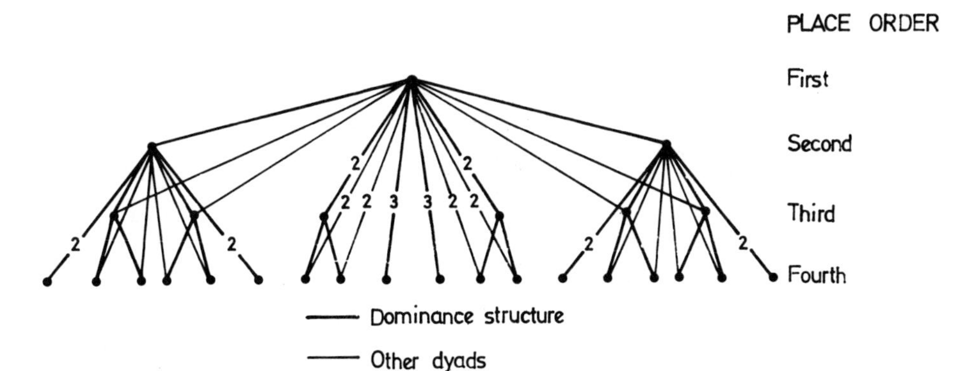

2: 10. Dominance Structure and Other Interaction Dyads in a Christallerian Urban System. (According to Allan Pred.)

Comments The central place theory treats the interplay between places on diffferent hierarchical levels. This interplay takes the shape of a so-called dominance structure. Such a construct can be illustrated by A. Pred's interpretation of W. Christaller's basic theoretical approach. The pair-wise linkage of places on different levels (dyads) can be seen in the Figure. These linkage patterns mean a simplification of the often rather complicated patterns of interrelation, which has been clearly illustrated in our migration studies. Cf. Figure 2: 11.

Source A. Pred (1975), p. 63.

In reality the distance zones used have been rather irregular since some parishes had part of their area in two zones and in that case their migrations have been attributed to the zone where the dominant part was situated. This means that it has not been possible to perform any individual measurement of the distance migrated in each case.

It is important to realize that the "dimensions" used here are not the same as cardinal points. They symbolize the level of urbanization and industrialization (according to the categories of the Myrdal Group). If we start in the "west" and move anti-clockwise we have an increased urbanization. The only inconsistency is the transocean migration which of course did not mean urban–urban migration in all instances. But our knowledge about the general character of the urban emigration makes it natural to locate these diagrams in direct connection with the metropolitan ones.

From the total migrational movement we can find that the age span 15–30 years was an extremely mobile one. Notice that the total fabric of migrations is represented in a ten times smaller scale in the upper (right) corner of the figure. The age sensitiveness of the migrations was, however, strongly dependent on the distance and the urbanization level.

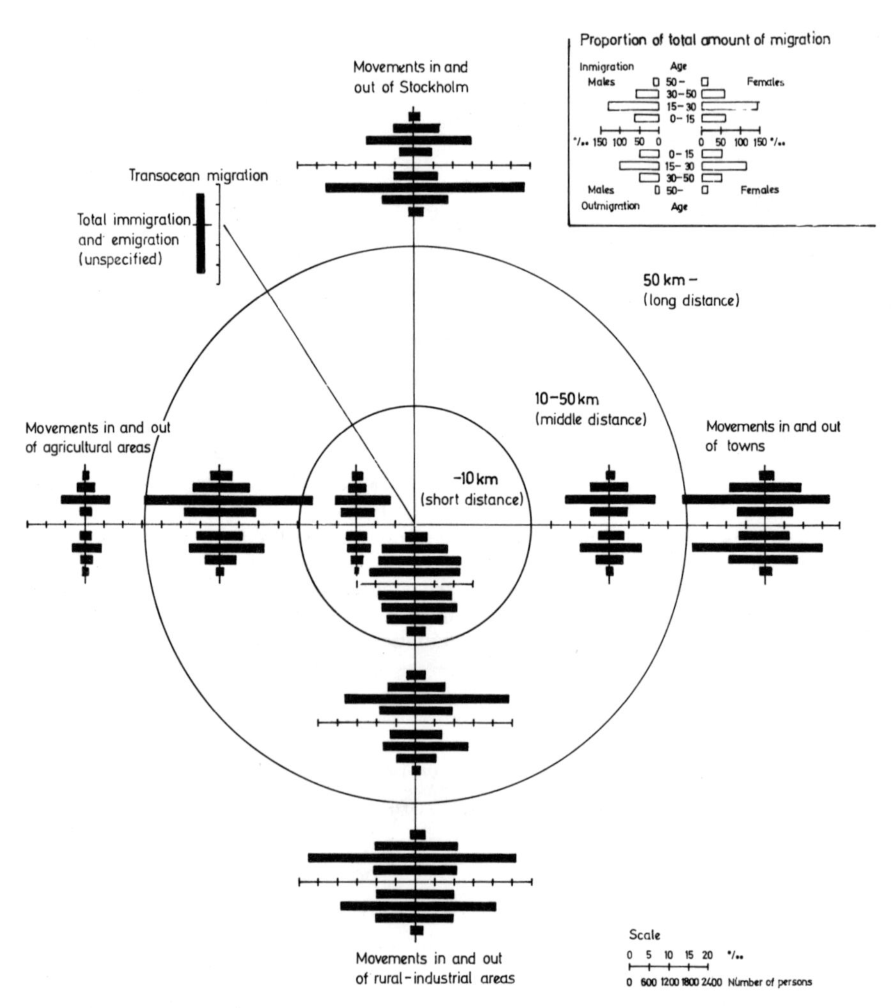

2: 11. The Total Population Movement of a Medium Sized City (Västerås in Västmanland, Sweden) 1895–1930 (N=120.440).
Source S. Åkerman (1975), p. 23.

Thus the proportion of older migrants was much bigger on short distances and especially in the exchange with rural-industrialized parishes. According to our tables these migrations are dominated by families. Inmigration is symbolized by the population diagrams above the graded demarcation lines and out-migration consequently by the lower part of the diagrams. The net changes too are much dependent on the distances migrated combined with the level of urbanization. The age structure and sex distribution vary to a great extent.

The effects of the total population movement are not very dramatic but they hide a complicated pattern characterized by huge losses in relation to the metropolitan areas especially in the age span 15–30 years and most apparent for the women. Such a pattern though on a smaller scale can be found in the external migration too. These losses were compensated for by strong gains in relation to pure rural parishes and to the *mixed* rural and industrialized ones of the intermediate zone. There was a strong female dominance in these net gains. Our city also registers substantial net gains in the interchange with cities except the metropolitan ones. These gains in their turn were dominated by male migrants. Thereby the distortions of the sex ratio coming from the exchange on short distances has been partly neutralized. The net losses to the metropolitan areas and North America had a female preponderance and gave the same effect. Notice how extensive the long distance migrations were for an expanding central place with a strong industrial growth like the city investigated.

An Economic Approach

Thorvald Moe has presented an explanatory model which exhibits some resemblance to Lee's fundamental ideas.[46] Moe has tested an econometrical model on mass emigration from Norway during the period 1873–1914.[47] He is the latest in a line of economists who have dealt with the problem of external migration.[48]

[46] It can be pointed out that macro-economic models have simply assumed that wage differences have been the real explaining variable for most international population movements. That is to say that the labor force has moved to those areas where the marginal value of labor has been highest. See e.g. C. P. Kindleberger (1967). Even if the opportunity structure of the labor market has not been entirely neglected in these studies it has not been sufficiently treated. In some more sociological economic analyses, however, the focus has been very much on employment–underemployment–unemployment, see e.g. H. S. Parnes (1968). This difference of opinion which has been revealed here is in a way the main theme of this chapter. It can be spelled out as a strong scepticism towards the assumption that the decision to migrate normally is based on simple benefit calculations by the individuals. Cf. the basic arguments in J. G. March and H. A. Simon (1958) and especially their views on "optimal behavior".

[47] T. Moe (1970), pp. 117–236.

[48] E.g. M. Wilkinson (1967) and J. M. Quigley presented by B. Odén (1971). Note the refinement of methods of analysis tried by M. P. Todaro (1973). To him the "disequilibrium situations" and their origin are worth special attention.

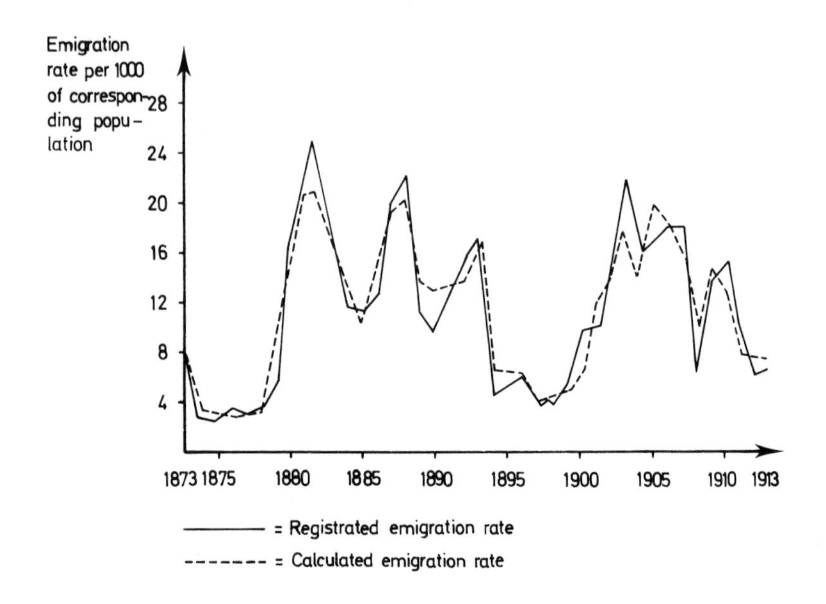

2:12. The Model of Thorvald Moe Tested Against the Norwegian Emigration of "Manpower" (15–35 Years of Age) 1873–1913.

Comments Moe uses the following function to predict the Norwegian emigration: $\text{LnMt}=\text{Lnb}_0+\text{b}_1\text{Ln PYt}+\text{b}_2\text{Ln COt}+\text{b}_3\text{Ln EUst}+\text{b}_4\text{UNt}+\text{LnV}$. The dependent variable Mt=the *emigration rate.* (Only persons in the prime working age (15–30 years) are included.) PYt=the *permanent income difference.* COt=the *cohort effect* measured by the relative number of Norwegians in the age group 20–29 years, living in Norway t-1. EUSt=*Job availabilities* in the US. (Frickey's index on production for trade and transportation is used as a proxy.) UNt=*Aggregate unemployment figures* for Norway (available from 1865). V=error term.

Source T. Moe (1970), pp. 163 ff.

Moe's migrational model implies that the inclination to migrate is, in the long run, a function of expected differences in income between the delivering and the receiving country as well as the supply of young, potential migrants.[49] The regional imbalance is temporarily adjusted for by means of the short-term costs of migration. Moe's model appears to offer an unusually good explanation of the annual emigration from Norway to the United States between 1873 and 1914. It also appears to forecast short- and long-term fluctuations in the emigration curve as well as the trend in the annual, unregulated series of emigration. Moe has also found that the variables utilized in this model individually forecast the long-term fluctua-

[49] T. Moe (1970), p. 155 ff.

tions in the total emigration of Norwegian manpower. However, this involves some chronological adjustements.

This conclusion is based upon regression calculations of emigration by means of one (or more) explaining variables. The remaining variables were held constant. Moe's interpretation can be spelled out in the following way: the observed, long-term fluctuations of emigration from Norway were caused by all explaining variables and not by one single economic or demographic factor.

I will analyze Moe's model in some detail. The dependent variable is the *emigration rate,* which is calculated on the professionally employed group. This variable is more precisely defined as emigrants in the most mobile age bracket of the labor-force (15–30 years) in relation to 1 000 persons of the same ages in the stationary population. These calculations have been made on an annual basis.

The emigration rate is, of course, of strategic importance for our evaluation of the model. Consequently, it is astounding that nowhere in Moe's presentation do we find a methodological discussion of the sources. The reader is left in the dark as to whether the Norwegian emigration statistics improved over the course of time from the early 1870s to around 1915. Moreover, Moe does not come to terms with a related question, namely the likelihood that the statistics may provide poorer coverage for the peak years of emigration as compared with its troughs. Moe presumably feels that the problem of source materials has already been adequately discussed by prior research, for example in the work of Ingrid Semmingsen.[50] In interpreting his results we must also pay attention to the omitted age spans.[51]

The permanent income gap is defined as the difference between Norway and the United States in the gross national product per member of the labor force. Moe does not hesitate to apply psychological interpretations which can shed light on the reactions of the emigrants. The emigrants' notion of the income gap is calculated as a mean value of the last five years' difference in the per capita income. Here we are faced with a difficult theoretical problem: how is it possible to convert a concept into a measurable variable? Sometimes Moe's treatment of this problem tends to be rather cursory. It is reasonable to define *the experience of a permanent income gap* as

[50] I. Semmingsen (1950).

[51] Another useful distinction has been suggested by J. M. Quigley who has tried to calculate the proportion between urban-industrial emigrants and rural ones.

influenced by the situation which prevailed over a five-year period prior to emigration. It might be even more realistic to take into consideration also the average age of the emigrants and their time period of labor market experience. A case in point is that the average age among emigrants was generally lowered during Moe's period of study.[52]

There are other problems here as well: for example, the distribution of income might have been different in Norway and the United States. Moreover, as Moe himself emphasizes, rates of exchange usually do not serve as a good measurement of the real purchasing power in different countries. Despite these reservations we must credit Moe with introducing an interesting variable, the permanent income gap. Moe regrets the fact that his calculations do not include those variables which can not be measured in monetary terms.

The so-called *cohort effect* is a new feature in Moe's model. He estimates this effect by means of the proportion of 20–29-year-old persons in the labor force. His purpose is to catch the variations in the labor force, particularly with regard to the most mobile sector. Here Moe works with a constant one-year lag. This is a more serious operative device than the time lag related to the income gap. Moe hardly explains this one-year lag nor its consistency over time. It would have been instructive if Moe had made his calculations in two separate sittings, one with the use of this weakly motivated "lag" and another without it. Still the cohort effect seems to be a most revealing variable.[53]

In addition to these long-term concepts Moe also discusses some factors affecting the *short-term fluctuations.* As has been mentioned, he is working with two special concepts here, namely the short-run cost of moving and the traveling costs. According to Moe, these costs can be divided into actual transportation costs as well as a period of unemployment in both the delivering and the receiving country.[54] This is something very difficult to

[52] In a situation, where we are dealing with 28-year-old emigrants on the average, the income gap can be calculated on the basis of the preceding ten-year period. Here we consider the fact that by the time someone had reached the age of about 18 he had often attained the wage level of an adult. When the average emigrant was e.g. 22 years of age, we apply this calculation on the basis of the previous four years, etc. It is also possible to balance different years: thus, the last two years, for example, ought to exert a stronger effect. T. Moe has toyed with the idea of a "distributed lag" calculation, but he abandoned it since the practical difficulties proved to be too big. It can be added that it is not self-evident to combine GNP with individual adults. Ideally, the living standard ought to be related to the number of *households* and their average size. Cf. R. Easterlin (1968).

[53] This phenomenon was first commented upon by E. Sundt (1857).

[54] T. Moe (1970), pp. 157–160.

grasp since we lack unemployment statistics in the United States and the Norwegian material seems to be very weak too.[55] It is of course rather unsatisfactory to use both a direct and an indirect method of measurement.

Considering these weaknesses, the application of lags, and a mathematical formulation (a double logarithmic equation) which both need further specification, Moe's claim to be able to explain as much as 87 per cent of the Norwegian labor emigration is rather exaggerated.[56] It could even be tempting to call in question whether econometricians face a blind alley here. Such a negative attitude, however, is unfair. It is obvious that further development work is essential both on a theoretical and an empirical level. Comparative analyses of the models are also badly needed.[57] In connection with Moe's serious attempt we ought to broaden the analysis to the vast debate about economic growth in general.[58] Hence it is most important to clarify the timing of the economic growth in Scandinavia compared with the United States. It is easy to beg the question and assume that the difference between the two regions was largest in the beginning of the investigation period and that it gradually evened out. Thus such a systematic change strongly must have influenced the pattern of external migrations. Calculations performed by S. Kuznets, however, seem to indicate

[55] For the American statistics T. Moe has had to be content with an indirect estimate of unemployment, Frickey's well-known index.

[56] A double logarithmic function seems often to give a better fit than other possible solutions. An improvement of the result in this way therefore tends to get an artificial character. Although it is more satisfactory than earlier econometric attempts, it can be added that T. Moe's model lacks *elasticity* enough to register the dramatic oscillations between years of high and low emigration. In the section below called "An Interdisciplinary Approach" this problem will be dealt with from a new point of view.

[57] E. Hamberg (Dept. of Economic History, Stockholm University) is preparing a study using a model very similar to T. Moe's, based on Swedish material.

[58] Research in this particular area began with a *single factor* model which was focused on production as related to the physical investments by way of *capital quota*

$$\text{Capital quota} = \frac{\text{investment}}{\text{GNP}}.$$

The previous over-confidence in the prognosis capacity of capital quota has now been abandoned, as research has found that only a part of the process of growth can be explained with the aid of physical investments. Consequently, scholars have initiated a search for other factors which can be of strategic importance. Among other things, they have pointed out such factors as education, health, research, technique, business management, and organizational structure. Special interest has been devoted to education. It would naturally be of great value to regard the role of migration from this vantage point. (G. Myrdal 1970).

that the economic development has been much more complex.[61] We will soon revert to this issue when analysing B. Thomas' well-known model.

A Center–Periphery Approach

We have discussed a two-country approach above; a further development of this construct can be found in a work by B. Thomas already in 1954 on migration and economic growth, later on elaborated in 1972. Thomas reacted strongly to the very simplified push and pull analysis which we have commented upon earlier.[62]

It was Brinley Thomas' ambition to go beyond the type of analysis which was common among economists at the time he began his research.[63] His

[61] S. Kuznets (1958). Thus the substantial gap between per capita income in e.g. Sweden and the US seems to persist still in the 1920s but as can be seen in the Diagram below the rate of growth of the Swedish economy was rather strong already in the late 19th century. Note that the dramatic movement of the English curve has strong implications for the discussion of B. Thomas' model:

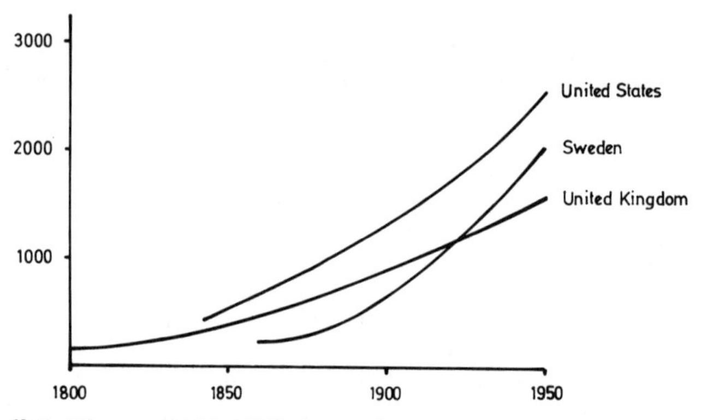

[62] B. Thomas (1954, 1972). In a rather comical manner American researchers stood on one side and argued for the dominance of pull factors, while European researchers stood on the other and, with equal stubbornness, argued in favor of push factors.

[63] Some efforts had been made to apply a different type of analysis though. Dorothy Swaine Thomas tried to weigh push and pull factors during each phase of emigration, and thereby she was able to provide a substantially more complex picture than earlier research. Brinley Thomas, meanwhile, found it possible to connect his discussion with certain observations made by J. A. Schumpeter in his well-known work, *Business Cycles* (1939), and give them a somewhat different interpretation. Simon Kuznets' classic study, *Secular Movements in Production and Prices* (1930), and several of his later publications assumed even greater importance in this context. Two cornerstones of B. Thomas' own contribution were, in fact, supplied by S. Kuznets: the long cycles and the capital investments sensitive to population developments. Valuable information and ideas were also supplied by A. K. Cairncross' work, *Home and Foreign Investment 1870–1913*, (1953).

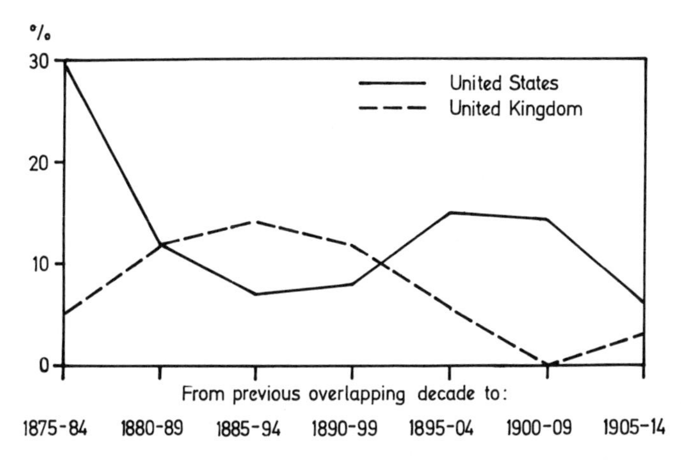

2: 13. Rate of Change in Real National Income Per Capita (from Decade to Overlapping Decade) in the United States and the United Kingdom, 1875–1914.
Source B. Thomas (1972), p. 14; Reprinted by the courtesy of Methuen & Co Ltd.

basic premise was spelled out by Schumpeter: "Capitalism itself is, both in the economic and the sociological sense, essentially one process, with the whole earth as its stage."[64] Railroad construction, electricity, etc., did not recognize any national boundaries, and such boundaries would, in all likelihood, pose no obstacles to research.

Another premise for Thomas' approach stemmed from his observation of a different timing of the economic growth of the United States and Great Britain. Drawing on Kuznets' well-known contributions, Thomas was inclined to explain this phenomenon with reference to cycles of approximately 20 years' duration, as shown in Figure 2: 13.

Instead of regarding the fluctuations as purely coincidental, Thomas maintained that they disclosed a connection between the American and British economies. Moreover, he claimed that North America and Western Europe was so integrated by the mid-1800s that they constituted an *Atlantic economy.* The most important factors in this process were migration, mobile capital, industrialization, and urbanization.

Thomas regards the demographic variables, and migration in particular, as the dynamic elements here. Demographic echo-effects coupled with migration lead, after a certain "gestation period", to increased housing construction and other infrastructural changes. This, in turn, affects in-

[64] J. A. Schumpeter (1939), Vol. I, p. 135.

dustrial production as well as general trade cycles, which engenders a temporary rise in production as a consequence of favorable developments in corporate profits.

It is not perfectly clear how Thomas visualizes the transfer of this economic expansion from the center to the periphery and vice versa. However, one important link is the idea that a powerful rise in housing construction, etc., in one country stimulates exports and other economic activities in another. Thomas lays great emphasis on the fact that English capitalists tended to withdraw some of their investments in countries such as the United States, Canada, and Australia when economic activities began to slacken. In such instances these investments actually stimulated Britain's domestic economy. The stage is now set for the same sequence of increased housing construction and improvement of trade cycles on the home front. "The see-saw movement arises fundamentally out of the inverse demographic cycles and the alternation of infrastructure and export upsurges, ... according to the rules of the gold standard game ..."[65]

From our own vantage point it is especially worth nothing that Thomas not only works with external migration but also theorizes that internal population turnover—particularly from the countryside to the cities—operated as an important prerequisite for the entire model. It could be expected that internal and external migration reflected the fact that both the United States and Britain periodically harbored the greatest rate of economic growth: in this way alternating swings might be observed, for example, between English in-migration to urban areas and British emigration to North America.

It would have been possible for the Uppsala Group to test Brinley Thomas' interesting model in a systematic way. But even if our research planning did not get this orientation we have made special investigations and analyses which possibly can help to evaluate the whole model. These observations can be combined with discussions and criticism which have been related to other parts of the model.[66]

As regards the center–periphery relation, it can be stated that the debate has neither adequately observed the definition problems involved, nor has the static character of the model been commented upon. For a center–

[65] B. Thomas (1972), p. 100.

[66] Critical from various points of view are: M. Abramovitz (1961); R. Easterlin (1968); P. O'Leary, W. A. Lewis (1955); H. J. Habakkuk (1968), and S. B. Saul (1962). I. Adelman (1965) even questions if the long cycles can be an artifact.

periphery model it is of course necessary to make clear how to understand these two concepts. At the same time we must decide how to perceive the interrelation between them on a theoretical level. Already here Thomas' construction clearly deviates from other similar theoretical attempts.[67] He seems constantly to equate center with England. This is a rather Anglo-Saxon centered view of the situation that may be motivated for the middle of the 19th century when Britain had a very strong position as the world's banker. But also countries like Germany and France have had center functions at least to some extent and their role in the model ought to be discussed more thoroughly.[68]

In general, Thomas attaches a strong importance to the investments. The monetary system that he describes with the Bank of England as leading part and the pound combined with the gold standard as regulators could not function more than one decade (the 1880s) of our investigation period. If this is a reasonable suggestion the model as it stands loses some of its value but remains interesting at least on a theoretical level.

Normally it is typical for a center–periphery situation, that the peripheral region has great problems in bridging the gap between its own *per capita* income and that of the center region. On the contrary this gap usually widens over time.[69] Capital investments in industry do not seem to have any "cobweb" effects on the whole economy. Instead we can find that these investments will be "absorbed" without much spreading effect to other sectors of the economy.[70] In this perspective the relation between Britain and the United States during the second half of the 19th century was very atypical. This calls for a more comparative approach than Thomas has used.

We may go further along this line. Thomas implies that the center–periphery relation also reflects the structure of the labor market of the Atlantic economy. If this is the case it must be pointed out that the periphery seems to have acted as the center! That is to say, the periphery attracts manpower to a greater extent than the center. This applies to the expanding industry as well as the commercialized agriculture of the Unit-

[67] See for example S. Langholm (1971).

[68] Generally speaking the relation between England and the more industrialized countries on the European continent has been almost neglected although France held an important center function on the European labor market and Germany had a certain position as banker on the European money market. A. K. Cairncross (1953).

[69] G. Myrdal (1957) and A. Hirschman (1958).

[70] G. Myrdal (1970).

ed States. Hence it is most important to notice how fast the United States gains a center position during her mass immigration period. It is reasonable to ask if this fact must not be reflected in the model. Time and again Thomas touches upon these circumstances but he never gives due attention to this complication.

It may be added that the whole periphery included Canada, South America, Africa, and Australia. Thomas presumes that the business cycles of this vast periphery have been synchronized, thus forming a link in his chain of evidence. He mentions that countries like Argentina, however, have sometimes acted as alternatives for English investments during recession in the United States. Thereby the concept of the Atlantic economy has become more complicated. As a matter of fact the general tendency has been for Britain to lose its dominating impact on the US and vice versa towards the turn of the century and so capital was released for Britain's still very important engagements in Africa and Asia.

This discussion also touches upon a problem of scale. Even if the British position on the money market was dominant—at least during the first part of the investigation period (1870–1913)—it is not self-evident that the British economy could balance such a resourceful and expanding continent. Hence there is a lack of *symmetry* in the model. It is not possible to talk about a real symmetry as regards the Atlantic labor market before the very last years of the period. At that time practically the entire European continent was involved in the mass emigration to North America.

In general this is a problem that is not sufficiently considered in the equilibrium constructs which have been tried by economists. The bias of Thomas' model is a feature typical of most economic analyses.[71]

The crucial point of Thomas' interpretation is the beginning of the migration cycles. Demographic echo-effects in Britain, e.g., could lead to

[71] The sequence population structure—migration→infrastructural activities—recovery of the construction sector→rise in business activity has also been much discussed and challenged by other economists. The criticism has been directed to certain points in B. Thomas' model but it is characterized by a general lack of creativity. The trade cycles in the United States have been singled out as the leading feature of the economic and demographic process, influencing the timing and volume of migration. In most cases migration and other demographic changes have hardly been attributed any decisive role. It is characteristic for this line of arguing that the pull factors in North America are looked upon as steering the whole development. The most representative of this school is probably Richard Easterlin who has shown how different regions and countries in Europe in a similar way responded to economic impulses from the US. To him this implies that the push factors can almost be disregarded. R. Easterlin (1968).

population sensitive economic activities at home but also to emigration! (Compare the so-called *cohort-effect* in Moe's model.) It ought to be embarrassing for Thomas that mass emigration from Britain and other European countries, as Richard Easterlin and others have pointed out, apparently also reacted strongly upon the American business cycles. It is hard to deny these facts. But how to solve this intriguing discrepancy between the scholars?

Maybe only a slight modification of Thomas' model is needed in order to harmonize the different interpretations! Instead of disregarding that the general business cycles can influence the timing of emigration we have to accept the empirical evidence implying such a causal relationship. Hence it can be supposed that the business cycles have an impact on the rise of immigration which in turn causes renewed infrastructural activities and a construction boom after a gestation period. The construction and housing industry must be considered a most important component in the whole process, as Thomas has pointed out. It is remarkable how well the focusing on the construction industry explains the paradox of a huge wave of European immigrants entering the American labor market exactly during the so-called *Great Depression* 1879–1893. It can be questioned, however, whether an external stimulus is needed. That must be dependent upon the state of the actual economy, its banking system etc., and the possibility of mobilizing capital for investments.

Some further comments are needed on this new interpretation. Those impulses for emigration which are initiated by the business cycles carry an inherent tendency of *overreaction.*[72] This will be commented upon in connection with a socio-psychological model attempt. Despite a sizable remigration across the Atlantic the receiving country gets an inflow of young labor, which tends to be disproportionately large compared with the labor market demands. It is reasonable to assume that this increase of an already considerable immigration has strengthened the important expansion of building and other infrastructural investments. One could also connect this phase of the cycle with the inherent growth of mass emigration, while on the other hand different short-term business cycles mainly lead to more casual fluctuations in the emigration curves. Thomas has a tendency to *separate* those phases which he has built up in such a logical and instructive way.

Reality is probably more complicated. A building boom can presumably

[72] A. Majava (1975) has also noticed this phenomenon.

in part overlap a period of prosperity in industry and could hence during certain periods, be especially favorable to the migrational movements.[73]

Concerning migration Thomas has made some very indirect calculations, which have been justifiably criticized. In his first book (1954), Thomas has used migrational data from Västmanland, a Swedish province in the vicinity of Stockholm. Thomas' choice of area was not the best one, since emigration from this part of Sweden was so insignificant that the assumed alternating swings between external and internal migration hardly could be expected.[74] The supposed pattern can, however, be discerned in areas of very intensive emigration.[75]

In his original version of his interaction model Thomas presumed that swings in external migration were inverse to swings in internal migration in countries of *immigration* as well as those of emigration.[76] He used the Negro migration as a proxy for the total internal migration in the US. His presumptions proved to be quite wrong in two important respects; the internal in-migration to cities in the US turned out to be synchronized with immigration and the Negro migration was atypical for the total internal in-migration.[77] Thomas could, however, abandon both these positions without getting any detrimental effects on the model as such. The counter-rhythm between external and internal migration which is consistent on the European side constitutes no necessary condition on the receiving continent. The fact that the black exodus, in slow progress during the final phase of the mass emigration, reveals a counter-rhythm, is an example of the socio-psychological barrier effects which might appear in connection with migration and which we commented upon earlier.

It is unfortunate that Thomas has had special problems with the empirical evidence about migration, which he gave such a central position. He is

[73] There are obvious difficulties in measuring the economic changes of the construction sector in a historical material. It seems likely, however, that the cause arrow does not necessarily point from migrations to construction in the simple way that is implied by B. Thomas. Constructing on a speculative basis might *per se* quite likely induce migrational effects.

[74] B. Thomas' internal migration analysis from 1954 has been criticized by S. B. Saul (1962) and others. With a somewhat improved empiricism but still with indirect calculation methods B. Thomas answers this criticism in 1972 on pp. 45–58. Other recent attempts by Scandinavian researchers to test his assumptions have given the same vague answer, probably due to the fact that emigration in most areas did not reach such an extent that it offered a real alternative to internal migration. S. Åkerman (1975), p. 25.

[75] B. Kronborg and T. Nilsson (1975), pp. 166–168.

[76] B. Thomas (1954), pp. 130–134.

[77] H. T. Eldridge and D. S. Thomas (1964), p. 224.

now formalizing his model in order to give it a more econometric shape. But it is questionable whether he is able to solve all those problems which have been discussed by doing so. On the contrary he might lose some of the flexibility which now characterizes his model.[78]

[78] There is no reason to assume that our theories become more "scientific" just because we give them the shape of a formal model. This misconception can be found e.g. in D. L. Meadows et al. (1972) in their well-known work "Limits to Growth". They define the non-formalized model as *mental models*. We may delimit another group of models—the *semi-quantitative* ones. In this new group we may include B. Thomas' model, for example, since his construct can only be tested to some degree with the aid of quantitative analysis. This type of model must be looked upon as especially useful to most historical studies. An interesting attempt to create a scheme of analysis for different theoretical approaches within social science research has been tried by R. Adamson (1975):

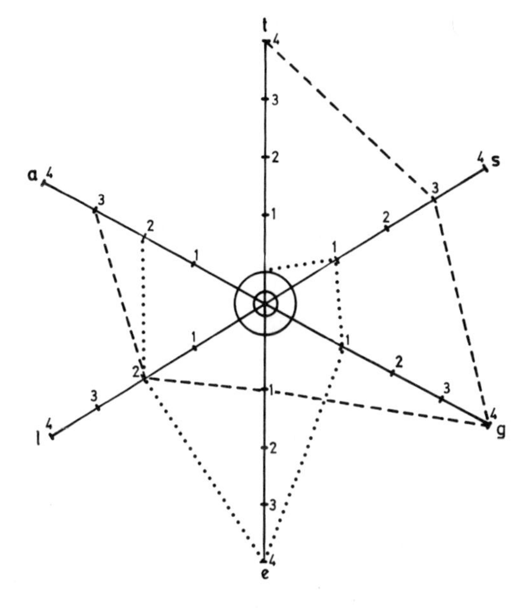

t=time dimension, s=spatial dimension, g=generalization dimension, e=empirical base, l=logical context, a=level of abstraction. Examples: --- K. Marx's short delineations of the materialistic idea of history. ······ a modern social science theory of a rather wide scope. 0=very low values, 4=very high values. (R. Adamson's interpretation.) As can be seen from the Figure, R. Adamson works with six dimensions. The judgements tend to be somewhat arbitrary, but nevertheless this tool seems to be very useful. In the section "Human Interactions in a Social and Geographical Setting" a three-step model of action spaces will be suggested. Such a model would rank high in the time, space, and generalization dimensions but low in the empirical, logical, and abstraction dimensions. It is possible that it could prove to be valuable to add a dimension of complication to the scheme of R. Adamson.

g. Behavioral Angles of Approach

Economists talk in figurative terms about "human investments", and there is good reason to shift the perspective and to center the study on the individual. Two avenues of approach can be chosen here; one sociological and the other psychological.

Sociological Approaches

J. J. Mangalam has tried a theoretical orientation based upon a sociological perspective. His point of departure is Talcott Parson's sociological theory. He distinguishes three structures which ought to be analyzed in migrational contexts: the social organization of the delivering country, of the migrant mass, and of the receiving country. Mangalam is inclined to give particular emphasis to the *interactive character* of migrational movements. In other words, it is unrealistic to treat migrants as isolated individuals. They are always involved in a process of socialization, and the framework for this process can be divided into three systems of components—a cultural, a social, and a personal system.[79]

As a phenomenon, social change occurs within or according to all of these systems. Norms, status roles, and institutions are important concepts in this functional analysis of society. Migration leads to social changes in both the delivering and receiving areas:

"But the greatest change is to be expected in S_M itself, because it is not only affected by the number and quality of the migrants but by variations in an indefinite number of elements in S_I and S_{II}. This change can sometimes be of an extreme nature. Also the structural strains involved in S_M as a result of migration are of a crucial nature. These strains can result, and actually do, from changes in practically all areas of functional problems. New ways of patterning, adapting, goal gratification, and integration hit the migrants almost all at once. Because of these considerations these two elements (social change and strain management) of S_M are printed in capital letters" (in Figure 2: 14).[80]

In his theoretical survey Mangalam does not deal very much with the

[79] J. J. Mangalam (1968) Introduction, pp. 1–19.

[80] J. J. Mangalam (1968), p. 15. Mangalam has of course been aware of the extensive debate and criticism on the so-called structural-functional analysis represented by T. Parsons and his school. Another starting point for this debate has been the well-known article by Robert Merton (1949).

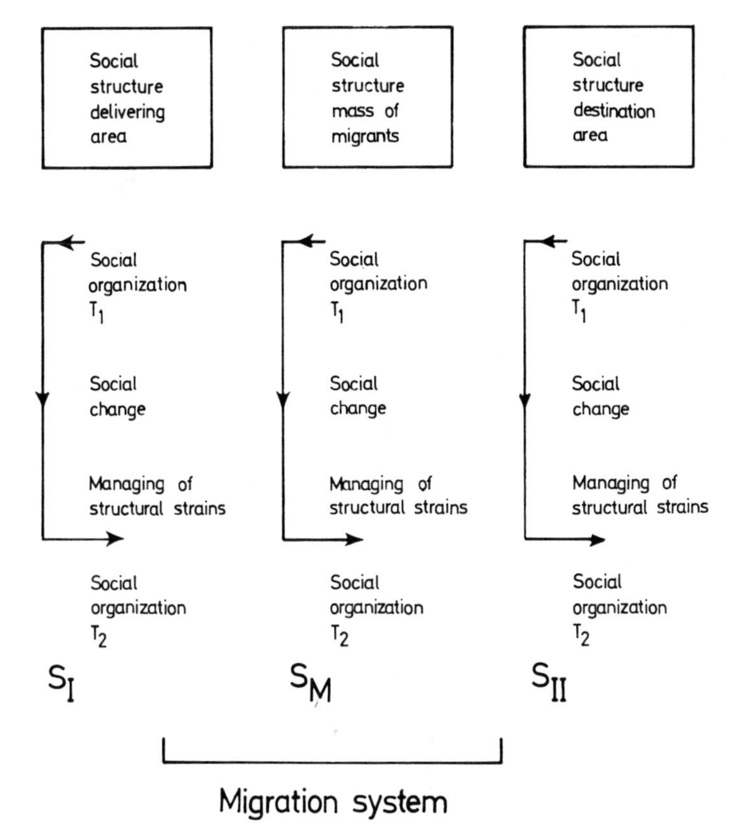

2: 14. The Model of J. J. Mangalam.

Comments S_I means delivering area, S_{II} means receiving area and S_M migration population. Note that the y-axis is the time dimension. This model is much simplified compared to the original.

Source J. J. Mangalam (1968), p. 18.

problem of quantifying and thereby testing research which has been organized on the basis of his recommendations.[81] Of course, we obtain a different type of test situation when we work with *structures* instead of *aggregates,* i.e., compact statistical data. It is not easy to find structural analyses of the kind Mangalam has in mind. Swedish researchers, however,

[81] The research team J. J. Mangalam, J. S. Brown and H. K. Schwarzweller has later on performed a small-scale study on the theme rural–urban migration within the same theoretical framework. H. K. Schwarzweller et al. (1971).

have performed a modest attempt to test another model of interpretation presented by the Dutch sociologist J. E. Ellemers who has the more specific purpose of analysing the decision to migrate.[82] Ellemers assumes that the concepts *structural strain, experience of strain and aspirations, migration offer, personality structure, and social control* develop decision to migrate into a so-called *value-added process.*[83] Hence, each step builds upon its predecessor and the entire "correct" combination is required in order for a decision to be reached. See Figure 2:15.

When applying a model we have to combine its concepts with suitable variables which is always a difficult technical problem. As a rule it is hardly possible to establish these connections in any perfect manner.[84] Of the ten demographic, economic, and sociological variables which could be used in this study we drew up the following attribution with Ellemers' concepts.

Concepts	Variables
structural strain (experience of strain and aspirations)	occupational category family size age civil status sex
migration offer	village (rote)
personal structure	ability to read number of migrations
social control	registration county of birth

Of the five variables which, by way of experimentation, were attributed to "structural strain" *occupational category* offers perhaps the best description of the strained conditions which can have prevailed in an agricultural area at the beginning of the industrialization. Occupational category encompasses such features as the differences between land-owning and propertyless persons and between skilled laborers—for example craftsmen—and others. Variables such as *age* and *civil status* are directly related to a certain individual's stage in the life cycle and may reflect more "normal" points of tension between the individual and his environment.

[82] J. E. Ellemers (1964).
[83] Compare also J. A. Jackson (1969), especially the article by R. C. Taylor.
[84] E. Nagel (1961), pp. 90–97. For a more general discussion about creation of concepts see R. Abler et al. (1971), esp. Figure 1:7.

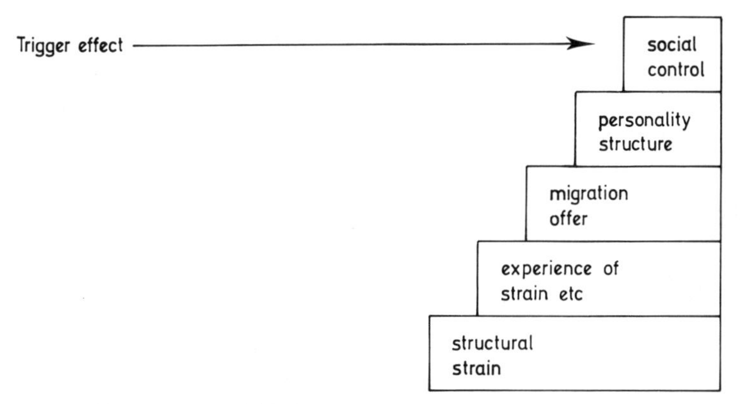

2:15. Ellemer's Value Added Process.
Source S. Åkerman et al. (1974), p. 34.

It appears rather obvious that the *ability to read* discloses features in the personality. The number of *previous migrations* has been attributed to personality structure as an indication of possible difficulties of adjustment, particularly for "overly mobile" persons. Of course, objections can be raised to this procedure. Moreover, it is not self-evident that migration offer can be captured by means of the *geographical variable* (village or rote). As mentioned other studies have documented the relationship between migrations from a well-defined region and the wealth of information on pertinent places of destination that reaches this particular region. Consequently, this pattern can support our interpretation.

It also seems conceivable that various types of *registration* in the church books can serve as a basis for determining the existence of social control. A person who was born and raised in a special social environment can be expected to react more strongly to social pressure than a person who has recently in-migrated or one who has only taken up temporary residence in the area.

The statistical method used in our study is AID-analysis (Automatic Interaction Detector) as formulated by Sonquist and Morgan.[85] Basically the technique is intended to help orientate the scholars in a vast and complicated mass of data. But at the same time it gives us a possibility to trace the interaction between quite a few variables. The great advantage of the new technique is that we can use variables also on the level of the

[85] J. A. Sonquist, E. L. Baker and J. N. Morgan (1973); J. A. Sonquist (1970). This technique is more thoroughly discussed in Chapter 6.

nominal scale in our analyses. We are able to do that by dichotomizing the predictors referring to the so-called criterion variable under study. This means that a study population is split into boxes consisting of groups of individuals of strong load on the criterion variable, e.g. *migration–no migration* or *emigration–internal migration.* The opposite development is registered on the other half of the so-called tree-output. The technique is also called data-split.[86]

By means of the resulting data cleavage (migrants/emigrants against residents) we can establish the fact that the variables *age* and *civil status* exerted a decisive influence. *Occupation* and *family size* enter in on the next level.[87] We defined these variables as integral components of structural strain. Migration offer, which we defined in terms of *geographical position,* occupied an intermediate level. Those which we judged to be personality variables do not enter into the picture until the fourth or fifth cleavage. It seems as if we have established the presence of the predicted interaction between Ellemers' concepts of structural strain, migration offer, and personality structure. Supposedly, these structural strains were more important than migration offer which, in turn, might have played a greater role than personality factors.

A Psychological Approach

As I mentioned above, the historian is handicapped compared with other social scientists who usually focus on current problems. We are painfully aware of this when we try to analyze the assimilation of migrants and move beyond external factors and situations. The Australian sociologist R. C. Taylor's inventive research of migrational situations can illustrate this. Taylor has isolated three major motives of migration or types of migrants, namely *Aspiring, Dislocated* and *Resultant.* Stated briefly, Aspiring re-

[86] Compare K. Mikkola (1974), who has tried the technique in a study dealing with recent internal migration in Finland.

[87] S. Åkerman et al. (1974) present the tree-output p. 48. Notice that this work can be done in two settings, one which takes care of structural contexts (background data) and another which takes care of various behavioral variables. This is of course most valuable for an in-depth analysis.

Our technique tries to come to grips with a very central problem within social science research in general: the relationship between the social, economic, and demographic *structure* and the *behavior* of the individuals involved. We often forget that differences of behavior can be as important for social change as the more easily studied structural differences. Cf. note 1, above.

fers to a conscious effort by a person to improve his own social and economic prospects or those of his family. This does not mean that the migrant necessarily considers himself as maladjusted in his present environment. On the other hand, the Dislocated type of individual views his situation as unsatisfactory. His present environment fails to match his needs and desires as related to the future of his children and other family members as well. The third type of migrant, characterized as Resultant finds himself redundant in his present economic and social situation, and this is not self-inflicted (compare unemployment). Consequently, this type shows the least inclination to migrate and, as far as possible, tries to find an alternative to migration. His behavior contrasts sharply with that of Aspiring and also Dislocated individuals, who deliberately conceive and plan their actions.[88]

In his empirical studies, Taylor has found logical differences between these three groups of individuals. These differences apply both to their attitudes towards information and the way in which the decision to migrate was realized. More importantly, the various motives for migration appear to have left a strong impact on their behavior and experiences in the receiving environments. Aspiring and Dislocated individuals, for example, seem to be more ready to adjust than Resultant individuals, who are also more inclined to re-migrate. Moreover, the three groups establish different personal networks in the new environment.

It must be admitted that it is rather difficult to analyze this attractive grouping of motivation for migration. Taylor ends up with a substantial residue which it is impossible to fit into these three main groupings. Hence there is a need to develop an even more sophisticated classification.

It may prove informative to connect Taylor's outline with our previous discussion on the development of mass emigration. We might assume that Aspiring and Dislocated individuals were more prevalent in the initial phases of movement than in the saturation phase. Moreover, we can expect that the regression phase was largely characterized by Resultant migration, with the exception of such categories as seasonal and educational migrants. It might also be possible to isolate certain occupational categories and social classes which dominate one or the other type of motive. Possibly, lower middle-class emigrants, for example, were largely Aspiring, whereas most emigrating small farmers were Dislocated and large numbers of emigrating artisans were Resultant. On the other hand, it

[88] R. C. Taylor (1969).

can prove more difficult to classify the extensive emigration of maid-servants, who presumably represented all three motives.

Human Interactions in a Social and Geographical Setting

By a systematic study of individuals it is possible to broaden the migration analysis. Our observation of geographic movements and other similar actions can reveal how different members of a society perceive their surrounding world. Such an angle of perspective might, in its turn, shed light on the basic conditions for the population mobility in general.

Research within social anthropology and geography and, for a long time, within genetics has begun to focus interest on this approach and new concepts like *action space* and *mental maps* have been coined. They are equivalent to *behavioral environment* and *perceptual environment* respectively.[89] Closely related to this research orientation are analyses based on concepts like *niche, network, neighborhood, marriage and migration fields.* We can imagine that a population of a country consists of several neighborhoods which theoretically can be described like this:

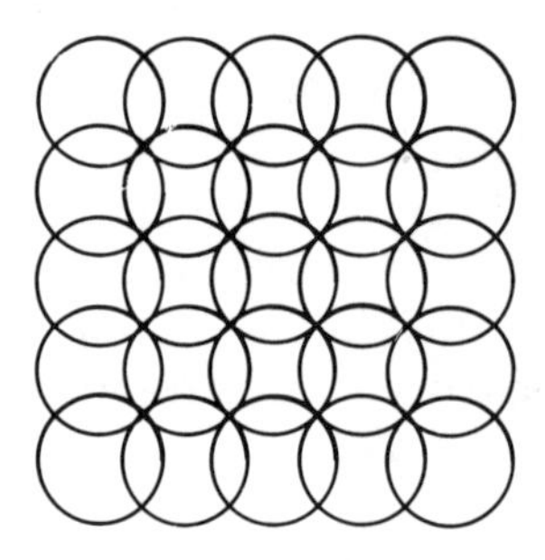

The overlapping of the areas implies that the different neighborhoods cannot be defined in a clear-cut manner (according to the social position of individuals and groups). Hence we have to use approximations.[90] We intend to capture the immediate social context of a group of individuals in the concept of *neighborhood.* This means that the most important personal interactions of this group take place within this sphere. On the next level we try to define a wider range of action for our population. We know that migrational movements, especially in a historical source materi-

[89] J. Sonnenfeld (1972).
[90] Cf. B. Hanssen (1952).

al, are the best indicators of such a field of action. Therefore we use the label *migration area.*[91]

But the contacts of the individual do not cease at this level. Knowledge and information which extend beyond an average migration area can be traced. This part of the surrounding world will be brought to the fore by more sporadic contacts (travels, seasonal migrations, correspondence, etc.). We have labelled it *experience area.* On the next level we find the huge remaining part of the world of which a person knows very little.

It is obvious that this theoretical construction will be restricted to a certain time period and that it presumably will function most satisfactorily before the 20th century. It is important for the practical value of this model that its concepts are satisfactorily delimited. This can be done by means of an average marriage field which can be equated with neighborhood. The frequency of migrations of varying distance can be used to define not only the migration area but also the experience area. In the latter case, of course, other data may also serve as information. For the sake of simplicity, neighborhood and migration area can be given a circular form whereas experience area can be allowed to take a more irregular shape.[92]

These ideas have as yet been tried in only one investigation but the assumptions about an interplay between the three areas seem realistic. This research, however, is still in a very preliminary stage. The dynamic character of this model is a most important feature. My intention has been to capture the changing interplay between the levels *neighborhood – migration area – experience area,* which may occur according to the suggested pattern. My theoretical point of departure has been the idea that changes in these "social spaces" might cause expansion as well as contraction.

h. An Interdisciplinary Approach

Time and again we have touched upon a basic difficulty for our model-building efforts. Hence, the severe fluctuations between peak and trough years of an emigration curve have not been adequately treated even by a

[91] Cf. the concept "mean information field" and "social space" which have been used more and more frequently in geographic research. R. L. Morrill and F. R. Pitts (1972), pp. 359–384, esp. p. 368.

[92] Calculations and some preliminary results in S. Åkerman (1976), Chapter 8. A serious complication is the fact that these areas often differ with social class, profession, age group, etc.

relatively sophisticated econometric model. We have noticed that such models lack sufficient *elasticity*. Another key observation has been the *overreaction,* which was commented upon in the analysis of the work of Brinley Thomas. All these observations indicate that there are social-psychological mechanisms which must be crucial for our understanding of migrational phenomena in general.

With this background in mind, then, we can try a new explanatory model which in some respects is more realistic than the models advanced in econometrics. In constructing our model we combine observations and factors from demographic, economic, sociological, psychological, and historical research. We take into account four groups of components:

A. Basic Factors and Conditions
B. Changes in the Basic Structure
C. Stimulators
D. Psychological-Sociological Multiplier Effects

It can be of advantage to regard some of Moe's constituent factors as constant here, at least if we are working with Kuznets' cycles. Consequently, the "permanent income gap" can be used in this manner. A closer study shows that there are other basic factors to consider, and these are not limited to the sphere of economy or demographic structure. Due to the scope of the present delineation we cannot discuss the arrangement of these factors in detail. However, it ought to be emphasized that presumably we must attach a great deal of importance to such factors as educational level, political power structure, religious conditions, possibilities for social advancement, etc. Moreover, the relationship between the *pace of economic growth* in the delivering country and that in the receiving country might be a better measurement of the constituent economic conditions than the factors which have been tested and examined up to this time.[93]

It is most important to keep in mind that the basic structure need not *change* for a mass emigration to occur. Emigration as such might even contribute to the perpetuation of a prevailing social and economic system. If changes in the basic structure of a society take place, however, they must be taken care of by the model. They form the second group of components in my scheme. The cohort-effect is a good representative of this set of variables. The fact that a series of basic factors promoting an extensive population movement do exist is not a prerequisite for the realization of

[93] Compare note 61 above.

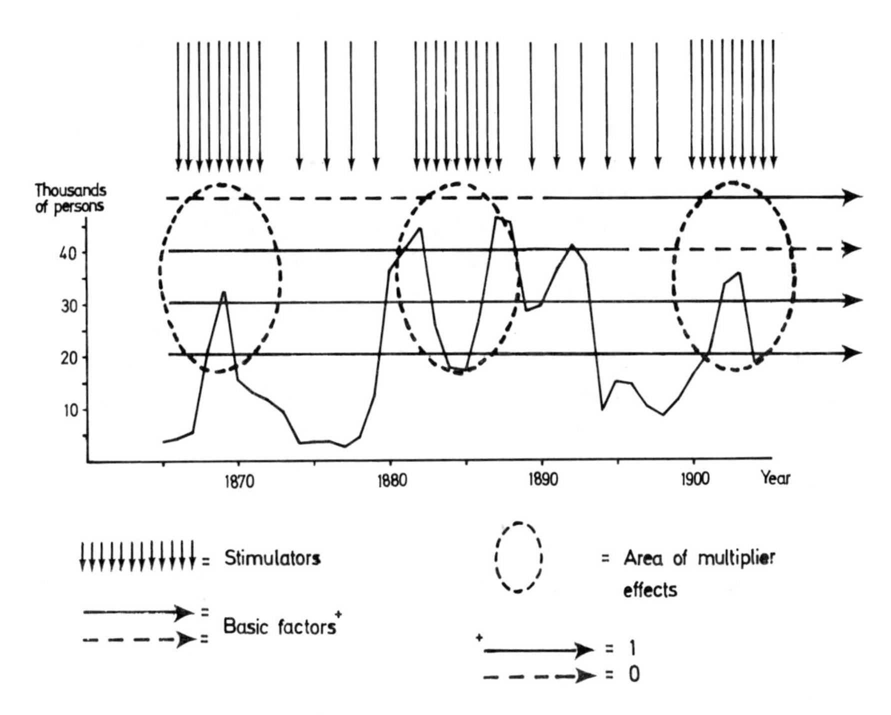

2:16. A New Model Approach.
Source S. Åkerman (1975), p. 32.

such movements. Nor will such a condition be created if we also add structural changes relevant for migrational movements. This statement is easy to verify by referring to the long passive period before the start of emigration in the 19th century—a period characterized by heavy population increase, pauperization of large sectors of society, etc. In addition another set of variables is needed. In my scheme it is called *stimulators*. Among these variables interest has primarily been focused on business cycles. Stimulator is, however, a broad concept deliberately chosen to mark various types of impact. The flow of information about an area of immigration belongs to this group of components. Isolated phenomena like the goldrush and the expected quota legislation in the 1920s must also be incorporated.

It seems as if it is possible to work with a value-added process (cf. Ellemers) also on the macro level. It is important to follow up the analysis even when the emigration is already triggered off. It can be empirically observed that mass behavior such as migration reacts upon itself.[94] We can talk about *psychological-sociological multiplier effects* (see Figure 2: 16). *When basic factors, relevant structural changes, and a set of stimulators interact favorably these multiplier effects can reinforce a dramatic growth in the volume of emigration and vice versa.* Hypothetically we may be able to register this mechanism both in a spatial and a social dimension. Thus, the implication is that the peak years show effects of reinforcements as well as of diffusion compared with the trough years. It remains to be investigated in detail how this mechanism works.[95] Without being able (for the moment) to test a general explanatory model of this type we can state that it may reveal more of the complicated realities behind migrational movements than would models of research restricted to a certain university discipline.

i. Summary

This survey of the theory and methods of migration research has taken the shape of a broad orientation about this extensive scholarly field. Some problem areas have been omitted deliberately and a real sharpening of the focus has been possible only on certain sectors. The strategy has been to give the discussion a broad interdisciplinary inclination. I have also questioned some very simplified models of explanation used in demography and economics and their basic assumptions. From the point of view of the theory of knowledge the stochastic approach has been questioned as well (compare the concept of *homo economicus*). It is worth emphasizing that I have not questioned the more elaborated model attempts performed in the field of economic research. It has been especially useful to criticize and evaluate the works of Brinley Thomas and Thorvald Moe both of whom based their research strategy on the findings of Simon Kuznets. Their works have raised expectations for a future development of a *predictive* model. Yet it seems as if such a model will not reach any

[94] My basic approach is parallel to the kind of business cycle analysis which has been tried by W. A. Jöhr (1952). Compare esp. his discussion about what he calls the core process of all business cycle fluctuations that he defines as a cumulative process of mass psychological influences which forces the analysis to concentrate on psychological mechanisms. Cf. esp. ibid. p. 520.

[95] The Nordic emigration scholars have been working for a long time with the data material from Iceland, Denmark, and Sweden. These analyses can be completed during 1976 at the earliest. Certain indications of relevance for our interpretations can be found in S. Åkerman (1974) and K. Söderberg (1974).

high degree of precision. Therefore general migration research cannot be content with the restrictions imposed on it by certain specialties.

My conviction has been that the social-psychological aspects of migrational movements have been too much neglected within this research. If we really try to reach something more than a superficial knowledge about population mobility, i.e. if we want to *understand* it, we must look upon this neglect as a very serious matter. We now face a body of empirical evidence based on social-psychological findings that we must take into account.

Important features of this new and growing body of knowledge are: individual decisions to move are made with a certain amount of resistance and without sufficient information on possible alternatives of migration. Moreover, many investigations indicate that information between individuals, especially on the primary group level, are of decisive importance for the realization of migration. Potential migration is generally widespread, and certain impulses or combinations of the same are evidently needed to trigger a definite response. Hence, we can expect that certain subpopulations in a given social, demographic, and economic structure will have stronger migrational tendencies. Personality factors also seem to affect migratory selection, but the outcome is highly dependent upon contextual frameworks. Finally we always have to consider a psychologically conditioned resistance to migrate, even where the context of migration appears to be favorable. The same applies to groups of individuals and entire subpopulations.

This is the frame of reference we have to take into consideration. An attempt has been made to integrate these various findings in a general interdisciplinary model approach which has only been outlined in a rather condensed way.

3. Sources for the History of Swedish Emigration

By Lars-Göran Tedebrand

It is a well-known fact that the study of international migration in its historical context is severely handicapped by deficient migration statistics. The discrepancy between various source series—for example, passport records and port statistics—takes significant proportions and varies both geographically, from country to country, and over time. As early as 1891 migration statistics were the focus of discussion at a series of international conferences on statistics, and prior to World War I, but especially during the 1920s and 1930s, the production of statistics considerably improved. Nevertheless, in 1947 the International Labour Organization could only characterize the mass of migration statistics as "still very imperfect and incapable of serving as a basis for international comparisons".[1]

However, since 1930, due to prominent contributions by Ferenczi and Willcox, comparative emigration research has access to statistical data which allow a rough territorial distribution and fluctuational analysis of overseas migration.[2] Re-immigration statistics undoubtedly exhibit the gravest deficiencies. At the same time, however, it must be emphasized that only a few countries possess emigration statistics based upon a consistent, differentiated, and reliable source collected during the period of mass emigration.

Naturally, there will never be sufficient source materials on the history of emigration to meet the demands of each special research orientation. But for a more diversified analysis of overseas emigration, the quantitative material ought to fulfill the following conditions. First, it should allow a time-series analysis on different aggregate levels with respect to local geography (villages, parishes, municipal districts) as well as regional and national geography. Second, it should allow a demographic and social differentiation of individual emigrants. Third, it should enable research to

[1] International Labour Office (1947), Chapter XI; I. Ferenczi (1929), p. 359; F. Thistlethwaite (1960), pp. 37 f.
[2] W. F. Willcox (1929, 1931).

profile emigration against the generally more expansive stream of internal migration, other streams of external migration, as well as the total population from which it originated. Finally, the transfer of primary data to the various statistical series must occur in a satisfactory manner and lend itself to controls.

In all of these respects Sweden's primary sources and its collection of emigration statistics meet high demands throughout the period of mass emigration. Moreover, demographers in other countries have long been aware of the fact that the Swedish church book material is well suited for historical population studies. Swedish researchers as well as a number of their foreign colleagues in various disciplines have won international reputations by virtue of their analyses of Swedish population data. These include such researchers of internal and external migration as D. S. Thomas, B. Thomas, and T. Hägerstrand and those who have dealt with problems of social mobility and issues of a more succinctly demographic nature, for example E. P. Hutchinson and G. Carlsson.[3]

Prior to a more detailed discussion of the basic sources for historical overseas migration, it is appropriate to outline the genetical growth and nature of Sweden's population registration.

Historical Background: The Local Material

For more than 200 years local population registration has served as the basis for Swedish national statistics. Demographic research in Sweden is particularly well equipped to make studies of the demography of late agrarian society and related developments during the various phases of industrialization. However, like his foreign colleagues the Swedish population historian encounters significant problems in drawing conclusions about population size and demographic changes during the first centuries of The Early Modern Era. The lack of both local and central census material has forced researchers to make indirect estimates of the trend in population development. To do so, they have primarily used various fiscal source series which show the development in settled areas.[4]

The most important nominative sources in Sweden prior to universal

[3] D. S. Thomas (1941); B. Thomas (1954); T. Hägerstrand (1957); K. A. Edin and E. P. Hutchinson (1935); G. Carlsson (1969).

[4] For the latest research in this area see L. O. Larsson (1972) and S. Lundkvist (1974). General information on Swedish population statistics can be found in B. Odén (1970) and *Minneskrift* (1949).

local parish registration are the *mantalslängder* (poll-tax registers), which date from 1628. However, prior to 1765 certain elements of the population are either underrepresented or altogether missing in these registers, and the reliability of the material fluctuates both chronologically and regionally. Yet, in fortunate cases these registers can serve as a basis for detailed historical and demographic analyses.[5]

More importantly, some clergymen in the early 1600s were influenced by registration methods in other countries and subsequently began records of ecclesiastical functions and their own parishioners. A church law enacted in 1686 paved the way for a uniform code of church registration in Sweden. In every parish priests were encharged with the task of recording clerical functions—i.e. baptisms, marriages and burials. The majority of Swedish parishes claim long and uninterrupted series of registers covering births, baptisms, marriages, deaths and burials since the middle of the 18th century.

The Church Law of 1686 also called for the recording of in-migration and out-migration in special books. Unfortunately, this regulation was not enforced over a long period of time. Not before the 1820s did parishes keep special records of migration on a more regular basis. Records of in-migration contain the date of registration; the current year and consecutive number of in-migration; the name, sex, and occupation of the in-migrant individual; the parish or country from which he or she migrated; and the new area of residence in the parish. The registers of out-migration contain the same information on out-migrants. The Swedish migration registers are suitable for longitudinal cohort studies, for example, of the relationship between geographic and social mobility.

The various individual data contained in the Parish Records of Ministerial Acts are collected in the principal record books of each parish. In addition to their ministerial records, priests also had the responsibility of keeping registers on adult parishioners. Known as the *husförhörslängder* (Parish Registers of Catechetical Examinations) these were originally used by priests in connection with annually held catechetical meetings. On such occasions priests recorded each parishioner's knowledge of the Catechism, reading proficiency, and abilities of comprehension. In Sweden's southernmost provinces, writing ability was also recorded to some extent. In 1748 a regulation was enacted, calling for the registration of children in these registers; this was already common practice in some parishes. The

[5] G. Lext (1968); D. Hannerberg (1940), pp. 40 ff.

Catechetical Registers contain a thorough range of individual data: name, date of birth, sex, civil status, occupation—and to a certain extent social status—place of residence (homesteads and villages), migration, marriage, and death. In reality, the Catechetical Registers came to function as population registers, where continuous individual notations were kept on the changes in the local population.[6]

As demographic research has come to focus increased interest on small groups and families the Catechetical Registers have drawn greater attention. Parishioners are listed in these registers by families. The names of individual family members (husband, wife, and children) are followed by those of relatives and domestic help who belonged to the main family household. By utilizing these registers the population historian is not only able to isolate the nuclear family structure but also study different forms of extended families. Recent quantitative studies have investigated notations in the Swedish church records regarding popular literacy prior to the introduction of compulsory school education. Such research has attracted attention from scholars in other countries.[7]

Historical Background: The Central Statistics

In the beginning the local parish registry material was used by Swedish government officials primarily as a countercheck to the poll-tax registers. After lengthy discussions, dating back to the 1730s, a royal decree was finally issued in 1748 instituting the *Tabellverket* (The Swedish National Bureau of Statistics). This inaugurated a differentiated type of population and social statistics in Sweden based on the local parish registers. The organization of this statistical bureau, which lacked any direct counterpart in other countries, was characterized by a decentralization of statistical processing. The tabulatory material on population and mortality, which parish priests recorded on special forms, was finally drawn up in the form of province-wide summaries (eventually by dioceses). Beginning in 1749 these were filed with the Chancellery in Stockholm. Seven years later, in 1756, the central task of organizing this material was assigned to a special

[6] A. Sandberg (1948); N. Friberg (1954); N. and I. Friberg (1971).
[7] E. Johansson (1972, 1973). The added interest in historical demography shown by various disciplines, together with the unique merits of the Swedish church book material, have recently initiated an extensive collection and computer storage of church records at a so-called data base. Cf. S. Åkerman and E. Johansson (1973).

commission, the so-called *Tabellkommissionen*. In essence, this was the world's first governmental department of statistics.[8]

This system was retained with minor changes until 1860, when the national census surveys (held every ten years between 1860 and 1930) were directly based upon nominative extracts from the Parish Registers of Catechetical Examinations. Annual reports on population statistics were now drawn from the entries in the parish registers of births, marriages, and deaths. However, parish priests were not entirely relieved of the task of producing statistics. At the beginning of each year they were to submit *Summariska folkmängdsredogörelser* (Condensed Population Reports) for their respective parishes which specified the various components of population mobility. This re-organization in 1858 of the Swedish system for statistics production saw the end of the old National Bureau of Statistics and its replacement by the *Statistiska Centralbyrån* (Central Bureau of Statistics).

Around 1900 the well-known statistician, Gustav Sundbärg, presented Swedish population data to an international audience. In so doing, he justifiably called attention to two important facts. First, the statistical material exhibited a long continuity of registration. Second, the production of statistics in Sweden was based upon accurate and detailed primary source materials and not, as in many other countries, upon census-takings whose reliability was frequently difficult to establish.[9] The centralization of responsibilities connected with the organization of these primary data in 1860 doubtlessly increased the reliability of Swedish population statistics.

Central Sources and Official Statistics

Swedish emigration research has frequently utilized the parishes primary source materials for case studies. However, this is an enormously time-consuming operation, and secondary sources must be used for timeseries analyses and more aggregated, structural studies. Therefore, it may be appropriate at this point to describe the Swedish migration statistics. Special interest will be devoted to the central source series and their relationship to local primary sources and officially published statistics.

Older Swedish population statistics harbored a weakness, namely the poor registration of internal and external migration. The primary tabula-

[8] For the oldest Swedish population statistics see H. Gahn (1916), pp. 15 ff. and A. Hjelt (1899, 1900).
[9] G. Sundbärg (1907), pp. 161 ff.

tory material of the National Bureau of Statistics only records migration for certain periods during the first half of the 1800s. For the period 1805–1835 the census tables contain five-year totals of in-migration and out-migration with respect to towns and rural deaneries (prosterier). Annual migration statistics are contained in the mortality tables between 1821 and 1844.[10] However, the *Tabellkommissionen* was primarily interested in net migration changes, and it is therefore typical that from 1840 on the Commission only required reports on net migration in connection with census-takings. It was not until the Condensed Population Reports were introduced in 1860 that Sweden acquired a central source series which registered annual in-migration and out-migration at the local parish level.

External migration is not separately registered in the Bureau of Statistic's figures on population turnover. The very absence of emigration figures led to an exaggerated picture of the extent of emigration in agrarian society. As early as 1780 Pehr Wargentin, the pioneer of Swedish population statistics, published certain estimates of emigration.[11] In recent years the whole issue of the extent of external migration during the 1700s has been discussed on the basis of new methodological standpoints. By utilizing the so-called difference method researchers have attempted to calculate the distribution of ages and sexes in Swedish emigration. This method involves the use of Lexis diagrams and population projections in various birth cohorts as a means of reaching a precise estimate of the population at given points in time—i.e. during census years. By subtracting the official population statistics from projected statistics one can reach an idea of the net population movements. However, this method encounters special problems in dealing with the 1700s. For example, input data pertaining to mortality risks, age-specific death rates, and age distribution must be based on modern reconstructions.[12]

The Initial Phase of Emigration. Passenger Fee Journals and Passenger Lists of Immigrant Ports

Official records of Swedish emigration statistics began in 1851. Despite the lack of central statistics one is not entirely limited to church book material for researching the initial decades of overseas migration. Passports were required of all travelers to and from Sweden as far back as the 1600s, and

[10] Cf. S. Carlsson (1973 *a*), pp. 190 ff.
[11] P. W. Wargentin (1780).
[12] E. Bernin, p. 1 ff.

this regulation was renewed by separate ordinances in 1811 and 1812. The passport journals kept by province government boards and civil magistrates naturally serve as primary source materials for any intensified, aggregate analysis of the early history of emigration. However, they are distributed among a large number of archives and also exhibit substantial gaps. Therefore, recent research has focused increasing attention on a central source series based directly upon the passport journals.

A fee was paid with each passport application; together with an extract from the passport journals, this was sent to the Royal Navy's Pension Fund. These passenger fee journals form a continuous series from 1817 to 1851 and provide names, occupations, dates of departure, home districts, and destinations, of travelers abroad.[13] However, they are hardly without their own share of deficiencies. Naturally, no record was kept of illegal departures from Sweden. It is uncertain whether the statistics on poor persons and children under 12 years of age, who were exempt from passenger fees, were made in a consistent manner. But this source series does have obvious merits. It allows the researcher to isolate emigrants to North America, and in contrast to the basic source material—the passport journals of the Swedish province boards—it is complete. Moreover, it appears that a systematic analysis of these passport journals can clarify the rhythm, geographical spread, and structural features of the early phase of emigration.[14]

In order to arrive at a true evaluation of the reliability of these journals the researcher must control their content in detail against the parish record books. However, the reports on emigrants to North America can also be juxtaposed with an independent, American source series. The United States Congress took legislative steps to control the emigrant traffic which flourished shortly after the Congress of Vienna. A law was passed in 1819, requiring commanding officers of emigrant vessels, upon arrival in American ports, to draw up a list (the ship's manifest) of all passengers' names, ages, sex, occupations, countries of origin, and intended countries of destination. Reports were also to be filed in the case of passengers who died at sea.

The ships' manifest are only partially preserved in their original manuscript form and on microfilm at the National Archives in Washington, D.C. However, the passenger lists for New York—the most important

[13] A. Friman (1974), pp. 18 ff; E. Nordström (1973).
[14] A. Friman (1974), pp. 29 ff.

harbor of immigrant traffic—are extant as an uninterrupted source series beginning in 1820. The American researcher, Nils William Olsson, has conducted a systematic inventory of all Swedish names contained in the New York ships' manifests.[15] From the 33 000 lists between 1820 and 1850 he has identified nearly 4 000 Swedish immigrants. In certain respects the ships' manifests are obviously deficient: passengers' names are distorted, and in some cases Sweden has been confused with Switzerland as the country of origin. In other cases persons who are definitely known to have emigrated are missing from these lists; for example the well-known emigrant pioneer and dissenting leader, Erik Jansson, altogether succeeded in concealing his true identity.[16] However, Olsson has expanded his analysis and linked the American reports with the Swedish passenger fee journals and church records. Naturally enough, considerable record-linkage problems arise in comparing such a variety of source materials.[17]

Olsson's book mainly has the character of a source publication. However, by identifying about 75 per cent of the Swedish names in the ships' manifests on the basis of the Swedish background material he has provided research with interesting aspects of personal history from the early years of emigration.

Sweden's First National Emigration Statistics, 1851–1860

Emigration to North America accelerated during the early 1850s. This increased government dissatisfaction over the lack of official statistics on this flow of migration. However, it was not until 1856 that the *Tabellkommissionen* required such information, not from parish priests, but from province boards. Sweden's first national statistics on emigration between 1851 and 1860 are based on these reports, which contain individual data on persons who applied for passports in connection with emigration and who were duly registered in the passport journals kept by *länsstyrelser* (province boards). However, as mentioned above, these journals do have deficiencies; individual data from certain areas were therefore extracted from the parish records. The Bureau of Statistics required the following information: the emigrant's name, age, civil status, occupation, home parish, and country of destination.

[15] N. W. Olsson (1967); cf. Beijbom (1969).
[16] N. W. Olsson (1967), pp. xi ff.
[17] Regarding this problem see, for example, E. A. Wrigley (1973).

These name lists are drawn from pass journals which were not originally intended to provide a basis for differentiated emigration statistics, and the various data were entered on a retroactive basis. There have been differences of opinion regarding the reliability of emigration statistics from the 1850s. In the early 1900s the *Emigrationsutredningen* (Commission on Emigration), appointed by the Swedish government, maintained that the nominative reports were incomplete, particularly during the latter half of the 1850s. The Commission estimated that unregistered emigration between 1851 and 1860 totalled not less than 119 per cent of the registered statistics. These estimates were drawn up by the Commission's Secretary, Gustav Sundbärg, and were based upon the relationship between estimated and recorded population increase during that decade.[18] More recent studies also indicate that the nominative reports exhibit lower emigration figures than church registers. One explanation cited in this context is that provincial officials, who organized the emigrant records on the basis of the passport journals, were not always able to isolate emigrants from the normal stream of foreign travelers and work migrants.[19] Naturally, the distinction between emigration and external work migrations has aroused many subjective judgements and evaluations. However, as is to be expected, this confusion appears to have primarily affected figures for the extent of European emigration.

All problems connected with the introduction of Sweden's first collection of emigration statistics have not yet been solved. However, this much seems to be clear: the official emigration statistics of the 1850s give a more reliable picture of emigration to America than was assumed previously.

The Condensed Population Reports and the Official Statistics on Mass Emigration

An ordinance issued in 1860 abolished the requirement of passports for travelers to and from Sweden. As a result, no statistics were recorded on Swedish emigrants over a period of several years. However, beginning in 1865 and retroactively from 1861, the Condensed Population Reports also contain nominative data on persons who filed address change certificates for the purpose of emigration. In other words, these emigrant lists represented extracts from the serial registration of persons who informed

[18] Emigrationsutredningen, Bilaga IV, pp. 248 ff.; Betänkande, pp. 595 ff.
[19] A. Wirén (1975), pp. 26 f.; H. Norman (1974), p. 130.

their parish priests of their intent to emigrate. The following individual variables are recorded in the emigrant lists of the Condensed Population Reports: the emigrant's name, occupation, year of birth, and country of destination. In 1870 a specially printed form was introduced which also indicated emigrants' civil status. An important supplement came in 1875, when separate lists of immigrants were included in the Condensed Population Reports. As a result, Sweden was able to establish national immigrant statistics long before other countries. The lists of immigrants and emigrants were improved in 1890, when widows and widowers received specific entries under the heading of "civil status". Up to that time such persons had been classified as "unmarried".

Since 1861 Sweden has produced emigration statistics which are indirectly based upon primary material from local parishes. Seen in an international perspective, these statistics not only predate others of the same type but also claim a high degree of reliability. The emigrant lists contained in the Condensed Population Reports serve as the basic source material for the official emigration statistics during the entire phase of mass emigration. Since these lists are based upon the migration registers of local parishes, research must control their registration of emigrants and check the accuracy and care taken by priests in filing annual reports with the Central Bureau of Statistics. A large number of special studies conducted by the Migration Research Project at Uppsala University has clearly shown that there is a great deal of conformity between the central and local source series.[20] On the other hand, it has been found that the local migration registers contained certain deficiencies which were subsequently transferred to the Condensed Population Reports. Thus, it is only natural that the payroll lists of industrial firms, for example, contain more specified occupational designations than the parish migration registers.[21]

Unregistered Emigration

Despite the high degree of conformity between the primary material of parishes and the central Swedish emigration statistics from 1861, breaks do occur in these records prior to 1885 but also to some extent later on. As late as 1884 persons were still at liberty to emigrate without filing address change certificates. The *Statistiska Centralbyrån* (Central Bureau of Statis-

[20] In particular, see L.-G. Tedebrand (1972), pp. 70 ff.
[21] B. Rondahl (1972), pp. 202 ff.

tics) was fully aware of the pre-1885 deficiency. In annually published reports it pointed out that the low figures reported by local priests were too low due either to emigrants' failure to file address change certificates or to their emigration on the basis of so-called work certificates or personal identification papers (*frejdebetyg*) issued in their home parishes. Consequently, such persons were still legally registered in the local church books.[22]

As indicated earlier, there were many difficulties in distinguishing between different forms of migration during the initial phase of mass emigration. In addition to registered internal population turnover there were movements by seasonal workers to extensive farming areas and rising industrial districts. Work migration represented a sizable share of Sweden's exchange of population with its Scandinavian neighbors.[23] Even emigration to North America gradually acquired some of the character of a transatlantic labor migration.[24] The Central Bureau of Statistics also observed that the statistics on immigrants from North America recorded by the Gothenburg Police outnumbered the figures reported by local priests; in 1885 the priests' statistics accounted for only 65 per cent of the Police Commissioner's.[25]

There are good possibilities of establishing the size of unregistered emigration. An indication of this is provided by the Central Bureau of Statistics' own condensed comparisons between port of embarkation statistics and the official emigration figures. They clearly show, for example, that overseas emigration from Sweden reached its peak in 1882 and not in 1887. However, research has primarily utilized various statistical methods in order to estimate the size of unregistered emigration. Sundbärg, in particular, used a rather simple, though hardly unobjectionable method as a means of charting unregistered statistics during various periods.[26] Having subtracted the surplus of births from population increase, he then compared the remaining migration loss with registered emigration and assumed that the difference between them represented unregistered emigration. A certain amount of unregistered emigration in proportion to registered statistics was charged to each calender year during the sub-

[22] *Bidrag till Sveriges Officiella Statistik* (Contributions to Sweden's Official Statistics), series A, 1882, p. XVI.

[23] L.-G. Tedebrand (1972), pp. 259 ff.

[24] L.-G. Tedebrand (1972), pp. 222 ff.

[25] *Bidrag till Sveriges Officiella Statistik*, series A, 1885, p. II.

[26] *Emigrationsutredningen* (The Report of the Swedish Commission on Emigration).

periods in his analysis. This procedure enabled Sundbärg to present the following figures for unregistered emigration in percent of registered statistics:

1860s	20 %
1870s	12 %
1880–1884	10 %
1885–1893	1 %
1894–1900	8 %

Naturally enough, Sundbärg linked the sharp decline of unregistered emigration beginning in 1885 with the Emigration Ordinance of 1884. On the other hand, he interpreted its rise up to 1900 as a direct consequence of sharpened legislation, passed in 1893, regarding emigration by military conscripts.

Recently, researchers have used more sophisticated methods for estimates of unregistered emigration prior to 1885. The official statistics show an annual emigration total of 20 526 persons (or 4.9 per mille of the average population) for the five-year period 1866–1870. The difference method, however, records a total of 23 828 persons (or 5.7 per mille of the average population).

It is altogether clear that Sundbärg exaggerated the importance of the Emigration Ordinance of 1884. According to the official statistics, a net external migration of 26 901 persons out of the 1866–1870 male birth cohorts took place from 1886 to 1890. However, by using a combination of so-called retrojection and projection methods research has discovered a net migration of no less than 35 600 persons.[27]

By utilizing these statistical methods research can largely clarify the magnitude of unregistered emigration and its changes over the course of time. However, objections can easily be raised to Sundbärg's techniques of measurement as well as the more modern methods. What Sundbärg calculated was not unregistered gross emigration but rather the unregistered loss of population due to external migration, as distributed according to particular years. His method entirely disregards one significant fact, namely that transatlantic emigration from Sweden was substantially characterized by work migrations. If re-immigration from America occurred within a two-year period after emigration, persons who left Sweden without filing address change certificates would be classified neither as

[27] E. Bernin, p. 7; H. Lundström (1975), p. 9.

emigrants nor immigrants. In other words, Sundbärg's net argument provides no information whatsoever on the total amount of unregistered gross emigration or its annual fluctuation. Although the more modern methods contribute certain important details regarding the structure of unregistered emigration, they too, fail to consider the disturbing effect of transatlantic work migration on the results of statistical measurements.[28]

More recent research has also criticized Sundbärg's period demarkations. As pointed out above, he seems to have exaggerated the significance of the Emigration Ordinance of 1884 and, at the same time, overestimated the effect which restrictive legislation in 1893 had on emigration by military conscripts.[29]

The Passenger Lists of Emigrant Ports

It is possible to isolate unregistered emigrants in the parish registers by concentrating interest on parish lists of so-called untraceable persons. However, there is source material which allows research to attack the issue of unregistered emigration on an aggregate level as well. A government ordinance was issued in 1869, requiring emigrant agents to submit to the port authorities a list of passengers who emigrated on a contract basis. These passenger lists (skeppslistor), have been preserved from the following Swedish ports: Gothenburg, the country's largest emigrant port, beginning in 1869; Malmö, in the southernmost province of Skåne, from 1874; and the capital city of Stockholm (transcript copies of the original documents), between 1869 and 1904.[30] Similar lists are also extant from Danish, Norwegian, and German ports from which Swedish emigrants embarked. In fact, the Danish and Norwegian emigration statistics are based either on these lists or on other police records of emigrant traffic.[31]

As mentioned above, the official Swedish statistics have underregistered the volume of emigration to North America. At the same time, however, the passenger lists cannot be used in their entirety for an annual control of the official emigrant volume. These lists themselves contain certain gaps and other imperfections. Nonetheless, excerpts have been drawn from all of the extant passenger lists with respect to a few, selected years of recorded high and low emigration (1874, 1882, 1885, and 1923). These are cur-

[28] L.-G. Tedebrand (1972), p. 322.
[29] A.-S. Kälvemark (1972), pp. 86 ff.; see also Chapter 6 c below.
[30] L.-G. Tedebrand (1972), p. 184; F. Nilsson 1970), pp. 261 ff.
[31] K. Hvidt (1971), pp. 65 ff.

rently being prepared for computer processing. At this stage certain preliminary results have been reached in the processing of the 1874 material from the emigrant ports of Gothenburg, Malmö, Kristiania (Oslo), Trondheim, and Copenhagen. Swedish emigration volume to North America by way of these five ports amounted to 4 736 persons in 1874; in contrast, the Condensed Population Reports only record 3 380 emigrants.[32] In other words, gross unregistered emigration to North America totalled at least 40 per cent of the registered statistics (compare Sundbärg's 12% figure). This point-analysis clearly reveals the weakness in Sundbärg's net argument.

It is only natural that Swedish emigration research has focused its attention on the Gothenburg passenger lists, which are altogether intact.[33] This material was drawn up according to a fixed page arrangement containing the following column entries: the contract number, the emigrant's name and occupation, birthplace (subsequently changed to home district), age, sex, place of destination, date of embarkation, lodgings on board ship, and the name of the emigrant agent. One weak point is that after 1870 occupations are only listed in exceptional cases.

Both during and after the 1870s all of this information was based upon oral reports from the emigrants themselves. There are discrepancies between the home districts cited by emigrants and the actual parish districts in which they were registered. Consequently, substantial linkage problems arise when one attempts to identify emigrants in the passenger lists and the local church records. Case studies have disclosed weaknesses in the Swedish registration of emigrant traffic. Even contemporary observers were aware of the fact that the 1884 Ordinance, which required persons to secure address change certificates before contracting overseas passage, did not prohibit emigrants from leaving the country as ordinary tourists bound for England. There they could subsequently arrange passage to America. However, this possiblity probably saw infrequent use, since emigrants thereby forfeited certain rights and benefits—for example, legal protection—provided by their passage contracts when stamped by the police commissioner in the port of embarkation. Nevertheless, the passenger lists do indicate that persons without address change certificates emigrated from Gothenburg after 1884 on the basis of emigrant contracts.

The Swedish Commission on Emigration sent a representative to Goth-

[32] I. Eriksson (1970), pp. 1–6.

[33] See L.-G. Tedebrand (1972), pp. 187 ff; B. Brattne (1973), pp. 72 ff.

enburg to oversee the Police Commissioner's handling of emigrant contracts and the attached address change certificates. It was his judgement, too, that the control procedure was exceptionally brief.[34] Even government officials were highly conscious of the fact that the Emigration Ordinance of 1884 did not prohibit unauthorized emigration from Swedish ports.[35]

In other words, the passenger lists claim obvious value as a corrective to the official statistics. Of even greater importance is the additional information offered by this source series. By studying emigrant destinations in America, as stated in the passenger lists, one can determine the preferences of various groups in selecting areas of settlement. Moreover, these reports clearly reveal that the official statistics have underestimated emigrant volume to Canada; this is due to deficient or incorrect information given by emigrants at the time address change certificates were filed.[36]

As far as the sociological study of migration is concerned, the passenger lists can serve as a basis for analyzing the group structure of emigration. Much remains to be done in this field of research. However, detailed regional analysis has already shown that Swedish emigration not only made the transition from family to individual emigration over the course of time but also shifted from large to small emigrant groups.[37]

Studies of mass emigration's group structure raise a number of issues. One in particular concerns the influence of former emigrants (so-called Yankees) who returned to Sweden for shorter periods of time. What role did they play as disseminators of information and recruiters of additional emigrants? Most Swedish-Americans returned to America on emigrant contracts. Consequently, the passenger lists offer unique opportunities for measuring this significant stream of tourist-travelers. In 1900 no less than 3 766 Swedish-Americans left Gothenburg for North America; this means that the "Yankees" represented about 1/4 of the emigrant volume in that particular year.[38]

In the past migration researchers have been somewhat sceptical about the possibilities of using the passenger lists for the purpose of emigration analysis. However, by using this material with the proper source-critical attitude one can essentially expand our knowledge of the way in which

[34] *Emigrationsutredningen,* Bilaga 2, pp. 73 ff.
[35] See, for example, *Svensk Författningssamling* (The Swedish Code of Statutes), 1904: 43.
[36] L.-G. Tedebrand (1972), pp. 211 f.
[37] L.-G. Tedebrand (1972), p. 188.
[38] L.-G. Tedebrand (1972), p. 188.

mass emigration from Sweden functioned in its historical context. At the same time, the source-critical examination of the passenger lists is of significant interest for international emigration research.

Sources for the History of the Transport Organization

As early as 1911 the American Dillingham Commission voiced the conviction that emigration from Southern Europe, which began in the mid 1880s, was an artificial phenomenon fostered by the North Atlantic shipping companies and their agents. Research has long been challenged by this statement, and theoretical discussions of volume changes in mass emigration have often questioned the intrinsic capacity of transport companies to accelerate emigration. However, studies of the transport sector's role in the emigration process have been thwarted by the lack of source materials. Shipping companies have either weeded out their archives or closed their doors to researchers, and only fragments remain of the material collected by emigrant agents.

Consequently, it was something of a sensation when the complete papers of an emigrant agency were discovered in Sweden in the mid-1950s. This material consists of letter copy files, original correspondence, account books, etc., from the Larsson Brothers' Company and covers the period between 1873 and 1914. It allows research to conduct highly intensified analyses of emigrant agent activities during the peak years of Swedish emigration, namely the 1880s.[39] Of particular importance is the fact that the archives contain information on the extent of potential emigration and the breakdown between cash and prepaid tickets for emigrant passage to America. In processing this material we have come to definite grips with the issue of emigration volume and the activities of emigrant agencies. The major finding is that the transport sector was incapable of accelerating emigration by wide-scale advertising or by price policies, not even for shorter periods of time.[40]

Background and Reference Data

Overseas migration represents only a residual share of the total (statistics on) population movement. Swedish emigration research has therefore devoted major interest to the study of emigration's structural contact sur-

[39] O. Thörn (1959); B. Brattne (1973). Recently, sections of smaller agent archives have been found in the small port of Kalmar, along the Baltic coast: see M. Höjfors (1971).
[40] B. Brattne (1973), *passim.*

faces in relationship to international migration. It is rather natural that researchers have also discussed Brinley Thomas' model for the relationship between urban in-migration and emigration within the framework of the "Atlantic economy."[41] Such studies are simplified in Sweden due to that fact that the central source series on migration, the Condensed Population Reports, contain annual statistics for external and internal migration on the parish level as distributed by men and women.

Equally important is the task of profiling emigrants against the total population in the delivering country. Cross-sectional data in the National Census Surveys covering the demographic and social structure of the Swedish population have been used to illustrate the selection mechanisms of emigration to America. Some of this background material can be found in the published population statistics. However, in dealing with individual parishes researchers have used the extensive tabulatory material kept at the Central Bureau of Statistics in Stockholm.

Swedish emigration research has devoted particular attention to the relationship between emigration and the processes of urbanization and industrialization in Swedish society. For this purpose parishes have been classified according to their industrialization level. Various fiscal sources have been used, primarily reports on the distribution of taxable income between agricultural property and industrial establishments.[42] This parish classification has also made use of other source series contained in the official statistics, such as reports on the number of craftsmen and industrial workers, agricultural and tenant farming conditions, *etc.*

Qualitative Sources

Although Swedish emigration research has a prominently quantitative orientation it has also dealt with the political, informational, and opinion-making aspects of emigration.[43] Attention has been given to the debate on emigration as reflected in *riksdag* publications, brochures and pamphlets, and the Swedish press. Studies have also been made of the shipping com-

[41] See Chapter 2f., above; L.-G. Tedebrand (1972), pp. 178 ff.; H. Norman (1974), pp. 108 ff.; B. Kronborg and T. Nilsson (1975), pp. 162 ff.
[42] This material has been used, for example, by D. S. Thomas (1941) and the so-called "Stockholm Study" which presented annual total statistics for internal and external migration in different types of administrative districts on the level of Swedish län for the period 1895–1930. *Cf.* L. G. Tedebrand (1972), p. 60 ff. and B. Kronborg and T. Nilsson (1975), p. 48 f.
[43] F. Nilsson (1970) p. 206 ff.; A.-S. Kälvemark (1972) passim.

panies' advertising tactics and their effects on the fluctuations of emigration.[44]

Some important phenomena can only be reconstructed sporadically, if at all, with the aid of the Swedish church book material. This applies to such issues as the diffusion of information on emigration, travel routes, the spread of migration traditions, as well as the major complex of problems connected with migrant assimilation. In this respect oral tradition can supplement extant sources to some extent. The Uppsala Group, together with the Emigrant Register in Karlstad, have also conducted an extensive inventory program aimed at collecting the oral traditions on emigration to America which live on in Swedish districts. Interviews with returning emigrants in particular have yielded a great deal of valuable information in this context.

[44] H. Norman (1974), p. 92ff.

4. Swedish Emigration Policy in an International Perspective, 1840–1925

By Ann-Sofie Kälvemark

One of the main prerequisites for the mass emigration from Europe in the 19th century was that people were *allowed* to leave their countries, that the emigration policies of Europe had turned liberal.

Policies of emigration are, of course, dependent on population policies generally and on the value attributed to a population in different times, civilizations and nations. The higher the evaluation of a large population, the more likely there will be a restrictive policy towards emigration. Where a large population, on the contrary, is seen as an encumbrance and a burden, emigration is likely not only to be permitted but also encouraged, perhaps even forced.

Emigration policies might also differ in other ways; they might for instance be selective. Some population elements might be seen as desirable and their emigration, consequently, prohibited; others might be considered burdensome and therefore allowed to emigrate.

But emigration policies are not only a concern of the different states. They vitally concern the rights of individual citizens. Emigration policies do not only reflect the wishes and ideals of the state with regard to population, but also reflect the situation of individuals and their freedom or lack of freedom.

In the following, research and results concerning Swedish emigration policy during the period of mass emigration will be briefly presented. Swedish emigration policy during this period was, however, far from an isolated phenomenon. It was part of a general and remarkably uniform European development and will accordingly be treated against a general European background.

The transition from mercantilist to liberal emigration policies in Sweden, as in other European countries, was part of a greater development. It should be seen not only in the context of the breakthrough of political and economic liberalism but also in the context of general population development. To begin with, this change from restriction of emigration to freedom of emigration will be briefly discussed.

a. Mercantilist Emigration Policy

In ancient times a large and growing population was nearly always seen as a valuable provider of labor, military force and as a sign of the greatness of the country and its ruler. Moreover, mortality in the shape of epidemics, famines, or war, constantly threatened the growth of population and often caused considerable decreases. A positive attitude towards population thus seemed natural. However, some Greek philosophers such as Aristotle and Plato, fearing overpopulation of their city-states, were advocates of stable or only moderately growing populations. But they are exceptions; the Roman policy and legislation reflect an increasing concern about the growth and maintenance of the population within the empire.[1]

Medieval European attitudes towards population and fecundity were religiously motivated and no conscious evaluation of population was involved.[2] But in the 16th and 17th centuries, in a Europe of national states and absolute monarchs, mercantilist thought and policy showed a deep interest in population—characterized by "an almost fanatical desire to increase population".[3] Population was conceived as a means to augment the power and glory of the state. An abundance of soldiers, sailors, and cheap labor would be the result of a growing population. Consequently, marriage and childbearing were encouraged and at times even emigration—but only to the colonies, where it was seen as a powerful means of increasing the wealth and influence of the mother country. Emigration to foreign countries, however, was seen as an evil and was generally restricted or prohibited. Still, important emigration took place during this period, often for religious reasons as when the Huguenots fled France in hundreds of thousands.[4]

[1] The history of population theories and population debate is treated by E. P. Hutchinson (1967). J. Overbeek (1974) also covers the period after 1900. Outlines of population thought and policy in ancient times are given in E. P. Hutchinson (1967), pp. 11 ff. and J. Overbeek (1974), pp. 23 ff.

[2] E. P. Hutchinson (1967), p. 15.

[3] E. Heckscher (1935), vol. 2, p. 158.

[4] J. Overbeek (1974), pp. 28 ff. An outline of population policy in several European countries during this period is given in D. V. Glass (1967), pp. 86 ff. A review of older theories on emigration policy is given in S. Lehmann (1949), pp. 12 ff. A review of older legislation on emigration is given in F. Fauchille (1922), pp. 828 ff.

Older legislation in Sweden reflects the European development. Restrictions on emigration were repeatedly issued during the 18th century. For example, emigrants were required to put up the sum of 100 Sw. *riksdaler* as security before leaving the country, quite a considerable amount of money during this period.

The restrictive policy against emigration is also reflected in a considerable number of publications which, in eighteenth century Sweden, dealt with population problems. They reflected the European way of thinking and "through all their writings ran a common conception of population as a prime productive factor, the source of national strength and prosperity". Emigration was given special attention in a contest arranged by the Swedish Academy of Sciences in 1765, on why so many Swedes left their country.[5] Quite in accordance with the development of a restrictive policy on emigration, the authors show great concern over emigration as a threat to population growth and consequently to national prosperity.

From Mercantilism to Liberalism

During the second half of the eighteenth century population development in Europe turned rapidly upwards; an almost unbroken trend of growth started which continued up to the 20th century. In some countries the rate of growth was especially high, as in Great Britain, where it coincided with the industrial revolution. Overpopulation and mass poverty threatened, and the greedy mercantilist concern over a large population was gradually reversed for fear of too numerous a population.[6]

One might see Malthus' Essay on the Principle of Population as a manifestation of this development. The Malthusian fear of a situation, where an exponential growth quickly increases the numbers of people above the means of subsistence, seemed to provide a good case for emigration as an alleviating factor. Malthus, however, saw population in a global perspective where emigration only could be a temporary remedy for overpopulation. He did advocate emigration as such a remedy especially when working on a royal commission on population problems in the 1820s.[7]

[5] E. P. Hutchinson (1967), p. 75.
[6] M. Reinhard, A. Armengaud, and J. Dupaquier (1968), pp. 197 ff.
[7] S. Lehmann (1949), p. 19. See also W. Petersen (1969), p. 254.

Other contemporary writers also recommended emigration as a remedy for overpopulation and mass poverty. Among these were also exponents of economic liberalism, who saw a free flow of capital and goods as the best way of obtaining a maximal return from industrial and other enterprises. And in the same way as a free exchange of capital and goods was believed to lead to the highest possible effectivity and prosperity, some of them considered the free exchange of labor, i.e. population, as a similarly expedient policy. Emigration, therefore, ought to be free.[8]

To the arguments of overpopulation and economic liberalism was, however, added another powerful influence which worked towards a greater freedom of emigration. The doctrines of the Enlightenment stressed the rights of the individual to decide on his fate and consequently, also, his right to decide where he wanted to live. Liberal thought, of course, ran along the same lines and actively sought to diminish government influence to a minimum.[9]

Political and ideological factors as well as practical ones, thus, worked in favor of a greater freedom of emigration. Consequently, virtually everywhere in Europe restrictions on emigration were abolished during the first half of the 19th century. Some specific restrictions persisted, however; the most important dealing with the emigration of soldiers and military recruits.[10]

In Great Britain a liberal emigration policy was introduced early as a means of alleviating population pressure and poverty—especially on Ireland—but also of getting rid of undesirable elements in the population. The restrictions were not only abolished, but emigration was actively supported, at times forced, with the policy of restriction followed by a policy of compulsion. In this policy another important element, surviving from the days of mercantilism, is discernible. Emigration served the double purpose of alleviating overpopulation and of increasing the British population element in the colonies, thus increasing the strength of the British empire.[11] Later this example was to be followed by other European countries. But a small country like Sweden, which had no colonies, could not use this solution to the problem of overpopulation. What was the Swedish reaction to the new situation?

[8] S. Lehmann (1949), pp. 20 ff.

[9] F. Fauchille (1922), p. 829; S. Lehmann (1949), pp. 20, 22.

[10] F. Fauchille (1922), p. 829 f.

[11] W. F. Willcox (1931), vol. II, pp. 234 ff.

The long period of restrictive emigration policy in Sweden was broken in 1840. The date is of importance, since the meeting of the Swedish *riksdag* that year was characterized by a general breakthrough of liberal and oppositional elements.[12] In fact, one of the leaders of the liberal fraction at this *riksdag* was also the principal author of a motion demanding greater freedom of emigration.[13] His reasons are interesting seen against the international development briefly outlined here. As the most prominent cause for relieving the restrictions on emigration he mentions "the demands of modern times for rights of the individual to decide over himself and his property". But other grounds are mentioned as well: freedom of emigration would be in accordance with national economic development and would furthermore eliminate the dangers of an over-population unable to support itself.[14]

Here nearly all elements of the European arguments outlined above are to be found—the right of the individual, the economic interests of the state and, furthermore, the threat of overpopulation. The demands were approved of by the *riksdag* but even before the formal decision was taken, a new law was promulgated cancelling the requirement of providing security before emigration.[15]

The background of the demand for greater freedom of emigration in Sweden may therefore be seen as an example of the current liberal policies and opinions spreading everywhere in Europe. But other circumstances, too, ought to have been influential as causes or conditions in this context. Sweden's population had grown rapidly since the beginning of the nineteenth century. The increase had been especially pronounced among the propertyless rural population: the numbers of crofters, cottars and dependent poor and old, at a rough estimate, increased fourfold from 1751 to 1850.[16] The growth of this group caused a substantial increase in the costs of poor relief, and this ought to have been a decisive motive for a ready acceptance of a greater freedom of emigration for the poor.

[12] S. Carlsson and J. Rosén (1970), pp. 373 ff.

[13] This leader was Lars Johan Hierta, editor of an oppositional and widely read newspaper. —N. Runeby (1969), pp. 131 f. Runeby gives here a thorough and valuable treatment of the role the United States played in contemporary political and social debate in Sweden and also of the discussion on emigration in the period 1820–1860.

[14] L. J. Hierta (1913), pp. 202 ff.

[15] *Svensk Författningssamling* 1840: 15.

[16] *Emigrationsutredningen,* Bilaga 11, p. 56.

In the Swedish debate on the problems of overpopulation and pauperism emigration was brought forward as a solution.[17] Private persons also initiated organized emigration; the most drastic proposal aimed at founding Swedish colonies, preferably in Australia.[18]

The abolition of one of the most restrictive measures on emigration from Sweden at the beginning of the 1840s was a consequence of the same conditions and arguments found in other parts of Europe—threatening overpopulation and mass poverty, liberal ideas on economics and the right of the individual to govern his own life.

The freedom to emigrate was, however, far from complete. The obligation of obtaining a passport for international travel—as well as for extended travel within the country—was still in force. Special groups, such as artisans, servants and workers at mines and foundries, had to obtain special permission in order to emigrate.[19] Furthermore, certain restrictions on the rights of recruited soldiers to emigrate were promulgated. Total freedom of emigration did, therefore, not prevail in Sweden during the 1840s and 1850s.[20]

A royal commission was appointed with instructions to scrutinize current legislation and make suggestions on suitable changes. The report of the commission was completed in 1852 but did not lead to any action.[21]

At the end of the decade, however, the passport issue was once more raised in the *riksdag,* first in 1857 and then again in 1860. The motions and discussions on the subject never touched upon its consequences for emigration, but exclusively dealt with internal and practical problems caused by the passports.[22] Finally in 1860 the requirement of obtaining passports for international and internal travel was cancelled.[23] A nearly total freedom to emigrate now prevailed in Sweden. As mentioned above men subject to military service had to obtain special permission in order to emigrate before the fulfilment of their service. Since their term of service at this time was very short, the restriction was of no great significance. It was, however, to become more and more important. It must also be added here that the actual legislation on emigration and the abolition of certain

[17] N. Runeby (1969), pp. 115 ff.

[18] N. Runeby (1969), pp. 172 ff.

[19] Cf. above p. 95.

[20] *Emigrationsutredningen,* Bilaga 1, pp. 11 ff.

[21] *Allmänna Besvärs- och Ekonomiutskottet:* 75, Riksdagstrycket 1856–8.

[22] *Allmänna Besvärs- och Ekonomiutskottet:* 75, Riksdagstrycket 1856–8 and *Borgarståndets protokoll* 1856–7, II, pp. 167 ff.; *Ridderskapets och Adelns protokoll* 1856–7, V, pp. 245 ff.

[23] *Svensk författningssamling* 1860: 34.

restrictive elements did not necessarily imply great changes in the legal practice. During the 1850s emigration from Sweden was quite considerable; in 1854 it reached a peak of 8 412 persons.[24] It remains to be investigated if, for instance, the passport regulations actually had any influence or if they were obsolete and not applied.

b. Liberal Emigration Policy

The new situation did not mean that all regulations concerning emigration ceased to exist. Various emigration ordinances were soon issued for the purpose of regulating the sale of tickets, the transport of emigrants, etc. This kind of legislation was primarily issued to protect the migrants from abuses by the steamship companies. It contained, for instance, demands for minimum comforts on board the ships, sanitary regulations, food, space, etc.[1]

In Sweden the first ordinance to this effect was issued in 1864, soon to be followed by another, more extensive one in 1869. In the ordinance of 1869 the activities of emigration agents, such as their obligations towards their customers, stipulations for getting a permit to establish an emigration agency, etc., were regulated.

Active Emigration Policy: Assisted Emigration

The absence of restrictive emigration legislation did not mean that the countries concerned ceased to have an interest in emigration and emigration policy. On the contrary several European countries saw emigration as a promising means of solving urgent population problems at home.

The custom of sending undesirable or superfluous population elements to the colonies, especially the British colonies, has already been mentioned. This policy of forced or assisted emigration was widely spread during this period.

As early as the 1820s British population pressure caused considerable activity in this field. The British government and private organizations assisted in the emigration of less desirable elements, people without employment, criminals, orphans, etc. The extent of this assisted emigra-

[24] *Emigrationsutredningen,* Betänkande, p. 62.

[1] Unless otherwise stated this survey is based upon A.-S. Kälvemark (1972).

tion, though considerable, never equalled "normal" emigration.[2] Commissions and committees were appointed to deal with the problem and in 1840 the Colonial Land and Emigration Department was instituted for the purpose of directing the emigration to the British colonies and getting rid of superfluous and burdensome population elements.[3]

These activities concerned all of Great Britain but especially in Ireland the principle of paying the fares for poor people was common. In 1890 the American consul in Queenstown reported that the British government had paid for the emigration of evicted farmers. Other American consuls at other places in Great Britain supplied information of a similar kind.[4]

In Switzerland several of the cantons used emigration as an effective means of getting rid not only of the poor, but also of invalids, the sick and the old, and criminals. This special Swiss export of burdensome population elements reached its peak during the 1870s. The policy at last caused an international scandal with protests from the receiving countries. To put an end to this kind of emigration, the Swiss government issued regulations concerning the transport and protection of individual emigrants. A national bureau for information to emigrants and for the protection of their interests when abroad was also created.[5]

Switzerland seems to provide the most far-reaching example of the use of this kind of assisted emigration. Although varying in extent, it existed almost everywhere. Italy, for instance, saw emigration as an opportunity to diminish social and political unrest among the farm laborers in southern Italy around the turn of the century.[6]

Also the Scandinavian countries provide examples of this special kind of emigration. Paying the tickets of the poor, criminals and otherwise burdensome elements of the population was a convenient and radical means of cutting down on a lot of expenditures and responsibilities.[7] The police of Copenhagen made it a habit to shorten the time of punishment for criminals who were willing to emigrate to America on tickets paid by

[2] H. J. M. Johnston (1972).

[3] W. F. Willcox (1931), vol. II, pp. 243 ff.; W. A. Carrothers (1969), pp. 242 ff.

[4] K. Hvidt (1971), p. 35, footnote 48, and O. Handlin (1969), *passim.—Special Consular Reports* 1890, pp. 283, 285, 287.

[5] S. Lehmann (1949), pp. 60 ff. and 74 ff. H. Meier (1963), pp. 105 ff.

[6] G. Dore (1964), *passim,* and especially pp. 69 ff.; Africa o America come soluzioni del problema contadino.

[7] Denmark: K. Hvidt (1971), pp. 36 ff. Norway: I. Semmingsen (1950), pp. 53 f. Sweden: F. Nilsson (1970), pp. 202 f.

the police, a practice which in time caused strained relations between the police and U.S. representatives in Copenhagen.[8]

To what extent this kind of assisted emigration was common in Sweden has not been investigated. The American consul in Gothenburg in 1890 asserted that "criminals, vicious characters, paupers and other objectionable persons" were continually sent from Sweden to America. There was no hamlet, parish or town in Sweden which had not been guilty of this misuse of the emigration.[9]

Selective Emigration Policies. Restrictions on Military Emigration

The use of an active support of emigration to get rid of certain parts of the population may be characterized as a selective emigration policy. This form of selective emigration policy had its counterpart in the remaining restrictive emigration legislation. Here we are dealing with the desire to *keep* the most valuable population elements in the country—in spite of the accepted principle of free emigration.

From the national point of view the most valued part of the population seemed everywhere to have been those subject to military service—the young men in their twenties. The emigration of these groups was generally restricted or prohibited in Europe—the main exception seemed to have been Great Britain. Thus, an important group of presumptive emigrants did not have the total freedom to emigrate.[10]

The extent of these restrictions is difficult to determine, since it is dependent upon the period during which the men were subject to military service. It also varied in relation to the practice of giving young men emigration permits. It is therefore difficult to decide which country maintained the most rigid policy and to what extent the policy was affected by changes in the length of military service or the practice of giving emigration permits.

It is strange that, generally, the effect of this restrictive legislation is neglected in the works dealing with European emigration. The influence is, for instance, easily discernible in the Swedish statistics on emigration. Towards the end of the century and afterwards, when restrictions were rigorously applied, the proportion of twentyone-year-old men among the emigrants was very low compared to the age-groups above and below twentyone. It also coincided with an increase in illegal emigration.

[8] K. Hvidt (1971), pp. 37 f.
[9] *Special Consular Reports* 1890, p. 277.
[10] *Emigration and Immigration* (1922), pp. 13 ff.

During the period up to 1884, when a new emigration ordinance was issued, the effect of the restrictions was probably small. The period of military service was short—a couple of weeks—and conscription did not play an important role in national defense which was based on a corps of professional soldiers. The enforcement of the legislation was also very slack.

During the following period the Swedish national defense was reorganized. The corps of professional soldiers was gradually dissolved and defense came to be based primarily on the principle of compulsory military service. Under these circumstances interest in restraining the flow of conscriptable emigrants rose. The new emigration ordinance in 1884 aimed at obtaining a better control over emigration and at preventing illegal emigration. To this end a statistical record of the conscripts' emigration was called for. The ordinance stated that the emigrant was required to present his certificate of change of address to the police authorities before he emigrated. Many emigrants had left the country earlier without such certificates and this was a situation which easily permitted of illegal emigration by conscripts. This also meant an underregistration of emigrants.[11]

In subsequent years the ordinance was supplemented by specific regulations to the effect that the conscript was obliged to have a special permit in order to obtain his change of address certificate for purposes of emigration. These regulations also prescribed the conditions under which such permits would be granted. The continuing and growing interest in preventing emigration of men subject to military service is reflected in the 1890s when at two different times proposals were made in the Swedish *riksdag*. These proposals regarding the emigration of conscripts, were without immediate results, although in 1894 the practice of issuing permits to conscripts who desired to emigrate was sharpened.[12]

The Army Organization Act of 1901 definitely transformed the Swedish defense into a system built upon compulsory military service. At the same time a new wave of emigration ensued. The problem of emigrating young men was again felt to be of importance. In 1901 the national defense capacity was discussed in the *riksdag* and the problem arose as to how the government could in some way require a person who "evaded" military

[11] See Chapter 3, above.

[12] Compare Chapter 6, below.

service by exemption or by emigration to fulfil his "economic military service", for example through the payment of a special tax. A committee was appointed to handle this question, although its main object was to tax conscripts who were exempted or emigrated, and though it was not primarily interested in putting an end to emigration, its proposal would, if carried, very likely have become an important deterrant to emigration.

Before the committee had finished its work, the problem of emigrating conscripts was again taken up in the *riksdag* when a conservative member of the First Chamber proposed that steps be taken to halt the emigration of conscripts. He also stated, that the State does not just have the *right* to hinder its subjects from emigrating, it is the *duty* of the State to do so. This proposal was rejected and reference made to the work of the above-mentioned committee. But the proposals of the committee were also rejected by the *riksdag*. The timely nature of the question also resulted in the appointment of another committee some years later, whose task was to investigate the manner in which remigration to Sweden might be encouraged by an easing of the regulations on compulsory service for those conscripts who returned to the country.

Consequently, the efforts which were made to sharpen the restrictions by means of legislation on the emigration of men subject to military service did not meet with success. On the other hand, beginning in 1902 there was an increase in the number of rejected applications for permissions to emigrate.

The restrictions on emigration of these young men which were in force also met with difficulties, since there were many possibilities to emigrate illegally by way of foreign ports, especially Copenhagen and the Norwegian harbors.[13] In 1902 the Swedish Consul-General in Copenhagen wrote a long memorandum to the Foreign Office in Stockholm, to draw the government's attention to this emigration which was assuming, in his words, very large proportions. He also demanded changes in legislation and a more effective implementation of the existing laws to bring a halt to the dangerous emigration of conscripts. His letter was sent to the Royal Board of Commerce (*Kommerskollegium*) for a statement.

Later that same year, the Foreign Office sent out questionnaires to the Consul-Generals in Bremen, Hamburg and London and to the Consul in Lübeck regarding the nature of emigration via foreign ports by Swedish men subject to military service. With the exception of England—where it

[13] See Chapter 6, below.

was reported that it was impossible to obtain correct information—all of the replies indicated that Swedish emigration by way of these ports was so insignificant that no appreciable emigration by military conscripts could be taking place. As on a previous occasion, the Swedish government appealed through its embassy in Copenhagen to the Danish government with the request of support in halting the illegal emigrant traffic out of Copenhagen. Again, the reply was negative.

Attention was also directed to emigration by way of Norwegian ports. At the initiative of the Provincial Governors of Jämtlands and Kopparbergs län, whose attention had first been drawn to the matter by clergymen in their provinces, requests were made for information on and measures against the illegal emigration by way of Norwegian ports. The Provincial Governor in Jämtlands län also appealed to the District Administrator of Trondheim province in Norway with the request for his co-operation. A cabinet-level decision was reached in the summer of 1904 to make a direct appeal to the Norwegian Home Office in this matter.

This same cabinet meeting discussed the Royal Board of Commerce's statement on the memorandum from the Consul-General in Copenhagen as well as the Board's suggestions for new regulations affecting the activities of emigrant agents. The Board rejected the Consul-General's proposals but suggested an amendment to the regulations governing the agents' activities and their propaganda. Such an amendment was issued, but the terms concerning the agents' propaganda were so vague that the effect of the amendment was probably insignificant.

Around the turn of the century there was thus considerable unrest concerning the emigration of men subject to military service. Immediate reasons for this interest were, as mentioned above, the increase of emigration and the re-organization of the Swedish army. But other reasons were powerful as well. The political climate of Europe was changing—growing nationalism, political confrontation and economic competition increasingly marked the years prior to World War I. Interest in the national defense accordingly increased. Furthermore tension between Sweden and Norway was growing, as the union between the countries was coming to an end.

National defense was felt by many to be of vital importance, and a high level of emigration was repeatedly mentioned as considerably weakening defense capacity. What was the truth behind this opinion? Was the emigration of conscripts and young men liable to conscription of such proportions that it actually weakened defense capacity?

To obtain an idea of the true reduction in the maximum number of expected military conscripts, the number of men born a certain year, arranged in age groups has been compared with the number still found in the respective age groups at the time these men became twenty years old. The result of the comparison indicates a considerable reduction in the age-groups. The remaining figure has then been compared with the number of those registering for military service at the time that their respective age groups became liable to military service. Here there were further reductions as a result of death, emigration, and primarily as a result of a high number of exemptions. This comparison is somewhat complicated because part of every age group was registered before or after the year in which it became liable to conscription, in other words upon reaching the age of 21. However, the result still remains that the original age groups were so greatly reduced as a result of death—above all as a result of the high infant mortality rate—emigration and exemption that considerably less than half of these actually fulfilled their military obligations. Seen in this context, those who were strong advocates of national defense ought to be considered highly justified in their uneasiness with regard to emigration.

c. Swedish Reaction against Emigration

This account of the discussion on emigration during the period of mass emigration has so far centered around only one particular part of the problem. At the turn of the century, however, demands were raised not only to stop the emigration of men subject to military service but to put an end to emigration generally. Emigration was considered as a threat to the country, draining it of its best and most valuable population. Contrary to the military interest in restricting emigration, which had made itself heard during a long time, these demands and the accompanying negative attitude towards emigration were something relatively new.

Emigration had, of course, caused a lot of debate and discussion earlier, especially during times of high emigration. But the different attitudes of the consequences of emigration for the nation were hardly unanimous, and there is evidence of both negative and positive attitudes. Among the advocates of a positive attitude toward emigration might be mentioned a member of the Swedish *riksdag* who in 1869 presented a proposal aimed at transforming the Swedish emigration into some form of colonization. This did not receive any support, but it is an interesting example of how the idea of setting emigration in a colonial context also had its spokesmen in Sweden.

In spite of the liberal emigration policy, the representatives of a negative attitude are mostly found among persons in official and administrative capacities. King Oscar II himself, for instance, advocated a negative position on emigration and called a meeting of the Swedish provincial governors in this matter in 1882. Among the statements on emigration issued by the governors later that year are also examples of a positive assessment, both in respect to the nation at large as well as to the individual.

Positive attitudes towards emigration appeared more frequently in the public debate on the subject, for example from the statistician Gustav Sundbärg, who was later to become the chairman of the large investigating committee on emigration. However, others adopted a more ambivalent position, for example the journalist and politician Ernst Beckman. One can also note that those economists who took up this question, among them Knut Wicksell, set emigration in Malthusian terms and saw it as a useful but temporary remedy to overpopulation.

The ambivalent position on emigration which is found in individual and official statements during the 1880s gave way to an almost wholly negative position after the turn of the century. During 1903 and 1904 a series of reactions against emigration ensued. In February 1903, the emigration issue was discussed in a protectionistic agricultural organization, *Sveriges agrarförbund*. A committee was appointed to investigate the situation and suggest appropriate measures against emigration. At the end of April 1903, a member of the First Chamber of the *riksdag* submitted a petition to King Oscar II signed by over a hundred persons requesting measures to be taken to halt emigration.

In November 1903, representatives for the Provincial Agricultural Societies (*hushållningssällskapen*) assembled at a so-called Farmers' Parliament (*lantbruksriksdag*). The Minister of Agriculture Th. Odelberg was present and took up the issue of emigration, opening the meeting for debate and statements on this matter. That same month a meeting was held by a society called Students and Workers which soon resulted in the discussion of emigration in the Second Chamber of the *riksdag* by the afore-mentioned Ernst Beckman, now chairman of the *Frisinnade landsföreningen,* which was the national organization of the Liberal Party.

With the exception of the last-mentioned initiative all these activities and the persons and organizations behind them advocated similar political positions and all emphasized the consequences of emigration for *agriculture.* Personal relations and contacts of the debaters can be traced, as well as their geographical connections, many of them coming from Västergötland where the greatest Swedish emigration harbor, Gothenburg, is situated. Emigration from Västergötland was, however, not especially great at that time. On the other hand, the internal migration of people from the country to the cities was high and resulted in a diminishing of the population in the rural areas.

Among the proposals issued by such organizational activities as a means of halting emigration was support for the Movement for Rural Resettlement and Home Ownership (*egnahemsrörelsen*). This led to promotion of farming interests held by persons and organizations involved in this connection by virtue of their capacity as employers. These same persons and organizations generally complained over the shortage of manpower in agriculture. Such complaints were unparalleled by anything which had taken place during previous periods of high emigration.

Was there actually a shortage of manpower in agriculture? The statistics on population and professional occupations at this time do not, unfortunately, permit of a precise answer to this question. On the other hand, there is a good deal which does point to a reduction in agricultural manpower. The general reduction in the rural population ever since the 1880s, the reduction in the number of crofters, cottars, and lodgers, the rise in wages for farm-hands, and the importation of foreign farm workers to the province of Skåne—all of these indicate that there was a diminishing of manpower. Employers began to feel that their interests were being threatened. It might be pointed out in this context, that the spokesmen for agricultural and military interests were primarily concerned with keeping the same category of emigrants within the country, namely young men aged twenty. On several points there is evidence that these interests and concerns were linked together.

Was the emigration from the agricultural areas greater than that from other areas around the turn of the century? There is much to suggest that such was the case during the first decade of the twentieth century. In her survey of population movements in Sweden, Dorothy Swaine Thomas has shown that the emigration from the farming regions between 1904 and 1909 increased in relation to the emigration from other areas. A comparison between the emigration from the countryside and that from the cities indicated a similar situation.[1]

[1] D. S. Thomas (1941), pp. 318 ff. Compare A.-S. Kälvemark (1972), pp. 135–141.

But it has also been pointed out that the effects of the internal migration from the countryside to the cities should have been about the same. The permanent migration of people from farming areas to industrialized areas resulted in a net reduction of the population in the former areas. It therefore seems likely that what employers in the agricultural areas were reacting to was just as much the effects of internal migration as emigration.

It is also possible to speculate whether or not emigration from rural areas differed from that in cities and industrial areas. This question is difficult to answer, but Sundbärg's account of the age and sex groups of emigrants from rural areas and in the cities during the period 1891–1900 reveals that the emigration of men between the ages of 20 and 25 from the countryside was considerably higher than their corresponding emigration from the cities.

As previously mentioned, in the fall of 1903 the emigration question was discussed by the organization called Students and Workers, which was leftist-oriented and espoused completely different political and social concerns than those organizations which had previously intervened in this issue. A committee was appointed by this organization with the task of persuading a member of the *riksdag* to take up the matter there. This resulted in the proposal on emigration which was presented by Ernst Beckman in 1904. In his proposal Beckman demanded the following: a statistical investigation of the social aspects of emigration; measures which would further remigration to Sweden; and study trips to the United States with the aim of acquiring information on trade, industry and education. Moreover, Beckman made constant reference to conditions flourishing in the United States at that time. Beckman concluded that reforms similar to those in America had to be introduced in Sweden if emigration were to be halted.

A closer examination of Ernst Beckman's own political program as well as the programs of the Students and Workers organization and the *Frisinnade landsföreningen* reveals that all of these demands are represented in each program. In one case Beckman has directly copied from one of his own political speeches from 1902. However, this speech does not make exhaustive references to emigration and American conditions. This means that Beckman and his associates used the emigration issue as a tactical, political means of presenting and emphasizing portions of their own political and social reform programs. However, it may be, of course, that their aim of halting emigration was sincerely intended. Their standpoint here means that an overwhelming part of the political parties represented in the *riksdag* at this time held a negative attitude to emigration.

At the same meeting of the *riksdag* a spokesman for the agricultural interests and right-wing sympathies which have been discussed earlier also presented a proposal regarding emigration. This member was rather insignificant within the ranks of his own Farmers' Party but did hold a certain position in the previously mentioned *agrarförbund*. Therefore, his proposal should be seen as another expression of this same interest. The proposal demanded support for the *egnahemsrörelsen* in Sweden, promotion of returning migration to Sweden, details on the dangers of emigration, and particularly for measures against the emigrant agents, who were felt to be the primary cause of emigration.

The proposals were referred to a committee in the *riksdag* and this committee retained only parts of Beckman's proposal in their report. Study trips to America and a statistical investigation of the social features of emigration were recommended. These demands were approved by the *riksdag* and were included in the written decision which the *riksdag* issued in this matter. After a cabinet meeting in the summer of 1904 the statistical question was sent on to the Central Bureau of Statistics and the question of study trips to the Royal Board of Commerce.

In its report the Central Bureau of Statistics expressed support for an investigation and also suggested ways in which such an investigation could be conducted. What is of interest here is that this report was written by the statistician Gustav Sundbärg, who was to become the leader of the actual investigating committee. On the other hand, the Royal Board of Commerce's report rejected the idea of special study trips to America, partly with reference to the fact that to a certain extent such an educational project was already in progress.

The Swedish Investigating Commission on Emigration

The investigating committee was appointed by the cabinet on January 30, 1907. The leading items on the agenda was presented by the Minister for Civil Service Affairs who strongly supported the suggestion from the Central Bureau of Statistics. He proposed that the investigation be conducted under the supervision of the Minister for Civil Service Affairs and be handled by a specially appointed staff of personnel. Gustav Sundbärg was appointed to head the investigating committee.

From the very beginning, the planning of the investigation reveals a primary orientation to questions of agriculture. This orientation is further emphasized in the final report, where questions of agriculture are given a wide scope of attention and are particularly stressed by the recommendations of the investigating committee. It was said that changes had to be made primarily in this area if emigration were to be stopped. Thanks to industrial development the sheer volume of emigration had efficiently diminished, but agricultural investments had not been sufficient to afford employment, housing, and other vital necessities for its share of the population.

In this context Sundbärg also discussed the complaints of employers over the shortage of manpower in agriculture and said that if such was the case, during this period of increased emigration and rising unemployment in the cities, then it had to be due to deficient conditions for agricultural workers. Those who were to blame for this were the employers themselves.

Sundbärg here mainly supported the liberal point of view, held by Ernst Beckman and others. The members of the investigating committee were, however, not unanimous in their standpoint on emigration. The secretary of the committee, the economist Nils Wohlin, maintained a much more right-wing view of the problem. In a special part of the investigation report Wohlin dealt with restrictions on emigration and suggested rather far-reaching restrictive legislation, especially on the emigration of military conscripts. Sundbärg, however, in the final report dismissed these suggestions and maintained firmly that all restrictions aimed at halting this emigration ought to be repealed.

The co-operation between Sundbärg and Wohlin broke down in 1910, when Wohlin left the committee and became intensely engaged in the work of a private organization, The National Society against Emigration (*Nationalföreningen mot Emigrationen*), which was founded in 1907. This organization, which above all represented agricultural and right-wing interests, concentrated its interest on the problems of *egnahemsrörelsen* and maintained that increasing possibilities to get a small farm in Sweden would be the best means to stop emigration.[2] This organization, of course, also recommended restriction on emigration, and spread its propaganda in pamphlets, advertisements and a monthly magazine. The effect of its activity, if any, is hard to evaluate.

The final report of the investigating committee was published in 1913, and as mentioned above, it rather recommended reform than restrictions.

[2] For information on this society see N. Runeby (1962) and F. D. Scott (1965).

Ironically, however, the report never laid the groundwork for a new, Swedish policy on emigration. The year after it was completed World War I broke out and set an effective barrier against emigration. Emigration from Sweden after the war never reached any considerable proportions; the country became more and more able to absorb and give opportunities to its population.

Trends towards Restriction: European Parallels

The British custom of sending its emigrants to its own colonies has been mentioned above. Towards the end of the 19th century this custom received new actuality. In 1886 an Emigrants' Information Office was opened on private initiative with governmental support. Its main purpose was to distribute information on the British colonies and support emigration to them. Other private organizations also gave their support to emigration to the colonies and dominions of Great Britain. The colonies and dominions themselves made efficient propaganda in their mother country; this is especially true of Canada.[3]

Ireland, however, continued to be an exception within the Commonwealth and sent its emigrants mainly to the United States. On Ireland a reaction against emigration, similar to that in Sweden appeared. At the end of the century an active propaganda against emigration was carried on by the Roman Catholic Church.[4] An Irish society against emigration was also founded.[5]

Germany, at this time a new and growing colonial power, also manifested a great interest in directing its emigrants to its own colonies.[6]

In the other Nordic countries the attitude towards emigration was for a long period, as in Sweden, passive and ambivalent; only military emigration was restricted. In Norway the high emigration of the 1860s was seen in terms of a Malthusian perspective and from the standpoint of a consistent, economic liberalism. Public opinion was resigned to the fact that emigration was inevitable.[7] But, as in Sweden, opinion changed towards the turn of the century and a national society against emigration was formed. After that, in 1912, a departmental committee was appointed with instructions to

[3] W. F. Willcox (1931), vol. II, pp. 243 ff.; W. A. Carrothers (1969), pp. 242 ff.
[4] A. Schrier (1958), pp. 45 ff.
[5] *Special Consular Reports* 1904, p. 159.
[6] *Emigrationsutredningen,* Bilaga 1, p. 164; M. Walker (1964), pp. 228 ff.
[7] I. Semmingsen (1950), pp. 415 ff.

prepare a new emigration ordinance. Its work was, however, prolonged and at last made to include a whole range of subjects which touched upon emigration, although its explicit purpose was to put an end to emigration.[8] Also in Finland a society against emigration was formed.[9]

Here only some examples have been given of different emigration policies and attitudes towards emigration in Europe at the end of the 19th century and the beginning of the 20th. They still might allow a few observations of a more general character.

The trend was obviously towards more restrictive policies of emigration—and consequently a higher evaluation of the population as an object of interest to the nation and state.[10] As previously mentioned this development conformed to the general political climate—tensions, confrontations, nationalism, economic competition and protectionism, which more and more dominated the European scene.

The reaction against emigration could take at least two forms. Countries which were colonial powers sought to direct emigration to their own possessions, thereby hoping not to lose but to gain manpower. High emigration countries without colonies—Sweden belongs to this category—experienced other forms of reactions, where demands for restrictions but also demands for reform took an important place.

This trend continued after the war and it was paralleled by a similar development in American immigration legislation, where restrictions and demands for restrictions gradually led to the legislation of 1924. European conferences on emigration during the 1920s provide many examples of the changing attitudes towards emigration.[11] Population was again something to cultivate and care for. The population policies of the 1930s, marked by the fear of depopulation, were not far away.

[8] I. Semmingsen (1950), pp. 434 ff.
[9] A.-L. Toivonen (1963), pp. 225 ff.
[10] Cf. W. Petersen (1964).
[11] M. Sanger (1927), pp. 256 ff. I. W. Gregory (1928), *passim*. Gregory strongly recommends restrictions on emigration.

5. Chronology and Composition of Swedish Emigration to America

By Sten Carlsson

a. The Chronological Course

The "New Sweden" Period

If one disregards the journeys of the Vikings to Vinland, in which a few Swedes may have participated, it might essentially be said that no Swede set foot in North America before 1638, when the two sailing vessels, *Calmar Nyckel* and *Fågel Grip*, landed at what is now Wilmington, Delaware. Between 1638 and 1655 a Swedish colony called "New Sweden" existed in the Delaware Territory (including parts of the present states of Delaware, New Jersey, and Pennsylvania). Judged according to our modern understanding of the term, the settlement was exceptionally sparse: the total population of Swedes and Finns in the colony probably did not exceed a level of roughly 350 persons. In 1655 the colony was lost to the Dutch, but the area still received an influx of population from Sweden, including around a hundred Finns from Värmland in 1656.[1] Swedish customs and ethnic traditions gradually disappeared from the scene, and the Swedish language was no longer spoken by any inhabitant by the time mass emigration began in the 1840s. However, the colony's historical landmarks have been preserved by such organizations as Swedish "colonial societies" in Wilmington and Philadelphia.

No direct connection can be said to exist between the New Sweden traditions and the waves of mass emigration during the 1800s which were directed to other parts of the United States. However, some Swedish American historians—represented, for example, by Amandus Johnson—have made frequent references to the "New Sweden" Swedes and their descendants, many of whom reached a substantially higher social status than the average immigrant of the 1800s. Some of the colony's descendants, such as John Hanson from Maryland and John Morton from Penn-

[1] A. Johnson (1911), Vol. II, pp. 710 ff.

sylvania, played prominent roles in the American struggle for independence. John Hanson presided over the Congress which met in Philadelphia in 1781 and has sometimes—though incorrectly—been called the first President of the United States.[2]

The Period 1820–1844

Although no quantitative statistics are available for Swedish emigration to North America during the 1700s, it is entirely safe to conclude that such movement was highly inconsequential. Statistics are available beginning with the year 1820 by virtue of the Swedish registration of passenger fees on sailing vessels and by way of the American registration of foreign travelers to the United States. For the period between 1820 and 1844, 563 passenger fees are recorded in the Swedish source material. Out of this total, 209 passengers are reported to have landed in New York.[3] However, many of these Swedes came for the purpose of tourism, business or studies and were not emigrants in the true sense of the term. More than half of these travelers belonged to the upper and middle classes. A minority consisted of craftsmen apprentices and seamen, while only a few were farmers.[4] At this time there was no group emigration from Sweden comparable to that which had started from Norway as early as 1825.[5]

However, some of these early emigrants subsequently influenced the phase of mass emigration from Sweden. Swen Magnus Swenson, a clerk from Småland, who arrived in New York in 1836 and went to Texas in 1838, founded the Swedish settlement in Texas with the help of his uncle, Svante Palm, who emigrated in 1844.[6] Carl Friman, a farmer and military registrar from Varnhem in Västergötland, came to Wisconsin in 1838 only to return to Sweden the following year. Yet, together with his five emigrant sons who ended their days in the United States, Friman became a pioneer in establishing Swedish settlements in the Middle West. Through his published writings Friman actively encouraged emigration to the new country.[7] The Finnish-born Gustav Unonius, who after studies in Uppsala

[2] A. Benson and N. Hedin (1950), p. 56. Even Franklin D. Roosevelt had some Swedish-American ancestors. However, as far as it is known, they did not live in New Sweden. Cf. V. Berger (1934).

[3] N. W. Olsson (1967), pp. 11 ff.; A. Friman (1974), pp. 23 f.

[4] A. Friman (1974), pp. 31 f.

[5] Cf. I. Semmingsen (1941), *passim*.

[6] N. W. Olsson (1967), pp. 18 f., 58 f.

[7] N. W. Olsson (1967), pp. 26 f.; N. Runeby (1969), pp. 164 ff.

left for Wisconsin in 1841, became a priest in the Episcopal Church and tried to induce his countrymen to cross the Atlantic. However, disappointed by the United States, and especially by the prevailing religious climate, he made his own way back to Sweden in 1858.[8]

The Pioneer Period (1845–1854)

The year 1845 can be said to mark the start of mass emigration from Sweden. Swedish passenger arrivals in the United States that year only totalled 65, of which 41 landed in New York.[9] However, among them was a group of 25 persons who were to play an important role in subsequent years. They were led by a master-builder named Peter Cassel, who came from Kisa in Östergötland, not far from the Småland border. Cassel learned of the United States through Gustav Unonius and an artillery officer by the name of Polycarpus von Schneidau, who first emigrated to Wisconsin in 1842 and finally settled in Chicago in 1844 as one of the first Swedes in the area.[10] Cassel's journey and destination were carefully laid out in advance. He went directly to Jefferson County, Iowa, where he founded the "New Sweden" colony. During the course of the next several years hundreds of persons from Östergötland and Småland joined him there.[11]

Aside from Peter Cassel, the "prophet" Erik Jansson assumed major prominence in the early history of mass emigration. Erik Jansson was born in Biskopskulla in Uppland but in 1843 settled in Hälsingland, where he founded a religious sect. After bitter conflicts with ecclesiastical and civil authorities he emigrated in 1846 to Illinois, where he established the Bishop Hill Colony. Between 1846 and 1854 about 1 500 of his followers, called "Erik Janssonists", crossed the Atlantic in large groups. Erik Jansson was murdered in 1850, and the colony was disbanded in 1860 following a series of crises, but the Swedish settlement remained.[12]

In 1846 a total of roughly 1 300 Swedes left for the United States.[13] The total for the entire 1845–1854 period can be estimated at 14 500. Estimates for the years 1851–1854 are based on the official Swedish statistics which,

[8] N. W. Olsson (1967), pp. 38 f., and cited references; N. Runeby (1969), pp. 161 ff.
[9] N. W. Olsson (1967), pp. 62 ff.; A. Friman (1974), p. 13.
[10] N. W. Olsson (1967), pp. 42 ff., and cited references; U. Beijbom (1971), pp. 43 f.
[11] N. W. Olsson (1967), pp. 64 ff.; R. Davidsson (1969), pp. 15 ff.; N. Runeby (1969), pp. 201 ff.
[12] N. W. Olsson (1967),, pp. 86 ff.; O. Isaksson and S. Hallgren (1969); article by O. Hellström (1973), and cited references.
[13] A. Friman (1974), p. 24.

Table 5: 1. *Registered Emigration from Sweden to Non-European Countries, 1851–1930*

Year	USA	Canada	Rest of the Americas	Rest of the non-European World	Total
1851	932			4	936
1852	3 031			4	3 035
1853	2 619			19	2 638
1854	3 980			9	3 989
1855	586			–	586
1856	969			3	972
1857	1 762			3	1 765
1858	512			3	515
1859	208			3	211
1860	266			2	268
1861	758				
1862	947				
1863	1 216			34	9 454
1864	2 593				
1865	3 906				
1866	4 466			9	4 475
1867	5 893			5	5 898
1868	21 472			15	21 487
1869	32 050			10	32 060
1870	15 430			27	15 457
1871	12 985		1	133	13 119
1872	11 838		–	77	11 915
1873	9 486		4	80	9 570
1874	3 380		1	136	3 517
1875	3 591		1	50	3 642
1876	3 702		–	39	3 741
1877	2 921		4	38	2 963
1878	4 242		–	130	4 372
1879	12 761		5	60	12 826
1880	36 263		12	56	36 331
1881	40 620		22	82	40 724
1882	44 359		16	159	44 534
1883	25 678		17	161	25 856
1884	17 664	2	15	178	17 859
1885	18 222	–	27	196	18 445
1886	27 913	4	170	154	20 241
1887	46 252	12	88	191	46 543

Year	USA	Canada	Rest of the Americas	Rest of the non-European World	Total
1888	45 561	6	99	176	45 842
1889	28 529	14	343	164	29 050
1890	29 487	12	470	148	30 117
1891	36 134	31	1 997	156	38 318
1892	40 990	113	17	155	41 275
1893	37 321	51	36	96	37 504
1894	9 529	25	36	88	9 678
1895	14 982	20	25	77	15 104
1896	14 874	37	68	196	15 175
1897	10 109	39	50	116	10 314
1898	8 534	35	29	85	8 683
1899	11 842	33	21	132	12 028
1900	16 209	93	17	115	16 434
1901	20 306	57	17	84	20 464
1902	33 151	185	16	125	33 477
1903	35 439	329	16	191	35 975
1904	18 533	333	22	80	18 968
1905	20 520	253	26	63	20 862
1906	21 242	364	27	59	21 692
1907	19 325	399	28	66	19 818
1908	8 873	244	43	86	9 246
1909	18 331	333	128	102	18 894
1910	23 529	655	346	117	24 647
1911	15 571	669	422	108	16 770
1912	13 896	611	49	133	14 689
1913	16 329	692	49	154	17 224
1914	9 589	311	30	76	10 006
1915	4 538	39	16	79	4 672
1916	7 268	153	15	52	7 488
1917	2 462	76	9	24	2 571
1918	1 416	57	3	22	1 498
1919	3 777	112	29	90	4 008
1920	6 691	254	39	109	7 093
1921	5 430	263	52	136	5 881
1922	8 455	303	60	167	8 985
1923	24 948	1 422	61	128	26 559
1924	7 036	1 192	48	125	8 401
1925	8 637	738	66	171	9 612

Year	USA	Canada	Rest of the Americas	Rest of the non-European World	Total
1926	9 693	1 154	71	144	11 062
1927	8 735	1 992	85	146	10 958
1928	9 179	2 306	65	133	11 683
1929	6 951	1 882	111	213	9 157
1930	2 868	606	113	132	3 719
1851–1860		14 865		50	14 915
1861–1870		88 731		100	88 831
1871–1880	101 169		28	799	101 996
1881–1890	324 285	50	1 267	1 609	327 211
1891–1900	200 524	477	2 296	1 216	204 513
1901–1910	219 249	3 152	669	973	224 043
1911–1920	81 537	2 974	661	847	86 019
1921–1930	91 932	11 858	732	1 495	106 017
Total	1 122 292	18 511	5 653	7 089	1 153 545

Source Bidrag till Sveriges Officiella Statistik. Serie A 1851–1900. Serie Befolkningsrörelsen 1901–1930.

however, can be presumed to be rather incomplete (Table 5:1). The majority of emigrants during this period were farmers—generally landed farmers and their families—whereas members of the upper and middle classes of Swedish society were now emigrating on a far lesser scale than before, as compared to the total number.[14]

Although religious dissent was the triggering factor of emigration in the case of the Erik Janssonists it was hardly the only one. Economic considerations also appear likely to have prompted their decision. In principle, the emigrants who made their way to the United States at this early stage were not driven by any material need. In many cases they were rather well-to-do individuals, and their objective at times seem to have been one of investing profitably in the expanding Middle West. It was a practice of emigrants from the Karlskoga mining district, for example, to sell their homesteads in advance of their departure.[15]

Emigration at this time was still greatly limited to certain regions within Sweden. Major areas of emigrant recruitment were Cassel's districts in

[14] *Ibid.*, p. 32.
[15] H. Norman (1974), pp. 76 ff.

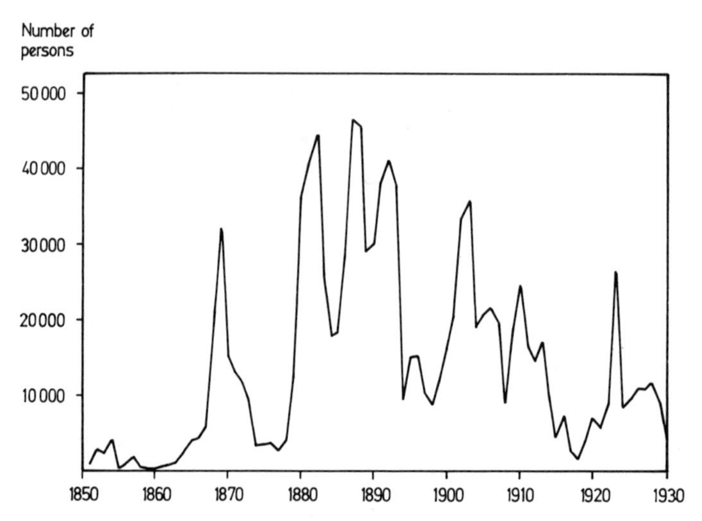

5: 1. Registered Emigration from Sweden to Non-European Countries, 1851–1930.
Source See Table 5: 1.

Östergötland and northern Småland and the Erik Janssonist regions in Hälsingland, eastern Dalarna, and northwestern Uppland. Other prime areas were the Karlskoga mining districts, the southern sector of Kronobergs län in Småland, and the Jämshög area in Blekinge.[16] Almost all of these emigrants settled in the Middle West. Though small in numbers, these pioneers assumed decisive importance for the future location of Swedish settlements in this part of the United States.

Emigration during the Famine Years (1868–1873)

A severe cholera epidemic in Chicago in 1854 along with a serious economic recession in the United States led to a decline in emigration figures.[17] The minor rise of emigration in 1857, which can be connected with the economic crisis in Sweden that year, was only short-lived. Between 1855 and 1860 only about 4 000 persons are registered as emigrants. However, the actual figure is probably somewhat higher. The statistics rise somewhat in 1861 and 1862 but are, nonetheless, inconsequential. The American Civil War acted as a deterrent on emigration. However, that the

[16] A. Friman (1974), p. 27; *Bidrag till Sveriges Officiella Statistik,* 1851–1855, Serie A; A. Wirén (1975), p. 43; see also below, Chapter 5: c.
[17] Cf. U. Beijbom (1971), pp. 53 ff.; H. Norman (1974), p. 86.

number of emigrants successively increased during subsequent years is probably due to the generous enticements offered by the Homestead Act of 1862. A total of over 12 000 emigrants is recorded for the years 1863–1867. The end of the Civil War in 1865 brought a certain, and rather moderate increase of emigration.

The greatest change in Swedish emigration came during the disastrous crop failures which struck Sweden in 1867 and particularly in 1868. While the early waves of emigration can primarily be seen as a result of pull-factors—i.e., the attraction of American economic and business cycles—this new period reflects the clear dominance of push-factors, namely deteriorated conditions in Sweden which made outcasts of large numbers of the population. For the period 1868–1873 registered emigration to North America totals 103 000 persons, of which 32 000 emigrated in 1869. Many of those who left Sweden between 1870 and 1873 were probably relatives of the 1869 emigrants.[18] The actual statistics were higher, since the technique of registration was still rather defective. Gustav Sundbärg has calculated that unregistered emigration during the 1860s was about 20 per cent, but his method have proved questionable.[19] In reality, an even greater amount of omissions must be taken into account.[20]

Emigration by large groups of people still took place during this period. Several examples can be mentioned: in 1866 around a hundred families, many of them Baptists, left Rättvik, Orsa, and neighboring parishes in Dalarna for Isanti County, Minnesota; and in 1869 a priest by the name of Olof Olsson, in the company of about 200 persons, left Värmland for Lindsborg, Kansas.[21] However, emigration by groups and families was less dominant than before. The majority of emigrants were single men and women.[22] The proportion of farmers was not as strong as before: from this point on sons and daughters who lived at home, farm-hands, maid-servants, trade apprentices, blacksmiths, and the like completely dominate the picture.[23]

Mass emigration was accelerated by crop failures in Sweden, but the extent of these failures in the various districts did not stand in direct proportion to the shortage of food. The northernmost districts in Sweden,

[18] U. Ebbeson (1968), p. 44.
[19] *Emigrationsutredningen* (1913) pp. 594 f., and Bilaga 4 (1910), pp. 247 ff.; L.-G. Tedebrand (1972), pp. 317 ff.; A.-S. Kälvemark (1972), pp. 105 ff. See also above, Chapter 3.
[20] L.-G. Tedebrand (1972), p. 291.
[21] H. Nelson (1943), pp. 196 ff.; E. Lindquist (1970), p. 29; L. Ljungmark (1971), pp. 217 ff.
[22] See below, Chapter 5: b.
[23] See below, Chapter 5: d.

Table 5:2. *Registered Emigration to Non-European Countries from All of Sweden's län, 1851–1930: Relative Figures for Each Decade*

Län	Annual mean figures per 1 000 residents								Mean figures
	1851 –60	1861 –70	1871 –80	1881 –90	1891 –1900	1901 –10	1911 –20	1921 –30	1851 –1930
Sth. City	0.67	1.82	1.88	6.50	4.87	3.74	1.45	1.47	2.80
Sth. län	0.03	0.18	0.43	1.88	1.33	1.34	0.67	0.79	0.83
Upps.	0.00	0.21	0.58	1.96	0.98	1.13	0.37	0.49	0.72
Söd.	0.01	0.42	0.79	2.82	1.61	1.52	0.47	0.55	1.02
Ög.	0.83	3.67	3.80	8.91	4.17	3.60	1.00	0.92	3.36
Jönk.	1.41	6.36	4.55	11.80	6.05	5.10	1.80	2.19	4.91
Kron.	0.96	3.47	3.96	10.48	6.21	5.57	2.44	2.60	4.46
Kalm.	0.24	3.55	2.91	9.56	6.79	6.75	2.82	2.91	4.44
Gotl.	0.11	1.17	2.48	8.51	4.30	4.05	1.33	0.98	2.87
Blek.	0.92	1.18	1.86	5.66	4.99	4.68	2.37	2.80	3.06
Krist.	0.88	2.89	3.25	8.10	4.96	3.84	1.56	1.62	3.39
Malm.	0.10	0.98	2.00	6.14	2.98	2.77	1.13	0.96	2.13
Hall.	0.32	1.61	4.19	12.08	8.11	7.47	3.29	2.97	5.01
Göt. Boh.	0.24	0.52	1.14	4.17	3.45	3.40	1.34	1.79	2.01
Älvsb.	0.51	2.25	2.28	9.89	5.89	5.47	2.06	2.11	3.81
Skar.	0.33	2.27	2.32	8.66	4.75	3.97	1.16	1.02	3.06
Värml.	0.07	2.76	2.88	10.83	6.25	7.35	2.65	3.22	4.50
Ör.	0.26	2.12	2.65	7.68	3.72	3.61	0.91	1.46	2.80
Västm.	0.08	0.82	1.38	3.15	1.57	1.54	0.48	1.03	1.26
Kopp.	0.08	2.74	2.54	6.26	2.65	4.46	1.38	2.69	2.85
Gävl.	0.94	3.83	1.57	5.13	2.81	4.72	1.53	1.65	2.77
Vnorrl.	0.07	0.93	0.99	2.94	4.46	4.85	1.52	1.87	2.20
Jämtl.	0.17	1.69	1.16	4.93	3.99	6.66	1.64	2.92	2.90
Vb.	–	0.45	0.38	1.80	1.49	3.67	1.32	1.56	1.33
Nb.	–	0.37	1.27	2.80	1.43	5.23	1.65	2.72	1.93
Nation-wide	0.40	2.18	2.36	6.94	4.14	4.21	1.51	1.76	2.94
Countryside	..[a]	..[a]	2.35[b]	7.14	4.04	4.36	1.54	1.85	
Cities	..[a]	..[a]	2.11[b]	6.46	4.52	3.73	1.41	1.55	

Sources For the period 1851–1900: *Emigrationsutredningens Betänkande* Bilaga V, p. 98, as complemented by rural and city statistics from *Sveriges officiella statistik,* serie A.
For the period 1901–1930: *Sveriges officiella statistik,* serie Befolkningsrörelsen 1901–1910, p. 184, Befolkningsrörelsen 1911–1920, p. 272, Befolkningsrörelsen 1921–1930, p. 134. Commentary see page 123.

which were hardest hit by famine, were still relatively unaffected by emigration. As shown by Map Diagram 5: 2 and Table 5: 2, the highest emigration rates are registered for northern Småland, southwestern Östergötland, the Karlskoga mining district, and sections of Hälsingland. However, the geographical spread of emigration was greater than before. High rates are recorded, for example, for large areas of southeastern Småland, western Blekinge, northern Skåne, central Västergötland, along with sections of Värmland, Dalarna and Jämtland. This does not mean that the major, regional distribution disappeared from view: during the 1860s Jönköpings län (northwestern Småland) had an emigration frequency which was more than 30 times that of Stockholms and Uppsala län. Emigration during the famine years was greatest in districts where a tradition of emigration was already rooted among the population.[24]

The Culmination of Swedish Emigration (1879–1893)

After reaching a first peak in 1869, emigration successively decreased during the course of the following years. In 1874 the number of registered overseas emigrants was down to 3 500, and emigration subsequently remained at that level up until 1879. However, it is likely that a relatively substantial amount of unregistered emigration took place during these years.[25]

A sudden rise of emigration occurred in 1879, when 12 800 overseas emigrants were registered. This figure rose sharply until 1882, when the total reached 44 500. Following a certain decline in subsequent years, the

[24] Cf. S. Carlsson (1967), p. 122; A. Wirén (1975), pp. 133 ff., 198 ff.
[25] I. Eriksson (1970), p. 1 ff. See also above, Chapter 3: b.

In estimating average population consideration has been given to reported figures on December 31 during the following series of years: 1900, 1905, and 1910; 1910, 1915, and 1920; and 1920, 1925, and 1930. Statistics prior to 1891 only apply to emigration to North America.

[a] No exact statistics are available on the distribution between rural areas and cities. With regard to all emigrants (including those destinated to countries within Europe), rural areas had 0.47 persons per year and 1 000 residents between 1851 and 1860 and 2.89 persons between 1861 and 1870. The corresponding figures for urban areas are 0.45 and 3.79: *Historisk statistik för Sverige* (First Edition 1955), Vol. 1, p. 69.
[b] No statistics are available on the distribution between rural areas and cities for the year 1871. The proportion has been assumed to be the same as it was in 1872. There are minor gaps in the statistical account of rural–urban distribution throughout this decade.

figure rose again in 1886 and, a year later, assumed its highest recorded level in history, namely 46 500. Emigration remained at a high level until 1893. For the period 1879–1893 a total of 493 000 overseas emigrants are recorded: this means that more than 40 per cent of the total overseas emigration between 1845 and 1930 was concentrated to these fifteen years.

A number of unregistered emigrants must be added to this total. Sundbärg estimated that unregistered emigration during the first part of this period amounted to 10 per cent of the registered statistics. On the other hand, in estimating omissions for the period 1885–1893 in light of sharpened legislation, he settled for a figure as low as 1 per cent.[26] However, there are grounds for suspecting that the number of omissions both before and after 1885 was greater than Sundbärg imagined.[27] Yet, under all circumstances the year 1885 does serve as a line of demarkation, and it must therefore be assumed that the omissions were far greater in 1882 than they were in 1887. Consequently, one should work on the premise that total registered and unregistered emigration reached an absolute peak in 1882 and not in 1887.

This tremendous transfer of Swedish manpower to North America was a result of co-operative pull and push-factors. The fluctuations can be correlated with the economic cycles in both Sweden and America. As far as push-factors are concerned, attention should be drawn to the crisis in 1879 which struck large sectors of the Swedish economy and was especially devastating to the timber industry in Northern Sweden. Västernorrland was the prime sawmill region in Sweden and up until that time was relatively untouched by emigration. Yet, during this crisis its emigration figures promptly increased tenfold and rose even more in subsequent years.[28] A similar effect, culminating in 1881, can be traced in the sawmill parish of Söderala in Hälsingland.[29]

The crisis of 1879 also struck the iron industry. The Finspång foundry in northern Östergötland—which, among other things, manufactured artillery cannons—suffered an exceptionally severe setback. However, as far as production quality was concerned, the Finspång foundry could not compete with other firms, such as the German Krupp works. This very same year the Swedish military authorities had placed an order of cannons

[26] *Emigrationsutredningen*, pp. 594 f., and Bilaga 4, pp. 248 ff.

[27] L. G. Tedebrand (1972), pp. 321 ff.; A.-S. Kälvemark (1972), pp. 105 ff. See also above, Chapter 3: c.

[28] L.-G. Tedebrand (1972), pp. 129 f.

[29] B. Rondahl (1972), pp. 43, 215.

with Krupp instead of the Finspång foundry. This led to a sharp increase in emigration from the area.[30] On the whole, the iron industry was characterized around 1880 by declining production and rising unemployment. An unusually large emigration of metal workers from Stockholm was also noted in 1879.[31] The same tendency can be traced among blacksmiths and other metal workers in Huskvarna in northern Småland, in the Karlskoga mining district, and at the Ljusne works in Hälsingland.[32]

However, the majority of emigrants during the 1880s represented the agricultural sector of the Swedish economy. This sector was in dire straits, partially as a result of the penetration of the Swedish market by Russian and American grain, which led to a sharp drop in prices. Between 1881 and 1887 the price of rye, which was incontestably the most important variety of grain, dropped by about 50 per cent. During the same period the number of bankrupcy applications filed in the countryside more than doubled.[33]

Some agricultural districts—for example, western Småland, Öland, Halland, and Dalsland—which had seen a rather moderate level of emigration up to this time were now gravely effected by the course of mass emigration.[34] The high emigration figures of 1886–1888 in particular must be seen as a consequence of the acute agricultural crisis, which was softened by the introduction of agricultural tariffs in 1888. Seven prime agricultural län—Jönköpings, Kronobergs, Kalmar, Hallands, Älvsborgs, Skaraborgs, and Värmlands—accounted for more than half of the overseas emigration in 1887.[35]

The emigration of 1891–1893 had a somewhat more industrial and urban character. During these three years the city of Stockholm recorded its highest emigration totals in history, and Västernorrland reached its maximum figures in 1892 and 1893.[36] The sizable emigration to Brazil in

[30] U. Ebbeson (1969), pp. 12, 45. The emigration from the Finspång foundry reverberated in the Swedish Parliament, where it was greeted with unfavourable commentary by one of the Farmer's Party leaders, Emil Key, an outspoken enemy of emigration. *Andra Kammarens Protokoll,* 1880, Vol. 14, pp. 4 f.

[31] F. Nilsson (1970), pp. 95 ff.

[32] S. Carlsson (1966–1967), pp. 46, 50, 62; B. Rondahl (1972), pp. 142 ff.; H. Norman (1974), p. 65.

[33] A. Montgomery (1921), pp. 135 ff.

[34] P. Noreen (1967), pp. 26 ff.; S. Carlsson (1966–67), pp. 54 f. Consult as well the Map Diagrams 5: 5 and 5: 6.

[35] Cf. the list of län in Ljungmark (1966), p. 185.

[36] F. Nilsson (1970), p. 287; L.-G. Tedebrand (1972), pp. 129 ff.

1891, accounting for about 2 000 emigrants, mainly came from the city of Stockholm and the Sundsvall district (Västernorrland).[37] The background was industrial stagnation and major unemployment.[38]

Generally speaking, emigration between 1879 and 1893 was characterized by increased geographical and social distribution. It can be added here that Finland, and the province of Österbotten in particular, were seriously affected by mass emigration during this period.[39] The shift from family to single emigration continued. One rather striking feature of the emigration between 1886 and 1893 is represented by the thousands of married men who left on their own for America, while their wives—the "America widows"—and children remained for a time in Sweden.[40]

Pre-War Emigration (1900–1913)

Improved economic conditions in Sweden and deteriorated opportunities in the United States contributed to the decline of emigration in 1894. In subsequent years both factors helped to keep emigration at a lower level than that recorded between 1879 and 1893. However, emigration did not lose its significance. A total of 72 000 overseas emigrants are recorded for the period 1894–1899. A new increase occurred around the turn of the century, culminating in 1903 (36 000 emigrants), and emigration retained a high level until the outbreak of World War I. The sum total of registered overseas emigrants between 1900 and 1913 was 289 000—i.e. only slightly half as many as between 1879 and 1893. The actual total was higher. However, the number of omitted statistics cannot have been as large as that during the pre-1885 period.[41]

Despite the extension of compulsory military service in 1901, when the normal training period for conscript soldiers rose from 90 to 240 days, the fear of military service seems to have claimed a clearly lesser degree of importance as a cause of emigration than labor market factors. A series of extensive strikes, culminating in the general strike of 1909, can be both directly and indirectly linked with emigration. On the whole, however, Sweden enjoyed a progressively improved economic situation during this

[37] K. Stenbeck (1973), pp. 126 ff.
[38] F. Nilsson (1970), pp. 36, 99 f., 106 f., 170 ff.; L.-G. Tedebrand (1972), pp. 129 ff. Cf. B. Rondahl (1972), p. 43.
[39] R. Kero (1974), pp. 24 ff.; E. De Geer and H. Wester (1975), *passim.*
[40] S. Carlsson (1968), pp. 107 ff.
[41] A.-S. Kälvemark (1972), pp. 86 ff.

period. This indicates that pull-factors—the strong attraction of the American labor market—were now dominant. An additional factor deserves mention in this context, namely the tremendous pressure which the growing ranks of Swedish-Americans brought to bear at this time on relatives and friends at home. In other words, emigration was not motivated now, as it was earlier, by overpopulation in Sweden. It also provoked far greater unrest than before: for the first time in Sweden a genuine debate rose on emigration which was largely characterized by the fear of insufficient manpower on the part of employers, especially those associated with agriculture.[42]

Emigration during this period mainly originated from the same sectors of the country as previously. However, a certain shift to the north can be observed: this can be related to the fact that the Finnish province of Österbotten now had a higher emigration frequency than the Swedish emigrant districts (see Map Diagrams 5: 9–11). Gävleborgs, Jämtlands and Västerbottens län recorded their highest emigration in history as late as 1903, while Norrbotten did not reach its peak figure until 1910.[43] Family emigration from northern provinces was still rather substantial at this time, but in other respects movements by single individuals dominated the picture more than ever before.[44]

An increasing share of the overseas emigration was now directed to Canada: according to official statistics, this country received over 5 000 Swedes between 1900 and 1913. This total is undoubtedly too low, since many emigrants who actually settled in Canada continued to report "the United States" or "North America" as their destination. Prior to 1900 only some hundred emigrants were recorded as having emigrated to Canada: on this matter of destination reports the statistics say nothing of real value. A detailed study has shown, for example, that in 1892 at least 190 persons left Västernorrlands län for Canada, whereas the official statistics only record 36 persons under the heading of "Canada" (and 113 from all areas of Sweden).[45] Nevertheless, Canada's share of Swedish emigration expanded sharply during the first three decades of the 1900s, and residents of Northern Sweden were particularly inclined to choose Canada as their place of destination.

[42] A.-S. Kälvemark (1972), *passim.*

[43] Cf. L. Ljungmark (1965), p. 187; see below, Chapter 5: c.

[44] See below, Chapter 5: b.

[45] L.-G. Tedebrand (1972), pp. 211 ff.

Post-War Emigration (1920–1929)

World War I curbed emigration to North America without entirely stopping it. Even the American entrance into the war in 1917 failed to bring a complete halt to emigration. However, the total figures were low: around 30 000 Swedes emigrated overseas between 1914 and 1919.

Emigration rose again in the early 1920s, partially as a result of Sweden's own share of difficulties during the first post-war period and by virtue of the new opportunities which seemed to open up in America. Registered overseas emigration for the period 1920–1929 amounted to 109 000 and was strongly concentrated to the year 1923 (26 600). Canada was reported as the place of destination for 11 500 emigrants during the 1920s.

The regional distribution in Sweden was approximately the same as at the beginning of the century: the old emigrant districts continued to play a major role, as did Jämtland and Norrbotten.[46] Emigration by single individuals was more dominant than before. One remarkable feature is the sex distribution of the emigrants. A certain surplus of men existed throughout the entire emigration period, with the sole exception of two five-year periods which had a relatively low emigration frequency (1896–1900 and 1916–1920).[47] However, the surplus recorded during the 1920s was far greater than in any other period. It was primarily concentrated to unmarried, rural emigrants in the age span of 15–29 years. The men in this category were up to three times the number of women. Seen as a whole, this group of single men between 15 and 29 years of age accounted for 44 per cent of the entire overseas emigrant stock.[48]

During World War I the United States sharpened its attitude toward German-Americans, Swedish-Americans, and other "hyphenated-Americans". The war itself generated distrust of Germans in particular, but even Scandinavians were affected. The end of the war evoked protectionistic labor market viewpoints: it was held that immigrants took jobs from native-born Americans. Southern and Eastern Europeans were looked upon with particular disfavor in this context, but Scandinavians were also affected by the change in atmosphere. The result was the introduction of immigrant quotas in 1921, 1924 and 1927. Aside from the emigrant contingent of 1923, Sweden never filled its annual quotas, and

[46] See below, Chapter 5:c. Cf. Å. Danielsson, T. Nilsson and B. Kronborg (1969), *passim.*

[47] *Historisk statistik för Sverige* (2nd edition), 1, pp. 129 f.

[48] *Sveriges officiella statistik,* Serie Befolkningsrörelsen, 1921–1930, p. 141. Cf. S. Carlsson (1968), pp. 113 ff., where the discussion includes emigration within Europe.

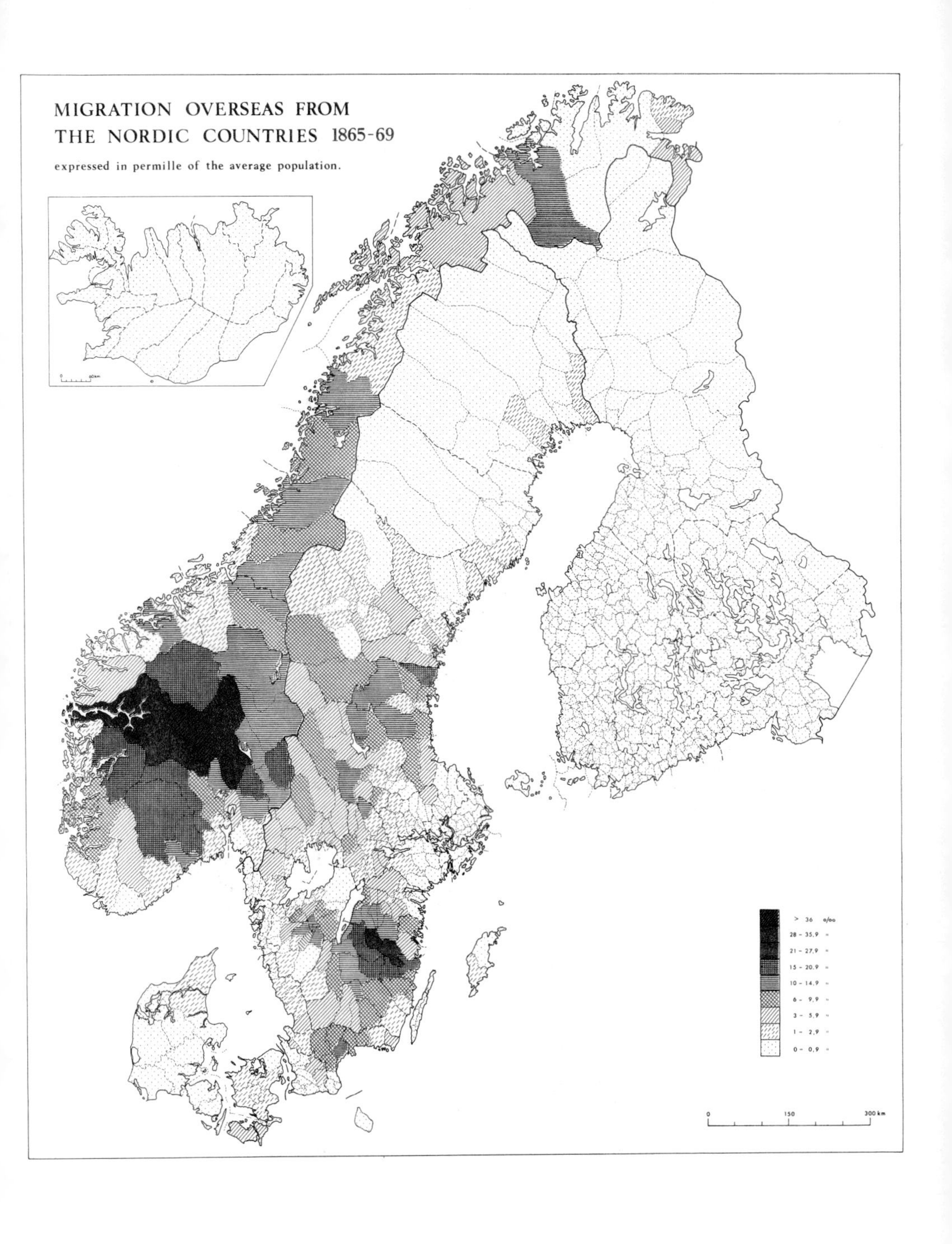
MIGRATION OVERSEAS FROM
THE NORDIC COUNTRIES 1865-69
expressed in permille of the average population.
> 36 o/oo
28 - 35,9 "
21 - 27,9 "
15 - 20.9 "
10 - 14,9 "
6 - 9,9 "
3 - 5,9 "
1 - 2,9 "
0 - 0,9 "
0
150
300 km

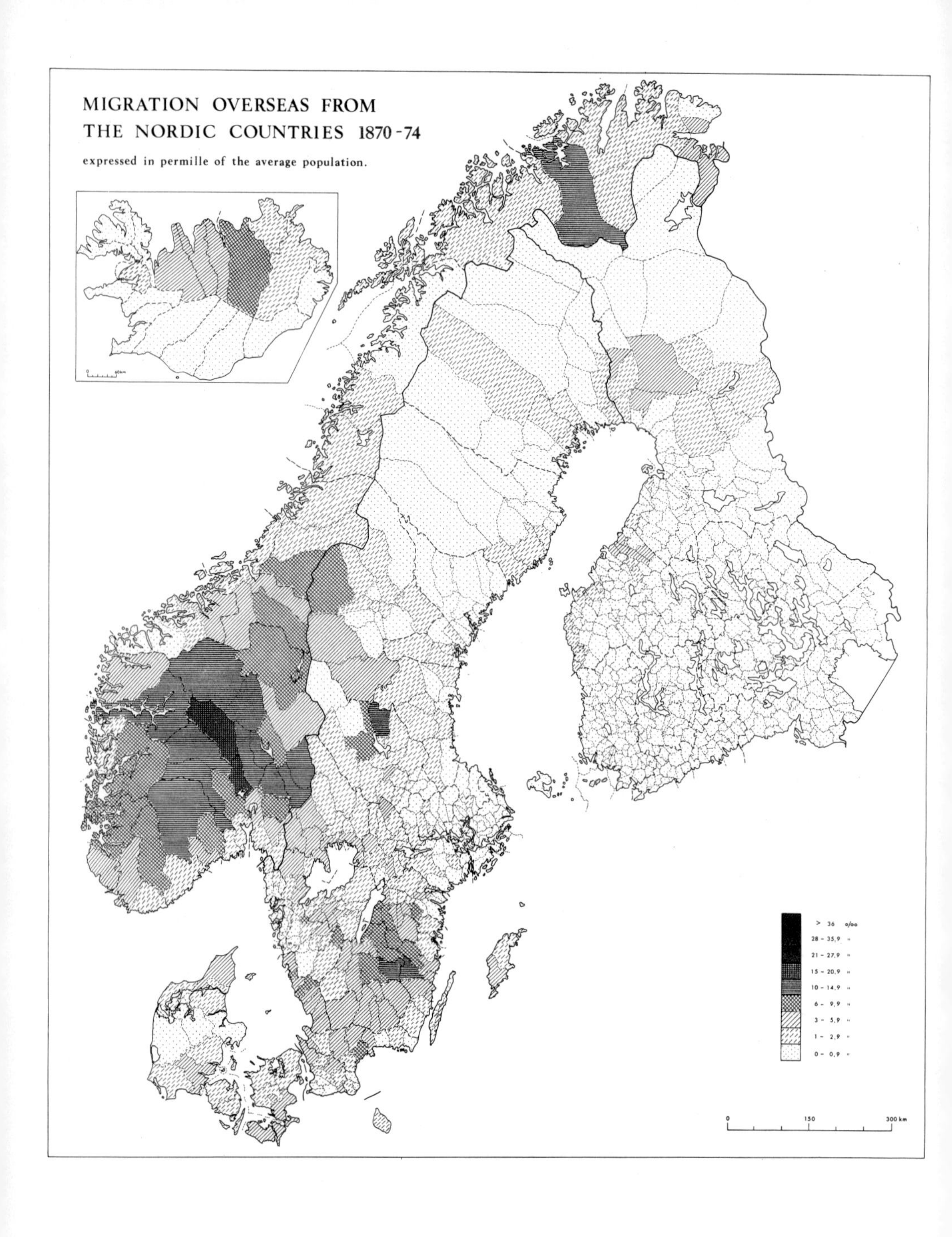
MIGRATION OVERSEAS FROM
THE NORDIC COUNTRIES 1870-74
expressed in permille of the average population.
> 36 o/oo
28 - 35,9 "
21 - 27,9 "
15 - 20,9 "
10 - 14,9 "
6 - 9,9 "
3 - 5,9 "
1 - 2,9 "
0 - 0,9 "
0
150
300 km

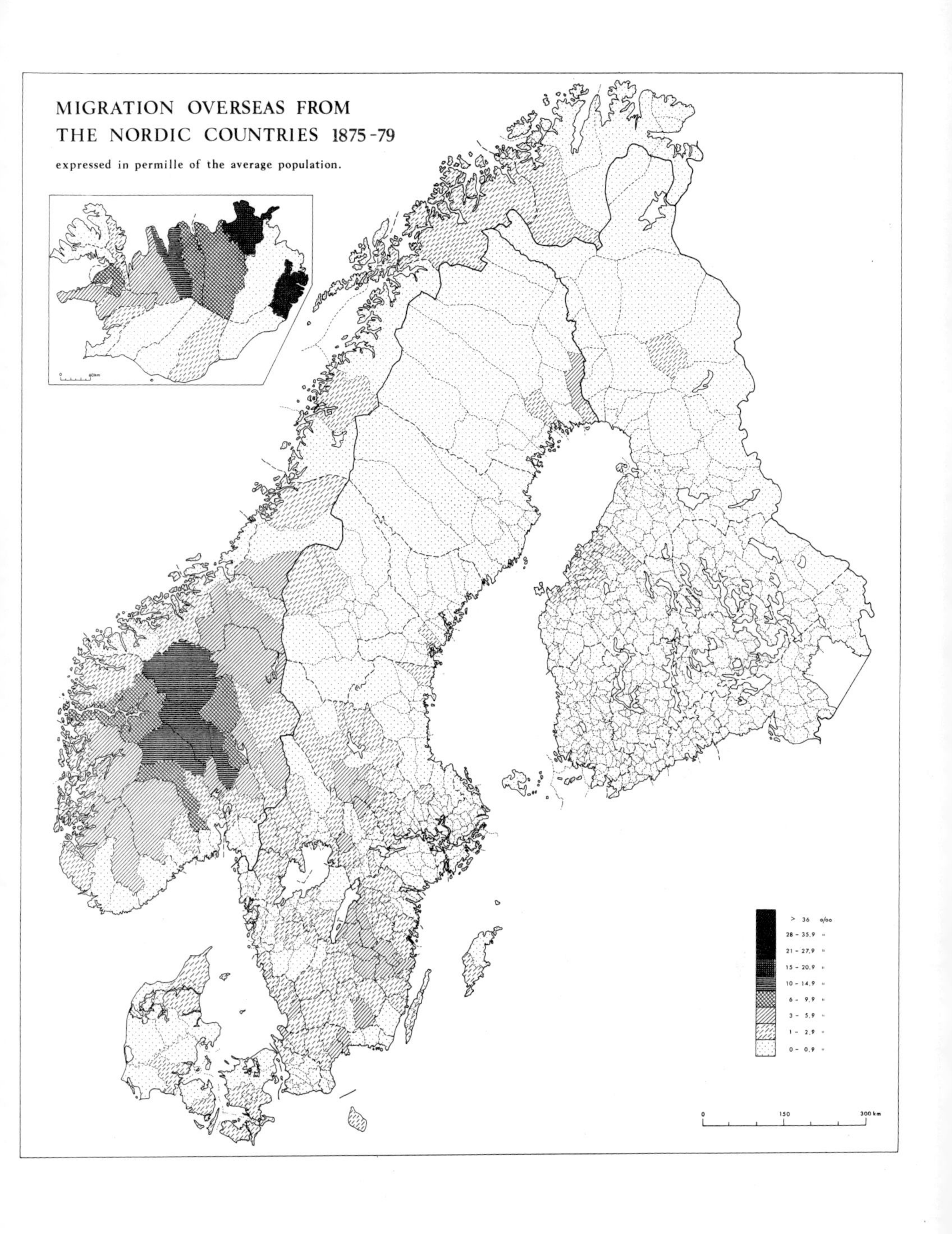
MIGRATION OVERSEAS FROM
THE NORDIC COUNTRIES 1875-79
expressed in permille of the average population.
> 36 o/oo
28 - 35,9 "
21 - 27,9 "
15 - 20,9 "
10 - 14,9 "
6 - 9,9 "
3 - 5,9 "
1 - 2,9 "
0 - 0,9 "
0
150
300 km

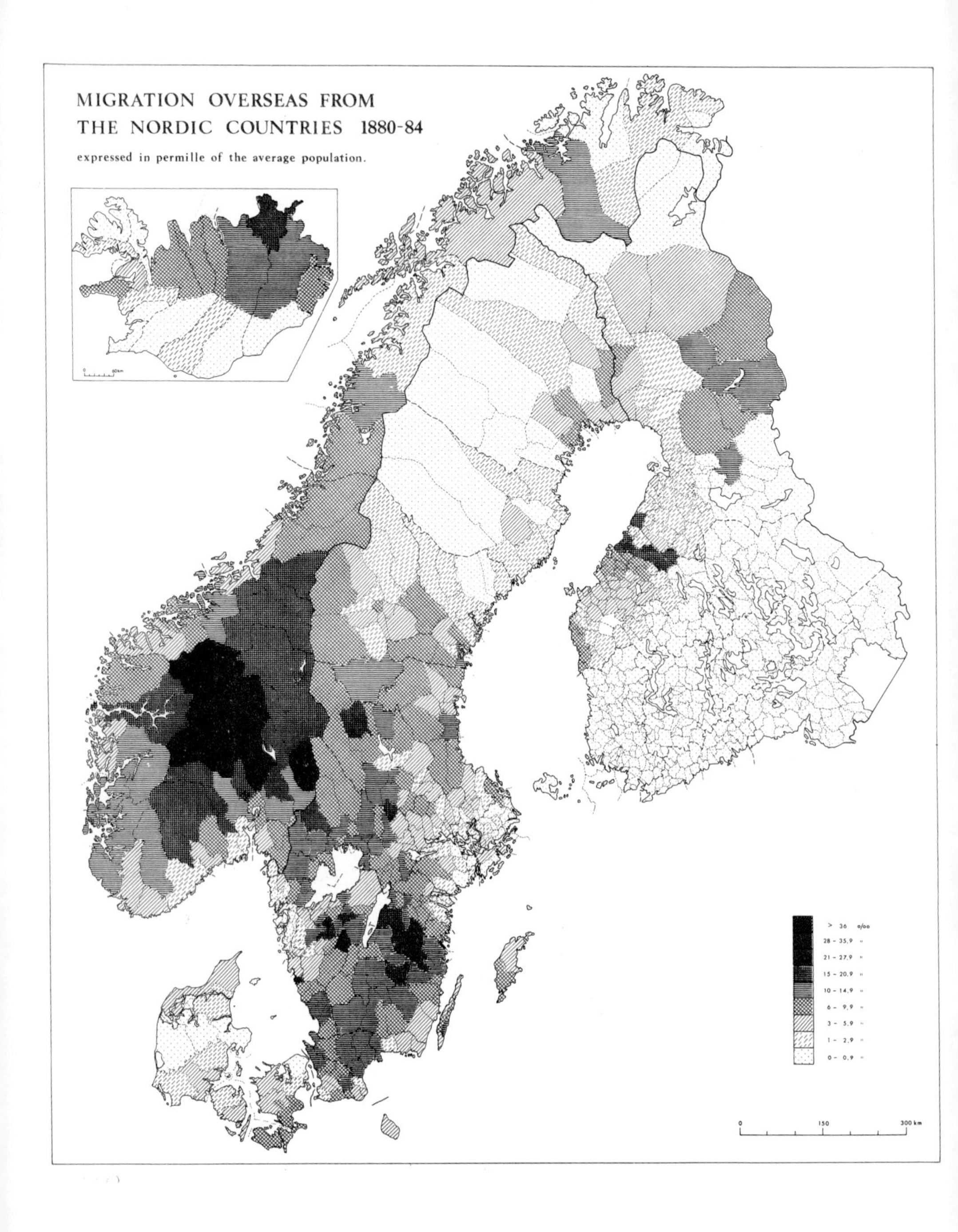
MIGRATION OVERSEAS FROM
THE NORDIC COUNTRIES 1880-84
expressed in permille of the average population.
> 36 o/oo
28 - 35,9 "
21 - 27,9 "
15 - 20,9 "
10 - 14,9 "
6 - 9,9 "
3 - 5,9 "
1 - 2,9 "
0 - 0,9 "
0
150
300 km
0
60km

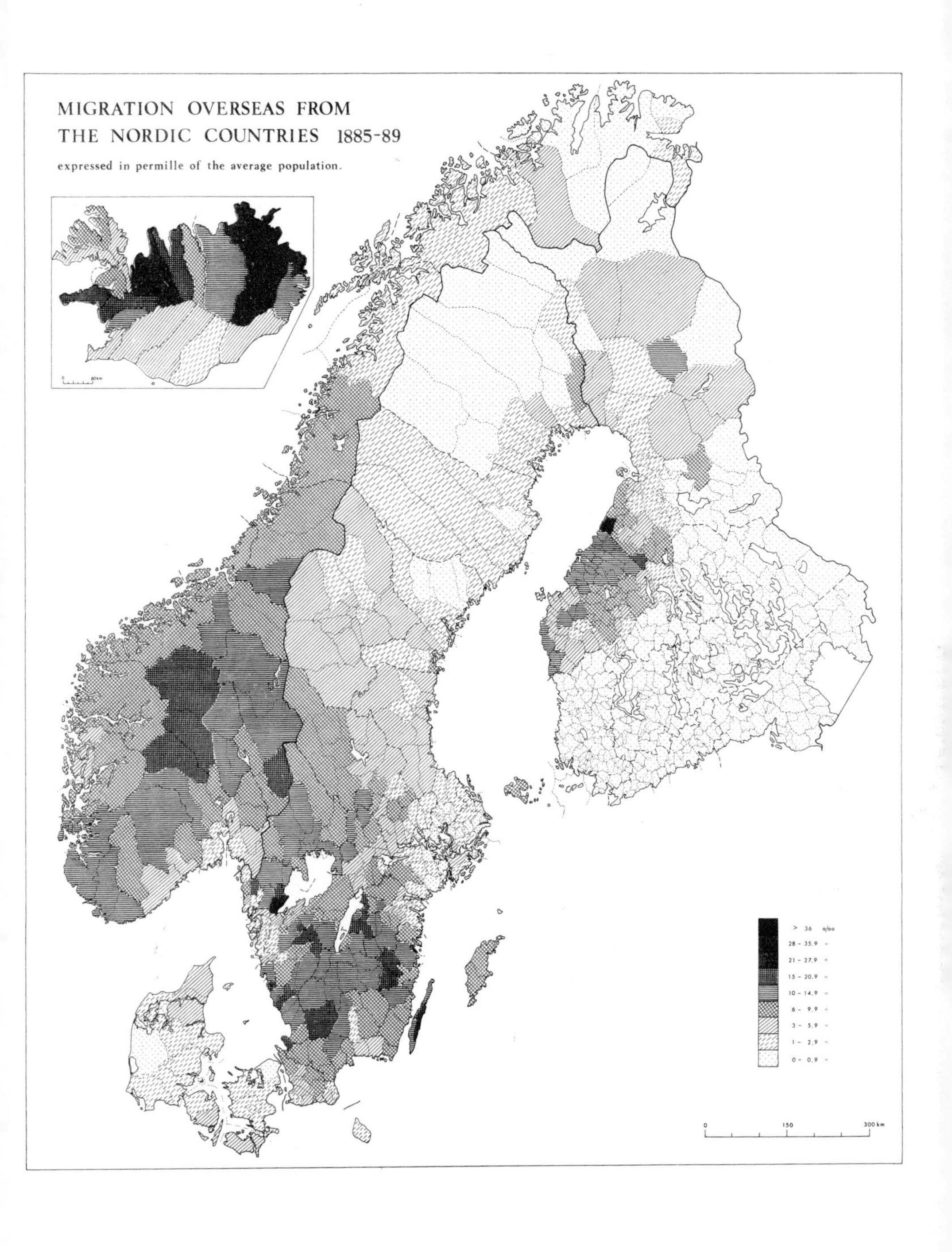
MIGRATION OVERSEAS FROM
THE NORDIC COUNTRIES 1885-89
expressed in permille of the average population.
0
60km
> 36 o/oo
28 - 35,9 "
21 - 27,9 "
15 - 20,9 "
10 - 14,9 "
6 - 9,9 "
3 - 5,9 "
1 - 2,9 "
0 - 0,9 "
0
150
300 km

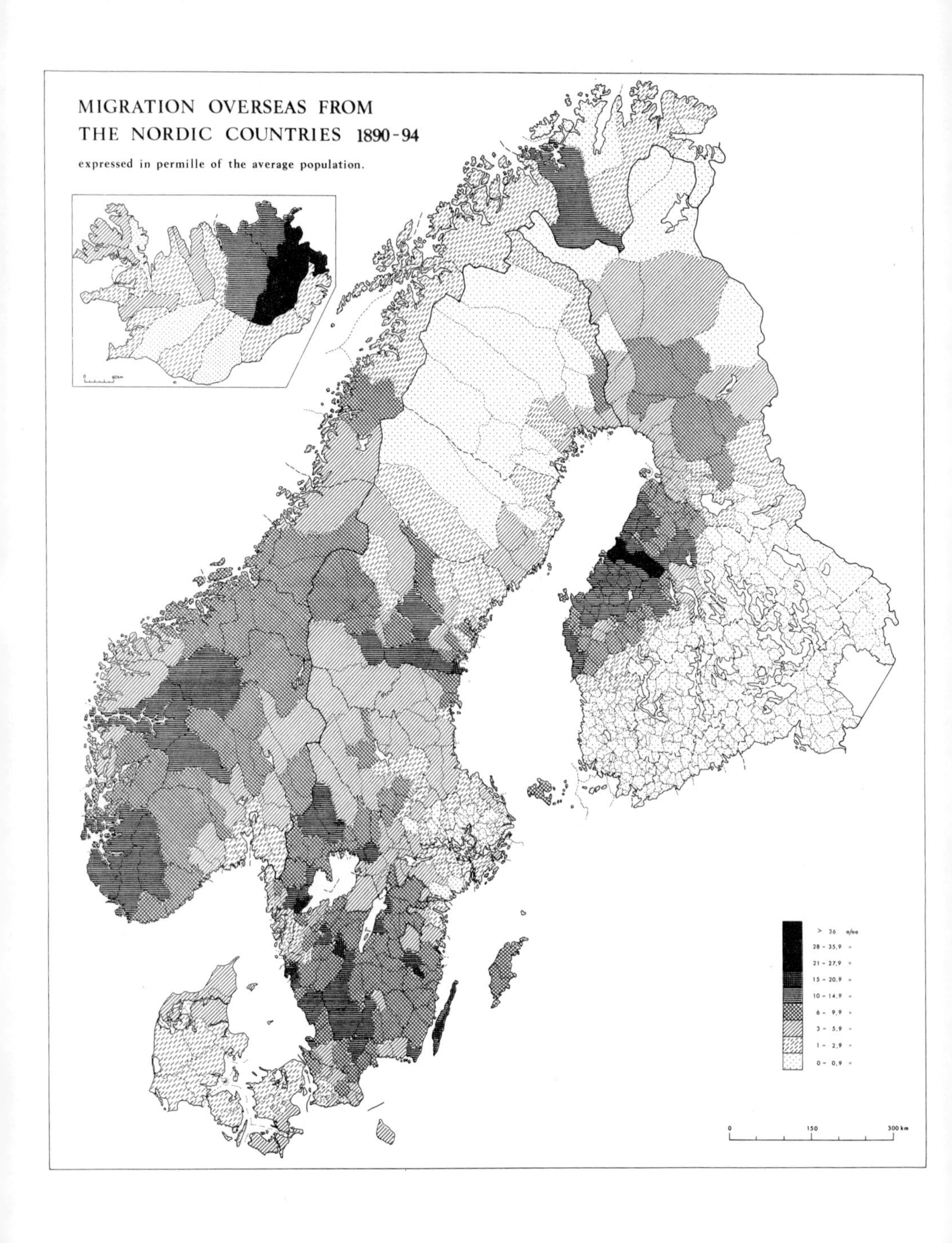
MIGRATION OVERSEAS FROM
THE NORDIC COUNTRIES 1890-94
expressed in permille of the average population.
0
60km
> 36 o/oo
28 - 35,9 "
21 - 27,9 "
15 - 20,9 "
10 - 14,9 "
6 - 9,9 "
3 - 5,9 "
1 - 2,9 "
0 - 0,9 "
0
150
300 km

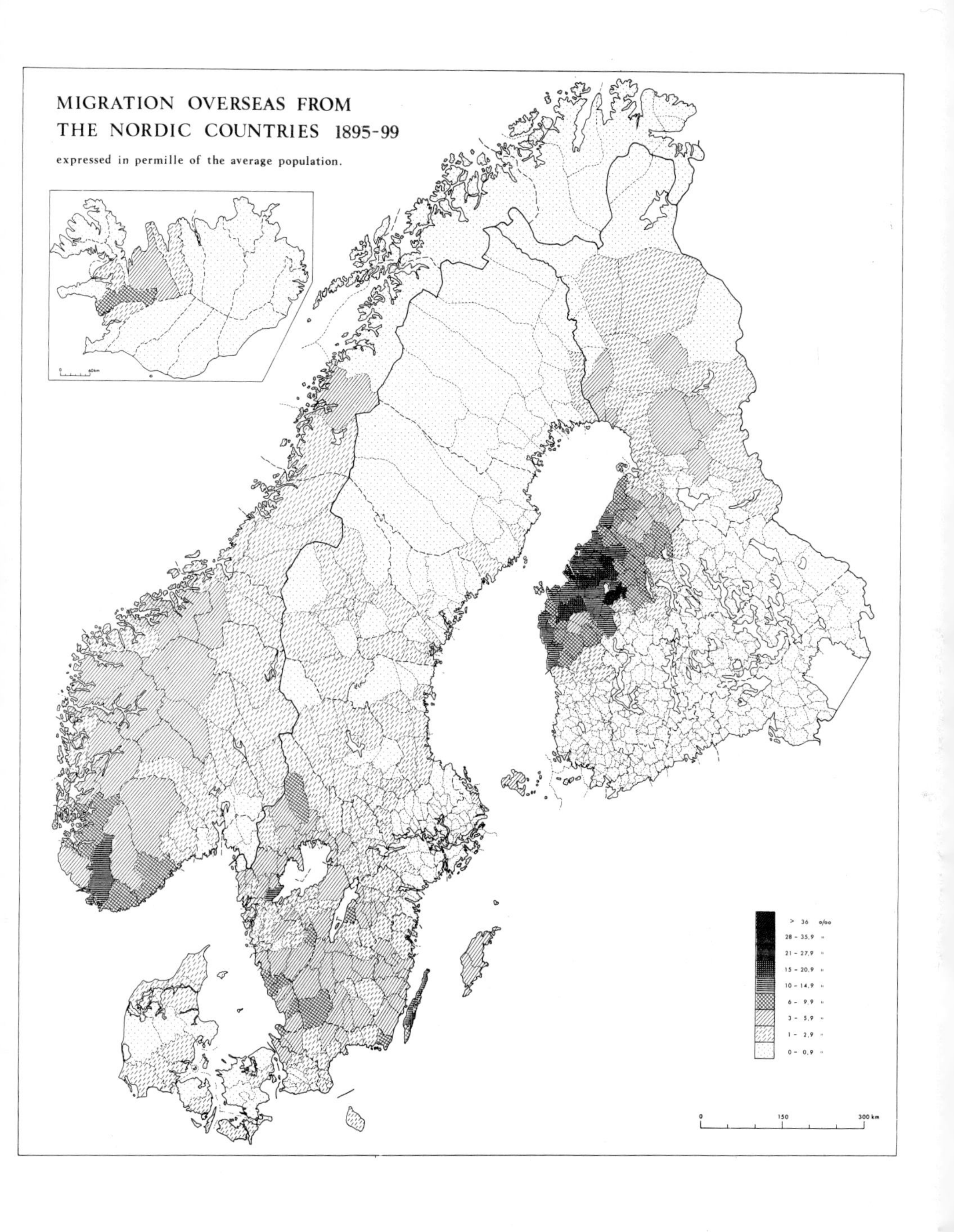
MIGRATION OVERSEAS FROM
THE NORDIC COUNTRIES 1895-99
expressed in permille of the average population.
> 36 o/oo
28 - 35,9 "
21 - 27,9 "
15 - 20,9 "
10 - 14,9 "
6 - 9,9 "
3 - 5,9 "
1 - 2,9 "
0 - 0,9 "
0
150
300 km

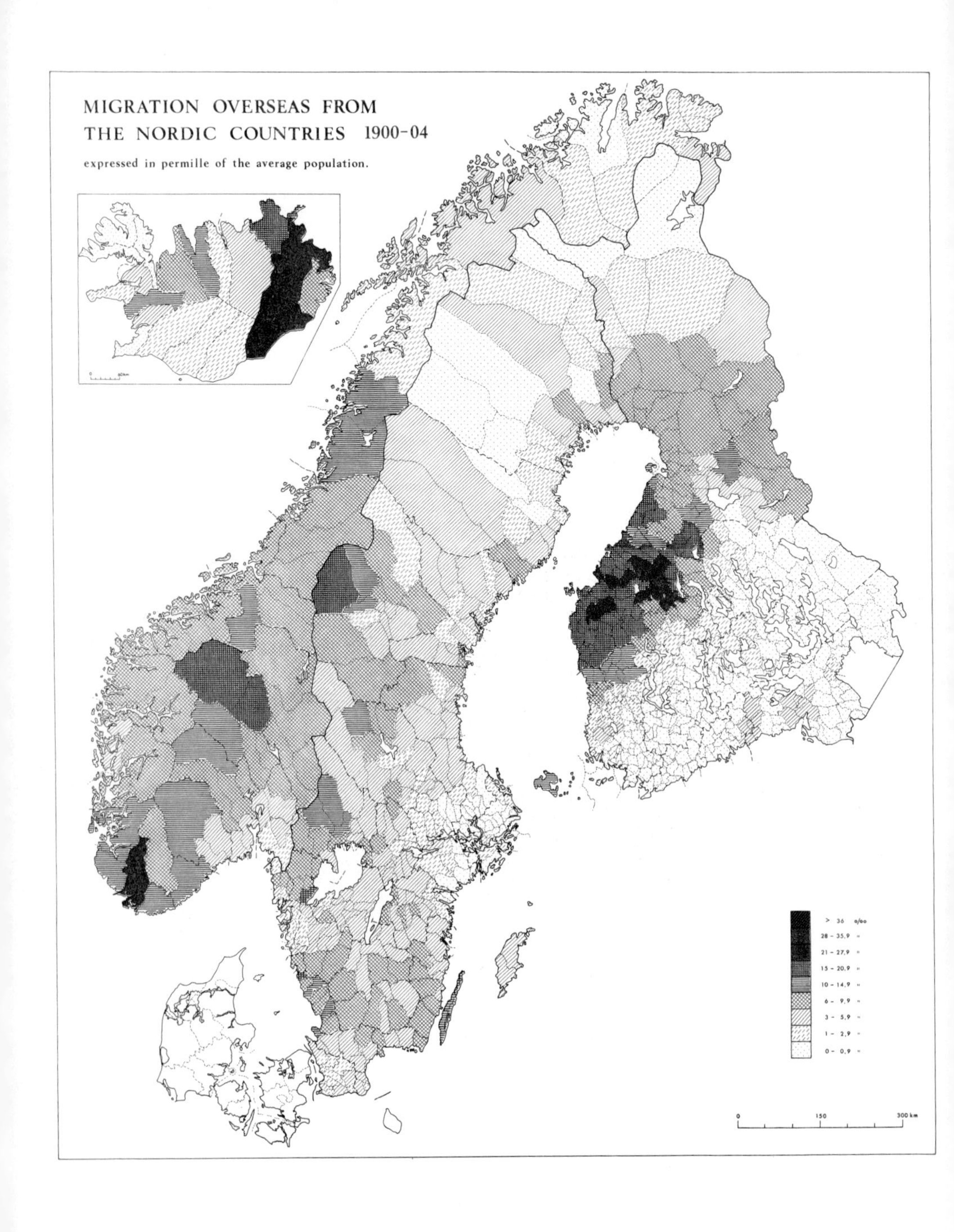
MIGRATION OVERSEAS FROM
THE NORDIC COUNTRIES 1900-04
expressed in permille of the average population.
> 36 o/oo
28 - 35,9 "
21 - 27,9 "
15 - 20,9 "
10 - 14,9 "
6 - 9,9 "
3 - 5,9 "
1 - 2,9 "
0 - 0,9 "
0
150
300 km

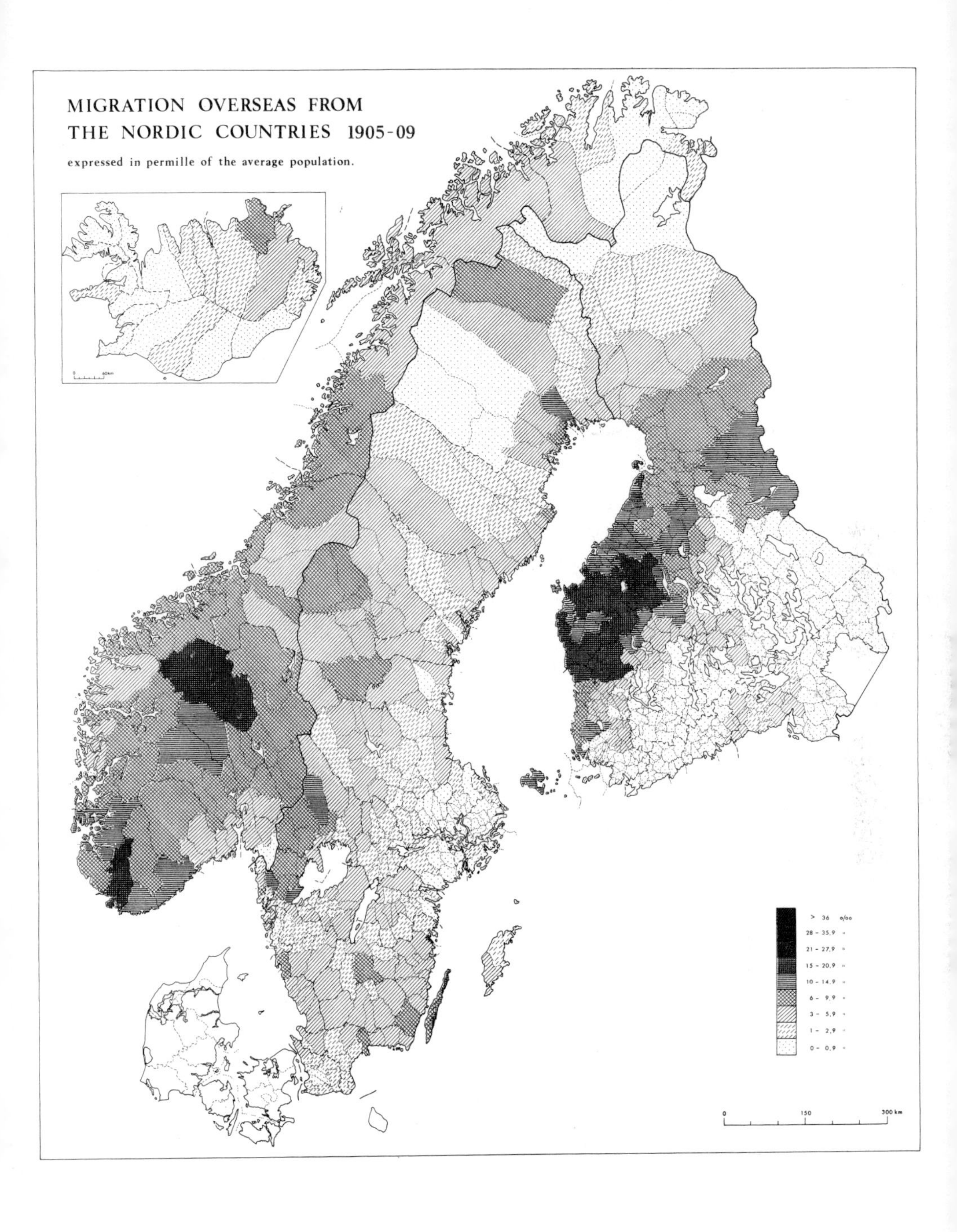
MIGRATION OVERSEAS FROM
THE NORDIC COUNTRIES 1905-09
expressed in permille of the average population.
> 36 o/oo
28 - 35,9 "
21 - 27,9 "
15 - 20,9 "
10 - 14,9 "
6 - 9,9 "
3 - 5,9 "
1 - 2,9 "
0 - 0,9 "
0
150
300 km

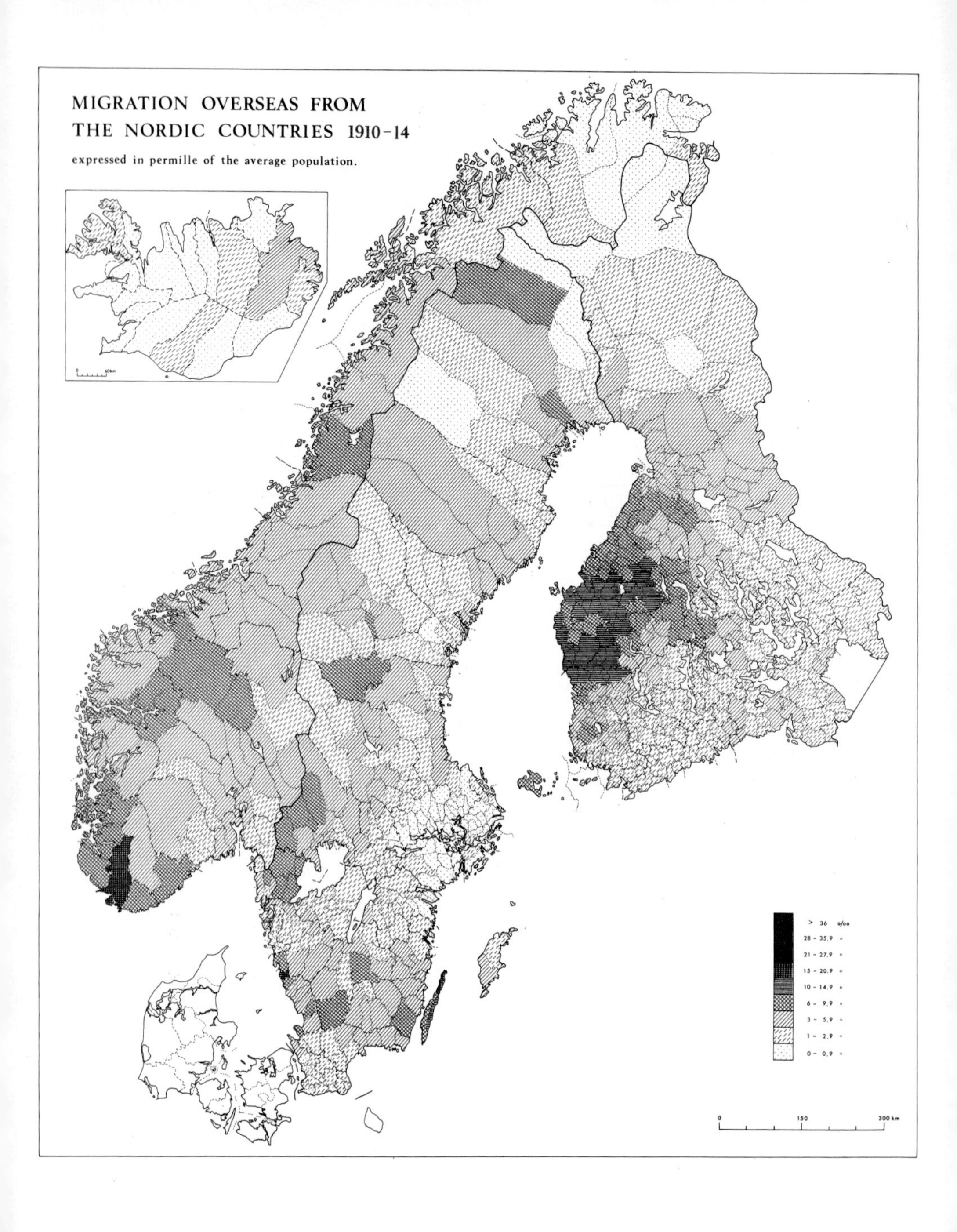

MIGRATION OVERSEAS FROM
THE NORDIC COUNTRIES 1910-14
expressed in permille of the average population.
> 36 o/oo
28 - 35,9 "
21 - 27,9 "
15 - 20,9 "
10 - 14,9 "
6 - 9,9 "
3 - 5,9 "
1 - 2,9 "
0 - 0,9 "
0
150
300 km
60km

therefore it can hardly be held that legislation was any direct cause of the numerical decline of emigration.[49] Of greater importance was the rise in Swedish economic and business cycles after 1923 and the start of the American Depression in 1929.

In 1930 only 3 500 Swedes emigrated to North America, of which 600 went to Canada. During the entire decade between 1931 and 1940 overseas emigration from Sweden maintained a total of 9 000 persons. Beginning in 1930 immigration to Sweden from countries outside of Europe, particularly from the United States, was far greater than emigration. The mass-emigration epoch was now at an end.[50]

Summary

The total registered emigration from Sweden to America between 1851 and 1930 amounts to ca. 1 150 000 persons. Calculations of the unregistered emigration during this period can only be very approximative but the unregistered may have been 100 000 persons. The combined gross emigration, then, comprised around 1 $^{1}/_{4}$ million people, of which upwards of 200 000 returned to Sweden before 1930.[51] In other words, the loss of population exceeded 1 million people. Expressed schematically, between $^{1}/_{5}$ and $^{1}/_{4}$ of all Swedes living during this period settled in North America.

Of all the European countries only Ireland and Norway, and possibly Iceland, had higher emigration frequencies than Sweden. Mass emigration did take a later start in Sweden than in Great Britain, Ireland, Germany, and Norway, but on the whole Swedes were among the early group of emigrants dominated by people from Northwestern Europe. It was only after the culmination of Swedish emigration that the second great wave of emigration emerged on the scene, dominated by Italians, Poles, Russian Jews, and other groups from Southern and Eastern Europe.

Chronologically speaking, Swedish emigration is unevenly distributed: 75 per cent of it is concentrated to three periods spanning 35 years (1868–1873, 1879–1893, and 1900–1913), while the remaining 50 years (1845–1867, 1874–1878, 1894–1899, and 1914–1929) only account for 25 per cent. This concentration is partially due to acute domestic crises, namely the years of famine in 1868 and 1869, the industrial recession of 1879–1880 and 1891–1893, and the agricultural crisis of 1886–1888. On

[49] S. Lindmark (1971), pp. 137 ff.
[50] *Historisk statistik för Sverige,* 1, pp. 122 ff.
[51] See below, Chapter 8.

other occasions a rise in economic and business cycles in the United States seems to have been the greatest operative factor. A more indepth discussion of the push and pull theory appears in another context.[52]

b. From Family to Individual Emigration

As originally pointed out by the Swedish Commission on Emigration (*Emigrationsutredningen*), the early emigration to North America was dominated by entire families and households which moved in tightly-knit groups and often in the company of other families. Later on, however, this pattern successively shifted in favor of emigration by single individuals, primarily consisting of young, married men and women.[1] It was this type of movement which increasingly dominated the scene as time went by. Left out of consideration here is the inconsequential emigration prior to the 1840s which was mainly characterized by movements of single individuals.[2]

The official statistics allow a rough categorization of emigrants: on the one hand, married persons and children under 15 years of age and, on the other, single persons over 15 years of age. The first group primarily consists of family emigrants, the second of individual emigrants. However, this categorization is not completely satisfactory. It means, for example, that widows, widowers, and divorced persons who emigrated together with their children are unjustly classified as single emigrants. Even unwed mothers with children receive this classification, despite the fact that even in their case one can speak in terms of a type of family emigration. In the same respect, children over 15 years of age who emigrated with their parents are incorrectly classified as single emigrants. However, this grouping shifts in the opposite direction while one counts as family emigrants the rather large numbers of married men and lesser numbers of married women who emigrated on their own, without their families, and those children under 15 years of age who also emigrated without the company of parents or other, older relatives. In all, these categories account for a few percent of the entire emigrant stock, and the errors involved largely cancel out each other. The greatest margin of error concerns the first decades of mass emigration, but here there are certain means of correcting the situation.[3]

[52] See below, Chapter 6.
[1] *Emigrationsutredningen*, Bilaga 4, pp. 50, 166.
[2] A. Friman (1974), pp. 29 f.
[3] S. Carlsson (1968), pp. 105 ff.

Between 1841 and 1850, 3 600 Swedes arrived in New York: they accounted for most of the Swedes who came to the United States during this decade. Of this figure 68 per cent can be classified as family emigrants.[4] This percentage successively decreased and during the 1890s it was down to ca. 29 per cent. It remained at a level of 25–26 per cent during the first decades of the 1900s. The decisive changes took place between 1868 and 1900. It is significant that the number of emigrant children under 15 years of age during the 1840s approximately corresponded to their percentage share of the total Swedish population (ca. 30 %). After that time children are strongly under-represented among emigrants (1921–1930: 9 % among United States emigrants, 27 % of the total Swedish population). One factor which enters into the picture is that the number of children per emigrant family drastically declined: the family emigrants of the 1920s largely consisted of relatively newly-wed couples without children.[5]

The general tendencies outlined here appear to apply to all of the Scandinavian countries. The course of Norwegian emigration ran nearly parallel to the Swedish.[6] As far as Denmark is concerned, the transition from family to single emigration can be schematically set in time to the period 1882–1896.[7] In Finland the percentage of family emigration rose up until the early 1890s but then fell drastically.[8]

The above percentage figures for Swedish emigration apply to the United States. Comparable estimates for Swedish emigration to Canada are available for the period 1901–1930—i.e. the period when emigration to that country was undoubtedly the most significant. Here the share of family emigrants fell from 56 per cent in 1901–1910 to 45 per cent in 1911–1920 and 29 per cent in 1921–1930. During these three decades emigration to Canada underwent basically the same structural change which characterized emigration to the United States between 1868 and 1900.[9] Since Swedish settlements in the United States were established at a far earlier date than those in Canada, it was natural that the following contrast arose: only after new settlements were created by entire families

[4] S. Carlsson (1968), p. 110, as based upon N. W. Olsson (1967).

[5] *Ibid.*, pp. 109 ff. As regards total population, see *Historisk statistik för Sverige* (2nd edition), 1, p. 68.

[6] A. Svalestuen (1971), p. 44.

[7] K. Hvidt (1971), pp. 202 f.

[8] A. Svalestuen (1971), p. 44; R. Kero (1974), pp. 119 ff.

[9] S. Carlsson (1968), pp. 112 f.

was it possible, on a much wider scale, to attract single, unmarried persons—often relatives of the earlier emigrants. It is conceivable that a similar contrast existed between the old Swedish settlements in the Middle West and the new areas of immigration on the American West Coast.[10]

The strong shift from family to individual emigration was almost entirely concentrated to the Swedish countryside. Family emigration from the cities consistently maintained a level of 30–40 per cent regardless of fluctuating emigration cycles. The greatest shift came in the typically agricultural districts with high emigration: Småland, Östergötland, Västergötland, and Värmland. Kronobergs län recorded the greatest shift (53 % of family emigration to the United States between 1861 and 1870, 22 % between 1891 and 1900). The largest amount of family emigration came from Västernorrland and Jämtland. In these areas the transition from family to individual emigration usually did not occur until after 1900. For a long time saw mill workers, lumbermen, and former homestead owners who sold their land and forest holdings to the timber companies accounted for a major share of the emigration from Northern Sweden.[11]

These patterns reflect an essential side of the emigration process. To a large extent, the early emigrants were driven westwards by "land fever". Small farmers, crofters and farm workers came to America in order to "take land" (compare the German term *Landnahme*). Behind them they left small plots and holdings: ahead of them loomed the opportunity of acquiring large amounts of acreage at very reasonable prices on the vast American continent. In time the American frontier moved westward, and the supply of cheap land diminished. Under these circumstances the small Swedish farmer and crofter had less cause to leave their native soil. The subsequent stream of Swedish emigrants included growing numbers of sons and daughters who lived at home, farm-hands, maid-servants, trade apprentices, blacksmiths, lumbermen, saw mill workers, shoemakers, tailors, seamstresses, etc. Their main objective was not to acquire land but to "take jobs" (compare the German term *Arbeitsnahme*) which paid well in comparison with wage conditions back home. While the early waves of emigration were characterized to some extent by a "folk migration", with all the implications and realities of an absolute and definite departure, the later phase of movement increasingly assumed the character of a gigantic, transatlantic "labor migration".

[10] *Ibid.*, p. 113. Regarding the general phase shifts of emigration, see S. Åkerman (1971), pp. 62 ff.
[11] S. Carlsson (1968), pp. 114 ff.; L.-G. Tedebrand (1972), pp. 165 ff.

c. Regional Distribution

Overseas emigration from Sweden was very unevenly distributed among various regions within Sweden. The differences can be viewed in broad outline in Table 5: 2, which shows the relative figures for each län and decade throughout the 1851–1930 period, though with reservation for the deficiencies in the statistics for the 1850s. The information in this table should be complemented with maps, which show the distribution by härader or their equivalents in all of the Scandinavian countries from 1865 until 1914 by five-year periods.[1]

Neither the län nor the härad *per se* represented a homogeneous entity in terms of emigration. In certain cases it would have been preferable to distribute emigration on the basis of the traditional, historical provinces. Had this been done, two small provinces—Dalsland in Älvsborgs län and Öland in Kalmar län—would have ranked first on the list. It would also have been natural to include the Karlskoga mining district, which lie in the province of Värmland but is part of Örebro län, under the traditional provincial heading instead of the län classification. The emigration from this district greatly resembled the pattern throughout Värmland and claimed a higher intensity than other sections of Örebro län.[2]

Whatever the guideline used, the regional differences of emigration distribution are still distinct. Halland had the highest value of all: between 1851 and 1930 an average of 5 per cent of the population emigrated per decade to America. Moreover, in proportion to its population Hallands län had seven times as many transatlantic emigrants as Uppsala län, the area least affected by emigration (0.7% in mean figures per decade). Halland was followed, in order of ranking, by Jönköpings, Värmlands, Kronobergs, Kalmar, and Älvsborgs län. Together with northern Skåne, western Blekinge, southwestern Östergötland, western Dalarna (Kopparbergs län), and the westernmost sector of Örebro län (including the Karlskoga mining district), these six län form a coherent *nucleus* of emigration. This section of the country, representing roughly 30 per cent of the Swedish population, accounted for around 47 per cent of all overseas emigrants.

[1] As a unit, a Swedish *län* may be regarded as smaller than an American state, but larger than a county. A Swedish *härad* is, generally speaking, smaller than a county.

[2] Regarding Dalsland see P. Noreen (1967), pp. 26 ff. Regarding Öland see S. Carlsson (1966–1967), pp. 54 f., and unpublished studies by M. Höjfors. Regarding Karlskoga see H. Norman (1974), pp. 16 ff.

The *peripheral* areas of emigration include the rest of Götaland, Närke, eastern Dalarna, Stockholm proper, as well as southern and central parts of Northern Sweden. These areas accounted for 50 per cent of the Swedish population but around 46 per cent of the nation's emigrants. The areas least affected by emigration were the Lake Mälar provinces (excluding Stockholm proper) and Västerbotten and Norrbotten, which included around 17 per cent of the Swedish population but only 7 per cent of the emigrant stock. These regions gain a rather distinct profile on the map diagrams, especially Diagram 5:6 (1885–1889). At the same time the "nucleus" of Swedish emigration emerges as part of a Scandinavian region, which also includes large sections of Southwestern Norway.

A substantial share of these regional contrasts can be seen as a result of so-called *urban influence fields*, as originally delineated by E. De Geer in 1959.[3] This means that expanding larger towns and cities attracted the population in the surrounding rural areas and thereby curbed the amount of emigration to America from the countryside which was otherwise strong in more outlying districts. Naturally, Stockholm (pop. 301 000 in 1900) had the greatest field of influence. The exceptionally low level of emigration from Stockholms, Uppsala, Södermanlands, and Västmanlands län was largely due to long-standing traditions of internal migration, whereby residents of these areas moved directly or by stages to Stockholm.[4] It is striking that the districts in the Lake Mälar provinces which lay farthest from Stockholm—for example, Oppunda in western Södermanland and Oland in northern Uppland—had higher emigration figures than those closer to the capital city (compare for example Map 5:9). Even cities such as Uppsala (pop. 23 000 in 1900) and Västerås (pop. 12 000 in 1900) attracted a large share of migrants from the immediate rural areas.[5]

Gothenburg (pop. 131 000 in 1900) had the second largest influence field. The low rates of emigration for western Västergötland, southern Bohuslän, and the northwestern districts of Halland can be directly related to Gothenburg's force of attraction on these areas.[6] This attraction was weakest in areas south of the city. This is undoubtedly due to the fact that central Halland became one of Sweden's most distinct districts of emigra-

[3] E. De Geer (1959), pp. 194 ff.
[4] Cf. I. Eriksson and J. Rogers (1973), pp. 80 ff.; M. Eriksson and S. Åkerman (1974), pp. 278 ff.
[5] I. Eriksson and J. Rogers (1973), pp. 80 ff.: H. Norman (1974), p. 133; M. Eriksson and S. Åkerman (1974), pp. 278 ff.
[6] E. De Geer (1959), pp. 199 ff.

tion already in the 1870s and that its migration pattern exerted an effect on the northern sectors of the province as well, despite their proximity to Gothenburg.[7] In some areas special shipping and navigation features can also have played a role.[8] Apparently the effectiveness of Gothenburg's attraction was limited to a few parishes in the northernmost sectors of the province (Lindome and Älvsåker). Moreover, Halland's own provincial center, Halmstad (pop. 15 000 in 1900), does not appear to have curbed emigration from its immediate surroundings, anyway not before 1890.[9]

Sweden's third largest city, Malmö (pop. 61 000 in 1900), was surrounded by parishes with consistently low emigration. The similarities between southwestern Skåne and the immediate adjacent sectors of Själland (the Copenhagen area) in Denmark are distinctly shown on the Map Diagrams 5: 6–7.[10]

At the turn of the century Norrköping (pop. 41 000 in 1900) was Sweden's fourth largest city. The areas surrounding the provincial center, i.e. northeastern Östergötland, had consistently low emigration—a pattern which was mearly similar to that in the Lake Mälar Valley region.

In-depth local studies have also disclosed that many of Sweden's provincial towns were surrounded by parishes with relatively low emigration, even though the influence fields were, of course, relatively small. A case in point is Örebro län, where a distinct difference emerges between parishes immediately adjacent to the provincial center of Örebro (pop. 22 000 in 1900) and those at a greater distance. Örebro län had 57 parishes: of the 19 with the highest emigration only one lay within a 20 km. radius from Örebro, whereas 13 of the 19 parishes with the lowest emigration were situated within this radius. In Värmlands län the provincial capital of Karlstad (pop. 12 000 in 1900) played a similar role.[11]

As far as Småland is concerned, parishes near Jönköping, Växjö, and Kalmar (respective pop. 23 000; 7 000; and 13 000 in 1900) had low emigration on the whole. The Småland parishes generally lost population through internal and external migration. However, while 37 per cent of the population loss in parishes near these three towns was due to emigration, the corresponding figure was 59 per cent in the most distant par-

[7] E. De Geer's reference (1959, p. 200) to contacts with Denmark appears less convincing, though not entirely irrelevant.
[8] C. Winberg (1969), pp. 55 ff.
[9] B. Kronborg and T. Nilsson (1975), pp. 140 ff.
[10] Cf. K. Hvidt (1971), pp. 133 ff.
[11] H. Norman (1974), pp. 104, 116 f., 126 ff.

ishes.[12] In Västernorrlands län the same phenomenon is registered not only for Härnösand (pop. 8 000 in 1900) and Sundsvall (pop. 15 000 in 1900) but also for areas around Sollefteå and Örnsköldsvik. In part this was essentially due to the attraction of industrial areas and not urban influence fields *per se.*[13]

In other words, urban influence fields had a distinctly curbing effect on emigration. Similarities can be found in other Scandinavian countries, at least in areas around Copenhagen, Oslo, Bergen, Helsingfors, and Åbo.[14] However, the situation is not all that simple, and it cannot merely be said that emigration frequency is directly correlated with factors of distance. First of all, it must be pointed out that in many cases the urban influence fields comprised large *flat land districts* which, by virtue of social and economic factors, offered relatively poor prerequisites for emigration. This was especially true of areas around Stockholm, Gothenburg, Malmö, and Örebro, whereas Östergötland seems to be an exception. The clearest analysis of these conditions comes from a study of Örebro län: it was found that parishes with large arable acreage had lower emigration than parishes with relatively little arable acreage. This grouping largely coincides with the distinction between central and peripheral parishes.[15] Aside from distance factors, it can generally be said that the low emigration from flat land districts was due to two separate factors. Those who owned land had strong ties with the soil and could expect a relatively favorable source of income. Those without land were caught up in a farreaching process of proletarization, primarily through the system of allowances granted to agricultural laborers, which obstructed emigration in many different ways.[16]

Secondly, it is obvious that the most peripheral and least settled areas of the country, namely Västerbotten and Norrbotten, had relatively low emigration, despite the absence of major urban fields of influence. Emigration in this distant part of Sweden mainly originated from the coastal areas, where a certain urban influence field was operative, and only to a very limited degree from the inland regions, where there were hardly any

[12] S. Carlsson (1966–1967), pp. 55 ff.

[13] L.-G. Tedebrand (1972), pp. 134, 144 ff.

[14] Cf. Map Diagram 5: 5–11. Also Budapest may be mentioned in this connection, according to investigations by J. Puskas.

[15] H. Norman (1974), pp. 124 ff. Cf. unpublished study by E. De Geer (1973) concerning Östergötland.

[16] See below, Chapter 5: d.

central municipalities to speak of. The most plausible explanation for this is the fact that in contrast to farming areas in South and Central Sweden these inland districts still offered opportunities for *land colonization,* both for agriculture and industry. In reality, they became a type of Swedish America during the 1800s. It is significant that both Västerbottens and Norrbottens län, as well as Jämtlands län, experienced peak emigration *after* 1900, when opportunities for colonization began to thin out. This stands in contrast to the pattern in all other Swedish provinces.[17]

Thirdly, mere reference to the distance factor cannot explain the reason why urban and industrial centers frequently had their own share of relatively high emigration. As shown by Table 5: 2, rural areas generally had a somewhat higher frequency of overseas emigration than cities and towns. However, this pattern did not hold in all cases: the 1890s are an exception to this and probably the 1860s as well. Moreover emigration to European countries was more intense from cities than rural areas: on the whole, then, the frequency of emigration was strongest in urban areas.[18]

Modern research has also abandoned the traditional outlook on emigration as a primarily agricultural and rural phenomenon.[19] In several cases local studies have shown that emigration was more intense from industrialized districts than from purely agricultural areas. For example the industrial districts in Örebro län ordinarily had a higher frequency of emigration than farming districts. Although this contrast may be partially due to the distance factor, it is clear that industrialization *per se* did not impede emigration. Rapid economic fluctuations, affecting such business sectors as the iron industry, prompted emigration from this part of Sweden.[20] In Risinge, a large parish in northwestern Östergötland, the most concentrated flow of emigration came from industrial communities and the least from villages in typically wooded areas.[21] In Västernorrland industrial parishes had a higher emigration frequency than farming parishes. Moreover, farming districts which were heavily affected by the expansion and land purchases of timber companies had more emigrants

[17] Cf. Chapter 5: a. Seen in terms of particular decades, Västernorrland can also be included among the countries which saw peak emigration after 1900. However, in terms of specific years its emigration culminated as early as 1892–1893.
[18] *Historisk statistik för Sverige* (First edition), 1, p. 69.
[19] In particular, see F. Nilsson (1970), pp. 11 ff; U. Beijbom (1971), pp. 11 ff.
[20] H. Norman (1974), pp. 104 ff.
[21] U. Ebbeson (1968), pp. 53 ff.

than purely agrarian areas which were relatively untouched by industrialization or corporate expansion.[22]

It is altogether clear that many urban emigrants were originally in-migrants from rural areas. Moreover, studies of Norwegian emigration, primarily from Kristiania (Oslo) and Bergen, have maintained that emigration to the United States essentially took place in stages; emigrants came from rural areas and never managed to establish themselves in an urban environment before crossing the Atlantic.[23] However, an in-depth study of emigration from two parishes in Stockholm between 1883 and 1891 has shown that while a clear majority of emigrants had in-migrated to Stockholm the greater part of them came from other urban and industrial environments. Moreover, a substantial number of the rural in-migrants had spent at least five years in Stockholm before leaving for North America. In sum, around 80 per cent of the Stockholm emigrants in this study had been under the constant influence of an urban environment at the time they decided to emigrate.[24]

It has also been found that a large proportion of these in-migrants and later Stockholm emigrants were born in provinces characterized by a heavy stream of emigration (Småland, Öland, Värmland). On the other hand, only a small share of in-migrants from the Lake Mälar Valley area, for example, eventually left Sweden for America. In this case the influence of relatives and friends on the other side of the Atlantic must have played a significant role.[25] In other words, the presence of a sizable *in-migrant* population with strong traditions of emigration from their home districts operated in favor of emigration from urban and industrial areas, especially those which were exposed to prominent economic fluctuations.

This brings us to the importance of the emigration tradition or the *stock effect.* Areas which established an early tradition of emigration—perhaps originally as a result of coincidences—frequently maintained a high emigration frequency in subsequent decades as a consequence of contacts in America. In Jönköpings län, the leading area of emigration up to the 1870s, a tradition of this type was established as early as 1836, when Swen Swenson emigrated to New York and settled in Texas two years later. In Swenson's footsteps came relatives and friends from northwestern Små-

[22] L.-G. Tedebrand (1972), pp. 132 f.

[23] I. Semmingsen (1940), p. 80; (1950), pp. 233 ff.

[24] F. Nilsson (1970), pp. 69 ff.; cf. K. Hvidt (1971), pp. 124 ff.; B. Kronborg and T. Nilsson (1975), pp. 139 f.

[25] F. Nilsson (1970), pp. 73 ff.

land and bordering regions in Västergötland.[26] The emigration from Kisa in southwestern Östergötland, inspired by Peter Cassel, had a similar effect on this district and bordering parishes in northeastern Småland. Up to the 1880s this region claimed one of the highest levels of emigration frequency in all of Sweden.[27] A strong, but chronologically limited effect was generated by the emigration of "Erik Janssonists" from Alfta, Hälsingland, and from Erik Jansson's home district in Uppland in 1846.[28] The direct relationship between this mass emigration and later emigration from southern Hälsingland is less clear.

The group emigration led by Erik Pettersson, a farmer's son, from Karlskoga to Wisconsin in 1853–1854 had unusually prolonged consequences. The contacts created by this movement lasted many generations, and their effect could still be traced as late as the 1920s.[29] A similar regional influence was generated by the group emigration led by Pastor Erland Carlsson from southern Småland in 1853.[30] The list of examples could go on and on. An attempt to weigh the statistical effect of the emigration tradition as compared with other factors resulted in a high rating for this tradition.[31] As far as Småland is concerned, the strong regional contrasts observed in the emigration during the famine years (1867–1869) cannot be correlated with the fluctuating degree of starvation from parish to parish. However, they can be correlated with movements by earlier emigrants prior to the period of mass emigration.[32]

The absence of such a strong tradition should essentially explain why certain districts had low emigration rates despite obvious prerequisites for a substantial level of emigration. This can be illustrated by a number of parishes located north, west and south of Lake Bolmen in western Småland. All of them lay at a great distance from urban centers, had underdeveloped agricultural sectors, and lacked appreciable means of land reclamation. At the same time their emigration frequency was far

[26] E. Severin (1919), *passim*; N. W. Olsson (1967), pp. 18 f., 58.; see above Chapter 5: a.
[27] N. W. Olsson (1967), pp. 64 ff., and "Index of Place-Names"; R. Davidsson (1969), pp. 15 ff.; see above, Chapter 5: a.
[28] N. W. Olsson (1967), pp. 68 ff., and "Index of Place-Names"; O. Isaksson and S. Hallgren (1969), pp. 32 ff.; B. Rondahl (1972), p. 8.
[29] H. Norman (1974), pp. 41 ff., 78 ff. See also A. Wirén (1975), pp. 168 ff.
[30] B. Boëthius (1927), p. 571.
[31] H. Norman (1974), p. 142 ff.
[32] S. Carlsson (1966–1967), p. 52.

below the average level for all of Småland.[33] The absolute minimum value is recorded for the tiny parish of Jälluntofta, whose frequency between 1861 and 1930 was only $^1/_{12}$ that of Stockaryd around 50 miles away.[34] It is evident that this relatively isolated Bolmen district remained rather unaffected by emigration impulses and never established any genuine tradition of emigration.

The local fluctuations of emigration cannot be totally explained with the help of variables which are available for measurement. However, the general pattern does appear rather clear. Basic factors effecting emigration from rural areas include *great distances* from larger urban or industrial centers, *the absence of fertile flat land areas,* and *the lack of possibilities for extensive land reclamation.* As far as cities and larger industrial areas are concerned, emphasis should be laid on the presence of *a substantial in-migrant population* and a large array of *industrial enterprises sensitive to changes in economic cycles.* It is true of both cities and rural areas that *a strong and lasting tradition of emigration* had a stimulating effect on emigration. The co-variation of two or more of these factors has nearly always resulted in a substantial level of emigration, above the national average.

d. Social Structure

In 1870, at the start of mass emigration to the United States, 72 per cent of all professionally employed persons in Sweden were active in farming, forestry and fishing, whereas only 13 per cent were active in industry and crafts. The remaining percentage shares were spread between commerce (3 %), transportation (2 %), public service sector (5 %), and non-farm domestic labor (5 %). In 1930, at the halt of emigration, the farming population's share was down to 38 per cent whereas industry and crafts now accounted for 33 per cent. Commerce (11 %) and transportation (5 %) were of more importance than in 1870, whereas the public service sector (6 %) and domestic labor (5 %) retained approximately the same percentage figures as before.[1]

[33] As a whole, Småland and Öland had an emigration frequency of 4.7 per decade between 1861 and 1930; this includes emigration within Europe. A series of parishes near or in the vicinity of Lake Bolmen had decisively lower rates: Dannäs 3.0; Torskinge 1.7; Ås 2.9; S. Unnaryd 2.9; Odensjö 2.5; Jälluntofta 1.0; Kärda 2.3; Hånger 2.5; Kulltorp 2.0; Lidhult 2.5. Higher figures are recorded for Bolmsö (an island in Lake Bolmen) and parishes east of Lake Bolmen.

[34] S. Carlsson (1966–1967), p. 52.

[1] S. Carlsson (1966), pp. 278 ff. Forestry is included in farming.

All in all, the greatest share of emigration occurred at a time when more than half of the Swedish population was active in traditional, mainline sectors of the economy. It was therefore entirely natural that the majority of emigrants came from *agriculture.* However, in proportion to its total share of the population farming hardly claimed any greater share of emigrants than industry and crafts. It is impossible to draw any genuinely strict comparisons on the national level between these two major economic sectors, as the official emigrant statistics do not provide a sufficient amount of exact information. The statistics from the 1800s are largely inapplicable for this purpose due to a highly cumbersome classification system. Despite improvements made in 1903, difficulties still confront research, especially when it comes to large groups of unspecified servants and workers.

During the first two decades of the 1900s industry appears to have had a somewhat higher emigration frequency than agriculture, whereas the opposite was true during the 1920s.[2] Local studies indicate that these conditions fluctuated both chronologically and geographically. In Småland agricultural and industrial emigration appear to have been rather evenly proportional between 1870 and 1900, although a certain shift may have occured in favor of agriculture toward the end of the 1800s.[3] On the other hand, industrial emigration was heavier than agricultural in Örebro and Västernorrlands län and in northwestern Östergötland.[4]

Significant differences existed between various categories of persons active in agriculture. Farmers and crofters played a leading role in the pioneer emigration of the 1840s, but their numbers thinned out as time went by. Between 1901 and 1930 they represented roughly 2 per cent of all emigrants, whereas their corresponding share of the total Swedish population stood at an average of 13 per cent. All local studies indicate that land ownership—whether the acreage was large or small—had a decisively curbing effect on emigration.[5] However, it should be pointed out that farmers and crofters were relatively inclined to emigrate in districts where timber companies acquired land and forest holdings around the turn of

[2] According to estimates based upon statistics in *Sveriges officiella statistik,* Serie Befolkningsrörelsen 1901–1910, 1911–1920, and 1921–1930, as compared with reports on the distribution of occupations and economic sectors among the total population (see S. Carlsson (1966), *passim*). However, the large group of "unspecified worker", who are clearly overrepresented among emigrants, gives rise to a substantial margin of uncertainty.

[3] S. Carlsson (1966–1967), pp. 44 ff.

[4] See above, Chapter 5: c.

[5] S. Carlsson (1966–1967), p. 49; P. Noreen (1967), p. 170; U. Ebbeson (1968), p. 66; B. Rondahl (1972), p. 143; L.-G. Tedebrand (1972), p. 172; H. Norman (1974), p. 62.

the century. This is true at least of districts in Ångermanland, where the timber industry was heavily concentrated. It was often common procedure for homestead owners to sell their property to the timber companies before emigrating to America.[6]

One group which had a very low emigration frequency were *statdrängar* or *statare,* i.e. married farmhands and farm workers who received, according to yearly contracts, most of their wages in kind and were granted free lodgings. Most of them lived in multi-family barracks often of extremely poor quality. A scant 300 *statare* are reported to have emigrated between 1901 and 1930.[7] On the other hand, it is worth noting that most *statare* lived in districts which had a generally low frequency of emigration—for example, the Lake Mälar Valley and southern Skåne. Yet emigrant *statare* were also rare in districts with high emigration, such as Småland and Östergötland (Risinge Parish).[8] *Statare* were nearly always married persons, and this had a curbing effect on the inclination to emigrate. Moreover, a lack of ready money made it difficult for them to secure tickets for passage to America. Another factor which must be taken into account is a general feeling of inertia or sluggishness in this very poor group.

The great mass of agricultural emigrants consisted of farmers' sons and daughters who lived at home, farmhands, and maid-servants. Nearly all of them were unmarried and their future prospects in an overpopulated agrarian society were uncertain. This was especially true of those who had many brothers and sisters; only one or possibly two of them could count on assuming possession of their parents' landholdings. Emigration frequency among this large group of people was consistently higher than the national average. As a rule, men migrated on a greater scale than women, and it appears that farmhands and maid-servants had a higher emigration frequency on the whole than young sons and daughters who worked on their parents' farms.[9] The proportion of farmhands and agricultural workers was especially apparent in the emigrant contingents of the 1920s. Of a combined total of 128 600 emigrants during this decade (including emigrants to countries within Europe), 20 400 have been classified as farm workers, of which only 600 were women.[10]

[6] L.-G. Tedebrand (1972), pp. 172 ff.
[7] *Sveriges officiella statistik,* Serie Befolkningsrörelsen 1901–1910, 1911–1920, 1921–1930.
[8] S. Carlsson (1966–1967), p. 49; U. Ebbeson (1968), pp. 64 f.
[9] S. Carlsson (1966–1967), p. 44; P. Noreen (1967), pp. 170 f.; U. Ebbeson (1968), pp. 64 f.; B. Rondahl (1972), p. 150.
[10] *Sveriges officiella statistik,* Serie Befolkningsrörelsen 1921–1930.

An in-depth study of emigration from Köla parish in Värmland has shown that children of well-to-do farmers emigrated to America only in exceptional cases. Although the frequency was higher among children raised on medium-sized farms it did not compare to emigration from small farms, crofters' holdings, and squatters' plots (*backstugor*).[11] The inclination to emigrate to America was proportionately greater for those sons and daughters living at home who had fewer prospects of securing by inheritance, some basic income from agriculture.

Young, unmarried workers and trade apprentices dominated the emigration from *industry and crafts*. There are no exact figures on the proportion of emigrant business owners: although their numbers were undoubtedly small they did increase over the course of time.[12] Salaried officials also emigrated on a very small scale but are not entirely unrepresented among emigrant contingents.[13] A study of Örebro län has revealed that increasing numbers of emigrants around 1900 were engineers. Personal contacts between Sweden and the United States improved with time and also led to a growing exchange of relatively skilled manpower.[14] Between 1901 and 1930 a national total of 4 000 engineers and foremen left Sweden for countries within and outside of Europe. In all respects their emigration frequency was higher than that of such categories as landowners and industrial *entrepreneurs*.

The metal and mechanical engineering trades made up the largest branch of Swedish industry and accounted for a relatively large share of emigrants over a long span of time. This was especially true around 1880, when a large number of blacksmiths emigrated from different parts of Sweden. This emigrant category subsequently diminished to some extent, no doubt as a result of improved conditions for Sweden's expanding mechanical engineering industry.[15] During the period from 1900 to 1930 the emigration frequency of this occupational group appears to have stabilized close to the national average.

Emigration frequency was relatively high among tailors, an occupational group which had relatively favorable prospects on the American labor market. Emigration by Stockholm tailors reached a peak between 1886 and 1893, when this sector suffered an economic relapse due, in part, to

[11] M. Nerander in *Emigranten* (1969), pp. 22 f.
[12] Cf. H. Norman (1974), pp. 66 ff.
[13] Cf. U. Ebbeson (1968), pp. 67 f.
[14] H. Norman (1974), pp. 67, 269. See also B. Kronborg and T. Nilsson (1975), p. 136.
[15] See above, Chapter 5: c.

growing competition from abroad.[16] Over 3 000 male tailors emigrated between 1901 and 1930, and their frequency exceeded the national average during the first two decades of this century. Extant statistics on emigration by seamstresses can be interpreted in different directions, but during the period from 1900 to 1930 their frequency was approximately the same as that of tailors.

Another large group of craftsmen were shoemakers. They were relatively well represented among emigrants, but their frequency was lower than that of tailors.[17] A rather moderate level of emigration originated from the Kumla shoe factory centers in Örebro län. However, a certain increase was noted in 1900 as a consequence of a brief crisis in the shoe branch.[18] Between 1901 and 1930 around 3 500 shoemakers emigrated from all parts of Sweden: their emigration frequency during this period was somewhat lower than the national average.

Swedish carpentry trades (carpenters, lathe-turners, and coopers) expanded heavily at the end of the 19th century. Economic unrest in this sector of the labor market periodically took large proportions and led to a rather high level of emigration, as that from Stockholm in the early 1880s.[19] Relatively high rates are also recorded in the 1910s and 1920s. However, reservations must be made for difficulties in classifying emigrants, particularly when it comes to demarkating carpentry trades from the construction branch.

On the whole, masons and other construction workers appear to have had a rather low emigration frequency. The scores of Swedes who were eventually employed by American construction firms were largely raised in farming homes. However, during certain periods of economic recession, such as the early 1890s, substantial numbers of construction workers left Stockholm for North America and Brazil.[20]

An important emigrant group were saw mill workers, the majority of which came from districts in Northern Sweden. At times their emigration frequency was extremely high, as for example during the crisis in the saw mill industry between 1891 and 1893.[21] A study of saw mill workers in Söderala, Hälsingland, has found that emigration around 1880 primarily

[16] F. Nilsson (1970), pp. 102 ff. Cf. S. Carlsson (1966–1967), p. 50.
[17] S. Carlsson (1966–1967), p. 50; F. Nilsson (1970), pp. 119 f.
[18] H. Norman (1974), pp. 46, 66, 89.
[19] F. Nilsson (1970), pp. 114 ff. Cf. S. Carlsson (1966–1967), p. 50.
[20] F. Nilsson (1970), pp. 107 ff.
[21] L.-G. Tedebrand (1972), p. 170.

consisted of skilled labor (sawyers, loggers, and pilers), whereas more unskilled saw mill and lumberyard workers altogether dominated those emigrant contingents up to 1900.[22]

Generally speaking, rather low emigration rates are recorded for the food processing sectors of the Swedish economy; these include such categories as bakers, millers, flour mill workers, butchers, etc. However, bakers appear to have been more inclined to emigrate than millers and butchers;[23] this is true even after the turn of the century.

On the whole, the differences between various industrial branches were relatively small. Variables such as age, civil status, and home district had a substantially greater impact than occupational designations. Nevertheless, it is evident—in altogether general terms—that emigration had the greatest effect on trade and industrial branches which were the most sensitive to fluctuations in economic cycles.[24]

Occupations connected with *trade and commerce* were generally under-represented among emigrants. In particular, business owners in this sector of the economy were disinclined to leave their firms or shops to seek their fortunes in America. Emigration frequency was higher among accountants, book-keepers, and shop clerks but hardly attained the level of the national average.[25] However, between 1911 and 1930 the emigration frequency of business employees appears to have exceeded the national average.

Low emigration rates are also recorded for the *transportation* sector. Emigration frequency was particularly low among railroad, streetcar, post and telegraph employees. Even those with extremely low salaries, such as station hands and mailmen, preferred to keep their jobs than make their way across the Atlantic. The inclination to emigrate was substantially greater among sea captains and seamen, whose professions naturally led to contacts with foreign countries and, more often than not, to residence abroad.[26] This is also true after the turn of the century.

Emigration was low among professionally employed persons in the *public works sector (allmän tjänst och fria yrken)*, i.e., salaried civil servants, teachers,

[22] B. Rondahl (1972), p. 143.

[23] F. Nilsson (1970), pp. 116 ff. Cf. S. Carlsson (1966–1967), p. 46.

[24] Cf. F. Nilsson (1970), p. 223.

[25] S. Carlsson (1966–1967), pp. 50 f.; F. Nilsson (1970), pp. 123 ff. Cf. U. Ebbeson (1968), p. 61; L.-G. Tedebrand (1972), p. 169; B. Kronborg and T. Nilsson (1975), p. 135.

[26] S. Carlsson (1966–1967), p. 51; F. Nilsson (1970), p. 131; L.-G. Tedebrand (1972), p. 169; U. Ebbeson (1968), p. 61; B. Kronborg and T. Nilsson (1975), p. 135.

priests, military officers, doctors, etc. Persons in this category played a rather prominent role during the initial period of emigration but were highly unconspicuous among later emigrant contingents. Many of them held relatively well-paid positions, and few chose to try their chances on the American labor market.[27] Between 1901 and 1930 the list of emigrants from this occupational category includes 95 priests and church attendants, 152 military officers, 248 non-commissioned officers, around 1 800 teachers and newspapermen, and roughly 700 salaried public servants, doctors, chemists and pharmacists, etc.

It is difficult to gain a statistical picture of emigration by persons listed under the heading of *unspecified labor (arbetare av obestämt slag)* in the contemporary source materials. These included persons who were not properly classified in respective registers as well as those who were essentially engaged in unskilled occupations of an indefinite and relatively seasonal nature. This group accounted for large numbers of emigrants and doubtlessly claimed a high emigration frequency.[28] However, it is impossible to make any strict estimates by virtue of the shifting terminology and classification used by different source materials.

Maids (*pigor* and *tjänarinnor*) made up a large occupational category, primarily those employed in non-farming homes where they totally devoted themselves to domestic tasks. Their emigration frequency was high, and the fluctuations from year to year were comparatively small. Changes in economic cycles did nothing to improve their wages or living conditions, which basically stayed at a very low level. For example, a maid who emigrated from Stockholm to Chicago to take employment in the home of an American family could clearly improve on her social status, wages, living and working conditions, as well as clothing standards.[29] This group was and remained one of the largest emigrant categories. Over 48 000 maids (*tjänstehjon*) emigrated between 1901 and 1930. This figure includes those who emigrated within Europe as well as maid-servants from farming homes.

The great mass of emigrants consisted of *young, unmarried* men and women. With the exception of the earliest periods of emigration, marriage

[27] S. Carlsson (1966–67), p. 51; F. Nilsson (1970), p. 131; U. Ebbeson (1968), p. 61; L.-G. Tedebrand (1972); B. Kronborg and T. Nilsson (1975), p. 135.

[28] S. Carlsson (1966–1967), p. 51; F. Nilsson (1970), pp. 138 ff.

[29] F. Nilsson (1970), pp. 132ff.; U. Beijbom (1972), p. 197. Cf. S. Carlsson (1966–1967), p. 51; U. Ebbeson (1968), p. 61; B. Kronborg and T. Nilsson (1975), p. 135.

and the building of families collectively operated as one of the most important factors in curbing emigration. Occupational groups dominated by young, unmarried persons—sons and daughters who lived at home, farmhands, maid-servants, servant girls, apprentices—had the highest emigration frequency, whereas groups with a large proportion of married and adult-aged persons had the lowest frequency. Purely economic factors played a more subordinate role. Agricultural workers (*statare*) and such categories as servants living-in and paupers (*inhyses- och fattighjon*) rarely emigrated.[30]

The lack of landed property or *the ownership of a business enterprise* were also important factors in this context. Persons who owned or leased plots of land—whether large or small—had no real cause to emigrate, especially during and after the 1870s. Landowners , farmers, and crofters are rarely mentioned in the emigrant lists. Property size was of little significance except for presumptive heirs of landed property, who did attach a great deal of importance to the amount of acreage they could expect from their holdings. As far as business owners are concerned, retailers and small-scale tradesmen and artisans had a higher emigration frequency than leading *entrepreneurs*.

A final point of consideration is the *lack of permanent employment.* The inclination to emigrate was most effectively curbed by relative or absolute guarantees of secure employment, irrespective of wage level—as, for example, in conjunction with government or public service. High civil officials, sergeants, and station hands were nearly equally disinclined to emigrate. However, employment on an annual basis did not prohibit farmhands and maid-servants from emigrating in large numbers. Engineers and master mechanics employed by private firms had a high frequency of emigration. Of all such groups emigration claimed its greatest contingents from young workers of both sexes in the areas of agriculture, forestry, seasonal employment and industrial branches which were sensitive to economic fluctuations.

The great majority of emigrants were poor and of limited means, but it was not poverty alone which drove them to America. The decision to emigrate also required the type of demographic and social factors discussed above. As a rule, this decision was based on an evaluation of the different prospects on the Swedish and American labor markets. An indi-

[30] S. Carlsson (1966–1967), pp. 49 ff.; A. Wirén (1975), p. 95.

vidual who decided to leave his native soil usually did so with the conviction or hope that he or she had something to offer America in the way of youthful vitality and physical strength and that he or she was reasonably familiar with the duties of qualified or unskilled jobs which awaited them in agriculture, industry, or private homes on the other side of the Atlantic.

6. The Causes of Emigration

a. An Attempt at a Multivariate Analysis

By Hans Norman

Central to the scientific discussion of emigration is its causal background. Even during the 1880s contemporary observers were seriously probing the forces behind the development of Swedish emigration as a mass phenomenon. Political and social debate on the issue culminated in Sweden shortly after 1900 with the appointment of the Swedish Commission on Emigration. Since that time international research has focused interest on the role of fluctuating economic conditions in the development of emigration. Much of this discussion has been devoted to the impact of push and pull factors, i.e. whether conditions in America or in emigrants' home countries were the decisive propellents of emigration. A previous chapter in this book has explored economic models as applied to an overall theoretical perspective on emigration.[1] Several case studies by researchers in the Uppsala Group have also centered on the causes of emigration and examined the general explaining value of these economic models. Local material has been used for the purpose of supplementing and diversifying the debate on the role of economic factors in the spread of emigration.

The first section of this chapter gives an example of the contemporary opinions of emigration. This is followed by a survey of the Uppsala Group's findings. The final section represents an attempt to combine economic and non-economic variables in terms of a multivariable analysis of the causes of emigration.

Contemporary Opinions

Examples of contemporary Swedish interpretations of the causes of emigration can be gained from reports by the provincial governors in 1882. At that time emigration from Sweden had accelerated with renewed intensity, and the government requested the provincial governors to

[1] See Chapter 2, above.

gather information and submit accounts of the reasons for this new surge. The contents and length of the governors' replies varied. Some of the governors based their reports on special investigations and inquiries made with lower officials in different sectors of their län.

One factor stands out in importance in that it was mentioned by nearly all of the governors, i.e. the general expectation which individuals had of improving their economic situation in America. The possibility of acquiring land in America is another cited propellent factor. Also mentioned was the favorable economic climate as well as prepaid tickets and travel money sent by earlier emigrants. Other incentives included newspaper advertising, emigrant agent propaganda, improved communications, cheaper passage fares, as well as the effect of returning emigrants who had made fortunes in America.

As far as conditions in Sweden are concerned, several governors mentioned heavy taxation as a cause of discontent. However, this factor was usually assigned little significance and was only listed as a contributing cause. It must be remembered that the governors' positions as representatives of the state probably influenced their answers. But still some mention was made of discontent over class distinctions, the high salaries of civil servants, and military service requirements.[2]

The first major scientific investigation of emigration and its causes was conducted by the Swedish Commission on Emigration from 1907 to 1913 under the leadership of the statistician Gustav Sundbärg. The Commission's report and its 20 appendices contain a wide range of statistical material, both Swedish and European. Primary focus was given to conditions in agriculture and less attention to the interplay between emigration and internal population mobility, industrialization, and urbanization. Sundbärg concluded that the ultimate causes of emigration were to be found in agriculture, with its economic stagnation and inability to maintain its share of the population.[3]

Push and Pull. Econometric Estimates

Even contemporary observers were struck by the strong chronological fluctuations of European emigration which, in their view, were related to

[2] A.-S. Kälvemark (1972), pp. 46 ff.

[3] *Emigrationsutredningens Betänkande,* pp. 663 f. The studies of two American researchers, J. S. Lindberg (1930) and F. E. Janson (1931) are largely based on the Commission's statistics. Their major findings on the causes of Swedish emigration fall well in line with the Commission's findings.

the cyclical pattern of economic development. After World War I, when the transatlantic economy suffered several economic crises, emigration and its relationship to international economic developments emerged as a lively topic of debate in research circles.

H. Jerome formulated a theory of push and pull factors, i.e. the impulses to emigration generated by conditions in America and in Europe. Jerome found that fluctuations in the curve of emigration fall more closely in line with economic trends in America and therefore concluded that the pull was stronger than the push.[4]

D. S. Thomas later expanded Jerome's theory on the basis of Swedish sources. She stressed two factors: The conditions in Sweden with its rapid population growth and slow industrial pace, created a latent push of emigration, while the American economic cycles gave rise to great variations in the emigration curve. Thomas also made a systematic analysis of Swedish population movement by classifying Swedish administrative districts according to their industrialization level as agrarian, mixed, or industrial. In this way she was able to demonstrate that a period of economic prosperity and subsequent in-migration to urban areas had a curbing effect on emigration intensity.[5]

Another important contribution to this debate came from the English economist B. Thomas. In an explaining model based on changes in the Atlantic economy Thomas maintained that a relationship existed between British and American capital investments, on the one hand, and manpower mobility, on the other. The transfer of capital from Great Britain to the United States during periods of economic prosperity stimulated emigration from Europe. On the other hand, the reduction of British investments in America led to a decline of emigration. Thomas concluded that the emigration stream followed the flow of capital.[6]

E. Lövgren has used local Swedish material as a means of determining the relationship between emigration and fluctuations in business cycles. He has compared American business trends with export cycles for lumber goods from the Sundsvall district, an area dominated by sawmill industries. In relating these measurements to the oscillations in the emigra-

[4] H. Jerome (1926), pp. 205–208.

[5] D. S. Thomas (1941), pp. 90, 165 ff., 318 ff.

[6] B. Thomas (1954), pp. 96 ff. Thomas' theory has been discussed in detail in Chapter 2, where S. Åkerman has presented new interpretations of relationships between capital flows and emigration streams. In a penetrative survey of all this research debate and its theoretical explaining models on emigration and business cycles, B. Odén (1971) outlines the development up to the latest econometric contributions.

tion curve Lövgren found that the pull factor, i.e. American economic developments, was somewhat stronger than the push factor, i.e. the weak export cycles for the Swedish lumber industry.[7]

Recent attempts to formulate econometric estimates of emigration include a study by the Norwegian economist T. Moe. He has worked with an explaining model where the inclination to emigrate is ultimately based on the spread of potential migration and on differences in income between the delivering and receiving countries. Moe also found that changes in emigrants' travel costs contributed to the short-term oscillations in the emigration curve.[8]

Several researchers connected with the Uppsala Group have questioned these econometric methods of measurement. In a study centered on Stockholm, F. Nilsson has pointed out the difficulties of substantiating a uniform pattern of economic development on a highly aggregated level. Different business branches may have had contrasting patterns of development. Nilsson contends that analyses based on such data are unavoidably uncertain. L.-G. Tedebrand has questioned E. Lövgren's estimates of emigration from the Sundsvall district primarily because of the comparison between a local pattern of lumber industry cycles and an accumulated American trade cycles index. S. Åkerman has criticized T. Moe's findings from a methodological standpoint. Åkerman contends that Moe's refined estimates were used on a source material which, according to a number of source-critical analyses, is too inexact for the purpose. Moreover, interpretations of volume changes in the emigration curve run into difficulties if they are solely focused in terms of an economic perspective. Such an approach can only help to explain the changes in volume trends. Emigration intensity was highly dependent upon the way in which individuals reached their decision to emigrate, and therefore our interpretations of these volume changes also must focus on psychological and sociological factors which may have contributed to a boom of emigration.[9]

In sum, migration researchers have not yet reached any generally

[7] E. Lövgren (1955), pp. 395 ff.

[8] T. Moe (1970), pp. 153 ff. E. Hamberg, of the Department of Economic History at Stockholm University, is preparing an econometric study of Swedish emigration. Her macro-study, covering the period 1870–1900, is based on wage reports and works on the hypothesis that the extent of emigration is related to both the degree of employment and wage levels. One important factor is the emigrants' income prospects relative to whether they stayed in Sweden or left for America.

[9] F. Nilsson (1970), pp. 253 ff.; L.-G. Tedebrand (1972), p. 178; S. Åkerman (1973), pp. 32 ff.

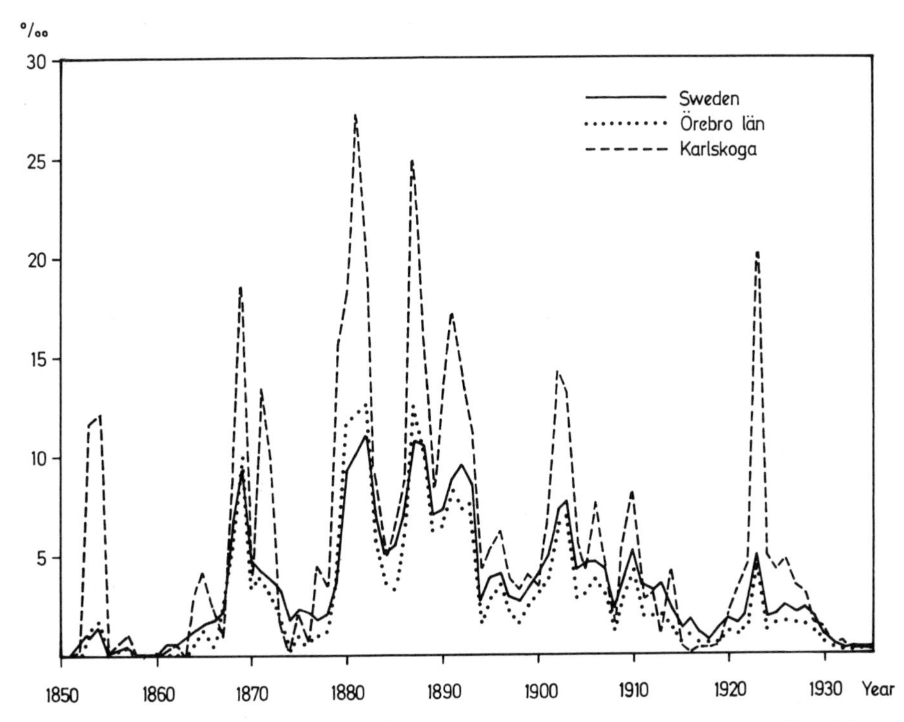

6: 1. Gross Emigration from Sweden, Örebro län, and Karlskoga Parish, in Per Mille of the Annual Mean Population, 1851–1930.

Sources *Historisk statistik för Sverige* (1955). *Emigrationsutredningen,* Bilaga 5; Condensed Population Reports, The Central Bureau of Statistics, Stockholm; H. Norman (1974), p. 42.

accepted explanation for the strong short-term fluctuations of emigration. On the other hand, they do agree that these fluctuations must be connected with changing economic patterns both in America and in emigrants' home countries.

Causes of Local Variations

The annual variations in the emigration curve give a strikingly uniform pattern, when comparisons are made between the developments in specific localities and regions in Sweden (see Figure 6: 1). This covariation also applies in some measure to the total emigration from Europe. There is much evidence that external factors decisively influenced the volume of emigration, thereby confirming Jerome's thesis that the pull was stronger than the push.[10]

However, there were prominent differences of intensity among different regions and sectors of the country despite the general coherence between peak and low years of emigration. The causes of these local variations have received major interest from migration researchers and have been explored in several local studies.

In the following discussion a multivariable analysis will be advanced for the local variations of Swedish emigration. This is prefaced by a summary of several research results which have tested the explaining value of different factors.

A study of Västernorrlands län has demonstrated differences in emigration intensity between dominantly agrarian and industrial parishes in non-urban areas. Emigration was strongest from the industrial parishes. These observations are confirmed by other regional studies which found that the industrial sector of the economy had a relatively higher emigration intensity than agriculture. However, there are exceptions: certain parts of the predominantly agricultural province of Dalsland, in southwestern Sweden, were among the most heavily affected areas in the entire country.[11]

Emigration intensity has also been related to the proximity of various regions to expanding urban industrial centers. In several cases it has been found that areas located within so-called urban influence fields had a low level of emigration. Investigated examples of Swedish cities with such strong influence fields are Stockholm, Gothenburg, Sundsvall, and Örebro. This phenomenon was discussed above in Chapter 5.

Researchers have often explored the possibility of connection between emigration and internal population mobility. Discussion has centered on the role of two specific factors behind emigration: (1) the extent of general population mobility in different regions and (2) the distribution of migration over various distances.[12]

Another apparently major factor is the prevailing tradition of emigration in various areas. Districts which, for some reason, had an early start of emigration usually developed a more extensive tradition of movement,

[10] Cf. H. Norman (1974), pp. 74–100.
[11] L.-G. Tedebrand (1972), p. 147; U. Ebbeson (1968), p. 61; H. Norman (1967), pp. 111 ff.; B. Rondahl (1972), pp. 140 ff.; P. Noreen (1967), pp. 26 ff.
[12] S. Åkerman (1971), *passim.*

including contacts and knowledge about conditions in America, than other districts where emigration started at a later date. Specific illustrations of this can be found in certain areas of Sweden which saw the departure of large groups of persons at an early stage of emigration: During the 1840s a group of religious dissenters emigrated from Hälsingland under the leadership of Erik Jansson, the "prophet from Biskopskulla", and a large emigrant contingent left Kisa in Östergötland led by the farmer and master carpenter Peter Cassel; during the 1850s Erik Pettersson, a farmer's son in Karlskoga Bergslag, headed a group emigration from this region.[13]

In a study of Risinge Parish in Östergötland, U. Ebbeson has tested D. S. Thomas' hypothesis that size of harvests was of decreasing significance for the extent of emigration in the late 19th century. A comparison between local crop yields and emigration failed to reveal any connection between poor harvests and increased emigration. If anything, a negative relationship emerged, indicating that poor harvests can have had a curbing effect on emigration. P. Noreen reached similar results in a study of Sundals härad in Dalsland. Poor harvests made it financially impossible for large groups to emigrate, and therefore a drop in crop yields cannot always be related to a rise of emigration.[14]

Researchers have also shown that religious oppression was not a strong impetus to emigration. S. Carlsson has studied the possible connection between religious separatism and regional variations in emigration to America during the 1860s. He compared the varying intensity of emigration from Småland with the spread of prayer chapels in Jönköpings län and the general dispersion of Low and Free Church assemblies. Carlsson concludes that religious factors cannot be considered a definite cause of the spread of mass emigration behavior. The statements of contemporary 19th century observers point in the same direction.[15]

[13] H. Norman (1974), pp. 142 ff.; L. Ljungmark (1955), pp. 31 ff.

[14] U. Ebbeson (1968), pp. 49 ff.; P. Noreen (1967), pp. 136 f. On the other hand it is clear that the exceptionally bad harvests of 1867 and 1868 contributed to the strong emigration of 1868 and 1869. G. Sundbärg also maintained that these harvests provided the necessary push to this wave of Swedish emigration (*Emigrationsutredningens Betänkande,* p. 155).

[15] S. Carlsson (1967), pp. 118 f. However, there are several examples of group emigration where religious factors contributed a propellent force, *i.e.* the mass exodus of Mormons from Denmark and the departure of Baptists from Hälsingland in Sweden. The American researcher G. M. Stephenson also concludes that Swedish emigration can largely be seen as a reaction to religious intolerance in Sweden (G. M. Stephenson [1932]).

A Multivariable Method of Analysis

In analyzing emigration researchers are often confronted with the problem of treating a wide range of variables. The following discussion represents an attempt to advance a multivariable analysis. Based on Örebro län, this study focuses interest on economic conditions, geographic location, as well as migration patterns and migration intensity. The 58 parishes in Örebro län were classified according to the following variables:[16]

Arable acreage in relationship to total acreage
Industrialization level
Proximity to the län center of Örebro (urban influence)
Size of cultivation units
Internal migration intensity
Parish acreage
Emigration tradition in individual parishes

The relationship between these variables and the intensity of emigration from the 58 parishes was tested in two ways: 1) by a stage analysis of the first three variables and 2) by means of a so-called AID analysis covering all 7 variables.

A brief description of the AID method, which stands for Automatic Interaction Detector, is warranted at this point. Elaborated and tested at the Institute for Political Research in Ann Arbor, Michigan,[17] this technique is primarily intended as an aid for researchers in approaching a vast and complicated mass of data. One of the advantages of this method is that it not only registers the effect of each individual variable but also records their interaction. Another advantage is, that research can use these variables on a nominal scale level. Moreover, the predictors (variables) with reference to the so-called criterion variable of study (intensity of emigration from the parishes) are dichotomized. This means that a study population is split into boxes consisting of groups of individuals, one half carrying a strong load on the criterion variable. The opposite is registered on the other half of the so-called tree-output. The cleavage process is presented in a cleavage diagram (Figure 6: 2). This technique is also called data-split.

[16] This account is based upon H. Norman (1974), pp. 102–147.

[17] For a closer presentation of AID analysis, see J. A. Sonquist and J. N. Morgan (1964) and J. A. Sonquist (1971), who developed this method. The abbreviation BSS below stands for Between Sums of Squares.

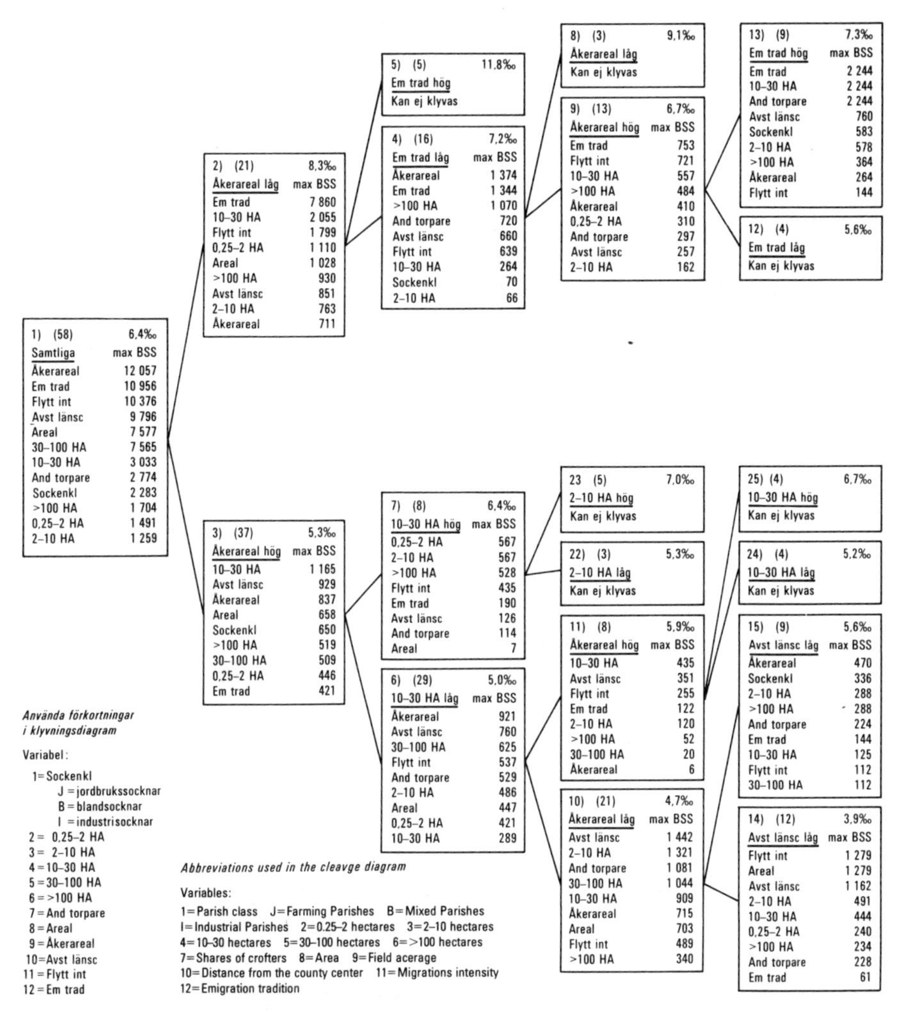

6:2. AID-Analysis Using Gross Emigration from the Parishes in Örebro län as the Criterion (N=58). Emigration Expressed in Per Mille of the Annual Mean Population. Mean Figures for the Decade 1881–1890.

Sources D. S. Thomas (1941), pp. 507 ff.; *Sveriges Officiella Statistik,* Serie Jordbruk och boskapsskötsel, 1913–1920; Condensed Population Reports, The Central Bureau of Statistics, Stockholm; H. Norman (1974), p. 125.

Although AID analysis can function as a search strategy, the researcher must thoroughly familiarize himself with his material from the very start and, preferably, also be able to test it with other statistical methods, since the use of AID analysis may produce pure artefacts.

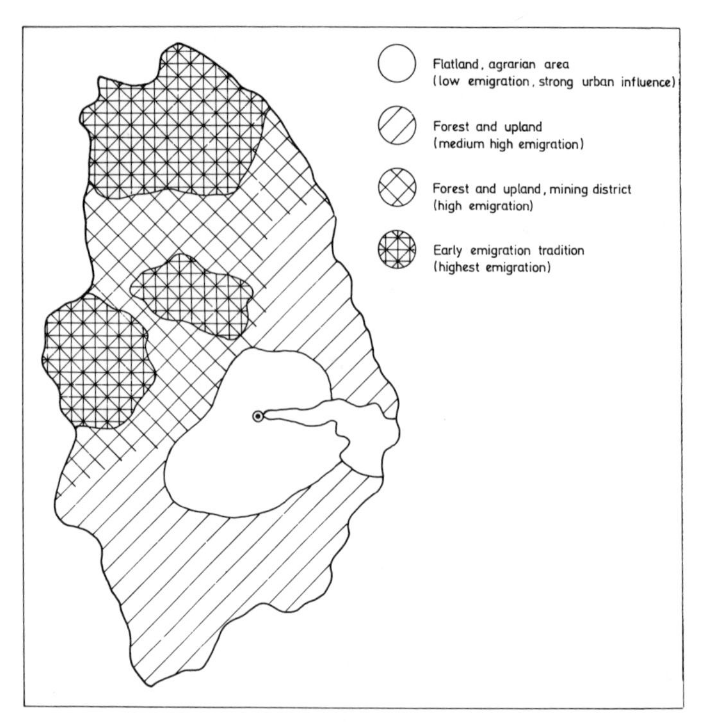

6:3. Main Emigration Areas in Örebro län.
Source H. Norman (1974), pp. 17 ff., 102 ff.

The present study of Örebro län was conducted with computer data processing. In the evaluation process the parishes were divided into two groups, one with higher emigration rates and one with lower. Cleavage was effected by the variable with the greatest explaining power, i.e. the greatest capacity for compounding emigration rates in two separate groups, each with the highest possible degree of internal homogeneity. This process continued with the emergence of new cleavages.

The multivariable analysis of Örebro län showed that the parishes can be classified in two major groups according to their emigration intensity. This pattern emerged both in the stage variable analysis and in the AID analysis. One group consists of flat land parishes, the majority of which are agricultural with large arable acreage, a low degree of industrialization, and a close proximity to the urban center of Örebro. Most of these parishes had a low emigration. In contrast is the other group of parishes with their higher emigration rates. These parishes are farther from the city of Örebro, have a higher level of industrialization and encompass a smaller amount of arable acreage. Emigration in this group of parishes was particularly strong from Bergslagen in the northwestern sector of Örebro län (Figure 6:3). The cleavage diagram (Figure 6:2) shows the data split process in detail. The uppermost variables in each box (underlined) have effected cleavage. The rest are arranged in order of their explaining power following each cleavage. The first cleavage was effected by the variable which expresses high or low shares of arable acreage in relation to total parish acreage. Cleavage resulted in a rough subdivision of parishes into two groups: the first consists of farming and flat land parishes with high field acreage and low emigration; the second of less distinctive farming parishes with higher emigration.

A follow-up study of the 21 parishes which account for the highest emigration after the first cleavage (upper branch on diagram) shows that arable acreage retained its explaining power by effecting cleavage again on the third level. Of prime importance, however, is the role played by emigration tradition, i.e. an early start of emigration, in these strong emigrant parishes. This variable effected cleavage on both the second and fourth levels. Moreover, as indicated by the order of priority in group 13, emigration tradition maintains a high explaining power even so far (high BSS-value). The highest emigration rates are recorded by five parishes in group 5 with a high tradition of emigration: Bjurtjärn (14.7 per mille of the annual mean population); Karlskoga (14.5 per mille); Ljusnarsberg (11.6 per mille); Nora Country Parish (11.4 per mille); and Hällefors (7.7 per mille). All of these parishes lie in the Bergslagen region (Figure 6:3).

According to the arrangement of variables in the initial position (group 1) arable acreage, emigration tradition, migration intensity, proximity to Örebro, and parish acreage rank in that order as the first five. That only two of these variables effected parish cleavage in this case is explained by the fact that all of them are coeffective. Here, and in similar cases, the following development applies: when one variable effects cleavage the others lose their position in the new groupings, since all of them operate in the same direction as that which effected cleavage.

On the lower branch of the diagram a selection has already been made to parishes with low emigration: here the results are not fully as clear as before. The lower the rates of emigration, the less possibility each variable has to show its explaining capacity.

Internal Migration and Emigration

Internal migration intensity showed a strikingly high explaining capacity in the combined AID analysis of Örebro, Värmland, and Västmanland län. This result is connected with special circumstances in the registration of migrants. In order to illustrate these conditions, more general discussion will be given to the relationship between internal migration and emigration.

Researchers are divided on this topic. Migration was extensive throughout Sweden during the 19th century. However, regional differences have been observed, and this has initiated a debate on the connection between internal migration and emigration. Two hypotheses have been advanced: 1) emigration was strongest in areas where the internal migration was high, i.e. a high level of internal migration stimulated people to emigrate; 2) emigration was concentrated to certain areas with lower levels of internal migration, i.e. emigration partially replaced internal migration.[18]

However, closer studies of the extent of internal migration have disclosed the difficulties in using parish migration rates as standards of measurement, since these are based on the number of registered migrants over parish boundaries. In making such estimates researchers ought to focus immediate attention on parish size. In a situation where several parishes have the same degree of actual migration intensity, those which are smallest in size receive the largest number of registered inter-parish migrants. An example of this phenomenon is the tiny parish of Upsala-Näs in Uppland, which registered a high migration intensity. Other complicating factors include the length of parish boundaries and the location of densely populated areas.[19]

The importance of parish size is borne out by S. Martinius' study of migration patterns in seven parishes of varying size in Southern and Central Sweden from 1860 to 1870. In relationship to the total migration in these parishes, intra-parish movement was greatest in parishes with the largest area. On the other hand, when intra-parish and inter-parish movement is combined the overall migration intensity proves to be remarkably equal in all seven parishes.[20] Therefore, the role played by internal migration intensity as an explaining factor in the above AID

[18] S. Åkerman (1971), p. 88.
[19] H. Norman (1974), pp. 108 ff.; I. Eriksson and J. Rogers (1973), *passim.*
[20] S. Martinius (1967), Tables 24 and 25.

analysis must be modified with reference to the way in which migrations were registered.

Conditions in Örebro and Värmlands län are illustrative in this context. In Örebro län the greatest emigration turned out to come from the outlying parishes with large areas but low registered internal migration. In Värmlands län the greatest emigration was concentrated to parishes along the Norwegian border, where a major share of internal mobility took the form of unregistered labor migration.[21] Thus, the observed relationship between high emigration and low internal mobility was only superficial and was due to the above conditions. These examples emphasize the importance of combining the results of AID analysis with detailed knowledge of source materials and local factors in the study populations before acceptance is given to a general explanation.

The Ljusne and Kumla Examples

Another variable in this AID analysis which was of major importance in explaining the presence of high emigration was the emigration tradition. The development in industrial areas such as Ljusne in Hälsingland and Kumla in Närke, in connection with local labor market crises, illustrates the impact of this variable on both emigration and internal migration. In his study of emigration from Ljusne B. Rondahl has shown that a local labor market and trade union conflict in 1906 immediately led to high emigration from this area. This ran entirely contrary to the prevailing trend of emigration in Sweden. The cause of the conflict was the proposed shut-down of sawmill operations in the area. This created tension between the company management and the workers, many of whom were members of a Social Democratic youth organization. The actual shut-down of sawmill operations in 1906 resulted in the emigration of 105 persons from Ljusne: this was the second highest annual emigration intensity for the area (36.6 per mille) and the highest in absolute figures. The majority of emigrants were members of the Social Democratic youth organization.[22]

[21] H. Norman (1974), pp. 127 ff. In an appendix to the nominative primary source reports on emigrants from Kila Parish in southwestern Värmland from 1851 to 1855, the local priest called attention to the laxity with which existing regulations were enforced. This had led to a situation where scores of working people emigrated annually to Norway and Denmark solely on the basis of work certificates. Some of them returned the same year, while others remained abroad for longer periods of time. Thus, despite many years' absence large numbers of persons were still listed as residents of their home parishes and not registered as migrants.
[22] B. Rondahl (1972), pp. 154 ff.

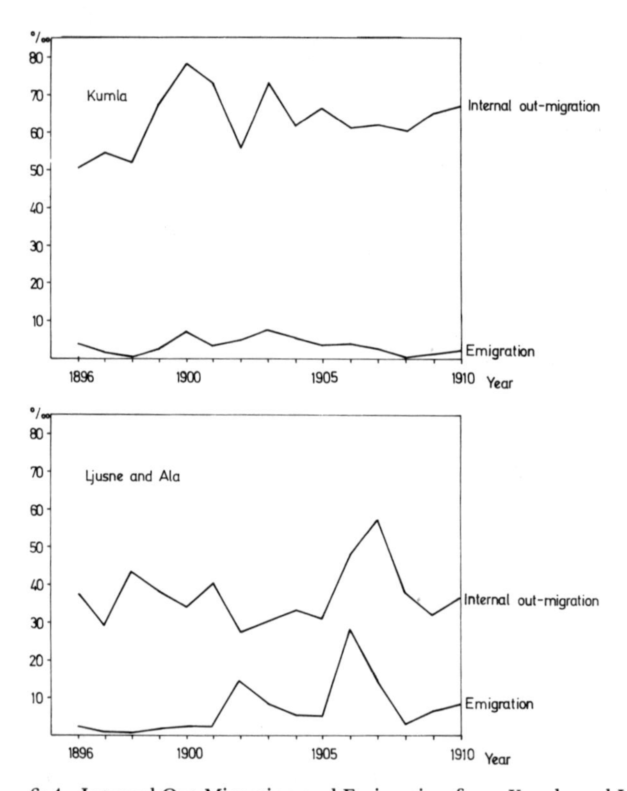

6:4. Internal Out-Migration and Emigration from Kumla and Ljusne-Ala in Per Mille of the Annual Mean Population 1896–1910.
Sources Parish Registers of Catechetical Examinations; Registers of Migration; H. Norman (1974), p. 90.

In Kumla an acute worsening of labor market conditions in 1900 led to the so-called "Kumla Crash". The ultimate cause was overproduction in the shoe manufacturing industry during the last years of the previous century. With the collapse of this branch 57 persons emigrated from Kumla in 1900. This resulted in a minor emigration peak for the area and again stands in contrast to the prevailing trend of emigration in Sweden.

The results of these local crises in Kumla and Ljusne were, however, markedly different in terms of internal and external migration intensity. Kumla recorded a minor peak of emigration but, at the same time, a powerful upsurge of internal out-migration. Ljusne also saw a strong increase of internal out-migration but primarily recorded a peak level of emigration. The number of emigrants from Ljusne was more than half that of internal out-migrants, whereas emigrants from Kumla only amounted to 9 per cent of internal out-migrants (see Figure 6: 4).

Previous migration patterns in both Kumla and Ljusne explain the different reactions of the population to a labor market crisis. Kumla's migrational exchange was strongly oriented to the surrounding regions and was particularly affected by the provincial center of Örebro and its urban influence field. As a result a great deal of its out-migration was channeled to Örebro and to other areas in Sweden. Ljusne, on the other hand, had maintained a prominent tradition of emigration ever since the initial period of emigration. Its population had developed close contacts with America, and in a special situation such as the crisis of 1906 emigration was a natural and viable alternative to internal out-migration.[23] Letter contacts, returning emigrants, prepaid tickets, descriptions of conditions in America by persons familiar with travel routes and the labor market situation there—all of these factors decisively influenced people in the area to move to America as well as to places in Sweden.

The multivariable analysis of the causes behind local variations in Swedish emigration has shown that the intensity of internal migration is an unreliable explaining factor. Before any conclusions can be drawn regarding its relationship to emigration intensity, certain corrections must be made with reference to the area of administrative units. In classifying internal migration as long- or short-distance movement, research may be immediately inclined to make a connection between emigration and long-distance migrations, since the latter resulted in effective streams of movement. However, investigations have shown that the distance factor played a subordinate role. What did carry weight in this context was whether internal migrants came from areas mediating impulses to emigrate.[24]

Generally speaking, the economic, geographic and demographic variables tested in this study point in the same direction. Figuratively they form two clusters: the first consists of areas with large arable acreage, low industrialization, and close proximity to the regional urban center; the second consists of areas with low arable acreage, high industrialization,

[23] Cf. the emigrant contingent led by Erik Jansson, p. 155 above. B. Rondahl (1972), pp. 154 ff.; H. Norman (1974), pp. 90 ff.

[24] Studies of emigration from Stockholm and Örebro have disclosed that in-migrants from traditionally strong emigrant districts had the greatest inclination to emigrate. See F. Nilsson (1971), pp. 75 ff.; H. Norman (1974), p. 144.

and greater distance to the regional center. In sum, the variables inside the two clusters were coeffective in this analysis and led to an amplified effect. Therefore, their separate roles in affecting the extent of emigration cannot be exactly determined. On the other hand, two factors continually emerged as significant for the rise of regional variations of emigration: a) urban influence fields and b) the prevailing emigration tradition in a particular area. In reality, both of these factors are functions of the same phenomenon, i.e. the consistency of migrational behavior. The migration patterns in Kumla and Ljusne illustrate how migration could either be channeled to America or to another part of Sweden. In effect, the prevailing migration pattern in an area was decisive for the destination, i.e. which one of the two migrational objectives that was the most viable alternative.

b. Fear of Military Service—A Cause of Emigration?

By Ann-Sofie Kälvemark

Economic conditions lay behind the great overseas emigration from Europe during the last two centuries. Other factors, such as a desire to escape political or religious repressions, have been considered important, but marginal as to their quantitative effects. Among these latter causes the desire to evade compulsory military service may also be ranged. Fear of military service may be marginal as a cause of emigration, but it still concerns one of the most vital and attractive groups of persons not only for the international labor-market but also for the demands of national defence. Military factors may also have been of growing importance over the course of time, considering the hardening political climate towards the end of the nineteenth century and its consequences in the form of lengthened military service in several countries. The assumption that fear of military service operated as a spur to emigration has never been thoroughly investigated and will therefore be given special attention here. The relationship between emigration and military service will be tested on Swedish evidence for the period 1887 to 1904, a period which saw both high and low emigration as well as several changes in the legislation concerning compulsory military service.[1]

[1] The main sources for this article are the following:
Unprinted: *Inskrivningshandlingar för värnpliktiga* [Enrollment lists] (The Royal Swedish Mili-

Contemporary interest in the problem is abundant and enlightening. Many reasons for the supposed abhorrence of military service were mentioned: the training period was too long, the payment was very low, instances of maltreatment were numerous, food and living conditions were generally bad, outbursts of contagious diseases in the encampments were frequent etc. Emigration was considered as the best way to avoid these unpleasant circumstances. The lively contemporary interest for the relationship between military service and emigration was much due to the prevailing discussion on the volume and organization of national defence. The corps of professional soldiers, which since the 17th century had constituted the main body of Swedish defence, was considered inefficient and out-of-date. Thus, there gradually developed a system of compulsory military service which finally resulted in the Army Organization Act of 1901, prescribing compulsory military service during 240 days, a period of considerable length. The risk of increased emigration was therefore often used as an argument by those who wished to curb the length and costs of military service, whereas the defenders of an extended period of military service maintained that emigration of military conscripts depended on the general trend in emigration and had nothing to do with the length of military service.

A complicating factor here is that emigration by military conscripts was prohibited in Sweden. This, by the way, was true not only of Sweden but of almost all European countries with the important exception of Great Britain. Strangely enough, however, this fact is overlooked by the general literature on emigration, where total liberty to emigrate is supposed to have prevailed in Europe during the period of mass emigration.

In Sweden the General Emigration Ordinance of 1884 also regulated the emigration of military conscripts. These were not allowed to emigrate as long as they were members of the *beväring* (recruited soldiers). It was, however, possible to apply to the Ministry of Defence for special permission to emigrate. The period during which the conscripts belonged to the beväring was initially six years—from the age of 21 to 26—but in 1892 it was prolonged to a period of twelve years. That same year the period of military training was prolonged from 42 to 90 days and subsequently, in

tary Record Office, Stockholm). Emigration surveys from the Police of Copenhagen (Provincial Archives of Sjaelland, Copenhagen).
Printed: *Emigrationsutredningen. Statistik rörande de värnpliktiga, utg. av Generalstabens statistiska avdelning* (Official Statistics on Recruits).

1901, to 240 days. With the lengthening of the period in the *beväring* the number of people subject to the legislation grew. At the same time the incentives to emigrate ought to have been increased by the considerably prolonged period of service.

The impact of the legislation, however, was to a large degree dependent on the general observance of it and also on the practice of giving permissions. Initially, permissions to emigrate were easily obtainable, but in 1894 the practice became restrictive. The conscripts had to fulfil a part of the training before receiving any permission. In 1902 the practice was made even more restrictive, which caused a considerable rise in the number of refused applications.

Thus the legislation against emigration of military conscripts ought to have been an important and growing restriction on emigration. But the observance of the law was considered far from satisfying. Foreign ports, notably Copenhagen, offered excellent possibilities to emigrate illegally. False papers or even false American citizenships are also mentioned as means of illegal emigration. The illegal emigrants were, of course, never registered in the official statistics, a fact, which complicates the testing of fear of military service as a cause of emigration. However, various ways of establishing the numbers of emigrating conscripts are available.

Under what circumstances is the influence of fear of military service on emigration discernible? One would naturally expect a high proportion of male emigrants at or just below the age of 21. In itself this would not suffice to establish a causal relationship. Opportunities to reveal such a relationship should be most favourable when changes in the conditions of military service took place. As has been suggested above, prolongation of the periods of service must have heightened the desire to escape military service. A sharpening in the practice of granting emigration permits to conscripts would probably result in a higher emigration among males below the age of 21. Times of political tensions or war would considerably increase and stimulate emigration, although actual combat, of course, creates a different situation from outright fear of military service.

Improved conditions, shortened periods of service, etc. would consequently probably have the opposite effect. Such changes, however, did not occur during the period studied here.

On the other hand, the dramatic prolongations of the training periods and the repeated sharpenings of the practice of granting emigration permits provide ample opportunities to study the problem.

The general trend of emigration might, however, somewhat complicate

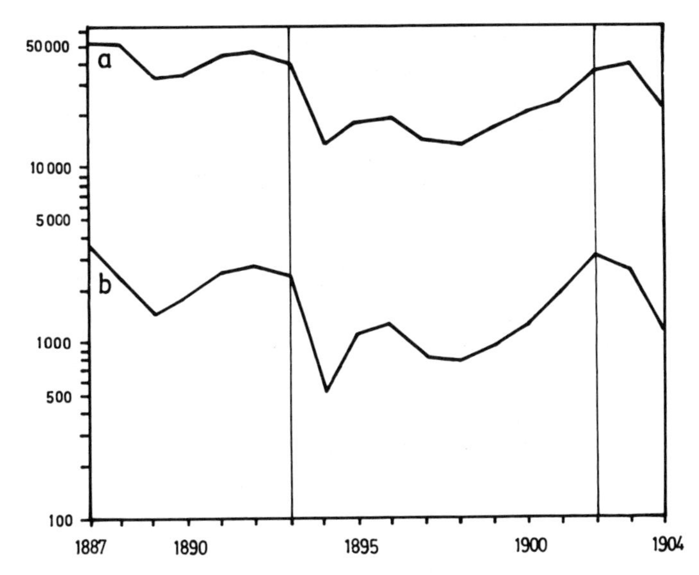

6:5. Total Registered Emigration, and Registered Emigration by Men One Year Prior to Military Conscription, 1887–1904.

Comments a=total registered emigration. b=emigration by men one year prior to military conscription. The vertical lines mark the introduction of the army organizational acts of 1892 and 1901. The vertical scale is logarithmic.

Source *Emigrationsutredningen.* Bilaga 4, Tables 49 and 78; A.-S. Kälvemark (1972), p. 89.

the situation. If, for instance, there occurs a general rise of emigration—due to economic conditions—simultaneous with changes in the conditions of military service, it might be difficult to isolate and discern the special influence of these changes on emigration. An ideal situation would be the following. In the middle of a period of low emigration a prolongation of the military service takes place. If military service had a decisive influence on emigration, a significant rise in the emigration of males in the ages concerned would follow. If the influence is weak, no changes should occur. Unfortunately, the period studied here not only contains changes in the conditions of military service but also great periodical variations in the number of emigrants.

The Swedish statistician Gustav Sundbärg at the turn of the century made a thorough investigation of Swedish emigration. In this context he touched upon the problem of military service and emigration. Studying the proportions of male emigrants at the age of twenty, he found a considerable increase from 4 per cent in 1866 to 16 per cent in 1908. Sundbärg saw this development as a consequence of the changes in conditions of military service and in the practice of granting emigration permits. He noticed peaks in the emigration of twenty-year-olds in 1887 and 1902, when changes in the army organization came into force. When estimating unregistered emigration he placed the main part of it after 1894, justifying this with a reference to the restricted practice of granting emigration permits.

Emigration of twenty-year-olds increased in 1887 and 1902. But we know that male emigration tended to conform much more to business cycles than the emigration of women. Therefore when emigration was high the proportion of emigrating males will be considerably greater than when emigration is low. Sundbärg's conclusion may therefore be somewhat rash, and a more detailed study of the problem is needed.

In Figure 6:5, emigration of twenty-year-old men from Sweden 1887–1904 is shown together with total emigration. The vertical lines mark the introduction of changes in military service. While emigration of young men rose steeply in 1902, it fell in 1892 and even more so in 1893. This trend conformed in all instances to the trend of total emigration. A connection between emigration and fear of military service would have resulted in a growing number of twenty-year-old emigrants, but the reverse is true. Indeed, in 1894 there was even a decrease in the proportion of young male emigrants from 11 per cent to 9 per cent of the total emigration. Strangely, in 1903 the emigration of twenty-year-olds diminished, even though total emigration continued to surge upwards.

Therefore, no evidence of casual relationship between emigration and military service may be concluded from the emigration of the twenty-year-olds. What other means are there of studying the problem of military service and emigration?

There are different ways of acquiring knowledge of the number of emigrant conscripts. The general statistics give the proportion of men emigrating in different age groups. These figures are, however, unsuitable for the present purpose, since they include persons who were exempt from military service—not less than 25 to 35 per cent of each age cohort were exempted from military service. The most satisfactory method of approximating the number of conscripts emigrating legally is to use the statistics on emigration permits from the Ministry of Defence. These statistics, however, usually tell nothing about the number of refused applications; that is, we know nothing of the total number of conscripts who wished to emigrate. Even this information might be rather useless, since it is probable that the number of applications destined for refusal declined, when

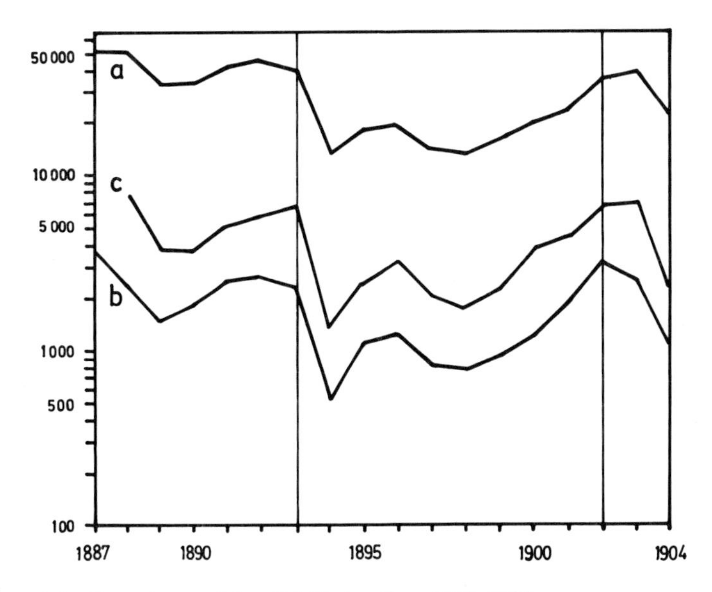

6:6. Conscripts and Swedish Emigration, 1888–1904.

Comments a=total registered emigration. b=emigration by men one year prior to military conscription. c=number of conscripts issued permits to emigrate. The vertical lines mark the introduction of the army organizational acts of 1892 and 1901. The vertical scale is logarithmic.

Source *Statistik rörande de värnpliktige* (Statistics Concerning Military Conscripts), Tables 10, 17, 23; A.-S. Kälvemark (1972), p. 94.

knowledge spread, for example, about a sharpening of the practice. The statistics, then, would probably not reflect the actual demand for permits.

Obtaining knowledge of the illegal emigration is more difficult: the statistics on Swedish emigrants transported from foreign ports must be researched, and the number of conscripts absent from enrollment warrants interest.

In Figure 6:6, emigration of conscripts according to the permit statistics is shown together with total emigration and emigration of twenty-year-old men. Some smaller differences may be noticed. In 1893, the number of permission grants increased somewhat whereas the other graphs go down. In 1902 the number of permission grants also increased somewhat, as did emigration in general, whereas emigration of twenty-year-olds decreased.

Of special interest are occasions when a restricted practice of granting permissions was introduced. In 1894 the number of permits strongly declined: in 1902 it rose slightly, despite sharpening of practice.

Since these changes conform with the development of total emigration, one cannot draw the conclusion that the change in practice caused the decline of permits in 1894. Probably the decline only reflected the actual emigration trend for both conscripts and all other individuals. Sundbärg was, therefore, wrong in designating 1894 as the start of considerable increase when calculating illegal emigration.

The observations made here indicate that emigration of conscripts is probably rather well reflected in the trends of emigration permits. The co-variation between this trend and the general trend of emigration implies that no casual relationship existed between fear of military service and emigration.

Yet the possibility of illegal emigration remains to be investigated. The migration statistics of foreign ports usually give information on emigrating Swedes. A small number of Swedes (as well as Norwegians) emigrated every year over Hamburg. Among these emigrants men were more numerous than women—above seventy per cent for the period 1893–1903. But since the numbers were small—the annual average for the same period is 178 emigrants—no emigration of conscripts worth consideration can have taken place from Hamburg.

The Norwegian statistics, unfortunately, do not distinguish between male and female emigrants and therefore give no clue to the problem. But the statistics on emigrants from Copenhagen, which was by far the most frequented foreign port of Swedish emigration do contain the necessary information. Table 6: 1 gives information on the percentage of male Swedes emigrating from Copenhagen as compared with the male share of all Swedish emigrants according to the official statistics during the same period.

Even before the demands for military service increased, the proportion of men emigrating from Copenhagen exceeded the proportion of men in the total emigration from Sweden. During 1886–1890 and 1901–1904 the proportion of men increased to over seventy per cent. In 1902 as much as eighty per cent of the emigrants over Copenhagen were men. These peaks coincide with the peaks of Swedish emigration in general, which may explain some part of the increased proportion of men. Still the difference is considerable between this emigration via Copenhagen and Swedish emigration in general. It seems very likely that some part consisted of illegal emigration by conscripts.

This might be more thoroughly investigated by combining information

Table 6: 1. *Percentage of Men in the Total Swedish Emigration and in Swedish Emigration via the Port of Copenhagen, 1876–1904*

Year	Sweden	Swedish emigration via the port of Copenhagen
1876–80	59.0	59.4
1881–85	55.3	64.2
1886–90	56.9	72.9
1891–95	53.9	69.7
1896–00	49.0	68.0
1901–04	55.3	74.2

Source Kälvemark (1972), p. 97.

on male and female emigration via Copenhagen with the months of departure during the year. The mustering of conscripts took place before the tenth of April, so in all likelihood illegal emigration ought to occur before this date.

Table 6: 2 and Figure 6: 7 give information on monthly emigration by Swedish men and women via Copenhagen for the years 1901, 1903, and 1904.[2]

As might be expected female emigration is lower than male during the whole period. But during the months of March, April and May emigration of men is many times higher than that of women. It seems therefore very probable that the Swedish emigration via Copenhagen partly consisted of illegally emigrating conscripts and, also, that an increase of this emigration took place when the new army organization came into force. This evidence then implies that conscripts actually emigrated illegally over Copenhagen—and the same might be true of Hamburg, even if the numbers there were small. It also seems clear that this emigration increased considerably at times of changes in the legislation. What does this mean? Did the conscripts emigrate to evade military service? Or did they emigrate illegally just because they were prohibited from emigrating legally?

Unfortunately, the periods 1886–90 and 1900–04 both coincided with considerable increase of emigration in general. It is therefore uncertain

[2] Figures for 1902 are not available.

Table 6:2. *Monthly Swedish Emigration via the Port of Copenhagen in 1901, 1903, and 1904, as Distributed by Sex*

	1901		1903		1904	
	Men	Women	Men	Women	Men	Women
January	20	7	32	3	25	5
February	64	14	119	13	67	14
March	122	16	380	24	155	13
April	137	25	346	41	163	32
May	107	20	235	58	109	34
June	48	22	126	52	71	41
July	50	16	99	25	59	26
August	41	26	114	43	72	34
September	41	26	82	34	42	20
October	39	14	69	29	41	17
November	37	16	40	20	63	17
December	14	6	13	4	15	3

Source General Surveys of Emigration over the Port of Copenhagen. The Copenhagen Police Archives. Provincial Archives of Sjaelland, Copenhagen.

whether the increased illegal emigration of conscripts via Copenhagen reflected a heightened loathing of military service. Increase might equally be due to an increase in the number of young men who wanted to emigrate; those subject to the restrictive legislation emigrated illegally.

Those conscripts who emigrated illegally were not removed from the population registers but were listed accordingly as absent at the musters. Statistics on the number of absentees ought therefore to reflect the course of the illegal emigration of conscripts. But it is difficult to determine the number of absentees who actually emigrated. Furthermore, a control of the muster lists has disclosed that among absentee conscripts were persons who had legally emigrated at the age of twenty.

Official military statistics are based on the muster lists and give information on absentees for two groups—twenty-one-year-olds and older ones. Members of the second group are recorded as absent every year up to age thirty-two. Since each member of this group was listed many times, the statistics are useless as a means of visualizing the chronological variations. Therefore, only the figures for twenty-one-year-olds will be treated here. Table 6: 3 gives the development from 1887 to 1904.

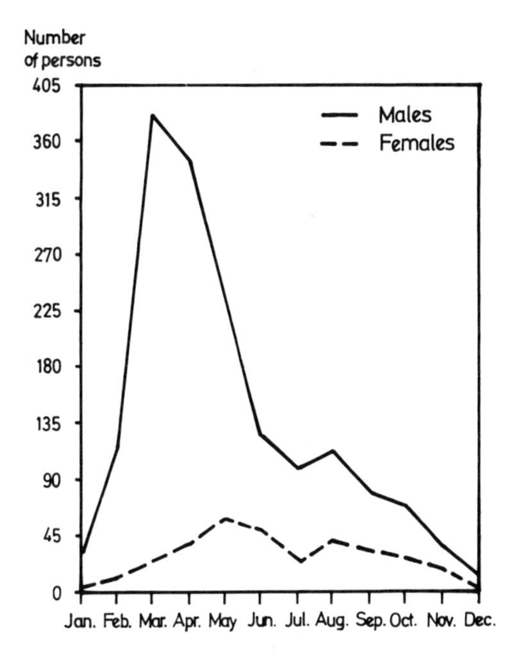

6:7. Swedish Emigration Over the Port of Copenhagen. Adult Males and Females.
Source The Copenhagen Police Archives; Provincial Archives of Sjaelland, Copenhagen; A.-S. Kälvemark (1972), p. 100.

The fluctuations during this period are interesting, since they actually reflect the same trend as emigration in general. Thus the proportion of absentees was high at the beginning of the century. The co-variation with emigration in general, is obvious. A comparison with the prolongation of military service gives the same result as before, on two occasions new legislative acts coincided with a rise in the number of absent conscripts, while on one occasion (1893) a new act was followed by a decrease. Generally, the emigration of conscripts increases when emigration in general rises. The events of 1893 strongly suggest that no correlation existed between dislike of military service and emigration.

Thus, the different ways of correlating fear of military service and emigration give rather similar results. There is no evidence of a strong casual relationship between fear of military service and emigration. The emigration of twenty-year-olds and conscripts increased at two instances of prolongation of military service—in 1887 and in 1902—but decreased in 1893 and in 1894 at another such prolongation. Furthermore, the emigration of this group corresponded closely with total emigration trends.

Table 6: 3. *Number of New Conscripts Absent at Enrollments in Per Cent of Total Number of New Conscripts, 1887–1904*

Year	Number of conscripts (21-year-olds)	Absent	Percent
1887	44 838	6 167	13.8
1888	38 456	5 542	14.4
1889	33 192	4 510	13.5
1890	37 414	5 057	13.5
1891	38 407	5 333	13.9
1892	40 360	5 076	12.6
1893	38 230	4 492	11.7
1894	37 827	4 811	12.7
1895	39 719	4 453	11.2
1896	42 369	4 827	11.4
1897	41 392	5 297	12.8
1898	43 867	5 655	12.9
1899	42 234	5 570	13.2
1900	44 532	5 725	12.8
1901	40 448	4 711	11.6
1902	39 747	6 584	16.6
1903	38 930	6 599	16.9
1904	39 412	6 289	16.0

Source Statistik rörande de värnpliktige 1887–1904. (Official Statistics on Conscripts.) See A.-S. Kälvemark (1972), pp. 102–3.

Economic conditions were the most influential causes of emigration even for conscripts. Still, one cannot deny the possibility that fear of military service might have been an *additional* impetus: when good economic conditions prevailed in North America, the inclination to emigrate might have been increased by the opportunity to evade military service. Then the increased emigration of conscripts over the course of time and also the increases which occurred at times of peak emigration generally could be explained in that way. It might also account for the considerable increase in illegal emigration around the turn of the century.

It is, however, extremely difficult to isolate or even to estimate the influence fear of military service had as an additional impetus to emigration. The very existence of restrictive regulations regarding the emigration of conscripts makes it almost impossible to determine whether young men emigrated in order to evade *military service* or to avoid the mechanical obstacles to their freedom of movement embodied in military *legislation*. Two things must be emphasized. First, men in these age groups traditionally have an extremely high rate of mobility, which becomes strengthened at times of high emigration and good opportunities in the countries of emigration. Second, emigration of individual young persons of both sexes increasingly came to dominate the emigration scene.

7. The Importance of the Transport Sector for Mass Emigration

By Berit Brattne in co-operation with Sune Åkerman

Status of Research

The revolutionary developments in communications in the middle and late 1800s had a strong impact on the exchange of population, goods, and information between continents. European emigration research has apparently taken for granted that the transition between sailing vessels and steamships was a special prerequisite for mass emigration. In several years at the beginning of the 1900s around 1 million persons annually crossed the Atlantic as immigrants to North America, and as early as the 1880s such movement had assumed a high level of intensity. The same was true of the extensive emigration and labor migration to Latin America, especially from Southern Europe, as well as emigration to South Africa, Australia, and New Zealand. The prerequisite for this type of movement was a newly organized maritime traffic and a tonnage capacity which was unthinkable during the 1850s. In turn, this fundamental transition presupposed a new production process for ship plate. The extension of railroad networks during the latter half of the 19th century was also of great importance in this overall context. It not only promoted safer and more rapid means of transcontinental transport but also played a decisive role for European expansion into inner Asia, as symbolized by the Trans-Siberian Railroad. It is important that we keep this particular transport dimension in mind, even though our major focus in this book is what Brinley Thomas has called "the Atlantic economy".

Migration researchers have generally paid too little attention or consideration to the relationship between geographic mobility and changes in the transport sector.[1] We mentioned these research tasks in Chapter 2 and emphasized that the traditional notions about the mass transport capacity of Atlantic shipping lines may need to be revised. In the following we will devote more intensified and systematic discussion to these issues, including

[1] A few exceptions: T. Taylor (1971) and K. Hvidt (1971).

A great part of the Swedish urban emigration were young unmarried women. Interior of a *bourgeoisie* home with a maid, Stockholm 1918. Nordiska muséet, Stockholm.

Railway construction workers in Nordmark Parish, Värmland, 1910. The North American railway companies often recruited Scandinavian labor. Nordiska muséet, Stockholm.

Sons and daugthers of rural proletarians represented a large part of the Swedish emigration. A Swedish crofter's son before his departure. Emigrantinstitutet, Växjö.

The Homestead Act increased social mobility chances for many Swedish rural emigrants. Farm in the vicinity of Belt, Montana. The owner was Jon Åkeson, born probably in Njura, Östra Broby, Skåne, who emigrated from Osby in 1882. Emigrantinstitutet, Växjö.

Until the Swedish farms were mechanized labor demands were considerable but wages were kept down by the landowners. Sugar plantation at the Säbyholm estate, near Landskrona in Southern Sweden. Emigrantinstitutet, Växjö.

Rationalization and mechanization occurred earlier in the U.S. farming than in the European. Reaper-binder on a farm in the Middle West. Emigrantinstitutet, Växjö.

The Swedish lumbermill industry, which was strongly expanding during the second half of the 19th century, was very sensitive to economic fluctuations. Pilers of sawn goods at the Vansbro sawmill, Dalarna, 1895. Nordiska muséet, Stockholm.

Many sawmill workers from the lumber districts on the northern Swedish coast moved to lumberjack districts in the U.S. and Canada. Lumberjacks in the State of Washington, around 1910. Emigrantinstitutet, Växjö.

the matter of emigrant agent activities which has won somewhat greater interest from researchers.

There are several major questions which emigration research confronts in studying the transport sector: (*a*) did the emigrant agents and their principal employers, the major Atlantic shipping lines, contribute in a decisive way to the massive flow of information which presumably paved the way for the spread of emigration behavior?; (*b*) did the emigrant agents' propaganda have the intrinsic capacity for accelerating emigration?; (*c*) did the shipping lines' pricing policies, primarily caused by bitter market competition, have any stimulative effect on emigration?

Both contemporary observers of the 19th century scene and modern researchers have offered relatively categorical answers to these intricate questions. In fact, some migration researchers and model theorists simply presuppose how such questions should be answered and use their interpretations as given premises in their work. Although researchers can often be forced to "beg the issue" they always run a certain risk. All things considered, such complexes as the transatlantic transport organization call for a direct contextual study. The real problem has been locating appropriate sources.

As mentioned above, contemporary observers were also well aware of the significance of emigrant agents for the development of emigration. In 1891, for example, an investigating committee of the U.S. House of Representatives made the following statement on the activities of the Atlantic shipping lines: "Their business is to bring as many people over here as possible ... they go through these countries with their agents and bring anybody as long as he is able to get the money to come over."[2] The Dillingham Commission, which in 1911 presented a 41 volume report on immigration, was rather blunt about its findings. It focused particular attention on the so-called new wave of immigration from Southern and Eastern Europe which, in its view, was an artificial phenomenon fostered by the Atlantic shipping companies and their agents.

One modern researcher who has devoted a great deal of interest to this problem is the Danish historian, Kristian Hvidt. In presenting his extensive research on the topic, Hvidt pointed out that no one had ever before taken on the task of conducting a closer analysis of the shipping com-

[2] 52d Congress, 1st Session, House Reports (1891–92), vol. 12, p. 792; also quoted by K. Hvidt (1971), p. 409.

panies' sales policies in Europe and using this analysis to determine whether the transport sector can be regarded as a third factor between "push" and "pull" or whether the emigrant agents merely channeled the pressure for emigration. Before launching into our own results, we will summarize the interpretation reached by Kristian Hvidt regarding the transport organization and its methods of operation.[3]

The study of the transport dimension of mass emigration is a neglected research field. Actually, this is somewhat surprising, for the wide range of works on European mass emigration contain a great many statements and speculations on the role of the transport sector. Econometric research has, at least theoretically, attached great importance to travel costs in connection with emigration.[4] These are considered short-term expenditures together with the temporary loss of income which usually follows emigration. One can also assume a period of unemployment for emigrants, both in the delivering and receiving country. According to this research, the decision to migrate is based on these short-term expenditures combined with an evaluation of the discounted future income. Hence the emigrants tried to estimate the difference between the alternative of migration and stationary residence.

Kristian Hvidt discovered the reason for the lack of prior research when he began his search for applicable sources. He found it almost impossible to obtain information on the activities and business methods of the emigrant agents. Archives which may have been established in connection with agency operations have either been destroyed or simply lost. There are some indications that the agents' activities hardly allowed the preservation of ordered archives. The situation was no more encouraging for the major shipping companies, especially in Liverpool, Hamburg, and Bremen. Although some sources appear to have been preserved, shipping lines generally refuse researchers access to useful information. Moreover, the heavy bombings during World War II destroyed practically all material in the ports of Hamburg, Bremen, and Hull. The latter was especially significant as a transit place for Scandinavian emigrants.

As a result, Hvidt was forced to scour the archives of the Copenhagen Police and other official archives. In 1868 the Danish authorities sharpened their control of emigrant traffic and agent activities, and this led to new legislation as well as emigrant registration. The emigrant pas-

[3] See K. Hvidt (1971), pp. 409–480.
[4] See especially T. Moe (1970).

senger lists are a remnant of the Copenhagen police control. In addition some documents pertaining to the organization of emigrant agencies have managed to be preserved.

In Denmark emigrant agencies began to organize at the end of the 1860s. Prior to that time certain merchants and commissioners had represented English and German shipping firms on a more or less part-time basis. Around 1870 the agencies had developed the type of organization which was to last until World War I. This consisted of ten or more major firms represented by head agents which, in turn, employed a large network of subagents throughout the country. The first on the scene was the Scottish Allan Line (1867) which, together with the Cunard, Dominion, Inman, Guion, Nation, and State Lines, belonged to the so-called Liverpool Circle. Other leading firms included *Hamburg-Amerikanische Packetfahrt A.G.* (HAPAG) in Hamburg and *Nordwestdeutsche Lloyd* in Bremen. American business concerns were also represented in Denmark, and their operations expanded heavily after 1900, when J. Pierpont Morgan acquired a substantial monopoly of the emigrant traffic. Moreover, there is nothing to indicate that American and other non-British capitalists were not attracted at an early stage by the highly lucrative prospects of emigrant transport. Even here we might find some substantiation for Brinley Thomas' theory of an Atlantic economy, whereby capital investments circulated between Great Britain and North America. The close co-operation between the major shipping lines and railroad companies in the United States and Canada might indicate one such pattern. Unfortunately, we have all too little knowledge of these large and fascinating intercontinental transactions.

The major emigrant transport agencies were joined by smaller ones, such as the American Beaver Line. Some Scandinavian companies also tried to establish themselves on this market, but their operations were short-lived. The exception was the Danish Thingvalla Line, which had its main office in Copenhagen. The Danish capital also came to play a major role as a transit port for emigration from Southern Sweden in the same way that the Norwegian port of Trondheim served as a point of embarkation for a rather substantial number of emigrants from Northern Sweden. However, the Swedish port of Gothenburg was most important for Swedish emigration as well as the major share of early Finnish emigration (see Figure 7: 1).

Various travel alternatives for Swedish emigrants around the mid-1880s are shown in Figure 7: 1. By that time railroad construction had made

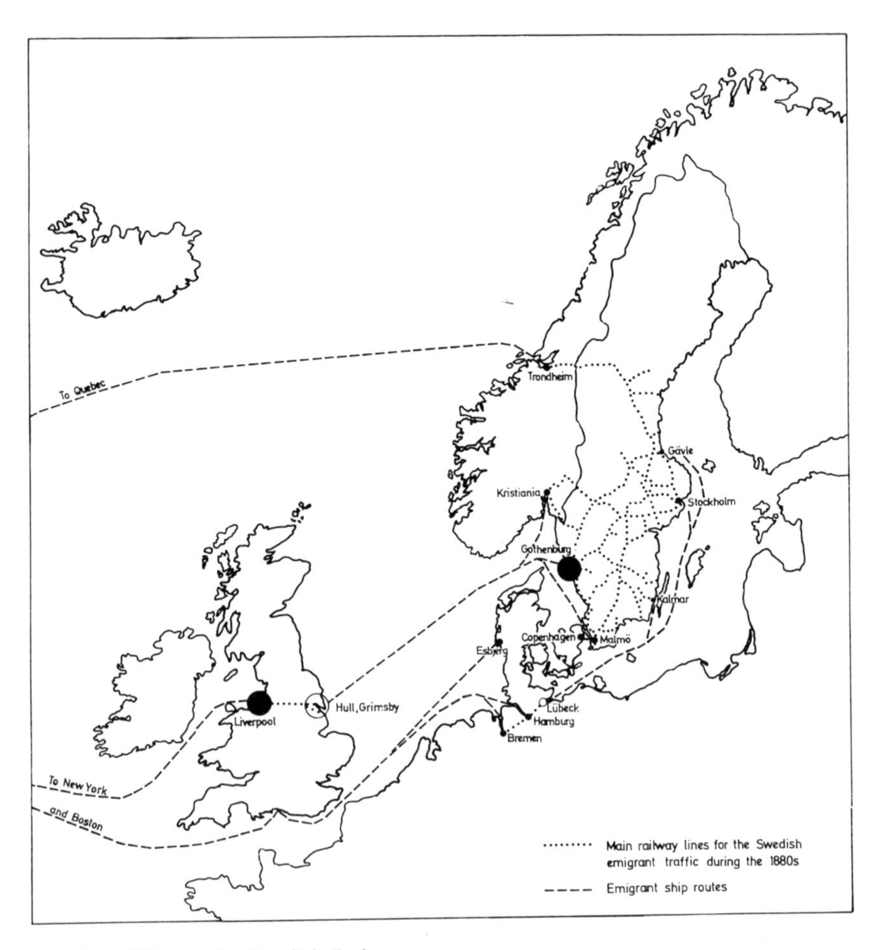

7: 1. Travel Routes for Swedish Emigrants.

major advances in Southern and Central Sweden but lagged behind in sparsely settled regions farther north. There, however, coastal shipping was relatively widespread and represented a comparatively comfortable, if not particularly rapid, means of transportation. The subsequent travel route entirely depended upon the particular transport organization in operation. Only the Thingvalla Line sent its emigrant passengers from Copenhagen directly to New York. As shown by the map, those who employed the services of the Liverpool or North German Lines were forced to make the trip in stages. For example, emigrants from Stockholm and the port city of Malmö, in Southern Sweden, traveled first by steamship to Lübeck; from there by train to Hamburg and Bremen; then by ship to the English ports of Southampton and Liverpool; and subsequently across the Atlantic. However, the majority of Swedish emigrants embarked from Gothenburg on special boats, run by the Wilson Line and destined for Hull in England, and then continued by railroad to Liverpool for final embarkation.

According to Kristian Hvidt, a period of bitter rivalry between the English and German mercantile blocks at the close of the 1860s apparently issued in efforts to establish co-operation on controlling the expanding European emigrant market. With the exception of Denmark, emigration from Scandinavia came under the control of the Liverpool Circle, whereas emigration from Central and Eastern Europe was dominated by the German lines. In effect, Kristian Hvidt has traced the sporadic formation of *cartels,* or so-called *conferences,* among the major shipping lines. These cartels, which Hvidt contends were intended to curb competition, also led to more formalized co-operative ventures, including minimum price agreements for Atlantic transport beginning in the late 1860s. However, Hvidt generally concludes that emigration was directly stimulated by the rivalry between shipping lines and the feverish activities of emigrant agencies with their wide-scale advertising and propaganda campaigns.

Hvidt's analysis of the advanced methods of emigrant recruitment seems to substantiate his argument. He calls particular attention to the network of thousands of subagents active in each emigrant country. Although Hvidt's overall description of the emigrant agents is a fairly balanced one, his conclusions are influenced by the accusations of some contemporary observers, especially foreign diplomats and police officials, who delivered a sharp criticism against the emigrant agents for their business methods.

In sum, the emigrant agents and the transport sector appear, according to Hvidt, to have played an independent role in accelerating emigration at least until 1900. He offers a similar interpretation for a separate but related issue, namely the role of price-fixing policies in the overall system. In his view, a constant reduction of ticket prices at the close of the 19th century made it possible for many prospective but relatively poor emigrants to carry out their intentions. He also contends that as late as 1904 a temporary drastic reduction in ticket prices caused an acceleration of emigration out of Copenhagen. At the same time he is a bit uncertain whether the 43 separate price statements, which were preserved somewhat by accident and happen to date from different periods of each year between 1866 and 1900, can provide an accurate picture of the entire process. Despite shortcomings, Kristian Hvidt has portrayed the working of a large emigrant agent system which encompassed all of Europe and represented an important stage in the process of emigration.

The Agency of the Larsson Brothers

The discovery of emigrant agent archives in Sweden has enabled Scandinavian research to shed further light on the various issues connected with the significance of the transport sector in the development of emigration. The archives were left by the five Larsson brothers who, at times collectively and at times individually, carried on emigrant agencies and other business concerns during the period 1873–1914. The preserved documents span a considerable period of mass emigration from Sweden to America, but their greatest coverage falls during the culminative decade, i.e. the 1880s, when the second major wave of emigration occurred. In effect, these documents are especially useful for research in studying both external and internal migration during the Industrial Era.[5]

Moreover, they inform about the structure and conditions of emigrant agencies during the 1880s. The framework of this business was shaped by the varying directives of official authorities and principal employers. Another contributing factor was the variable nature of mercantile conditions affecting emigrant transport, which was strongly dependent upon the demand for passage. The contents of the Larsson archives together with the principles used by the emigrant agents in marketing their services provide succinct illustrations. The emigrant agents constitute an important element in the structure of the transport organization, but the central issue at stake is whether they actually functioned as emigrant recruiters, capable of influencing the extent of emigration.

In certain respects, primarily commercial, the same conditions prevailed for emigrant traffic throughout Scandinavia. Therefore, the present findings on the relations between the North Atlantic shipping companies and their representatives can also be considered valid for Norway and Denmark. Moreover, as Finnish emigrants largely passed through Swedish ports during the 1880s it can be assumed that their travel conditions were the same as those of emigrants from the rest of Scandinavia.[6]

[5] The Larsson Brothers' emigrant archives were found by Olof Thörn, who in two articles (O. Thörn 1959a, 1959b) has described their contents and discussed the organization of this agency. In a doctoral dissertation B. Brattne has treated the activities of this agency.
[6] H. Wester (1970).

A study of the Larsson agency can also shed light on additional problems within the general scope of emigration research. The archives provide a unique opportunity to analyze potential emigration, to determine the distribution of emigrant volume in terms of cash and prepaid tickets, as well as discuss certain travel problems which directly affected emigrants.

The Larssons themselves originated from one of the social groups, crofters, which sent scores of emigrants overseas. Four of the five brothers emigrated in their youth to America on separate occasions during the 1860s and 1870s. Their visits not only gave them a knowledge of English but also provided an education and practical experience in business. After their separate returns to Sweden during the 1870s and 1880s, the brothers used their experiences and contacts in America to devote a greater part of their professional careers to the emigrant agency business. The youngest brother, Samuel Larsson, represented emigrant transport firms for 37 years, which meant that by the beginning of the 20th century he was the "grand old man" among emigrant agents.

The Representative Features of the Larsson Agency

During the 1880s ten British shipping companies were engaged in the emigrant traffic business. The Larssons represented the Guion Line which, in terms of passenger volume, was of medium size. Business income varied sharply and was directly dependent upon the changeable volume of emigrants during different years. The Larsson agency made substantial profits during peak years of emigration. On the other hand, income from other business activities was of considerable significance for total earnings during low years.

The possibility that the Larsson concern was representative of emigrant agency operations in Sweden can be studied from four angles of approach. An examination of Elis F. and Samuel Larsson's taxable business income during the first half of the 1880s shows that they can be regarded as representative in this respect. The same is true of the business activities they conducted on the side. In terms of continuity, the Larsson agency can be most closely compared to representatives of the leading shipping companies who held agencies for the same firm throughout this decade.

An examination of the Larssons' agency's passenger volume shows that the Guion Line was fourth largest among the British shipping firms on the Swedish emigrant market. On both the Swedish and Continental markets, however, the company was clearly outdistanced by the leading Cunard,

White Star, and Inman Lines. The Guion Line's average share of emigrant traffic from Sweden during the 1880s was approximately 10 per cent: a medium passenger volume. On the other hand, the Larsson agency was not representative in terms of passenger distribution between cash and prepaid tickets. Of all British shipping companies the Guion Line transported the lowest percentage of emigrants with prepaid passage.

Although they lacked the positive factor of prepaid tickets in their total sales results, the Larssons gradually managed to increase their share of the market. Despite fluctuations in the volume of transportation the market shares were fairly constant for the majority of shipping firms. The successes of the Guion Line can be attributed to the intimate collaboration of the Larsson brothers and their strong, personal investment of resources and energy.

Prepaid Tickets and their Significance for Emigration Volume

By comparing the information supplied by different source-series on emigrant volume during the 1880s one can determine the reliability of the statistics drawn up by the emigrant agents under the heading of the "Return of Emigration."[7] If these statistics prove to be applicable they can supplement the relatively imperfect details on the distribution of emigrant passage between cash and prepaid tickets. Emigration research attaches great interest to this possibility in discussing the propellent force behind emigration. In reality, the discrepancy between the "Return of Emigration" and the official statistics is percentually very small. Consequently, the information provided by the first mentioned statistics on the total passenger volume of each shipping company can essentially be regarded as correct. According to comments made in the correspondence of the Larsson archives, the distribution of cash and prepaid tickets recorded by respective shipping companies contains inaccuracies. Therefore, research should interpret the recorded share of prepaid tickets for individual companies as an approximation of the actual figures. The percentage of emigrants with prepaid tickets who sailed from Gothenburg can be estimated at roughly 50 per cent for the years 1883–1886 and around 40 per cent for the years 1888–1889 (see Table 7: 1).

[7] The reliability of the official Swedish emigration statistics can also be studied by way of a comparison with material in the Larsson archives. In addition to reports on emigration volume, research can also focus on the official statistics' record of emigrants' ages, places of destination, and travel costs.

Table 7: 1. *Passengers with Prepaid Tickets in Per Cent of all Passengers Traveling with British Shipping Lines from Gothenburg 1883–1889*

Shipping Lines	1883	1884	1885	1886	1888	1889
Allan	50.9	37.9	37.2	36.7	39.3	48.7
American	63.4	66.8	68.7	52.9	59.1	64.2
Anchor	38.4	55.4	37.5	40.5	37.8	48.9
Cunard	54.7	53.2	52.2	35.6	40.1	44.4
Dominion	48.7	39.0	38.8	36.8	41.7	58.0
Guion	25.9	33.3	19.6	8.4	21.2	18.5
Inman	50.0	46.2	62.0	38.8	38.1	45.9
National	56.5	55.7	48.8	13.6	28.0	34.5
State	37.4	48.4	17.7	10.5	32.0	58.0
White Star	48.7	54.6	64.9	46.0	53.2	50.7
All Shipping Lines	50.2	50.6	54.4	34.3	40.5	43.3

Sources Bröderna Larsson & Co:s arkiv, The Provincial Archives, Gothenburg; B. Brattne (1973), p. 101.

Once comparisons are made between Danish and Swedish statistics, the role of prepaid tickets as a pull factor appears to be much more difficult to interpret than researchers have been led to believe.[8] That a larger percentage of persons emigrated with prepaid tickets during low years of emigration than during peak years is probably a false connection which, in turn, can lead to an overemphasis of the importance of prepaid tickets for emigrant volume. In discussing prepaid tickets one must take consideration to the varying commercial conditions under which the North Atlantic transport organization operated during the 1880s. It can be assumed, but not proved, that ticket price-cutting took place to a greater extent on the American than on the Scandinavian market in times of hard competition.

Naturally enough, it must have been more difficult for a company to maintain a fixed passenger fare on the expansive American market as compared with the more limited and controllable Scandinavian market. It is hardly likely that the European market situation was solely responsible for the gradual co-operation between British and Continental shipping firms during the latter half of the 1880s. Close collaboration was also a prerequisite for price control on the American market where, according to Swedish statistics, 40–50 per cent of emigrant tickets were purchased. The statistical material lends some support to the hypothesis that changes in the

[8] K. Hvidt (1971), p. 348; I. Semmingsen (1941), p. 57.

number of prepaid tickets are partially due to more advantageous prices in the United States. During the years of collaboration between shipping companies, from 1888–1889, the portion of prepaid tickets was 10 per cent lower than during the mid 1880s when no collaboration was in force.

Furthermore, a dispatch of prepaid tickets from the country of immigration can, in many cases, be interpreted as the implementation of a decision made prior to emigration or as a purely technical measure aimed at simplifying the process of emigration. Prepaid tickets did constitute a substantial pull factor but not to the extent that its percentual distribution might easily indicate.

Legal and Commercial Conditions for Emigrant Agency Operations

One way of evaluating the significance of legal regulations for emigrant agencies is to study the Larssons' permits to act as emigrant agents from 1875 to 1885. According to the Swedish Commission on Emigration, official control of this business was both conventional and ineffective.[9] An examination of the annual agency permit applications shows that Elis F. Larsson was apparently refused permission twice and that his permit was strongly in question on two other occasions. Samuel Larsson's permit was withdrawn on one occasion, but since the brothers held these permits on an alternative basis, the Guion Line agency could function without interruption. Consequently, official intervention did not terminate their business. However, the knowledge of official control and the risks of losing an agency generally gave rise to more careful observance of existing regulations. The market competition greatly contributed to law enforcement efforts, in that agents drew the attention of the authorities to offences committed by business competitors. In this way official supervision was more efficient than it might otherwise have been.

The commercial demands of the North Atlantic transport organization had a far more decisive impact on the marketing of emigrant agencies and the structure of emigrant traffic than laws and ordinances. A close relationship existed between the internal affairs of the North Atlantic shipping lines and the marketing procedures of individual companies. A study of the relationship between the commercial demands of the North Atlantic transport organization and the marketing procedures of individual firms must be based upon an analysis of the competitive market conditions

[9] *Emigrationsutredningen, Bilaga 2,* pp. 43 ff.

affecting emigrant traffic. The Larsson archives can be used to supplement what has been known about the collaboration between shipping companies. Contrary to the situation in Great Britain's coal and steel industries,[10] the British succeeded in establishing cartel agreements in the shipping industry and thereby alleviated the increasing rivalry among the industrialized countries on the European continent in the last decades of the 19th century. This form of collaboration was probably not foreign to shipping representatives on the emigrant market. During this particular period trust formations also increased rapidly in the United States, and even in Sweden cartel agreements emerged as a new feature in the sphere of business economics.[11] The so-called Liverpool Conferences maintained co-operation between British shipping companies on the Swedish market from 1880 up to the middle of 1884 and again from 1888–1889, when the leading Continental companies were also incorporated in this venture.

Economic considerations were the primary impulses to collaboration between shipping companies. During conference periods they managed to maintain a considerably higher level of ticket prices than would otherwise have been possible. Agents' commissions were also more favorable during such periods, in that a specific renumerative sum was stipulated for each transported emigrant. During non-conference periods, however, commissions were directly dependent upon the demand for sailings on the home market.

To ensure the realization of their ultimate goals, the shipping companies forged plans for economic and organizational co-operation. Directives were issued regarding the organization of emigrant agencies to reduce local competition and establish a controlling body. Mutual price and provision terms, coupled with periodical agreements on dollar exchange rates and advertising principles, led to an appreciable limitation of eventual competition. The imposition of economic co-operation on local agent associations largely created guarantees for compliance with the above directives. Regulations beyond those of a purely economic nature were also observed, which shows that the control procedures were effective.[12]

[10] A. J. Taylor (1968), p. 65.

[11] L. Jörberg (1966), p. 29.

[12] This study means in general a sharpening of the focus on the monopolistic tendencies during this stage of the capitalistic development. Further research ought to be done on this theme. Information about different systems of trust building can be found in D. Echel (1966), P. Laager (1959) and E. H. Chamberlin (1962), which also treat the definition problems involved.

Price Policies and Emigration Volume

The price-fixing policy of the shipping companies provides a basis for a study of the connection between price levels and emigrant volume in line with the hypothesis that the demand, and not the supply, of sailings was decisive for price-fixing. Travel costs and emigration volume show a fairly similar variation during the 1880s (Figure 7: 2).

Travel costs were high during the first four years of this decade and again in 1888–1889, all of which were years of peak emigration. The prerequisites were a large number of passengers and organized collaboration between shipping companies. Passenger volume, which successively declined after 1883, caused a reduction in travel costs and an interruption in market co-operation. By the middle of the decade prices had dropped to such an extent that they amounted to only two-thirds of the cost level at the beginning of the decade. Emigrants had the opportunity of negotiating low ticket prices and other favorable terms of travel. Nevertheless, the volume of emigrants could not be maintained to anything approximating the level which existed in the early 1880s. In 1885 it constituted barely one-third of the volume in 1882. A strong upsurge of emigration in 1887 led to a successive rise in price levels, and during the next two years travel costs were the same as at the beginning of the decade. The price directives issued to the emigrant agents by the shipping companies, combined with insufficient passenger tonnage, indicate that there were factors beyond their control which affected emigrant volume. The development of travel costs can be shown to be a direct consequence of the changes in the development of emigration. Even with the adoption of a periodically elastic price policy the transport sector represented by the shipping companies and their agents could not accelerate emigration. Thus, in this respect it cannot be credited with the role of a propellent force in the development of emigration.[13]

Emigrants' travel terms were also greatly dependent upon fluctuations in emigrant volume. During years of considerable emigration travel costs were comparatively high and stable, despite seasonal fluctuations in passage demands. At times there was a certain shortage of passenger tonnage which led to a further depreciation of travel terms. On the other hand,

[13] K. Hvidt (1971), p. 456. Hvidt contends, to the contrary, that passage prices were elastic for both the shipping lines and their agents and that prices were low throughout the 1880s. He explains the latter with reference to the fact that the companies' passenger tonnage exceeded the actual demand for passage.

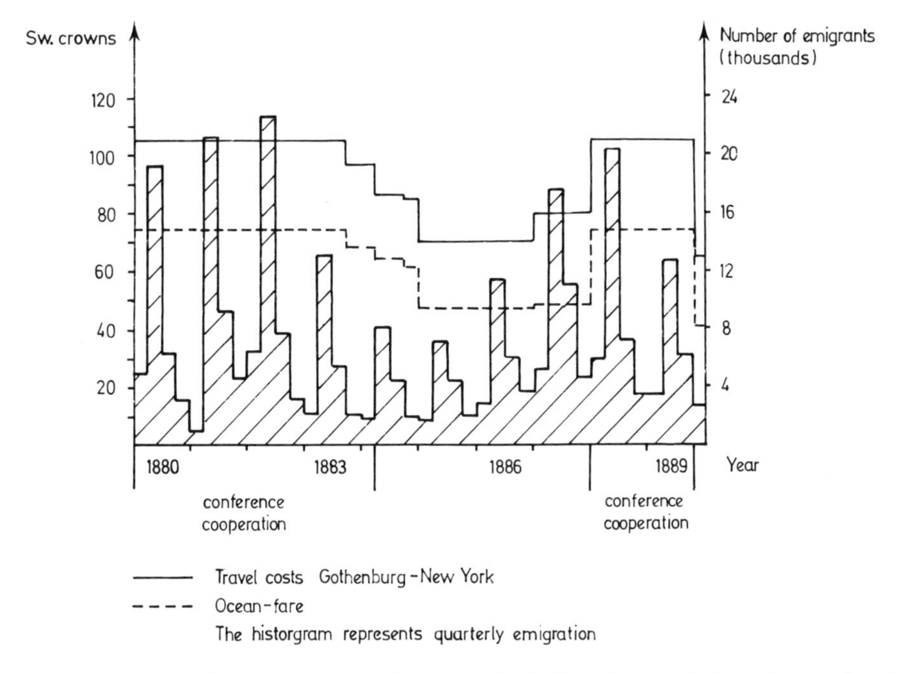

7:2. Ticket Prices for the Travel Gotenburg-New York. Total Costs and Ocean Fares Related to the Volume of Emigration in the 1880s.
Sources Göteborgs Poliskammares arkiv, and Bröderna Larssons arkiv, The Provincial Archives, Gothenburg; B. Brattne (1973), p. 143.

emigrants had greater opportunities of solving travel problems to their own advantage during low years of emigration. Prices were elastic, and the bitter rivalry between emigrant agents made it possible for emigrants to negotiate lower fares, particularly for group travel and for children under 14 years of age. They were also able to obtain relatively comfortable lodgings on board emigrant ships.

The Subagent Organization

Legal and commercial factors governed the framework of the emigrant agency. A study of the agents' information activities can shed light on the practical aspects of the business in terms of customer contacts. Of particular interest are the technical set-up of the agency, the source and contents of the information, as well as the nature of the agents' market contacts. By examining these factors research can determine whether the information issued by the emigrant agents actually had a decisive influence on the extent of emigrant volume.

From an organizational standpoint the agents' most important channels of information in the early 1880s were their own representatives, the subagents. In light of its information on the numerical strength of this organization, prior research has assigned considerable significance to the subagents for the sales results of individual agents and, consequently, for total emigrant volume.[14]

The documents in the Larsson archives facilitate a study of the subagents' organization with regard to numerical strength, opportunities of establishing customer contacts, and the importance of familiarizing the market with specific shipping companies. It has been found that the Guion Line was represented by approximately 150 subagents in 1882. Consequently, the entire corps of shipping companies was represented by roughly 1 500 subagents on a nation-wide scale at the beginning of the same decade. Subagents were mainly recruited among persons who, by way of profession, social status or place of residence, had opportunities of making contacts with large groups of people. The organization of subagents in Sweden followed the same structural principles applied throughout Scandinavia.

The emigrant agents did not actually expect the subagents to recruit emigrants on their own. Their hope was that through the work of the representatives the company name would become known on the market and that emigrants would book passage in advance. The outcome of the enterprise proved a disappointment. Emigrant agents received few advance bookings through direct action by subagents, and as a result subagents received very little economic benefit from their assignments. The lack of continuity in the activity of individual subagents reflects the disappointment over meagre profits.

The role played by the subagents in familiarizing the market with the shipping companies can be examined by studying the relationship between the number of subagents in different Swedish areas and the volume of emigrant passengers. The subagent network was generally most compact in districts with a high total of emigration. For the Larssons there was a clearly negative relationship between the number of subagents and the shipping lines' passenger volume. On the whole, not even an increase in

[14] K. Hvidt (1971), pp. 434 ff.; L. Ljungmark (1971), pp. 70 ff; *Emigrationsutredningen, Bilaga 2*, pp. 56, 60.

representatives had any positive effect on their share of emigrant volume from separate districts. On the contrary, their share was fairly constant during the last two years of the 1880s. Consequently, this study shows that the information supplied by the subagents had hardly any significance for the extent of emigrant volume.

The development of the subagent organization during the 1880s is closely connected with the changing conditions of the emigrant agencies. There was a larger number of company representatives during years of heavy emigration. The formation of the subagent network was occasioned by the difficulties of delivering direct "word of mouth" information during the period of collaboration between shipping companies. The emigrant agents should logically have concentrated on their subagents during years of low emigration. Due to small profit margins and the knowledge that subagents were of little importance, emigrant agents explored the possibilities of a more open collaboration with considerably more effective sales promoters, i.e. Swedish Americans. As a result, the subagents were bypassed altogether.

Direct Contacts with the Emigrant Market

The large quantity of informational material which the emigrant agents distributed in various ways during the 1880s was mainly produced in Sweden and paid for by the Atlantic shipping companies. Up to the middle of 1883 material of foreign origin was also made available to the emigrant agents by representatives of immigration promoters in America. After that point the Swedish authorities prevented the distribution of material which contained detailed information about conditions and prospects of settlement in America. Consequently, the majority of material distributed during the greater part of the 1880s was of native origin.[15]

Most of the information supplied by the emigrant agents concerned transatlantic travel. Brochures and circulars emphasized in propaganda fashion the advantages and popularity of the particular line represented by the agents. Much space was also devoted to the services provided by emigration offices at ports of embarkation and to sound general advice for prospective emigrants. Details about conditions in the United States were brief and can hardly be regarded as idealized descriptions.

[15] K. Hvidt (1971), pp. 353 ff. However, Hvidt contends that material of foreign origin was also distributed on a wide scale during this period.

In addition to the subagent organization, newspaper advertising constituted an important channel of information for written or direct personal contact with the emigrant market. Though distributed nation-wide, advertising was concentrated to sectors of the Swedish press which were presumed to reach specific segments of the population receptive to emigration. Advertisements were monotonously repeated week after week during peak years of emigration, and their content was very stereotyped. The prime aim was to give publicity about the specific emigrant agents and the shipping companies.

The response of the market to this flow of information can be studied in light of the correspondence contained in the Larsson archives. More than 1 000 letters have been examined from the period 1882–1884 and 1887–1888. Particular attention has been devoted to the correspondents' inquiries and the agents' replies as a means of exploring two specific issues: (*a*) what role did the emigrant agent play in the development of emigration? and (*b*) can the information supplied in these letters be characterized as emigrant recruiting? To shed further light on these questions, interest has been focused on the agent's role from the point of view of the time lapse between the establishment of written contact and the departure of emigrants. Consideration has also been taken to emigrants' destination choices. The analysis of this correspondence provides a basis for discussing the inclination for emigration during this decade.

The clients' letters disclose that individuals were primarily interested in obtaining general information about America and details on travel costs and departure times. During the latter part of the 1880s these inquiries became more specific: the demand for information about America diminished somewhat, and requests for details on sailing vessels, conditions on board ship, departure times, and travel costs to specific destinations predominated. The shifting nature of these inquiries reflected the correspondents' heightened awareness of emigration conditions during the latter part of the 1880s. More specific inquiries about working conditions in America, land purchase terms, and employment opportunities were percentually very low throughout the decade. In effect, it can be said that the market had limited expectations of the information supplied by the emigrant agent. Letter writers were primarily concerned with travel details and any additional services provided by the agent in terms of emigrant transport.

The replies of the emigrant agent disclose a similar attitude on his part. Approximately three-fourths of the letters were simply answered by means of a printed information sheet. The amount of written replies during these two periods (1882–1884 and 1887–1888) appears to covariate with the level of business competition on the emigrant market. There were few replies during periods of heavy transport demands and collaborative ventures between shipping firms. On the other hand, agents were more inclined to answer letters during periods of open market competition.

A study has been made of extant replies, in all 166, with regard to specific content and possible differences in the number of replies to certain groups of individuals. Written answers were sent to 11 per cent of all correspondents who never emigrated; 32 per cent to persons who did emigrate; and 39 per cent to Swedish Americans. The marked numerical difference between the first two groups can be explained by the fact that a considerable share of the replies to persons who eventually emigrated contained acknowledgements of paid deposits. The relatively high percentage of replies to Swedish Americans is due to the fact that the agent considered them as more inclined to travel and that he anticipated the prospect of transporting an entire group.

As far as content is concerned, there are no differences between replies to individuals who never emigrated and those who did. On the whole, such replies have a stereotype format and contain purely general information. Even when the letter writer asked more precise questions about discounts, deferred payments, and aid in seeking employment, the agent seldom furnished him with a full reply. The same applied to inquiries about the need for official emigration documents and the possibility of illegal emigration. Emigrant agents did offer their services for securance of the Emigration Certificate. After 1887 this procedure became especially complicated for men subject to military service. However, agents always avoided mentioning possible loopholes in emigration stipulations. In cases where agents showed compliance with correspondents' requests, i.e. a departure from existing legal and commercial regulations, their promises and pledges were carefully formulated. On the other hand, in his correspondence with Swedish Americans the emigrant agent did not follow his employers' directives but showed a positive attitude to negotiating favorable terms of travel.

Naturally, these study results do not exclude the possibility that agents, by virtue of their office contacts with emigrants, were able to act in a more decisive manner to facilitate emigration and thereby increase their sales. Since the majority of persons who visited the agents at the ports of embarkation had already decided to emigrate, it is outside the purpose of this study to examine personal conferences between contracting parties. Even these are, of course, very difficult to substantiate.

The results of the study on the time lapse between correspondents' initial contacts with the emigrant agent and their subsequent departures and choice of destinations add further support to the contention that the emigrant agent was more of a travel agent than an emigrant recruiter. The time-lapse analysis is based on the assumption that a decision to emigrate was usually such an important undertaking that there would have been a considerable time difference between letter contact and possible departure if the agent's information had had any significance for the decision-making process. The study shows that more than half of the correspondents who never emigrated and almost 70 per cent of those who did prepared plans of departure within a four-week period. Although a certain postponement of the actual departure date can be noted for the latter category, a clear majority did depart as planned.

Consequently, it is highly conceivable that correspondents had already decided to emigrate before contact was made with the emigrant agent. The correspondence offers no opportunities to determine the causes behind the decision to emigrate nor explain the choice of shipping company. The information distributed by the emigrant agent and the correspondence carried on with him cannot have been triggering factors and are hardly sufficient stimuli for a decision to emigrate.

The destinations of emigrants in the United States have a comprehensive yet uneven distribution. Slightly more than half of the destinations were located in the states of Illinois and Minnesota, which were the most attractive areas of settlement by Swedish emigrants during the 1880s. There is a certain congruity between the geographical spread of emigrant destinations and the location of areas about which agents could supply more detailed information. This applies to Chicago, Minneapolis, and St. Paul, all of which were popular destinations for Swedish emigrants.[16] Yet, as there is no sufficient correspondence between emigrant destinations and those areas with which agents maintained contact, it can only be concluded that agents' opportunities of supplying more detailed information were either not exploited or had little effect on emigrants.

Due to the terms governing commissions, it was economically more advantageous for agents to book emigrants to destinations as far inland as possible from the American ports. A study of possible influences on

[16] Compare Chapter 9: b, below.

emigrants' choices of destination has focused on individuals who changed their travel plans after establishing contact with the emigrant agent. It was found that agents could not have successfully influenced emigrants for reasons of their own economic gain, in that this particular group of individuals reduced its travel costs on the whole. The suggestion that agents did not exercise influence on the choice of destinations is also borne out in a case study by Lars Ljungmark of the emigrant agent Karl Möllersvärd and his assistant. Ljungmark analysed the agency's possibilities of directing an emigrant contingency, recruited for the Northern Pacific Railway Co., to settlement areas selected by that company in the early 1870s. It became apparent that the emigrants' own countrymen exercised the greatest influence on their destination choices once they had arrived at ports of disembarkation.[17]

In sum, the general impression seems to be that the emigrant agents followed correct business procedures in dealing with clients' inquiries on travel costs, various transport problems, and general informative details. To survive they had to create a climate of goodwill for their business on the emigrant market. In this respect parallels can be drawn between the representatives of the shipping companies and the representatives of American firms with a commercial interest in immigration. Agents responsible for recruitment of Scandinavian emigrants to the Land Grant Railroads were fully aware of the importance of reporting the facts correctly and seeing to it that promises were kept in order to achieve successful results.[18]

Potential and Actual Emigration

The correspondence between the emigrant agents and their clients also sheds light on the potential inclination for emigration during the 1880s. This is operationally defined as the percentage of letter-writers who did not emigrate but excludes persons with prepaid tickets. The average share of non-emigrant letter-writers was about 80 per cent. If one assumes that all of the representatives of the British shipping companies corresponded with the emigrant market to the same extent as the Guion Line, this would mean that approximately 100 000 persons corresponded with the emigrant agents during the 1880s without implementing a decision to emigrate. It

[17] L. Ljungmark (1971), pp. 185 ff. This result corresponds to "the stock effect", discussed in Chapter 2, above.
[18] L. Ljungmark (1971), pp. 137 ff.

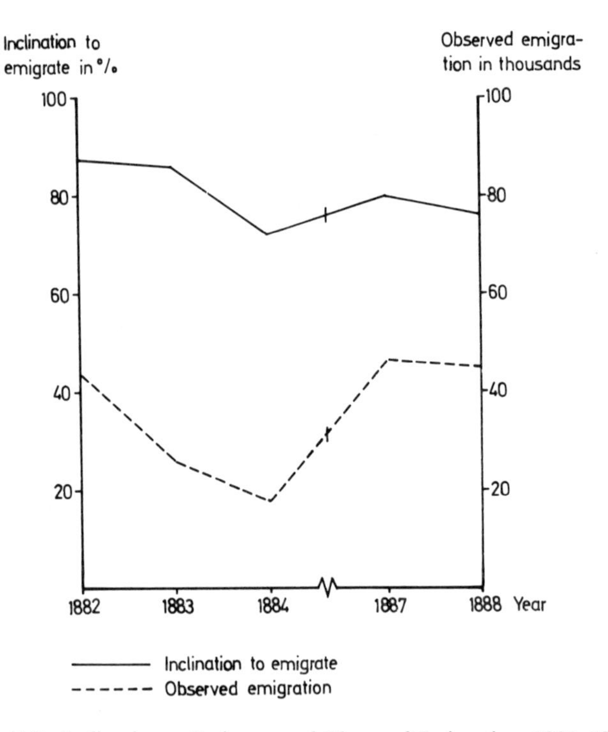

7: 3. Inclination to Emigrate and Observed Emigration, 1882–1884, 1887–1888.
Sources Bröderna Larssons arkiv, The Provincial Archives, Gothenburg; *Bidrag till Sveriges Officiella Statistik,* Series A: XXIV–XXVI, XXIX–XXX; B. Brattne (1973), p. 216.

can also be shown that letter-writers normally made inquiries on behalf of other individuals as well. An examination of the results of written contacts with the Guion Line representative reveals that each prospective emigrant contributed on an average of one additional emigrant and each Swedish American with five.

The projected relationship between potential and actual emigration vis-à-vis the Guion Line provides a basis for estimating the total inclination for emigration in Sweden during the 1880s (Figure 7: 3). It can be said that the idea of emigration was considerably more established in Swedish society than statistics on actual emigration would lead one to believe. There ought logically to have been a positive correlation between the variations in potential and actual emigration. Although the basis for studying this correlation was relatively limited in terms of potential movement, the results indicate an almost identical variation of intensity.

By examining different combinations of inquiries from all prospective emigrants it is possible to comment upon the level of potential emigration. Prospective emigrants who did not detail their requests are regarded as less inclined to emigrate. There are many points of uncertainty connected with such a study, and therefore the aim must be restricted to trace the tendency in the inclination to emigrate. During the early 1880s approximately one-third of our prospective emigrants can be classified as less inclined to emigrate. During the latter part of the decade this group constituted somewhat more than one-tenth of the total. Consequently, a larger share of all potential emigrants was decidedly more inclined to emigrate by the end of the 1880s. Out of this study population only one-fourth emigrated. However, the correspondence does not provide any answer to why departure plans were shelved or may be postponed for the time being.

Ship Building and Emigration

In general, the emigrant agents experienced a favorable market situation during the 1880s. Between 12 and 17 agents were active every year during this period. Ten of them represented British firms which handled approximately 90 per cent of the emigrant traffic passing through Swedish ports. As mentioned, cartel agreements during most of this decade helped to eliminate one of the major causes of competition, i.e. an elastic price policy. Under these agreements the emigrant agents could also expect to receive a fixed commission for every transported emigrant which was independent of the total passenger volume.

During the decade more than 350 000 persons, whose passage was arranged by emigrant agents, were transported through Swedish emigrant ports.[19] At the same time we have found an extensive amount of potential emigration. With respect to this great demand, the emigrant agents consequently had theoretical opportunities of increasing the sales volume. However, neither their information activities nor their elastic price policies, when permitted, could affect the size of emigrant volume.

Though it is conceivable that transport capacity *per se* could stimulate emigration in the way K. Hvidt has proposed, we have observed one factor which can pose problems for such an interpretation, namely a certain lack of tonnage at the close of the 1880s. It is possible that this situation was only temporary. Nevertheless, it appears more likely that ship construction reflects fluctuations in emigrant volume and not vice versa.

[19] *Bidrag till Sveriges officiella statistik, serie A,* XXII–XXXI.

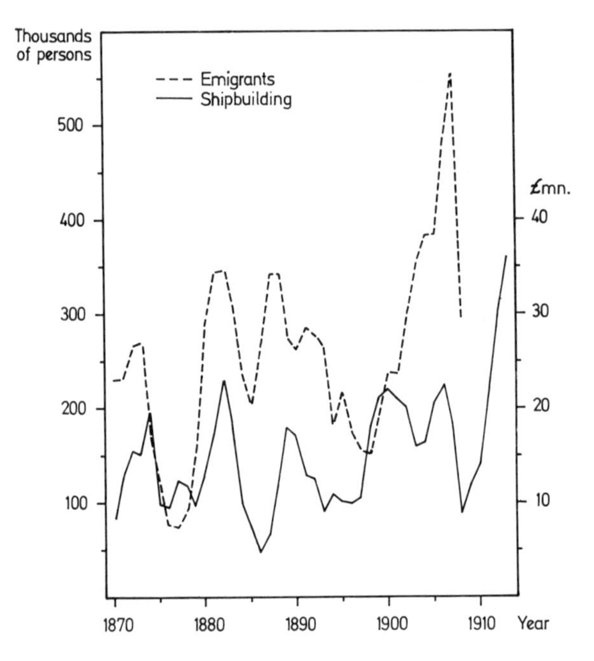

7:4. British Ship-Building Related to Emigration Via British Ports, 1870–1913. Annual Figures.
Sources A. K. Cairncross (1953), p. 169; *Emigrationsutredningen*, Bilaga 4, p. 117.

Figure 7:4 illustrates the volume of ship construction in England during the central period of mass emigration, as measured in sales prices instead of tonnage. This curve has been correlated with the most relevant share of European emigration, i.e. that which crossed over English ports. However, this estimate of fluctuations in ship construction includes other vessels besides those which plied the transatlantic emigrant routes. The same applies to merchant ships in general. Nevertheless, it seems reasonable to assume that the large fleet of transoceanic vessels constructed by the Liverpool lines in particular during the second part of the 19th century represented a substantial share of the total ship construction in England.

Judging from Figure 7:4, we might draw the conclusion that the prominent peaks of emigration were followed by peaks in ship construction with a lag of two years. This situation appears to have held at least until the end of the 1890s. After that the picture becomes somewhat more diffuse, and we can probably work on the assumption that other types of tonnage again played a greater role than emigrant steamships. As mentioned earlier, American shipping interests took the initiative from their European counterparts at this point. It is possible that the accumulated volume of ship construction prior to the mid-1890s, as well as new construction at the end of that decade, had an impact on the enormous emigration peak which emerged shortly after 1900. Moreover, it is likely that the re-organization of the entire transport sector in the late 1860s, which is not covered by our diagram, had a more dynamic significance for the strong growth of emigration than we have been able to register in this particular study. Unfortunately, it is hardly conceivable that future research can shed much more light on the play of conditions during this early period. The fact that shipping lines had already formed cartels by the late 1860s might indicate that the dynamic elements of an altogether open market were eliminated from the scene even at this early stage of mass emigration.

Concluding remarks

The spread of information about North America as a migration alternative has been discussed both in this chapter and in Chapter 2. Judging from our empirical evidence, the new transport organization, which was built up at the end of the 1860s, and its extensive propaganda, do not seem to have had more than a marginal effect on emigration. An established flow of information was already a reality. Still, the agents' massive if somewhat monotonous advertising campaigns could of course remind people of the existing possibility to emigrate.

It is no longer possible to maintain that the propaganda of the emigrant agencies could decisively strengthen the inclination to emigrate. At least concerning the mass emigration to North America, a series of investigations seems to show that the activities of the agencies and their method of operation were dictated by the strong fluctuations of emigrants. These fluctuations were caused by external factors.

The price policy of the transoceanic steam-ship companies did not play a very active role either. Through cartel agreements between the shipping companies ticket prices were raised substantially during the peak years of emigration, while at several times attempts were made to stimulate emigration during the trough years. This pricing policy was hardly successful in stimulating transatlantic emigration. On the other hand, the well developed cartel organization which had its counterpart within the coal and steel industries was remarkably successful. This means that the strong capital interests which were engaged in the North Atlantic shipping industry on a big scale managed to take more excessive ticket prices than they would have been able to in a more open competition. Those who suffered from this were the multitudes of poor European emigrants, who sought a better future in the New World.

8. Remigration from America to Sweden

By Lars-Göran Tedebrand

According to official statistics, 981 017 Swedes emigrated to the United States and 178 251 persons remigrated to Sweden between 1875 and 1930. This means that remigration during this period totalled 18.2 % of emigration. The stream of returning emigrants reached all delivering countries of emigration, and it was therefore a well-known fact that emigration did not always lead to permanent settlement and assimilation. Even the American naturalization statistics showed the varying degree of assimilation among different ethnic groups. Not until 1908 can we establish a certain comparative perspective on the territorial distribution of remigration. In that year the American statistics begin to provide direct reports of registered remigration by way of American ports. Between 1908 and 1931, a total of 4 077 263 persons returned from the United States to European and Asian countries. Among non-European nationalities Chinese and Japanese exhibit a high remigration frequency. This is hardly surprising, considering the formulation of American immigration policy and the psychological attitudes toward immigrants of these nationalities. Table 8: 1 shows remigration statistics for the most represented European nationalities and folk groups.[1]

In proportion to emigration, remigration was strongest among Southern and Southeastern European immigrants. Italians and Greeks in particular reveal a high return frequency. The high figures of remigration among nationalities which made up the so-called "new generation of immigrants" are partially due to the fact that around 1900 emigrants rarely settled in farming areas but rather in large cities and industrial regions—i.e. in labor markets which were the first victims of economic recession. However, this is only part of the picture. Of greater significance is probably the fact that mass emigration during the early 1900s contained contingents of trans-

[1] The American statistics apply to the fiscal year beginning July 1 and ending June 30.

Table 8: 1. *Remigration from the U.S. to Europe, 1908–1931, Distributed According to Nationalities and Folk Groups*

Nationality	Number	Nationality	Number
Italians	1 240 884	Hungarians	156 019
Poles	339 428	Slovaks	132 763
Englishmen	208 081	Scandinavians	125 308
Greeks	197 088	Croatians-Slovenes	118 129
Germans	161 342	Russians	115 188

Source *Annual Report of the Commissioner General of Immigration, Fiscal Year Ended June 30, 1931, U.S. Department of Labor.* Washington, 1931.

atlantic labor migrants. These particular migrations were part of an established pattern and, among other things, explain the exceptionally strong remigration to poor sections of southern Italy. Italian farm workers and farmers' sons who returned home as "Americani", after spending some time on the American labor market, resemble large numbers of their countrymen, the celebrated *golondrinas* (the swallows), who left for Latin America during the harvest season. The substantially repetitive element in Italian emigration is also shown by the fact that 10 % of Italian immigrants in 1904 had already been in the United States before.[2]

The rise of an Atlantic labor market must be set in a larger context, where the expansion of American industry and the late industrialization of certain European countries comprise the major components of the explaining pattern. International manpower mobility was a well-known phenomenon in Europe both prior to World War I and during the 1920s and 1930s, and it only reflected the varying developmental stages of different regions. The absolute figures of labor migrants are amazingly high. As early as 1886 a quarter of a million Italians were working in France, which was the most important center of international labor migration. In 1931 no less than 900 000 Italians, 500 000 Poles, 330 000 Spaniards, and 300 000 Belgians resided in France. From this international "visiting worker perspective" we must see a great deal of remigration from North America.

[2] R. F. Foerster (1919), p. 36.

a. Status of Research

Frank Thistlethwaite has rightly characterized this interesting research field as "the further face of the moon".[3] A glance at the international research situation hardly contests this statement. Despite the extent of remigration international research on the topic is conspicuously meagre: most countries totally lack such statistics or only have deficient material. Studies of Norwegian, Irish, Italian, and Greek remigration, for example, are based on census reports, fragmentary statistics, and interviews. It is true that such research has made a few interesting structural observations and presented findings regarding the capital investments of returning migrants and the effects of remigration on receiving countries. However, the quantitative sources are so weak, and the methods of measurement sometimes so unfortunate, that the results are both contradictory and problematic in terms of generalized evaluations. Several examples can illustrate this point. Censuses taken in Norway in 1910 and thereafter required information on returning Norwegian Americans. In an irreproachable study the Norwegian historian, Ingrid Semmingsen, has worked with remigration statistics in the 1910 Census. She found that 40 % of these individuals had been employed in American industry and mining enterprises, whereas only 10 % had been farmers. After return to Norway these figures were reversed: 40 % were farmers and only 11 % worked in factories and mines.[4] The transition among returning emigrants from industrial to agricultural occupations shows that the directional movement of Norwegian re-immigration broke with the migrational tendencies in Norwegian society, at least during the pre-World War I period.

The Greek-American historian, Theodore Saloutos, is the only researcher who has devoted an entire monograph to the topic of remigration. He has found an entirely different connection between returning emigrants and social trends.[5] Saloutos maintains that the urban life of remigrants in the United States dictated their choice of residence after their return to their native country. Although some remigrants returned to rural villages, the majority settled in cities such as Athens, Saloniki, and Pireus. In other words, the directional movement of Greek remigration would not only diverge from the Norwegian pattern but also—and more surprisingly—from the Italian.[6]

[3] F. Thistlethwaite (1960), p. 40.
[4] I. Semmingsen (1950), pp. 460 ff.
[5] T. Saloutos (1956), *passim*.
[6] F. P. Cerase (1967), pp. 67 ff.

Another example of this somewhat confusing research situation can be mentioned. With regard to the 1920s historians have made a clear connection between remigration and the radicalization of the Norwegian labor movement. On the other hand, the Italian researcher, F. P. Cerase, maintains that return migration played a conservational role in Italian society. G. R. Gilkey, however, reaches a different conclusion: the returning "Americani" established new attitudes towards the traditional fabric of society in their native country.[7]

Return migration can, of course, have changed character over time. Moreover, it is rather obvious that its effects on receiving countries varied in proportion to its intensity and the stages of development in these countries. However, it is difficult to free oneself from the suspicion that these differences of opinion among researchers can largely be explained by the confusing array of source materials at their disposal.

The relationship between return migration and the Americanization process—i.e. the technical and cultural impulses from America to Europe—is a complicated and important research topic. However, as long as we know so little about the structure and function of remigration, its effects on receiving countries must be considered an ancillary assignment. The major deficiency here is the inability of research to conduct systematic, statistical and demographic analysis of return migration from North America. In contrast to his international colleagues, the Swedish researcher of return migration has access to source material suitable for this purpose. Immigration was systematically recorded by parish priests in appropriate registers. Moreover, beginning in 1875 priests were instructed to transfer these reports to special immigrant lists in the *Summariska folkmängdsredogörelser* (Condensed Population Reports), which were submitted annually to the Central Bureau of Statistics in Stockholm.[8] These lists contained the immigrants' names, occupations, years of birth, and countries of emigration. From this year published records of Swedish population statistics contain aggregated immigration data based on this central source series.

Several theoretical and methodological considerations are appropriate before we describe remigration to Sweden from North America.

[7] G. R. Gilkey (1968), pp. 44 ff.

[8] See Chapter 3 above.

b. Return Migration as a Counter-Stream

Return migration from North America is not an isolated phenomenon in migration history. As early as 1885 the English statistician Ravenstein pointed out that every stream of migration gives rise to a compensating counter-stream.[9] Counter-balanced streams of movement always appear in connection with internal and external migration. Two Swedish examples can suffice as an illustration here. During the course of industrialization after 1860 hundreds of thousands of people migrated from agricultural districts to urbanizing areas. However, this population drain occured in stages and over a long period of time. The annual net shifts of population between the countryside and densely populated areas were rarely dramatic: nearly an equal amount of persons migrated in the opposite direction. Unemployment, assimilation difficulties, and other psychological factors forced many persons to return to the agrarian environment. Therefore, the direct return migration is very conspicuous with regard to internal population turnover. A study has shown, for example, that around 40 % of the migrants who left a number of typically forested parishes in western Sweden during the period 1930–1944 returned to the parishes of out-migration.[10] This counter-balance effect assumed even greater importance in the context of external migration. The substantial immigration to Sweden from neighboring Scandinavian countries during the latter part of the 1800s was balanced by a nearly equal amount of movement in the opposite direction.[11] What distinguishes Swedish emigration to North America in this context is the relatively weak counter-movement and the highly substantial, net population loss as compared with other countries.

It is, of course, unsatisfactory to regard return migration from North America as a mechanical counter-stream to emigration. Remigration as a self-perpetuating phenomenon can never be accepted as an historical explanation. The fact that we have called attention to obvious strains of labor migrants in the context of return migration demonstrates our accustomed objection to such a mechanical perspective.

A theoretical outline (Figure 8: 1) can prove useful in discussing the stages of remigration. The arrows do not symbolize any exact chronological sequence but merely theoretical changes in trends. Two components are included as explaining variables: 1) differences in levels of economic

[9] E. G. Ravenstein (1885), p. 199.
[10] J. Wallander (1948), p. 140.
[11] G. Sundbärg (1885–1886), pp. 37 ff.; L.-G. Tedebrand (1972), pp. 259 ff.

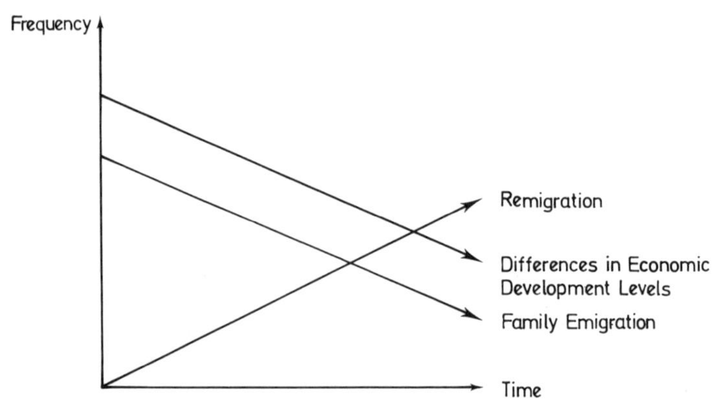

8: 1. Background Factors for the Rise of Return Migration.

development between the United States and Sweden; and 2) changes in the structure of emigration. New pioneer settlements, railroad construction, and industrial expansion in the United States up to 1890 should have had a sharply repressive effect on return migration. In this phase return to Sweden occurs at a relatively slow pace. It is not until the American industrial recessions of the 1890s and the acceleration of Swedish industrialization during the same decade that we can expect a strong intensification of return migration. Since mass emigration from Sweden had already culminated by this time it is likely that return migration also culminates at a rapid pace but retains a high level of intensity after 1900 as a result of increased numbers of labor migrants among emigrant contingents. In other words, the regression phase should be more evenly structured than in other types of growth processes. Improved communications and strong "America traditions" in certain areas can also have counteracted the regressive curve of return migration. The economic equalization between delivering and receiving countries of migration was most extreme during the international depression of the early 1930s. There is reason to assume that at this point return migration was even stronger in volume than emigration.

As mentioned above, we also need to emphasize the significance of emigration structure for the growth in volume of return migration. We cannot *a priori* expect any sizable degree of return migration during the early phase of Swedish emigration, which was dominated by family movements and concentrated to areas of colonization in the United States. In other words, the counterbalancing features of early Scandinavian emigration should have been far weaker than those of the early waves of emigration from Southern and Southeastern Europe. However, as emigration made the transition from family to individual movements the labor migrant element was automatically amplified in Swedish emigration. Another important fact is that individual emigration, more so than family emigration, was directed to areas which were sensitive to economic market fluctuations. Other factors as well can, over time, have amplified these counterbalancing features of transatlantic migration. After 1900 agrarian emigration from Sweden rises again. There is reason to assume that this phase of emigration contained substantial numbers of individuals who, for social and psychological reasons, preferred movement to America to proletarization in Swedish cities and industrial districts. Moreover, there is much to indicate that the repetitive element is amplified during the late phase of transatlantic migration.

Although it is possible to list general economic and structural causes of this remigration, the majority of returning emigrants made their decision on the basis of rational considerations. It seems reasonable to work with two major motives for return migration. Some emigrants can have regarded a certain period of residence in America as an interesting alternative to unfavorable labor market conditions in Sweden and can therefore have originally intended to return. One can expect a certain regulated phase shift between high emigration and high return migration. Yet, for various reasons many emigrants may never have been able to fulfill their original intentions of returning but remained in America for the rest of their lives. But return migration can also be seen as a process of rejection from American society. For various psychological and social reasons some emigrants never gained a foothold in the hard American environment and were forced to return to their native countries. Naturally, it is extremely difficult to distinguish between these two individual causes of return migration. However, detailed studies of remigration structure and its connections with American economic recessions can enable us to isolate some of these causal contexts.

c. Method

The Swedish source material allows us both to pose and answer a whole set of questions. What was the relationship between the volumes of emigration and return migration, and how did this relationship change over time? What impact did American economic recessions have on the intensity of remigration? What was the relationship between the regional distribution of return migration and major social transformations—i.e. industrialization and urbanization? Was return migration strongest to rural areas or was it primarily an urban and industrial phenomenon? In other words, was return migration positively or negatively correlated with social trends? Once these central issues have been approached with the aid of aggregated data, we can focus attention on individuals and study the relationship between places of emigration and return migration, the duration of residence in America, the structure of remigration, as well as the distribution and change of return frequency among different emigrant cohorts.

A convenient way of answering these questions is to conduct a "three-stage" analysis. Structures and contexts which can be established on the national level are tested and diversified by a gradual narrowing of interest to local and individual studies. A first stage involves processing mass data from official national and län statistics, as they apply to the relationship between the frequencies of emigration and remigration and between urban emigration and remigration. In this way we can shed light on the relationship of remigration to general migration tendencies in Swedish society. In a second stage we intensify the regional analysis by establishing connections between re-immigration to a large number of rural districts and their social and economic structures. Västernorrlands län in northern Sweden was selected for this intensive study. There are two main reasons for this regional limitation. First, emigration from Northern Sweden did not accelerate in intensity until the 1890s—i.e. during a period when a sharp rise of remigration began to countervail emigration. Second, Västernorrland comprises regions which in economic and social respects are clearly distinct from each other: this stems from the explosive expansion of the saw mill industry during the latter part of the 1800s. In a third stage of analysis we determine return frequency for a large number of emigrant cohorts. The Sundsvall district, which has Europe's and perhaps the world's largest compact area of timber industries, has been selected for this detailed analysis. Chronologically the study encompasses the period 1875–1913, but certain lines are extended up to 1930, which marks the end of mass emigration from Sweden.[12]

[12] This discussion is primarily based on L.-G. Tedebrand (1972), pp. 222–258. Remigration to Sweden has also been treated briefly by H. Nelson (*Emigrationsutredningen*, Bilaga VIII, pp. 77 ff.); E. De Geer (1959), p. 215; B. Odén (1963), pp. 270 f.; L. Ljungmark (1965), pp. 176 f.; S. Carlsson (1968), pp. 103 ff.; and in more detail by B. Kronborg and T. Nilsson (1975), pp. 144 ff.

Mass emigration resulted in considerable technical improvements and an increase in the capacity of the Atlantic passenger traffic from small sailing ships to big liners. The brig Ella built in Rostock 1867. Emigrantinstitutet, Växjö.

The Rollo, a steamer which carried many Swedes to America at the end of the 19th century, Emigrantinstitutet, Växjö.

A European emigrant liner, The White Star Olympic, built in 1911, 45,324 tons. Emigrantinstitutet, Växjö.

B. B. PETERSON

Befullmägtigad för Konungariket Sverige.

GÖTEBORG

Några allmännyttiga råd för utvandrare till AMERIKA.

N:o 1. Den som har god utkomst i Sverige, bör stanna der, heldre än söka det obekanta, skulle deremot förmärkas, det ej inkomsterna motsvara utgifterna, res då till Amerika medan medel finnas dertill då möjligen något öfverskott kan beredas vid framkomsten, för att der börja en ny verksamhet, och har Amerika bland sina svårigheter, fördelar att erbjuda, som intet annat land kan göra det stridigt.

N:o 2. Hvar och en som fruktar kroppsarbete bör ej utvandra.

N:o 3. Hys inga öfverdrifna förhoppningar, och du skall lyckas.

N:o 4. Var nykter, redbar och flitig, och du skall lyckas här bättre än annorstädes, ty dessa egenskaper äro de som aktas och betalas i Amerika, ty der nedsätter lättjan och arbetet adlar.

N:o 5. Börja resan under ett fast beslut, att med tålamod, kraft och ihärdighet bereda dig ett hem och du skall lyckas.

N:o 8. Jordbrukare, handtverkare och arbetskarlar samt tjenstflickor kunna alltid beräkna en säker och god utkomst.

N:o 9. Haf medförda kistor och säckar väl och tydligt märkta, nedlägg ej penningar uti dem.

N:o 12. Tag väl vara på lösa tillhörigheter och lemna dem aldrig utan tillsyn ty någon medpassagerare torde då undansticka dem, särdeles då de Irländska kommit ombord.

Martin Olsson
Kontor Sillgatan 44, Göteborg

Pris: ota

gällande från Göteborg till nedannämnda platser i Amerika.

Städers namn	Staters namn	Rdr.	öre
Boston	Massachusetts	132	50
Chikago	Illinois	173	25
Detroit	Michigan	164	—
New-York	New-York	132	50
San Francisco	California	353	—

Barn under Ett år betala endast landstigningspenningar.

John Millar,

TILL CANADA!

På grund af den nuvarande dåliga penning- och arbetsställningen i Amerikas Förenta Stater tillåter jag mig att fästa utvandrares uppmärksamhet på Canada, hvarest denna kris icke utöfvat något inflytande. Den Canadensiska regeringen tillbjuder utvandrare, som bosätta sig der, 200 acres land fritt för hvarje familj och 100 acres för hvarje ogift person. Jemväl erhålles ett understöd af 18 rdr, som frådrages det vanliga passagepriset, äfvensom fri resa på jernvägarne i Canada från landstigningsplatsen till bestämmelseorten.

Goda löner och arbetsförtjenster kunna alltid påräknas. Den 1 Maj afgår en expedition till Canada under ledning af kapten Heller, hvilken är bosatt derstädes.

Öfverste H. Mattson,
Ombud för Canadensiska regeringen,
adress Göteborg.

30

Emigrant advertisement from the National Steamship Company in 1873. Soberness, uprightness and diligence are mentioned as good qualities for an emigrant while those afraid of hard labor are recommended not to go to America. Emigrantinstitutet, Växjö.

During the earlier phase of mass emigration most emigrants from Scandinavia settled in the frontier areas. Street picture from Helena, Montana, 1870. Emigrantinstitutet, Växjö.

Chicago, which was a center for the large farming districts of the Middle West received a considerable Swedish urban population. The Aug. Jacobson store, 182 N Halsted Street, Chicago West, about 1885. Emigrantinstitutet, Växjö.

For a longer or shorter time many immigrants experienced conditions in the poor quarters and slums of the big and rapidly growing cities like New York, Boston, and Chicago. Such environments have been photographed by a Danish social reporter. (R. Hassner (1970), *Jacob A. Riis. Reporter med kamera i New Yorks slum*). These people in a backyard on Jersey Street in New York in the 1880s belonged to the anonymous "other half" of the population. They contrast sharply with the successful immigrants and with the more well-to-do farmers, who formed the broad popular base of the Augustana Church (see below).

Whether they settled in towns or in rural districts the Swedish immigrants were soon ready to found congregations and to build churches. Church associations were of the greatest importance for the immigrants' social contacts. The Lutheran Church in Smoland, Kansas. Emigrantinstitutet, Växjö.

Table 8: 2. *Emigration and Remigration, Sweden and the United States, 1881–1930. Remigration in Per Cent of Emigration. Distribution by Decades*

Years	Emigration	Remigration	Remigration in per cent of emigration
1881–1890	324 285	18 766	5.8
1891–1900	200 524	47 138	23.5
1901–1910	219 249	44 029	20.1
1911–1920	81 537	37 153	45.6
1921–1930	91 932	27 474	29.9
Total	917 527	174 560	19.0

Sources Bidrag till Sveriges officiella statistik, Serie A; Sveriges officiella statistik, Ut- och invandring.

d. Remigration to Sweden

Frequency and Course of Development

The natural point of departure for a time-series analysis of remigration to Sweden from America is the relationship between return migration and emigration. Table 8: 2 presents decade statistics of emigration from Sweden to the United States and remigration from the United States to Sweden during the period 1881–1930. Included are percentage figures of remigration in relationship to emigration. A graphic picture of remigration frequency in per mille of the average population during the period 1880–1913 is presented in Diagram 1, where comparisons have also been made with total immigration to Sweden and immigration from countries outside North America. The graph curve of American business cycles has also been charted directly above the bottom line in Figure 8: 2.

The countervailing features of this transatlantic movement are still rather weak during the 1880s, and there is nothing to indicate that they might have been stronger during the early phase of mass emigration. The weak countermovements during the initial emigration decades were typical of Scandinavian emigration but may also have applied, for example to German emigration, which never appears to have had any substantial amount of labor migrants.[13]

[13] P. Marschalk (1973), p. 95.

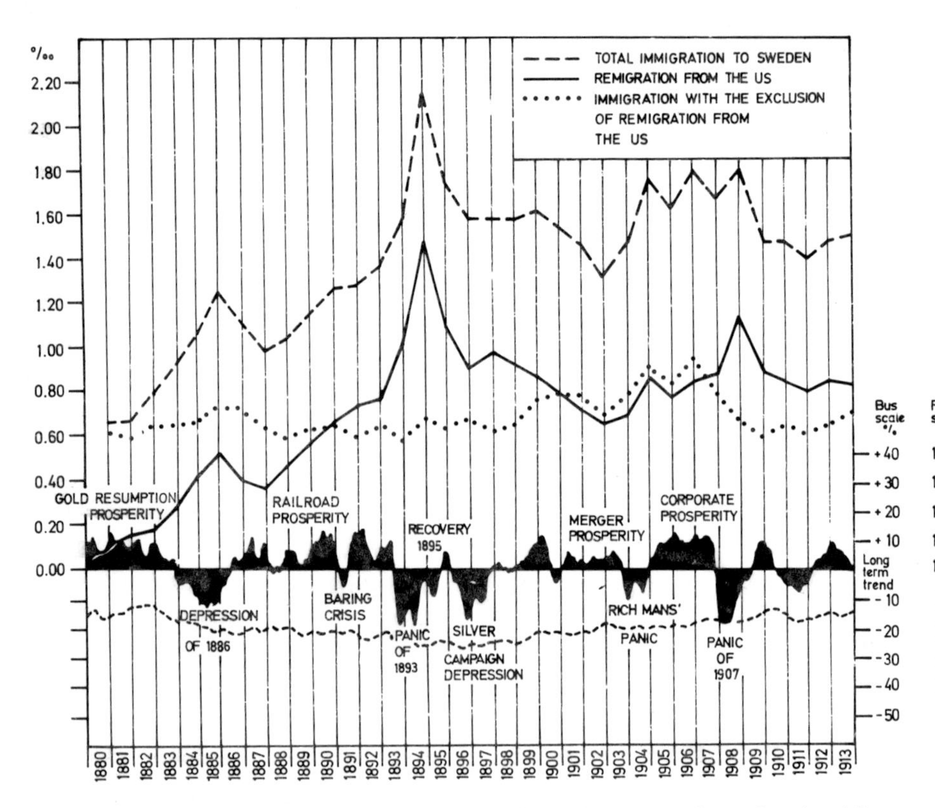

8: 2. Total Immigration to Sweden, Remigration from the U.S., and Immigration Minus Remigration from the U.S. in Per Mille of the Median Swedish Population, 1875–1913. American Trade and Business Cycles.

Sources Bidrag till Sveriges Officiella Statistik, Serie A; Sveriges Officiella Statistik, Ut- och invandring; J. A. Estey (1956), p. 20; L.-G. Tedebrand (1972), p. 225.

As shown by Figure 8: 2, the trend of remigration is already increasing during the 1880s. Return frequency reaches a peak in 1893–1895: this comes as no surprise, considering the American economic recession at this time and the structural changes in Swedish emigration. This is followed by a falling trend up to 1902, when re-immigration rises once again to reach a new peak in 1908. The rate of returning subsequently remains high.

Since remigration is dependent upon the strength of the preceding emigration flow, we cannot observe any mathematically regulated growth of remigration volume over time. However, the heavily counterbalancing features in this late phase of mass emigration are visible. At the same time

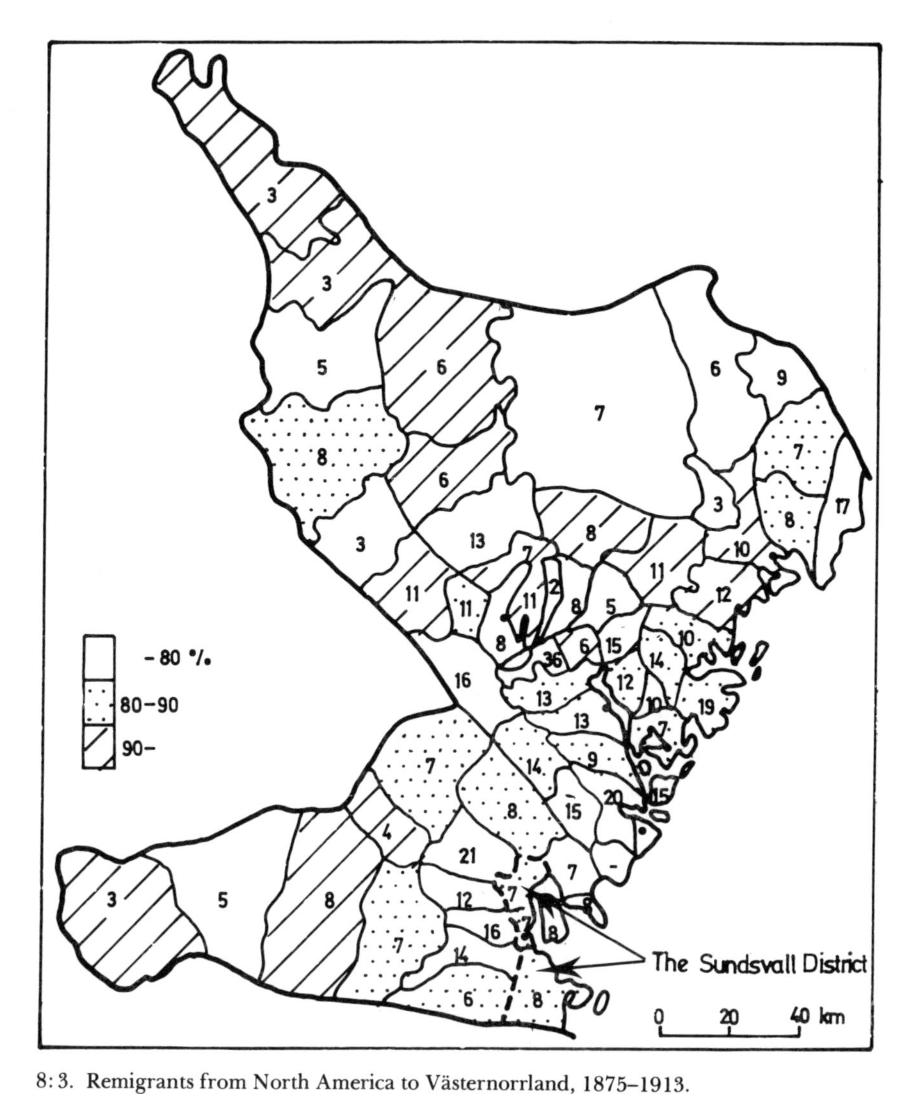

8:3. Remigrants from North America to Västernorrland, 1875–1913.

Comments Remigrants from North America in per cent of emigrants from Västernorrland parishes to North America, 1875–1913 (Figures). Remigrant principal persons from North America to original parishes of emigration in Västernorrland, 1875–1913, in per cent of all remigrant principal persons (hatches).

Source Registers of Migration, Parish Registers of Catechetical Examinations, and Parish Record Books from Church Archives in Västernorrlands län; Condensed Population Reports, The Central Bureau of Statistics, Stockholm; L.-G. Tedebrand (1972), pp. 236, 239.

it is evident that remigration to Sweden never reaches the frequencies established by the "new" immigrant nationalities.

Prior to World War I remigration frequency never exceeds 1.5 per mille (in 1894) and is never less than 0.1 per mille (in 1879). During years of particularly high frequency returning migration nearly equalled emigration—as, for example, in 1894 and 1898, when remigration volume amounts to over 70 % of emigration volume. Remigration exceeds emigration for the first time in 1918, as a result of the special conditions which prevailed during the war years. However, as was assumed previously, it is not until 1930 that remigration definitely surpasses emigration.

The rise of remigration occurs in obvious stages. The first occurs in 1882–1885, following the heavy wave of emigration in 1880–1882; the second in 1888–1892, following the prominent emigration of 1887–1888; and the third in 1892–1895, following the high emigration of 1892 and 1893. Remigration also increases after the heavy emigration of 1902 and 1903. As indicated earlier, the successive rise of remigration frequency reflects the fact that prominent years of emigration recruit large numbers of returning immigrants, partially independent of American economic developments. For example, remigration frequency rises in 1887–1890 despite economic prosperity in the United States during that period. In other words, there is a phase-shift connection between high levels of emigration and remigration, where the time interval is primarily explained by the length of migrants' stay in America.

On the other hand, the oscillations in the graph curve of return immigration are mainly due to American economic conditions. A comparison between remigration fluctuations and American business cycles reveals a very close inter-relation. American recessions triggered remigration, whereby Swedish immigrants were effectively removed from the American labor market. Remigration increased, for example, at the outset of American recessions in 1884, 1893–1894, 1904, and 1908. An extremely heavy wave of return immigrants occurred in 1894, when over 7 000 Swedish Americans returned home. In the fall of 1893 the American economy suffered its greatest crisis of the century, and the nearly 40 000 Swedes who emigrated that year met with wide-scale unemployment on the American labor market.

In contrast to the course of remigration, the curve of immigration to Sweden from countries outside of North America reveals a relatively even development. The oscillations here are to be seen primarily as a result of cooperative economic trends in Sweden and the other Scandinavian countries. Moreover, the curve of total immigration to Sweden is distinctly profiled by the curve of re-immigration, with its characteristically ascending oscillations.

This survey of Swedish emigration and remigration on the national level has shown that the countervailing features of early family emigration were relatively weak. Furthermore, an increase of emigration consistently leads to an increase of return migration after a certain length of time, greatly independent of conditions on the American labor market. The oscillations in the curve of remigration can be directly correlated with the alienating effects of American recessions on immigrant manpower. Due to improved economic conditions in Sweden mass emigration culminated before the turn of the century, and as a result return migration rapidly enters a saturation phase. However, an increased amount of labor migrants in this late phase of mass emigration helped to stabilize return frequency at a rather high level. Yet, remigration to Sweden never assumed the same proportions as it did to countries representing the so-called "new generation of American immigrants". Finally, the economic equalization between delivering and receiving countries led to a situation during the final phase of mass emigration where remigration surpasses emigration.

Regional Distribution

Table 8: 3 charts Sweden's population exchange with the United States for the period 1875–1913, as distributed by Swedish län and the city of Stockholm. It also shows remigration in per cent of emigration, the population growth of each län, and their share of the national totals of emigration and remigration. In relationship to emigration, return migration is weakest to heavily forested län in Northern Sweden and strongest to agricultural län in Southern and Western Sweden. The relatively low level of remigration to Northern Sweden is due to two factors: first, the prominent pattern of family emigration among saw mill workers and farmers in this area even after 1900; second, the economic stagnation in the sawmill industry after 1890. Generally speaking, then, there is an obvious connection between the strength of remigration and the regional phase shift of family emigration.

Naturally, the län which assumed a larger share of the nation's remigration statistics compared with emigration occupy the greatest interest in this context. Table 8: 3 shows that agrarian län with high emigration figures—for example, Kalmar, Gotlands, Älvsborgs, and Hallands län—had a

Table 8: 3. *Population Exchange of Swedish Län and the City of Stockholm with the United States, 1875–1913. Remigration in Per Cent of Emigration. Percentage Shares of National Emigration and Remigration by Län. Population Growth in Respective Län*

Area	Emigration	Remigration	Remigr. in % of Emigr.	Emigr. in % of Nat. Tot.	Remigr. in % of Nat. Tot	Population Growth
Stockholm	42 631	7 606	17.8	5.0	6.0	+146.5
Stockholms län	8 486	1 636	19.3	1.0	1.3	+62.6
Uppsala län	5 409	585	10.8	0.6	0.5	+24.9
Södermanlands län	10 333	1 731	16.8	1.2	1.4	+29.3
Östergötlands län	53 445	5 879	11.0	6.3	4.6	+12.7
Jönköpings län	52 797	6 218	11.8	6.2	4.9	+14.9
Kronobergs län	42 047	5 215	12.4	4.9	4.1	−5.0
Kalmar län	61 085	10 322	16.9	7.2	8.1	−4.9
Gotlands län	10 451	2 698	25.8	1.2	2.1	+1.4
Blekinge län	25 104	4 475	17.8	2.9	3.5	+13.8
Kristianstads län	44 016	7 232	16.4	5.2	5.7	+1.6
Malmöhus län	52 061	7 616	14.6	6.1	6.0	+40.6
Hallands län	44 130	9 131	20.7	5.2	7.2	+11.4
Göteborgs o. Bohus län	38 364	8 261	21.5	4.5	6.5	+62.1
Älvsborgs län	66 765	12 380	18.5	7.8	9.7	+1.9
Skaraborgs län	48 344	6 191	12.8	5.7	4.9	−4.8
Värmlands län	71 379	10 259	14.4	8.4	8.1	−2.6
Örebro län	32 514	4 381	13.5	3.8	3.4	+17.7
Västmanlands län	10 688	1 357	12.7	1.3	1.1	+29.6
Kopparbergs län	32 716	3 849	11.8	3.8	3.0	+27.6
Gävleborgs län	30 641	3 061	10.0	3.6	2.4	+57.8
Västernorrlands län	28 635	2 520	8.8	3.4	2.0	+70.8
Jämtlands län	17 129	1 434	8.4	2.0	1.1	+60.2
Västerbottens län	10 468	1 355	12.9	1.2	1.1	+69.4
Norrbottens län	13 706	2 027	14.8	1.6	1.6	+102.6

Sources Bidrag till Sveriges officiella statistik, Serie A; Sveriges officiella statistik, Ut- och invandring.

substantially higher share of remigration than emigration. During the peak year of remigration in 1894 the last three län had an even greater percentage of remigration than emigration.

Return migration amounted to 15 % of emigration for the nation as a whole from 1875–1913. However, the corresponding figures for the above län were 17 %, 26 %, 21 %, and 19 % respectively. In other words, remigration was strongest to agrarian län with a relatively slow pace of industrialization. Since this concentration does not decrease over time, it falls well in line with our prior assumption of a strong labor migrant strain in late agrarian emigration. Another immediate factor here is the significance of a long tradition of energetic "commuting" to America from farming districts in Southern and Western Sweden. External migration losses are somewhat reduced in the agrarian län if consideration is given to total emigration statistics—i.e. emigration minus remigration.

The lack of co-variation between the regional strength of remigration and the general migrational tendencies in Sweden during the industrialization period can be seen in the relationship between regional population growth and remigration frequency. The population growth of Sweden as a whole from 1875–1913 amounted to 29.0 %. Of the 9 län which assumed a greater share of national remigration than emigration, 6 have a population growth which is substantially under the national average. During this period Kalmar län, with its large amount of returning emigrants, suffered a population loss of 5 %, the second largest in the nation after Kronobergs län. On the other hand, population growth in Älvsborgs and Gotlands län was limited to 2 % and 1 % respectively. In other words, there is no positive connection between population increase and remigration frequency on the level of Swedish län.

Urban Emigration and Remigration

During the decades up to World War I agrarian Sweden was successively broken down by industrialization and urbanization. The urban share of the population rose from 15 % in 1880 to 26 % in 1913. This process continued during the 1920s, and in 1930, 33 % of the Swedish population lived in cities. As a means of illustrating the relationship of remigration to urbanization, a comparison will be made between the growth of Swedish cities and the strength of urban remigration. Table 8:4 shows the percentage of urban residents in the total population and the cities' share of emigration and remigration for the periods 1881–1910 and 1921–1930. All figures are expressed as a five-year median.

With the exception of the five-year periods 1891–1895, 1921–1925, and 1926–1930 the cities' share of remigration is somewhat larger than their share of emigration. However, during the remaining five-year periods there are rarely any pronounced differences in the strength of urban emigration and urban remigration. The sole exception is the period

Table 8:4. *Urban Share of the Swedish Population. Urban share of Emigration and Remigration between Sweden and the United States. 1881–1910 and 1921–1930. Five-Year Median Figures*

	Urban share of		
Years	Total population	Emigration	Remigration
1881–1885	16.3	14.0	21.8
1886–1890	18.1	17.9	20.6
1891–1895	19.4	22.7	19.1
1896–1900	20.9	20.3	24.1
1901–1905	22.3	20.2	21.4
1906–1910	24.3	21.1	21.6
1921–1925	30.3	27.3	24.8
1926–1930	31.8	30.6	30.6

Sources *Bidrag till Sveriges officiella statistik, Serie A; Sveriges officiella statistik, Ut- och invandring; Historisk statistik för Sverige,* Vol. I, Table A:4.

1881–1885 which, on the other hand, was generally characterized by rather weak remigration. On the whole, it is striking that return to urban areas did not intensify during years of high return migration. In other words, there is no positive correlation between the general course of urbanization and the directional movement of remigration. Urban remigration was only significant during the initial phase. During the period of mass remigration, beginning in the late 1880s, the cities' share of returning migrants only exceeds their share of emigrants by a very small margin. Despite the prevailing pattern of urbanization, there is no rise in the amount of remigration to urban areas. Table 8:4 clearly shows that even up to 1930 the cities were incapable of attracting a share of returning emigrants which corresponded to their share of the total Swedish population. These findings indicate that the proportion of urban and industrial workers among returning emigrants cannot have been as great as prior research has been led to believe.

The above analysis, based on aggregated national statistics, has demonstrated that the regional distribution and directional movement of remigration diverged in essential respects from the transformative tendencies in Swedish society. In this context remigration to Sweden seems to possess tangible similarities with, for example, remigration to Norway but diverges from the pattern in Greece.

The Remigration Frequency of Rural Districts

The above results relative to the directional movement of remigration can be examined and reinforced by a study of returning migration to Västernorrland.[14] Figure 8: 3 shows remigration in per cent of emigration to Västernorrland's 63 rural parishes. All parishes in this län have been divided into 4 main groups in order to relate remigration frequency in greater detail to social structure and industrialization level: 1) industrial parishes; 2) rural-mixed parishes; 3) agricultural parishes; and 4) corporation parishes. The term rural-mixed parishes refers to areas with a certain degree of industrialization, whereas corporation parishes represent areas in which the lumber industry had acquired more than one-third of farm and forest acreage by 1900. The following chart shows remigration in per cent of emigration among rural regions of Västernorrland for the period 1875–1913.

Parish	Emigration	Remigration	Remigration in % of emigration
Industrial	14 188	1 204	8.5
Rural-Mixed	3 482	306	8.8
Agricultural	1 680	213	12.7
Corporation	6 840	512	7.5

Source Summariska folkmängdsredogörelser, The Central Bureau of Statistics, Stockholm.

In Västernorrland as a whole remigration totalled 9 % of emigration. Remigration was substantially stronger to agricultural parishes than other parishes. Remigration to some agricultural parishes totalled substantially more than 1/5 of emigration. Remigration to industrial parishes lay under the average for Västernorrland, whereas that of rural-mixed parishes equalled the average. It is not surprising that corporation parishes have the lowest figures of remigration: in these areas the proletarization process was wide-spread among former landowning farmers. Remigration to certain outlying corporation parishes amounted to only 3 % of emigration.

[14] The analysis of return migration to Västernorrland includes the small numbers of immigrants from Canada.

In sum, the results of the national and regional analyses of remigration with regard to its geographical distribution confirm each other. Remigration is clearly concentrated to agrarian areas. In other words, remigration is strongest in areas which made the swiftest transition from family to individual emigration and had the greatest amount of labor migrants among emigrant contingents. Therefore, in certain emigrant districts where a phase shift occurred—as, for example, in the above corporation parishes—remigration was still remarkably weak after the turn of the century.

Residence in America: A Step in an Urbanization Process?

A central issue is whether returning Swedish Americans remigrated to their home districts or to other areas in Sweden. Similarly, to what extent did residence in America constitute a step in an urbanization or industrialization process among individuals? The agrarian orientation of remigration and its lack of correlation with social trends would indicate that such was not the case. However, on Figure 8: 3 a large number of individual studies can help to illustrate this complex of problems. The diagram indicates the per cent of returning principal persons (over 15 years of age) who settled in their parishes of emigration in relationship to all persons returning to Västernorrland during the period 1875–1913.

Figure 8: 3 clearly shows that remigrants from America moved in a static direction toward parishes of emigration. Around 80 % of Västernorrland's Swedish Americans returned to parishes of emigration. In other words, remigration reveals a remarkably "conservative" pattern. The most striking feature is that industrial parishes did not attract more remigrants from other regions of emigration than agricultural parishes. While 790 (or 84 %) of the 946 principal persons who returned to industrial parishes in Västernorrland originally emigrated from these areas, the corresponding figures for agricultural parishes were 136 (or 78 %) of a total of 175 returning emigrants. Nearly 90 % of those who returned to the wide-scale sawmill district around Sundsvall had originally emigrated from the area. These figures even indicate a certain return movement to agrarian regions by persons who had migrated to Swedish industrial parishes prior to emigration. All things considered, these results must be interpreted as follows: at the time of their remigration to Sweden, Swedish Americans did not settle in more urbanized areas than those from which they originally emigrated. In other words, cities and industrial parishes did not make sizable population gains at the expense of agricultural parishes in connection with return migration. This, of course, does not exclude the possibility that occasional returning emigrants did not settle in their old home districts or areas of emigration. However, as a rule this has not happened.

The "conservative" pattern of return migration is of substantial interest from the standpoint of migration psychology. Though not generally the case in migration contexts, it does appear that factors of social psychology can explain remigration. It is tempting to draw comparisons between returning emigrants' ties with their home districts and seasonal labor migrations within Sweden to extensive farming areas and rising industrial districts. A parallel can be made to the "rural-industrial barrier" which has been demonstrated in several local studies of internal migration in Sweden during the early phase of industrialization.[15] All of these phenomena symbolize the resistance of numerous agrarian groups to a permanent change of social and physical environment during the process of industrialization. A period of stay in America can have held far greater attraction for many farmers' sons than the proletarization process in Swedish cities and industrial areas. In many cases the "subjective" distance to America can have been shortened by a long tradition of emigration among agrarian groups. This interpretation provides a natural explanation for the strength of agrarian remigration and the surprisingly weak numbers of urban and industrial workers involved in the transatlantic migration of Swedish manpower.

Remigration Frequency

The functional nature of remigration can be illustrated in more detail by an analysis of its frequential distribution and change among different emigrant cohorts. The Sundsvall saw-mill district is suitable for this special analysis. It must be said at the outset that individual motives for the decision to remigrate are definitely hard to establish and usually defy meaningful analysis. Church records sometimes disclose very personal reasons behind the decision to remigrate. For example, four persons who returned to the Sundsvall district died only one or two months after their arrival, and in one case the cause of death was tuberculosis. Three women were reported to have suffered severe mental disturbances shortly after their return, and one of them was admitted to a regional hospital for care.[16]

[15] See, for example, B. Rondahl (1972), p. 259.

[16] The relationship between physical health and changes in workers' physical environment during the course of industrialization constitutes an interesting and important research topic.

Table 8:5. *Remigration Frequency Prior to 1913 among Emigrant Men and Women over 15 Years of Age from the Sundsvall District, 1875–1909*

Year	Male emigrants	Male remi-grants	Remigra-tion frequency %	Emigrant women	Female remi-grants	Remigration frequency %
1875	1	–	–	1	–	–
1876	2	–	–	1	–	–
1877	–	–	–	–	–	–
1878	1	–	–	1	–	–
1879	103	2	1.9	64	–	–
1880	96	6	6.3	91	3	3.3
1881	134	5	3.7	104	1	1.0
1882	109	8	7.3	88	2	2.2
1883	41	1	2.4	38	2	5.3
1884	22	1	4.5	18	1	5.6
1885	22	3	13.6	16	1	6.3
1886	18	–	–	13	–	–
1887	120	9	7.5	46	–	–
1888	105	9	8.6	77	3	3.9
1889	30	4	13.3	26	–	–
1890	40	4	12.5	21	1	4.8
1891	230	17	7.4	108	4	3.7
1892	365	47	12.9	235	20	8.5
1893	374	53	14.2	252	15	6.0
1894	39	9	23.1	87	3	3.6
1895	32	4	12.5	55	2	3.8
1896	24	4	16.7	41	1	2.6
1897	5	1	20.0	22	3	15.8
1898	20	–	–	27	1	3.7
1899	30	3	10.3	59	5	8.9
1900	36	2	5.6	72	9	13.0
1901	104	10	10.0	66	6	9.1
1902	305	29	9.5	203	15	7.4
1903	226	20	9.0	176	14	8.2
1904	62	5	8.1	90	8	9.8
1905	107	4	4.2	82	–	–
1906	175	15	8.6	107	9	9.1
1907	127	12	9.4	112	11	9.8
1908	42	2	5.4	52	3	6.5
1909	159	14	8.8	90	4	4.6
Total	3 304	305	9.2	2 541	147	5.8

Tabulatory material enables us to isolate more general tendencies. Table 8:5 shows the per cent of returning emigrants prior to 1913 in each emigrant age cohort (men and women over 15 years of age) from the Sundsvall district during the period 1875–1913. As indicated above, we cannot expect to see any mathematically regulated growth of remigration frequency. Hypothetically speaking, the following factors can have been significant for the fluctuations of this frequency. Large emigrant populations, especially after 1890 when family emigration began to decline, contained many labor migrants for whom the journey to America was only a temporary alternative to unfavorable prospects on the Swedish labor market. The American recessions promoted remigration by alienating immigrant manpower, and female remigration rose over time as a result of increased emigration by unmarried women after the turn of the century.

Few emigrants who came to America before the middle of the 1880s returned to Sweden (Table 8: 5). The expansion of the American economy during this period, together with the strong element of family emigration among sawmill workers, had a curbing effect on remigration. However, a powerful increase of return migration can be observed among those emigrants who confronted the American depression in 1885. Major interest here is directed to the return frequency among large emigrant contingents from the Sundsvall district in 1892 and 1893, which met with the American economic crisis in the fall of 1893. The frequency of remigration among male emigrants in 1892–1894 varies between 13 and 23 % as against 9 % for the entire study period. Even the few male emigrants who confronted the depression in 1896–1897 show a high frequency of return. After 1900 we can observe a relatively high frequency of remigration among the large, male emigrant populations of 1901–1903. On the other hand, the frequency decline among those who immigrated to America during favorable economic cycles in 1905–1906.

The frequency of remigration among women reveals less correlation with fluctuations in American business cycles than the frequency among men. This is particularly evident in 1893 and 1894 and is definitely related to the fact that women were employed in branches which were less sensitive to economic fluctuations. Large numbers of them worked in private homes. However, their frequency of remigration grew gradually. Of those

---

Sources Registers of Migration, Parish Registers of Catechetical Examinations, Parish Record Books, Parish Church Archives in the Sundsvall District; *Summariska folkmängdsredogörelser,* The Central Bureau of Statistics, Stockholm.

who emigrated during the period 1880–1889, men accounted for a 7% frequency of return and women 3%. From 1890 to 1899 the sexual composition of remigration frequency was 12% for men and 6% for women, whereas from 1900–1909 the frequency of women was not appreciably lower than that of men—i.e. 7.5% as opposed to 8%. In other words, there was a strong phase shift of remigration by women as compared with that by men. This reflects the chronological phase shift of emigration by unmarried women in relationship to emigration by unmarried men.

The functional nature of remigration can be further illuminated if we expand this study to include the distribution of remigration frequency among different emigrant age groups. The statistical section of this study is omitted here.[17] Male emigrants aged 35–44 years have the strongest frequency of return. Only during the strong family emigration of the 1880s do these age groups show any weak return frequency. A particularly high frequency is noted among middle-aged males who came to America during peak years of emigration. Of those aged 35–39 and 40–44 years who emigrated in 1892, 1893, and 1902—i.e. during years of severe economic recession in the sawmill industry—remigration accounted for respective figures of 17%, 10%, and 19%; and 15%, 18%, and 22%.

The fluctuations of remigration frequency among employed middle-aged males are instructive examples of the way in which periods of high unemployment in Sweden forced some married workers to seek temporary employment in America. One should also note that the assimilation capacity of middle-aged men may have been less than that of younger males. However, this factor does not explain the short-term fluctuations of remigration frequency among middle-aged workers.

The remigration frequency of middle-aged female emigrants was strikingly low. Most of them emigrated with their families, and therefore their share of what can be called the transatlantic labor migration of middle-aged men is eliminated.

A measurement of remigration frequency among older emigrants appears of little value due to the low, absolute figures recorded for these groups. However, it is clear that older emigrants who were retired did not return to Sweden. It is likely that such persons came to America in order to join their children who had emigrated at an earlier date.

This analysis of remigration frequency among different emigrant age cohorts has been limited to one sawmill district in Sweden. However, it is

[17] This study is based on Table 66 in L.-G. Tedebrand (1972), p. 249.

probable that the results can be generalized. Due to the family character of Swedish emigration the frequency of remigration was low among men and women up until the middle of the 1880s. During the period of mass remigration in the 1890s the frequency among male emigrants was strikingly prominent, especially with regard to middle-aged cohorts. The migrant labor character of emigration was amplified during economic recessions in Sweden. This led to a tangible rise of remigration frequency among middle-aged male cohorts. The effects of American business recessions also heightened this frequency by alienating immigrant manpower from the American labor market. Remigration frequency among females increased after 1900. Older emigrants, finally, had a low frequency of return.

The Demographic Structure of Remigration

We should naturally expect that the migrant labor strain in remigration led to an even stronger overrepresentation of men among remigrants as compared to emigrants. Remigration to Sweden from America was, in fact, a clearly male phenomenon. The following chart shows the sexual distribution of adults (children under 15 years of age are omitted) in the population exchange between Sweden and the United States for 3 ten-year periods. The proportion of married migrants of both sexes is also indicated.

During the 1880s, 3 out of every 4 returning emigrants were men. Although this male dominance later declined, men still accounted for 64 % of adult returning emigrants during the 1920s. The increased remigration of women was not, of course, due to a weakened frequency of return by migrant labor. Rather, it should be connected with short-range evaluations of employment prospects which had become more common among female emigrants.

	Emigrants				Returning emigrants			
	Men %	Married %	Women %	Married %	Men %	Married %	Women %	Married %
1881–1890	57.6	21.7	42.4	24.5	74.2	30.0	25.8	42.6
1891–1900	52.7	17.9	47.3	16.3	65.5	33.6	34.5	34.4
1921–1930	65.8	15.7	34.2	24.9	64.0	27.7	36.0	38.9

Table 8: 6. *The Age Structure of Swedish Overseas Migration, 1891–1900*

Ages	Emigrants		Remigrants	
	Number	%	Number	%
0–14	29 578	14.5	6 851	14.2
15–19	48 603	23.8	1 504	3.1
20–24	56 940	27.8	6 754	14.0
25–29	27 628	13.5	9 774	20.3
30–34	15 246	7.5	8 833	18.4
35–39	9 056	4.4	5 588	11.6
40–44	5 248	2.6	3 317	6.9
45–49	3 411	1.7	1 929	4.0
50–	8 733	4.3	3 571	7.4
Total	204 513	100.0	48 121	100.0

Sources Bidrag till Sveriges officiella statistik, Serie A.

The relatively high percentage of married persons among returning emigrants may come as some surprise. We can, in fact, illustrate the mechanisms of remigration by focusing special attention on the civil status of returning males. The Sundsvall district can exemplify this situation: 124 (or 74 %) of the 168 married men who returned to this district from 1875 to 1913 emigrated and remigrated without their families. The per cent of married men who returned on their own culminated from 1890 to 1894. The distribution of civil status among returning emigrants can thus also shed interesting light on the migrant labor strain in remigration.

In light of the principal interpretation of remigration outlined above, we should not expect any dramatic differences in the age distribution of emigrants and returning migrants. Table 8: 6 presents a comparison between the age structure of emigrants and remigrants during the decade 1891–1900.[18]

Remigrants represented able-bodied age groups to a very strong degree. The type of "pensioner-immigrant" common to the 1960s and 1970s was very rare during the period of mass remigration. The major difference between these two populations is a rather prominent shift of gravity

[18] The table includes the relatively moderate exchange of population with other overseas countries besides the U.S. and Canada.

Table 8: 7. *Lengths of Stay in America for Male Principal Persons Who Emigrated from Västernorrland to North America and Remigrated from 1880–1913. Five-Year Distribution*

Length of stay in years	1880 –84	1885 –89	1890 –94	1895 –99	1900 –04	1905 –09	1910 –13	1880 –1913
1	6	20	86	10	80	75	76	352
2	8	7	42	32	13	54	43	199
3	5	9	13	41	10	45	39	162
4	2	6	8	35	2	52	30	135
5–9	2	17	11	67	44	65	66	272
10–14	–	–	6	10	16	8	12	52
15–19	2	1	–	1	3	5	4	16
20–24	–	–	–	–	–	1	4	5
Total	25	60	166	196	168	305	273	1 193

Sources Registers of Migration, Parish Registers of Catechetical Examinations, Parish Record Books, Parish Church Archives in the Sundsvall District. *Summariska folkmängdsredogörelser,* The Central Bureau of Statistics, Stockholm.

toward older age groups among remigrants. Remigrants aged 15–19 are particularly few in number, 3.1 % as opposed to 23.8 % for the same age group among emigrants.

The Length of Stay in America

The age distribution of returning Swedish Americans did not diverge dramatically from that of emigrants. This is due to the short amount of time which most remigrants had spent in America. The longest period spent in America by males was 24 years and by females 21 years. However, these are both extreme cases. Most remigrants returned to Sweden after only a few years overseas. If we regard returning migration as a stage in a transatlantic labor migration, then we can expect to find overseas stays of relatively short duration for the majority of remigrants. Table 8: 7 charts stays in America among male principal persons who returned to Västernorrland from 1880–1913. These statistics do not include returning migrants who settled in parishes other than those from which they originally emigrated. However, there is no reason to assume that this category of individuals would have diverged from the rest in terms of length of stay in America.

In most cases remigration occurred only one or two years after emigration. Not less than 71.7 % of these remigrants stayed in America 4 years or less, and only 6.1 % stayed more than 10 years. The reason for the low percentage of long-term stays in America is somewhat obvious. Long periods of stay ought to have led to substantial social integration in America and increased resistance to remigration.

Few stays of medium duration (5–9 years) are recorded among the strong wave of remigrants from 1890–1894. This is probably due to the fact that those who emigrated in the middle or late 1880s managed to become integrated in American society and resistant to the idea of returning before the depression of 1893–1894.

There are indications that the length of stay in America was socially selective. Over 40 % of the remigrants to some agricultural parishes in Västernorrland stayed for periods of 5–9 years in America. A number of studies have also shown that many farmers' sons bought farms in Sweden with money saved in America.

Improvements in communications or reductions in travel costs do not explain the long-term changes and short-term fluctuations affecting lengths of stay in America. This is demonstrated, for example, by the fact that extremely short periods of stay show no tendency to rise over time. Of decisive importance for the distribution of short periods of stay was the situation on the American labor market and its character of a temporary alternative to unfavorable employment prospects in Sweden. Peak years of emigration primarily recruit remigrants with short periods of stay in America. During the peak emigration years of 1890–1894 and 1900–1904 remigrants who spent one year in America amounted to 51.8 % and 47.6 % respectively, as opposed to 29.5 % for the entire 1880–1913 period. The clearest examples of labor migrants are doubtlessly to be found among those who spent only a few years in America. Generally speaking, the short periods of stay in America highlight the specific character of remigration as an integrated part of an atlantic labor market. Moreover, there is much to indicate that the repetitive element in this transatlantic migration was largely concentrated to remigrants with short periods of stay in America. All things considered, this "commuting" element comprised a substantial share of late transatlantic migration. Not less than 10.6 % of those who emigrated as passengers on the Swedish American Line in 1922–1923 had been in America previously.[19]

[19] *Sociala Meddelanden* (1924), 3, p. 173.

The short periods of stay in America contributed to the rather consistent pattern of movement by migrants returning to original districts of emigration. For most remigrants a period of stay in America was not a step in a process of social adjustment. A special study of remigration to the city of Halmstad, on Sweden's West coast, can illustrate this point. Of those who returned to Halmstad from 1870–1899, 93 % had not changed their social position during their time in America.[20] This finding falls well in line with the strikingly static and "conservative" character of remigration to Sweden from North America.

[20] B. Kronborg and T. Nilsson (1975), p. 158.

9. Swedes in North America

By Hans Norman

Nearly one million Swedes settled on the North American continent during the epoch of mass emigration from Sweden. At the start of this epoch the American farming frontier had extended as far as the Mississippi and St. Croix River Valleys. The time of arrival for various ethnic groups largely decided which areas of the continent they would eventually settle. At the beginning most Swedish immigrants came to America to acquire land. Therefore, they mainly settled in the Middle West.

European immigration to North America occurred in several major waves. The first came in the late 1840s and early 1850s. The majority of immigrants in this period originated from Ireland and Germany. The remarkably strong emigration from Ireland is usually linked with crop failures in the 1840s. A minor peak of emigration can also be observed at this time from a large number of areas in Sweden, particularly in 1853 and 1854. A new major wave of emigration followed the end of the American Civil War and was dominated by immigrants from northwestern Europe. At this point the proportion of Scandinavian emigrants took significant dimensions.

Immigration from northwestern Europe, the so-called old immigrant contingents, mainly consisting of Irishmen, Scots, Englishmen, Germans, and Scandinavians, culminated in a third wave during the 1880s and early 1890s. This was followed by still another period of extremely high immigration between 1900 and 1914. However, this stream of movement was dominated by immigrants from southern and southeastern Europe, the so-called new immigrant contingents.

A major share of the early immigrants intended to settle in the inner regions of the American continent to exploit the rich possibilities of farm land. Later immigrants, however, largely settled in the industrial cities of the Eastern United States; now the choicest land was already taken. This was true of Scandinavians and other groups from northwestern Europe but specifically applied to the great waves of immigrants from southern and southeastern Europe.

The present account of Swedish settlement in America begins with a source-critical study of individual data contained in the U.S. Federal Census as compared with church registry material of Swedish Lutheran congregations in America. A second section deals with the geographical distribution of the Swedish immigrant population as well as urban and agrarian immigration in concentrated areas of Swedish settlement. A third section analyzes issues regarding ethnic and social structure, the persistence of the Swedish population, and patterns of intermarriage. Examples are also given of activities in Swedish-American organizations and the Swedish-American press, of Swedish group consciousness, and of the controversial transition from the Swedish to the English language. A final section deals with demographic conditions among the Swedish-American population on the basis of a detailed methodological study of reproductive capacity in some areas of settlement.

a. The U.S. Federal Census and Swedish-American Church Records. A Comparison

The U.S. Federal Census has served as a basic source for studies of Swedish-American settlements and for issues regarding the settlements' ethnic, social and demographic structure. Therefore a systematic control of this source will be presented by the way of introduction.

The accuracy of the U.S. Census has often been questioned, but few attempts have been made to control it against other sources. The present method involves a control of the Census Manuscripts against church registration material held by Swedish-American congregations. In Pepin and Burnett counties, Wisconsin, the testing ground of this study, only the Lutheran congregations had a continuous registration of members. Therefore, the Census Manuscripts have been checked against this set of material.[1]

[1] Since 1968 the Emigrant Institute in Växjö, Sweden, has made an inventory and microfilm record of membership lists kept by Swedish-American congregations. An inventory conducted in Minnesota and Wisconsin in the Spring of 1968 revealed that the Lutheran congregations' membership lists best suited the needs and purposes of migration research. The applicability of this material was evaluated with respect to the amount of detail furnished on individual church members, their birthplaces, and parishes of emigration. The record books of the Mission Covenant and Methodist congregations have less applicability, since they, as a rule, lack the consistency of the Lutheran material. The Baptist Church records usually lacked all of the information essential for migration research. Their membership lists began at the time each person was received into the Church by adult baptism. However, there

The Federal Census material exists both in manuscripts and printed form. Use of the manuscripts census is indispensable for studies on the individual level. However, the census data for 1890 and 1900 could not be used in this investigation. At the time the original research was made the Census Manuscripts of 1900 had not been released and furthermore, much of the Census Manuscripts of 1890 was destroyed by fire. Therefore, the investigation of census manuscripts could be persued only up to 1880.[2]

Under the auspices of the Federal government censuses were taken for all states in the Union, every ten years, beginning in 1790. At times individual states have also conducted their own censuses, the so-called Local Census, during certain intervening years.

The original purpose of the United States Census was twofold: it was to serve the needs of internal revenue and provide a basis for state representation in the Congress. As an institution the Census successively expanded, and the method of assembling population reports gradually improved. The first Census only registered free persons (non-slaves), and specific names were mentioned solely in the case of each family head. Additional information included the number of individuals in each household, their sex, age groups, and race. As time went by the Census gradually covered a greater share of the population. In 1810 a factory census was introduced, followed by an agricultural census in 1840. Starting in 1850, when a thorough revision was made, special censuses were created to cover mortality and social statistics. From then on, the Census can serve as a wide source of demographic, economic, and social data. One important feature dates from 1850, namely the entry of country or state of birth of all registered persons. Therefore the 1850 Census can be used for research dealing with ethnic conditions in the United States.[3]

Among the information contained in the Census after 1850 the following can be mentioned: names of all persons; their age at the last birthday prior to June 1; sex; occupation (for persons over 15 years of age); value of real estate; value of personal property; place of birth (designated by state,

are exceptions: for example, the Baptist congregations in Isanti County, Minnesota (those in Cambridge and Stanchfield) kept consistently detailed membership records. (L. Ljungmark 1971, p. 254.)

[2] The Census Manuscripts of 1900 was made available to research in 1974. For the investigation of ethnic and social structure the local manuscript census of 1905 from the state of Wisconsin has been utilized. There is no comparable material for Worcester, Massachusetts.

[3] C. D. Wright (1900), pp. 12–50.

territory, or country); contract of marriage and schooling during the previous year.[4]

Other improvements came in 1880. In that year records were taken of the relationship between family members (members of households) and the individual stated as the family head. The civil status of registered persons became more detailed than before: individuals were listed as single, married, widowers, or divorced. The state or country of birth is also recorded for the parents of each registered individual.[5]

When the accuracy of the census material has been called into question attention has been drawn to one weak point: the census is based upon oral reports. Moreover, it has been held that the system of dispatching an enumerator to collect information on a house to house basis can have contributed many errors to this material. This would have especially applied to the pioneer era, when language difficulties were prevalent and surveyed individuals were not always permanently settled in an area. It is true that each enumerator was required to testify in writing and under oath on the census manuscript that the census registration had been "duly and truthfully made in accordance with law and my oath of office". Each citizen was required by law to provide the enumerator with correct information. However, it must be assumed that the mobile conditions of the American population often made it extremely difficult to record accurate statistics. In particular, the chaotic conditions following the Civil War have been cited as partially responsible for the errors contained in the Census of 1870.[6]

The procedure followed in this source-critical study of the Census involves a test of individual data against comparable information in the membership records of Swedish-American congregations. Consequently, it has first been necessary to establish the reliability of these church records. For this purpose they have been compared with the data on individuals contained in the *Summariska folkmängdsredogörelser* (Condensed Population Reports) at the time emigrants left Sweden for America.[7] A certain amount of out-migration by members of the Swedish-American congregations to neighboring Lutheran congregations took place. There-

[4] C. D. Wright (1900), p. 147.

[5] C. D. Wright (1900), pp. 58 ff., 166 ff.

[6] W. Petersen (1969), pp. 45 ff.; E. Ehn (1968), pp. 119 ff. For a more detailed description of the United States Census, its origin and construction, see U. Beijbom (1971), pp. 20 ff.

[7] For a more detailed presentation of the Summariska folkmängdsredogörelser, see Chapter 3 above.

fore, it has been necessary to scrutinize the accuracy and care taken with membership data in these instances of migration. Controls have been made in three successive stages, as diagrammed below.

1.	2.	3.
Swedish Church Records (Summariska folkmängdsredogörelser)	Swedish-American Church Records, (Membership Lists from Swedish Lutheran Congregations. Membership Lists from Swedish-Lutheran Sister-Congregations)	U.S. Federal Population Census Manuscripts 1860 1870 1880

The system of entering information in the membership records of Swedish Lutheran congregations in America resembles the system used in the Swedish parish registers. The most important difference is that the American records do not list individual occupations. Column entries with the greatest value for migration research are: full name; year of birth; place of birth; date of baptism; date of confirmation; date of marriage; date of arrival in America; notation of the parish from which emigration occurred; date of arrival in American congregation and name of the previous congregation from which internal migration occured; destination of subsequent migration. There are also special column entries on the cause of death, exclusion from the congregation, etc. Special records were also kept of baptisms, marriages, and burials (Records of Ministerial Acts).

The Lutheran congregations studied here are Sabylund in Pepin County, founded in 1856, and Zion Congregation in Trade Lake, Burnett County, founded in 1871. Certain records have also been controlled in two adjacent congregations, Little Plum in Pepin County and West Sweden in Polk County, both of which were founded in 1873.

As a rule, the congregations' membership records exhibit careful registration. A general impression gained from this type of Swedish-American church record is that the above system of membership enrollment was used until the turn of the century and often even longer. However, the exactness of certain membership data tends to diminish over the course of time. For example, the names of parishes of birth or emigration are sometimes replaced solely by the names of the home province or län or simply with "Sweden". Sabylund Congregation used these membership records until the 1920s, and even then the registry procedure was generally well performed. In Trade Lake this older type of church register was used until the early 1930s. Congregations gradually abandoned membership record books for membership card files. Thus the Records of Ministerial Acts in Sabylund were converted to file cards as early as 1911.[8]

There are three specific objectives of this source study. First the reliability of the Swedish-American Church records must be established. In this context interest is directed to controls of names, ages, and sex as compared with equivalent data in the Summariska folkmängdsredogörelser. Second, the United States Census must be investigated as a source of population statistics for the demographic structure of Swedish settlements in Pepin and Burnett Counties. Comparisons can be made for the number of children aged 0–14 years, sex distribution, ages, and civil status—all of which are contained both in the Census and the Lutheran congregations' registers. Third, the source control aims to provide a more general range of information concerning the conformity between the Census and the church registry material. This comprises a study of factors which are important when linking these sources: birthplace, various name spellings, name changes, and possible variations in accuracy between different census-takings.

The first stage in this source control procedure was a card-file registration of all persons in the Swedish Lutheran congregations from the time of the congregations' founding until 1880. This was followed by a process of record linkage: membership data in the Swedish-American church registers were matched for identification with equivalent material in the Census. In Pepin County the control procedure included the years 1860, 1870, and 1880. In Trade Lake where in-migration and settlement occurred later, the control was limited to the year 1880.[9] Using information on the parishes of birth and emigration from Sweden as well as the date of arrival in America, a certain degree of identification linkage was also possible with the Summariska folkmängdsredogörelser.

However, the possibility of comparing and identifying data between these bodies of source material was limited for several reasons. First, the Lutheran congregations in Sabylund and Trade Lake represent only one of the religious denominations in their respective counties. In Pepin

[8] Church Records from Sabylund and Zion, Trade Lake. For a discussion of the source value of the Swedish-American records, with particular attention to conditions in Chicago, see U. Beijbom (1971), pp. 346–363, and K. Olin (1973), pp. 3 ff. (chapter by U. Beijbom).

[9] In Pepin the identification process comprises the entire county, whereas in Burnett it is limited to one township, Trade Lake.

County there were two Mission Covenant congregations (Stockholm and Lund) in addition to a smaller Lutheran congregation (Little Plum). In Trade Lake Township a thriving Baptist congregation existed side by side with the Lutheran. Other denominations were also active in both study areas during this period.

Second, the areas from which these congregations secured membership did not conform to the counties' administrative boundaries. Third, membership in a church congregation was entirely voluntary: consequently, it must be assumed that some persons were never members of any congregation whatsoever.

All of these factors indicate that the persons registered in these congregations' membership lists only comprise part of the population surveyed in the United States Census.

Problems also arise in linking information from the congregations' registers backwards in time to data in the Summariska folkmängdsredogörelser. The American records do not always list the parish of emigration for their members. In certain instances only the parish of birth is indicated. Of 341 family heads in Sabylund 275 are listed with their parish of emigration. In Zion, Trade Lake, the corresponding figure is 88 to 51.[10]

This investigation revealed very small divergencies between the Swedish church records and the records kept by the Swedish-American congregations up to 1880. The names of members in the American congregations have almost always retained their Swedish form and spelling. This applies both to emigrants and their children, even those born in America. Names ending in *-son* are common, and most are spelled with a double *ss*. The old form of *-dotter* (daughter) was used in women's names, for example *Nilsdotter* (Nils' daughter).

There is a surprisingly large conformity between these two sources. This is particularly true for the stated years of birth, but is also largely true for the month and day of birth (see Table 9: 1).

Many of the birthdate deviations appear to be clerical errors.[11] The

[10] The difference in magnitude between these two sets of figures reflects the size and age differences between the two congregations.

[11] For example:
10/28 instead of 10/23 6/18 instead of 7/18
3/15 instead of 3/13 10/2 instead of 11/2.
There is a reason for the substantially fewer comparisons between birthdates in relation to stated years of birth. During the period studied the records of many parishes in the Summariska folkmängdsredogörelser only list years of birth.

Table 9: 1. *Conformity between Data in the Summariska folkmängdsredogörelser and the Membership Lists of Swedish-American Lutheran Congregations*

Congregation	Total number of persons covered by data	Conformity N	Conformity %	Deviation (N)
Birth Year Reports				
Sabylund	408	404	99.0	4
Zion	105	103	98.1	2
Birth Date Reports				
Sabylund	131	111	84.7	20
Zion	26	22	84.6	4

Sources Membership Lists of Sabylund and Zion, Trade Lake. *Summariska folkmängdredogörelser,* Central Bureau of Statistics, Stockholm.

registration procedure followed by these Swedish-American congregations was probably based upon the *flyttningsbetyg* (address change certificates) which emigrants may have brought with them from Sweden. On the whole, this section of the Swedish-American church records exhibits a high degree of accuracy and organization.[12]

Notices of transfer to other congregations also leave a very solid impression. All of the 65 studied individuals who moved from Sabylund to the neighboring Little Plum Congregation had completely uniform reports as to date and year of birth. Only one of 39 birthdates is incorrect among persons who moved from Trade Lake to the neighboring West Sweden Congregation.

Comparisons between the United States Census and the records of Swedish Lutheran congregations were based on the premise that discrepancies were due to in-accuracy in the Census Reports. As has already been stated, there is a considerable conformity between the records of Swedish-American congregations and the Summariska folkmängdsredogörelser. The minor deviations noted above have been taken into account when drawing comparisons with the Census. In cases where the deviations proved to be important they have been corrected on the premise

[12] A similar comparison between the registers of Lutheran congregations in Chicago and those of the Swedish Church has shown a conformity of 83 per cent. U. Beijbom (1971), p. 360.

that the accurate information is contained in the Summariska folkmängds-redogörelser.

Identifying information between these sources is often difficult and time-consuming. Several outside factors also complicate the picture. As mentioned earlier, the congregations' memberships were not always limited to the administrative county boundaries. Furthermore, the listed names of individuals do not always agree with one another. Those listed in the Census are often Americanized: for example, Karl becomes Charles, Johanna becomes Jennie, Kerstin becomes Carrie. Similar changes affecting surnames include Lawson (instead of Larsson) and Bear (instead of Björn). At times the spellings distorted because of language difficulties. There are cases where Gerda is written as Juda, Kajsa as Cioser in one Census and Kesith in the next. In extreme cases the only means of establishing identity of a family is to examine the relative age positions of the children.

Finally, it can be said that the problems of identification fluctuate, depending upon the person who functioned as the census enumerator. An appreciable difference was observed for Pepin County between 1860 and 1870, on the one hand, and 1880, on the other, when a Swede served as enumerator in Stockholm Township. During his term of office many names which were formerly unrecognizable regained their Swedish spelling. On the whole the Census Reports of 1880 are more intelligible than those of 1860 and 1870. This is probably due to the fact that the person in charge of the census-taking could speak the language, was familiar with conditions in the area, and was apparently well-known to the resident population. A similar improvement occurred in Burnett County, where in 1880 a Swedish enumerator was responsible for Trade Lake and Wood Lake Townships.

The accuracy of the Census Reports with respect to birthplaces appears to be good: only a few deviations have been noted. Also in other respects there is very little disagreement. The sex designations for a total of four children vary between the Census and the church registers.

Some demographers have questioned the accuracy of age reports in the census material. There are a number of common errors usually cited in this context. Children's ages tended to be exaggerated. Therefore, children are often under-representated in the Census. Furthermore, middle-aged persons, especially women, were inclined to understate their ages; some women even refused to give their age. It has also been argued that many people were uncertain as to how old they really were and therefore gave rounded-off ages like 30, 40, 50, etc., regardless of whether they were actually somewhat older or younger. This leads to accumulations in these even age groups.[13]

At this point a more detailed analysis will be made on the conformity between the age reports of the United States Census and the church registers.

In Pepin County a total of 157 households, consisting of 687 individuals, were investigated. Of all the 1 335 Swedes residing here in 1880 no less than 51 per cent were identified in both the Census and the Lutheran congregations' membership records. A similar investigation for Burnett County comprised a smaller population, since this study was limited to one township, Trade Lake, which was the first area to be colonized by Swedes in that county. A total of 27 households, consisting of 118 individuals from the township's 477 Swedes, were successfully identified in both source series (25 %).[14]

There was no accumulation of certain ages in the census material for Pepin and Burnett Counties. On the other hand, there were other inaccuracies, one of which appears to be of a systematic nature (Table 9: 2). Data on ages in the two sources conform in approximately 60 per cent of the total number of controlled individuals (1 154). In about 25 per cent of the cases the ages given by the Census are one year higher than those given in the church records, and in nearly one-tenth of the cases they are a year lower. These discrepancies comprise the same pattern and are of approximately the same magnitude in each census-taking studied. The results are uniform in Pepin County and Trade Lake Township. The lowest percentage of tallies between the sources (40 %) occurs in 1870, and this confirms what was said earlier about the unreliability of this particular census.

In other respects the discrepancies are not extensive, although they are spread over as long a period as 10–11 years. Of differences greater than one year, 48 can be singled out as too low and 36 as too high, in other words, about the same in both directions.

Two general types of census errors are conceivable. There are those

[13] W. Petersen (1969), pp. 61 ff. In passenger lists regarding Danish emigrants K. Hvidt has in fact reached such results. The accumulation of children below twelve years of age is probably due to the discount applied to passenger tickets on emigrant vessels for persons below this age limit. (K. Hvidt 1971, pp. 148 ff.)

[14] Many of the Swedes in this township were members of other denominations, primarily Baptist congregations.

Table 9: 2. *Conformity between Ages Given in the Federal Census for Pepin County and Trad Lake Township, Burnett County, Wisconsin, and in the Membership Lists of the Swedish Luthera Congregations in Sabylund and Trade Lake, 1860, 1870, and 1880*

	Number of persons	Number of persons with lower ages, given in the census (y.=years)						Con-formity	Number of persons with higher ages, given in the census					
		6–*w* y.	5 y.	4 y.	3 y.	2 y.	1 y.		1 y.	2 y.	3 y.	4 y.	5 y.	6–*w* y.
Pepin County														
1860 Men	32	2	–	–	–	1	3	17	7	–	2	–	–	–
%								*53.1*						
Women	31	1	–	–	–	–	1	22	6	–	1	–	–	–
%								*71.0*						
1870 Men	143	–	1	2	3	3	13	57	55	6	2	–	–	1
%								*40.0*						
Women	143	4	2	2	–	4	12	58	51	4	3	2	–	1
%								*40.6*						
1880 Men	372	–	1	1	–	4	26	257	77	4	1	–	1	–
%								*69.1*						
Women	315	1	1	2	2	4	30	202	66	5	1	1	–	–
%								*64.1*						
Trade Lake Township														
1880 Men	64	–	1	–	2	–	9	43	8	1	–	–	–	–
%								*67.2*						
Women	54	1	1	–	1	1	5	32	13	–	–	–	–	–
%								*59.3*						
Total														
Men+women	1 154	9	7	7	8	17	99	688	283	20	10	3	1	2
%		*0.8*	*0.6*	*0.6*	*0.7*	*1.4*	*8.6*	*59.6*	*24.5*	*1.7*	*0.9*	*0.3*	*0.1*	*0.2*

Sources United States Census of 1860, 1870, and 1880; NA; Membership Lists of Sabylund a Zion, Trade Lake.

traceable to incorrect reports from the surveyed individuals, either as a result of deliberate intention or lack of accurate knowledge. There are others, however, which indicate that the enumerator himself was negligent or misinformed as to the regulations governing the census survey.

The major age discrepancies probably represent the first type of error.

It can be assumed that some persons were unsure of their own age and of the ages of their family members. According to census regulations, it was sufficient if one family member answered the enumerator's questions. Every person 16 years of age or older was legally required to answer. From 1880 on this age was raised to 20.[15]

One cannot exclude the possibility that, for whatever reasons, some persons intentionally gave false information. Due to an uneven sex distribution in these areas there was often a large age difference between married couples. Eight cases of large discrepancies between stated and actual ages have been found, varying from 3 to 11 years. These are concentrated to marriages where age differences between husband and wife were considerable. In all of these cases the stated ages tend to diminish the age differencies.

However, the second type of error, due to the enumerator's lack of accuracy, had considerably greater consequences in the long run. According to regulations, the ages of individuals were to be recorded on the basis of their last birthday prior to June 1 during the year of the census-taking.[16]

This regulation seems to have met with a varying degree of compliance. The census surveys were taken during the summer, after June 1, and in some cases over a considerably longer period of time. Consequently, the age reports have frequently been made with reference to a later point of time. This means that a sizable share of the population has been recorded as being one year older than it actually was.[17]

It is difficult to pinpoint any real consistency in these age designations. Apparently some census-takers took age designations lightly. The following two examples from the Census of 1880 are illustrative: (next page).

The way in which the census surveys were recorded during the months following June 1 entailed the risk that many persons were listed at altogether high age specifications. The uniformity of the ages filed during these years in Pepin County and in 1880 in Trade Lake Township indicates that these results are not coincidences. Theoretically, there should have been small risks that declared ages would be one year short of the actual ages, for such cases would reflect conditions prevailing more than

[15] C. D. Wright (1900), p. 169.

[16] C. D. Wright (1900), pp. 152, 157, 166.

[17] In Pepin County most of the census-taking occurred during June and July. In 1870 it lasted until the latter half of August. In Burnett County on the whole the process took place during June and July, but in one township it lasted into the month of September. Cf. U. Beijbom (1971), p. 25 regarding conditions in Chicago, where the census surveys in 1860 and 1870 occurred during June and August and in 1880 throughout the month of June.

Name		Date of birth according to church records	Age at last birthday prior to June 1 given in the census	Census reports, discrepancy in years
Gabrielsson,	Olof	38 01 21	41	−1
Wife	Margaretha	45 01 03	33	−2
Son	Erland	66 09 21	14	+1
Daughter	Hilma	73 05 30	7	–
Son	Edvard	76 05 08	4	–
Son	Ernfrid	78 04 25	1	−1
Andersson,	Carl	36 03 06	44	–
Wife	Johanna	36 12 26	43	–
Son	Karl-Erik	61 04 06	19	–
Daughter	Selma Bernhardina	63 07 31	17	+1
Daughter	Wilhelmina J.	66 07 04	14	+1
Son	Carl Johan	68 12 24	12	+1
Son	Carl Edvard	71 05 22	9	–
Daughter	Alvina Christina	73 09 14	6	–
Son	Carl August	76 01 05	4	–
Son	Carl Aron	78 03 20	2	–

one calender year prior to the census-taking. Nevertheless, it is true that 10 per cent of the listings are one year lower than the correct ages.

Two principal results of this source analysis deserve special mention here by way of a summary. First, the individual data recorded by the Swedish Lutheran congregations in American have a high degree of conformity with contemporaneous Swedish population material. This demonstrates the importance of the fact that the Swedish tradition of population registration was adopted at an early stage by the Swedish Lutheran congregations. Inasmuch as these individual data were also consistantly well kept for persons moving from one congregation to another, it can be said that this registry material is a reliable source for demographic and genealogical research.

Second, the deficiencies observed in the census material for Pepin and Burnett Counties are not those for which it usually receives criticism. There are no age accumulations at even years, and there is no tangible difference between the number of incorrect age reports for children and those for adults. However, there is one systematic error caused by the condition that the census surveys were to cover the situation on one specific day (June 1). Since the majority of census surveys took one or more months to complete, some of the information was incorrectly recorded with reference to later points in time. Moreover, in some cases accuracy of age specifications was further reduced as a result of intentionally incorrect information or ignorance. On the whole the agreement between the United States Census and the church records is about 60 per cent. Almost 13 per cent of the ages are too low, while nearly 28 per cent are too high. The greatest accumulation of errors occurs within the range of one year below to one year above the correct age.

There is much to indicate that these findings have a general range of application: the regulations governing census-takings were the same all across the country, and the same seems to have been the case for the time of the census-taking (compare the conditions in Chicago). If this holds true, then the age structure of the American people as it appears in the census has actually shifted somewhat in the favor of lower age groups.

Age discrepancies given in the Census of 1880 have also been examined for different age groups. The discrepancies are rather evenly distributed. To a great extent those ages which are too high nullify the effect of those ages which are too low. However, there is an error of 10 per cent in 1880 due to overly high age specifications. Consequently, the demographer must be aware of the fact that an average of every tenth person in an age group is actually one year younger than his stated age in the Census of 1880.[18]

Since the majority of errors only represent one year's discrepancies upwards or downwards this defect in the census material ought not to be overestimated. Therefore, these findings hardly diminish the applicability of the United States Census as a demographic source. If one revises the age groups affected by each separate calculation one cannot only correct these errors but subsequently use the Census as an extensive source for statistical and demographic research.

b. Regional Distribution

Introductory Perspective

The underlying factors of the regional distribution of Swedish immigrants in America have been frequently discussed. Some members of the Uppsala Group have dealt with problems of this nature. They have examined the

[18] H. Norman (1974), pp. 346 f.

Table 9:3. *The Distribution of the Swedish-Born Population in the U.S. in 1880 and 1900 According to the U.S. Census. Distribution of Emigrants from the Sundsvall District, Västernorrlands län, 1875–1913, and from Örebro län, 1879–1882 and 1901–1903, According to Destination Reports in the Gothenburg Passenger Lists*

	All Swedish-born in the U.S.		Emigrants from the Sundsvall District[a]	Emigrants from Örebro län[a]	
States	1880 %	1900 %	1875–1913 %	1879–82 %	1901–03 %
Northeast	*15.01*	*23.09*	*21.79*	*26.31*	*37.11*
Maine	0.51	0.34		1.04	0.15
New Hampshire	0.07	0.35	0.18		0.88
Vermont	0.03	0.02	0.12		
Massachusetts	2.45	5.60	9.31	12.57	20.74
Rhode Island	0.40	1.06	0.06	0.06	0.98
Connecticut	1.07	2.81	0.06	0.21	2.29
New York	5.74	7.43	7.43	5.74	7.43
New Jersey	0.83	1.28		0.09	
Pennsylvania	3.90	4.20	4.63	6.61	4.63
Middle West	*76.54*	*64.21*	*67.50*	*72.65*	*58.99*
Ohio	0.61	0.69	1.00	0.18	1.51
Indiana	1.61	0.81	0.23	0.80	0.34
Illinois	21.83	17.25	11.78	21.41	25.18
Michigan	4.84	4.69	15.11	14.90	6.19
Wisconsin	4.19	4.56	14.29	2.14	3.46
Minnesota	20.16	20.10	20.80	18.77	14.35
Iowa	9.04	5.20	1.00	6.70	2.68
Missouri	1.63	1.00	0.06	1.69	0.98
North Dakota		1.47	0.88		0.83
South Dakota	1.63	1.50	0.35	1.01	1.12
Nebraska	5.23	4.30	1.46	1.07	1.56
Kansas	5.77	2.64	0.53	3.98	0.78
South	*1.71*	*1.55*	*0.76*	*0.51*	*1.12*
Delaware	0.03	0.05			0.24
Maryland	0.09	0.06		0.51	
District of Columbia	0.02	0.04			
Virginia	0.02	0.03			
West Virginia	0.01	0.02			
North Carolina	0.01	0.01			

States	All Swedish-born in the U.S. 1880 %	1900 %	Emigrants from the Sundsvall District[a] 1875–1913 %	Emigrants from Örebro län[a] 1879–82 %	1901–03 %
South Carolina	0.03	0.01			0.29
Georgia	0.06	0.03			
Florida	0.12	0.09			0.05
Kentucky	0.05	0.04			
Tennessee	0.13	0.06	0.06		
Alabama	0.06	0.09			0.05
Mississippi	0.16	0.05			
Arkansas	0.11	0.06			
Louisiana	0.14	0.06	0.06		
Oklahoma		0.09			0.05
Texas	0.67	0.76	0.64		0.44
West	*6.72*	*10.50*	*9.96*	*0.54*	*2.79*
Montana	0.14	0.93	0.53		0.19
Idaho	0.16	0.49	0.12		0.15
Wyoming	0.13	0.30			0.10
Colorado	1.12	1.87	0.59	0.33	0.98
New Mexico	0.02	0.04			
Arizona	0.05	0.06			
Utah	1.93	1.22	0.06		0.05
Nevada	0.16	0.05			
Washington	0.33	2.22	6.03		0.83
Oregon	0.51	0.79	1.58		0.15
California	2.17	2.53	1.05	0.21	0.34
Alaska and Hawaii		0.27			
	100.0	100.0	100.0	100.0	100.0

[a] New York figures are recalculated. This procedure is described on p. 249.
Sources H. Norman (1974), pp. 218 f.; L.-G. Tedebrand (1972), pp. 208 f.

likelihood of a connection between the economic structure in an area of emigration and emigrants' choice of settlements in the country of immigration. In the same respect, they have tried to estimate the role played by a special occupational orientation among the population in the delivering area of emigration. One question is whether emigrants' selection of first

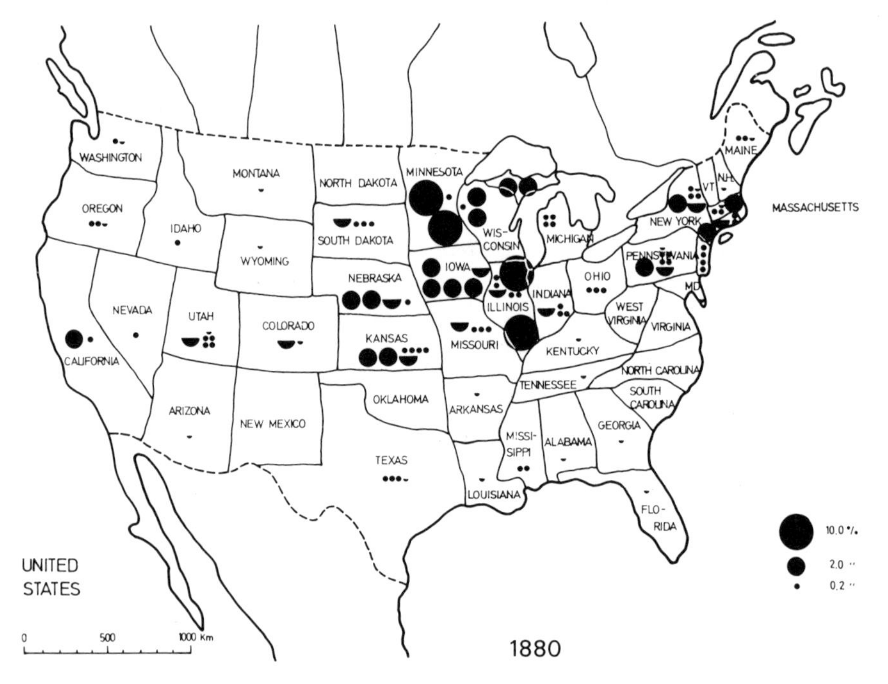

9: 1. The Distribution of the Swedish-Born Population in the U.S. 1880 and 1900.
Sources U.S. Census 1880, 1900, Part I; H. Norman (1974), pp. 218 f.

settlement areas stemmed from their judgement of prospects on the labor market and whether their emigration constituted an attempt to fulfill certain social expectations. Several research findings have disclosed how important the first place of settlement was, since it often happened that emigrants from the same home districts followed in the footsteps of the first pioneers. On the whole, this research has documented a number of cases in which a connection emerged between certain areas of settlement in America and certain specific regions in Sweden.[1]

The Regional Distribution of Swedish Immigration

Information on the general distribution of ethnic groups can primarily be found in the U.S. Federal Census, conducted every ten years, and in the local state census surveys which were frequently taken during intervening

[1] M. Eriksson (1971), pp. 7 ff.; L.-G. Tedebrand (1972), pp. 207 ff.; H. Norman (1974), pp. 224 ff., 235 ff., 265 ff.

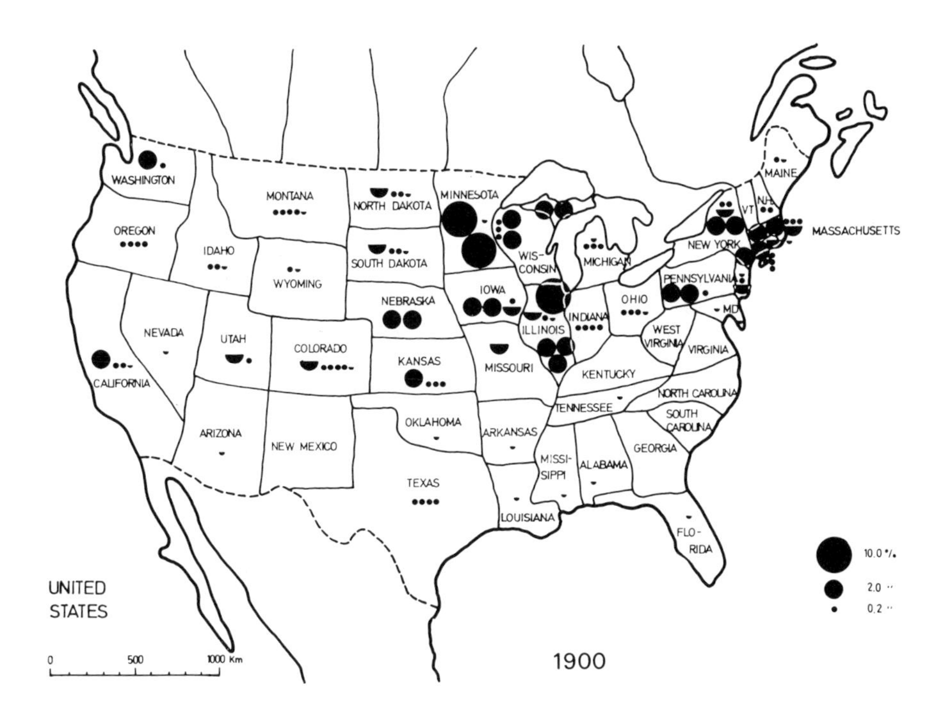

years. The U.S. Census gives the birthplaces of each individual but specifies only the state of birth for native-born Americans and the native country of immigrant persons. More detailed information on individuals' places of origin can be found in some church records—i.e. in cases where persons did belong to such religious denominations which conducted a thorough membership registration. The Swedish-American Lutheran Church was one of the denominations which kept such records. As a rule, this material indicates the birthplaces (*län* and parishes) of all Swedish immigrants as well as the areas in Sweden from which they emigrated. Notations on subsequent movements by immigrants to other parts of America are often included in these records.[2]

Table 9:3 and Figure 9:1 show the distribution of Swedish settlement based on the U.S. Census of 1880 and 1900. In 1880 Swedes were primarily concentrated to the Middle West, while around 1900 they were more

[2] See above, Chapter 9:a.

distributed in the industrial states to the east, such as New York and Massachusetts, but also in the states of the West Coast.[3]

Of all states in the Middle West, Illinois and Minnesota were the prime areas of settlement for Swedish immigrants. A rather substantial proportion also settled in the prairie states of Iowa, Nebraska, and Kansas and in the more forested states of Wisconsin and Michigan. As emigration progressed, the Midwest states lost some of their status as prime areas of Swedish settlement. The strong concentration of Swedes was further reduced by the early 1900s as a result of inter-state migration. A great deal of first and second generation Swedes migrated from farming districts to more industrialized areas nearer the East Coast. Relatively large numbers of them also moved to the Pacific Coast and, in some measure, to the South. This was especially true of pensioners and retired persons who were attracted by the warm climate of California and Florida.[4]

A comparative study of the regional distribution of Scandinavian immigrants in 1910 shows that Norwegians were most concentrated in the Middle West. At that time 65 per cent of all Norwegian immigrants resided in Minnesota, Wisconsin, North Dakota, Illinois, and Iowa, with the greatest proportion in the first three states. In contrast, these five states had only 45 per cent of all Swedish immigrants, 40 per cent of the Danes and 27–28 of all Finnish immigrants. The Danes were almost equally distributed among the typical farming states of the Middle West but also had strong numbers in Nebraska and California. The Finns were primarily concentrated to Minnesota and Michigan. Nearly $^1/_4$ of all Finnish immigrants settled in Michigan (Table 9: 4).[5]

On the whole, the chronological sequence of immigration by ethnic groups substantially reflects the area in which they settled. One example of this is immigration to Wisconsin. Like the overall pattern of American colonization from east to west, immigrant settlement in Wisconsin largely spread westward from the southeastern sectors and subsequently northward along the Mississippi. This explains why the Germans have their greatest concentrations in eastern and southern Wisconsin, whereas the Norwegians have theirs in the southern and southwestern sectors. The greatest concentration of Swedes is found in the western and northwestern

[3] Regarding Swedish emigration to Canada, see Chapter 5 above.
[4] L. Ljungmark (1965), pp. 129 ff.
[5] A. Svalestuen (1971), pp. 52 ff.

Table 9:4. *Concentration of Scandinavian Minorities in the U.S. in 1910. Distribution by States with at least 5 Per Cent of Each Minority Population. Foreign-Born Persons*

	Minnesota	Illinois	Iowa	Wisconsin	North Dakota	South Dakota	Michigan	Nebraska	New York	Massachusetts	Washington	California
Swedes	18.4	17.2							8.1	5.9		
Norwegians	26.0	8.2	5.4	14.1	11.4	5.2			6.2		6.9	
Danes	8.8	9.5	9.9	9.0				7.5	6.9			7.8
Finns	20.5						24.0		6.8	8.2	6.7	

Source A. Svalestuen (1971), p. 53.

sectors, whereas the Finns largely settled in the northernmost portions of Wisconsin where colonization had begun at a comparatively late date.[6]

The Reliability of Emigrant Destination Reports

Swedish passenger lists provide the source material for this study of emigrant destinations. These lists include notations of the *län* and parish of emigration and the place of destination in the country of immigration as stated on emigrant tickets. Since the majority of Swedish emigrants embarked from Gothenburg, the passenger lists of this port have been used.

Source analyses show that these lists are preserved nearly intact and that the destination reports fully conform to the emigrant contracts signed by emigrants and shipping representatives. Moreover, some emigrant agents evidently received a commission on tickets issued for passage on American railroads. It was therefore profitable for them to arrange emigrant destinations as far west as possible.[7] This fact might contribute to the relatively high degree of conformity between destination reports in the passenger lists and the actual goal of emigrants upon arrival in America.

It is difficult to make detailed comparisons between the reported destination and the actual areas of settlement due to the fragmentary and

[6] H. Nelson (1943), Vol. I, p. 184, Vol. II, Map 22; C. C. Qualey (1938), p. 65; C.-H. Smith (1931), pp. 419 ff.
[7] See Chapter 3, above; B. Brattne (1973), pp. 74 ff., 244.

problematic nature of the American source materials. However, a number of observations regarding emigration from Örebro län can serve as the basis for more fundamental conclusions.[8]

During an early phase of emigration large numbers of emigrants traveled westward over Chicago to the Mississippi River and then by steamboat to Wisconsin and Minnesota. Since many of the steamboat landings were located on the Minnesota side, this state is overly represented in the destination reports. In reality, however, many emigrants were traveling to areas on the Wisconsin side.

The numerous emigrants from Örebro län who settled in Stockholm, Wisconsin are illustrative. In 1879–1883 none of them was officially reported to this destination. On the other hand, as many as 146 persons were reported destined for Lake City, a steamboat landing on the Minnesota side of the Mississippi.

A further example is represented by the scores of emigrants from Ljusnarsberg parish in Örebro län who settled in Trade Lake, Burnett County, Wisconsin. Prior to 1897 none of these emigrants was reported in the passenger lists as destined for Trade Lake. The commonest destination was Rush City in Minnesota, which was the nearest station stop on the railroad between St. Paul and Duluth. After 1900 the accuracy of the destination reports improves. In 1903, for example, 13 immigrants are reported as destined for Grantsburg in Burnett County.[9]

Both examples show that the passenger lists' destination reports are misleading in those cases where a steamboat landing or station stop was in one state and the intended area of settlement lay in a neighboring state. This explains why Minnesota was the reported destination of many emigrants actually bound for Wisconsin. However, these distortions in the registration of destinations must be assumed as exceptions to the rule. Other studies reveal a substantially greater conformity. The Långasjö study, for example, which closely follows emigrants on the American continent, observes that destination reports in the passenger lists usually correspond to the actual areas of settlement. It also underlines, however, that emigrant arrivals in New York distort this conformity. M. Eriksson has reached similar results in studying the conformity between individual data

[8] This account is based on H. Norman (1974), pp. 221–224.

[9] An improvement is also observed with respect to New York. From 1879–1883 not less than 44 per cent of the emigrants from Örebro län who embarked from Gothenburg are reported as destined for New York, whereas from 1901–1903 this figure falls to 26 per cent.

in the city directory of Worcester, Massachusetts, and the destination reports for emigrants from Örebro län.[10]

The overrepresentation of American ports, especially New York, among emigrant destinations must be considered. Nevertheless, the destination reports as a whole provide a relatively accurate picture of the actual geographical spread of primary settlement areas of Swedish emigrants. Once the New York figures are normalized, the value of these destination reports seems to be essentially reinforced when the comparatively equal distribution of emigrants from Örebro län and the Sundsvall district throughout the United States is compared with the distribution of all Swedish immigrants according to the U.S. Census.

Relationship between the Economic Structure in Areas of Emigration and Immigration

The regional distribution of immigrants from the Sundsvall area and Örebro län, as based on the destination reports of Swedish passenger lists, discloses a connection between the economic structure of emigrant districts in Sweden and choices of settlement in America (Table 9:3). The large overrepresentation for New York as a reported emigrant destination has been eliminated in this table by a statistical recalculation where New York state has been assigned emigrant percentages in relationship to its share of the total Swedish immigrant population in 1900.[11]

A comparison with the distribution of the entire Swedish immigrant population shows that emigrants from the Sundsvall district settled on a proportionately large scale in Michigan, Wisconsin, and Washington but to a lesser degree in Illinois. Emigrants from Örebro län settled on a wide scale in Massachusetts, Michigan and, to a certain extent, in Pennsylvania. On the other hand, they have a proportionately smaller representation in Minnesota and in other farming states like Iowa, Nebraska, and Kansas.

These deviations from the total distribution of the Swedish-American population can be explained with reference to the economic structure of emigrant districts in Sweden. Sundsvall was a major saw-mill district and most of its emigrants settled in lumber and industrial regions of the Middle

[10] *En Smålandssocken emigrerar* (1967), p. 709; M. Eriksson (1971), pp. 3 ff.

[11] It might be assumed that the large proportion of Swedish emigrants in Massachusetts, primarily those from Örebro län, was due to Boston's overrepresentation as a port of emigrant disembarkation. However, this was actually due to a significant volume of in-migration to that state. Cf. H. Norman (1974), pp. 220 ff.

West. After 1900 substantial numbers of them settled in the western United States, especially in the saw-mill districts in Washington. In other words, the spread of emigrant destinations from the Sundsvall area contrasts sharply to emigration from agrarian areas in Västernorrlands län, which was almost exclusively oriented to farming areas in the Middle West.[12]

A similar connection between the economic structure in areas of emigration and immigration has been found for emigrants from Örebro län. The parishes in this län were classified in two groups, a) agrarian economies and b) industrial economies. The emigrants from these parishes during the period 1879–1882 were distributed in two different categories of states, a) those with a high degree of industry (Massachusetts and Pennsylvania) and b) those which were essentially farming states (Iowa and Kansas). Emigrants from agrarian parishes in Örebro län settled to a great extent in Iowa and Kansas, whereas the majority of those from industrialized parishes settled in Massachusetts and Pennsylvania.[13]

A similar tendency is observed for the period 1901–1903. However, at that time an even greater share of the emigrants settled in Massachusetts and Pennsylvania. This reflects the chronological sequence of emigration outlined above. During this later phase emigrants did not settle in farming districts on the same scale as before but were more inclined to immigrate to American industrial regions.

Another example of the relationship between the economic structure of emigrant parishes and the choice of immigrant settlement areas is a study of emigrants from five parishes in Örebro län during the period 1869–1905. These parishes include Karlskoga, a prominent iron industry region; Ljusnarsberg, an area of wide-scale mining operations; Kumla, a shoe industry center; Stora Mellösa, a typical agricultural parish; and the city of Örebro.[14]

Table 9: 5 shows the percentual distribution of emigrants from these areas in some states with major settlements from Örebro län. Also included are four Prairie States (Iowa, Kansas, North Dakota, and South Dakota) which saw prominent immigration by Swedes.

[12] L.-G. Tedebrand (1972), pp. 203 ff. A remarkable large share of emigrants from Västernorrlands län settled in Canada: from 1885–1909, for example, nearly 1/5 of all emigrants from this part of Sweden went to Canada.

[13] M. Eriksson (1971), pp. 7 ff.

[14] This account is based on H. Norman (1974), pp. 226 ff.

Table 9:5. *Percentual Distribution of Emigrants from Karlskoga, Ljusnarsberg, Kumla, Stora Mellösa, and Örebro in Selected American States, 1869–1905*

	Illinois	Iowa, Kansas and the Dakotas	Massachu-setts	Michigan	Minne-sota	New York
Karlskoga (iron)	21.2	5.1	24.0	3.8	5.8	28.6
Ljusnarsberg (mining)	12.1	5.7	10.2	20.7	12.6	30.9
Kumla (shoe)	26.8	4.9	7.7	3.4	6.5	39.1
Stora Mellösa (agrarian)	20.0	16.9	10.0	2.0	13.3	28.0
Örebro (län centre)	14.5	4.6	9.2	1.9	6.8	52.4

Source Passenger Lists, Gothenburg

Three prominent concentrations emerge in this table. Emigrants from the agrarian parish of Stora Mellösa dominate the distribution in states with agricultural economies. The greatest proportion of emigrants on Minnesota was from this community. Moreover, emigrants from this parish settled in the Prairie States on a much wider scale than emigrants from the other four areas. Other striking features in this table are the high percentage figures for Karlskoga emigrants to Massachusetts and for Ljusnarsberg emigrants to Michigan. Kumla parish has the greatest share of emigrants to Illinois, where Chicago was the principal area of settlement. The city of Örebro shows equally high percentage figures to New York. Minnesota, the "Swedish state", plays a very limited role in this context, despite the fact that it was designated as a destination for some of the immigrants who settled in Wisconsin.

The strong orientation among Karlskoga and Ljusnarsberg emigrants to Massachusetts and Michigan respectively reflects similarities of economic structure in areas of emigration and immigration. In 1869 a large number of workers from Värmland and other mining districts were attracted by offers of employment in the iron industries of Worcester, Massachusetts. Many of them came from the Bofors and Degerfors foundries in Karlskoga parish. This led to a consistently high level of immigration to Worcester and other industrial regions in Massachusetts from iron foundries in Sweden.

Emigration from Ljusnarsberg to Michigan also reflected the economic structure of this Swedish parish. Ljusnarsberg was a center of extensive mining operations, and the group emigrations from the area in 1868–1869 were almost exclusively oriented to the mining ranges of northern Michigan. Although some of these emigrants moved on to a new area of settlement in Trade Lake, Wisconsin, the Michigan colony proved large enough to attract continued immigration from Sweden. As a result, the northern Michigan mining ranges assumed a strong concentration of emigrants from Ljusnarsberg.

A similar pattern emerges in the emigration from Småland and Öland. Industry and artisan trades had a significantly stronger position among the immigrants from these parishes to Chicago than among all emigrants from Småland and Öland. A parallel with respect to social differentiation is the overrepresentation of women (maid-servants) aged 15–29 years: this indicates a planned immigration to the big city environment with its ample opportunities for female workers.[15]

Danish emigration also provides examples of the role played by economic structures in emigrants' choice of settlements. Emigrants from rural Denmark mainly settled in the farming states of Wisconsin, Minnesota, Iowa, and Nebraska. On the other hand, urban emigrants, particularly those from Copenhagen, had a proportionately weaker representation in these states.[16]

Urban Settlement

Two case studies in the Uppsala Project deal with Swedish immigration to American cities: one concentrates on Chicago, the other on Worcester, Massachusetts.[17]

During the entire emigration period *Chicago* functioned as the major stopping place for Swedish immigrants on their way west. The railroads and waterways of the Eastern and Western United States converged here, and the city was a center for land sales offices and employment agencies. Moreover, many Swedes settled in Chicago for longer or shorter time periods and formed a sizable Swedish enclave. In 1900 one out of every ten Swedish-Americans lived here, and next to Stockholm Chicago ranked as the largest city in the world with a Swedish population.

The Swedish settlement of Chicago can be divided into three main

[15] U. Beijbom (1971), pp. 141, 338 f.

[16] K. Hvidt (1971), pp. 321 f.

[17] The account of settlement in Chicago is based on U. Beijbom (1971), pp. 74 f., 99 ff., 111, 141 ff. and U. Beijbom (1973), p. 179 f. The account of settlement in Worcester is based on H. Norman (1974), pp. 237 ff., 261 ff., and 291 ff.

periods. The first period saw the rise of immigrant slums along the north bank of the Chicago River during the 1840s and 1850s. The Swedish population here lived under very poor and highly disordered circumstances. The area was marshy and unhealthy, and the expansion of the city's industrial sector gave the settlement a highly temporary character. The majority of the Swedes belonged to the working class, and many were unemployed. Gustaf Unonius, one of the prominent Chicago pioneers and church leaders, described them as primitive squatters, the majority of which lived in a state of destitution. According to the U.S. Census of 1850 the Swedish population in Chicago numbered about 200 persons. In 1860 this figure had increased to about 1 000.

From the 1860s on the Swedish population was increasingly concentrated to a permanently rooted enclave farther north in the city, the so-called Swede Town along Chicago Avenue, which became the North Side's "Swedish Farmers' Street". The population increase in this part of Chicago was largely due to non-Anglo-Saxon immigration. Although the Irish were the first to settle, the Germans soon became the dominant ethnic group. Smaller numbers of Swedes and Norwegians also moved in at an early stage. However, the Swedish colony assumed the fastest rate of growth, and by 1890 it was one of the largest immigrant groups in the city. In 1870 Swedes numbered 7 000 persons; in 1880 no less than 18 000. Swede Town was characterized by a large and low-paid working class which, however, usually had permanent employment and their own homes. At the beginning even this area posed a dismal picture, but the rise of industrial zones offering jobs within walking distance and the prospects to acquire their own homes attracted a poor immigrant population. The establishment of leading Swedish-American social and cultural institutions in this area, as well as the rise of a Swedish business center, contributed considerably to the maintenance of a certain ethnic consciousness. Despite a strong through-current of immigrants traveling farther west, Swede Town retained its ethnic character due to a relatively permanent core of ministers, newspapermen, club people, craftsmen, and businessmen.

The third phase of Swedish settlement in Chicago includes the gradual shift of population from the Swede Town enclave to more outlying residential districts. This movement was initiated by the more well-established part of the population. An increasing social differentiation among Swedish immigrants, together with improved economic circumstances, subsequently dissolved the old ethnic cohesion in Swede Town. These same factors also diminished the prospects of retaining Swedish customs and

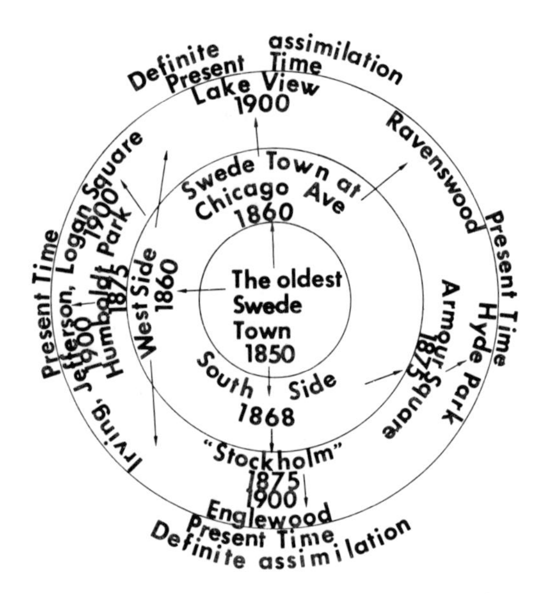

9: 2. Swedish Immigrant Settlement in Chicago: From Swedish Enclave to Suburban Residence.
Source U. Beijbom (1971), p. 100.

traditions among Chicago Swedes. As Swedes moved out of the area, Swede Town was populated by other ethnic groups representing the new waves of immigration. Large numbers of Italians settled first and were later followed by Southern Blacks and Puerto Ricans. Figure 9: 2 illustrates the Swedish settlement phases, from the original Swede Town to a gradual exodus to outlying residential areas.

As was often pointed out by health officials, cramped housing conditions were a characteristic feature of urban immigrant enclaves. This was especially true in Swede Town. Similar conditions have been found among Swedish immigrants in Worcester, Massachusetts, where a great many newcomers, often relatives to earlier immigrants, were lodgers or boarders.

Such housing accomodations are probably related in great measure to the intensive pattern of immigration and the subsequent shortage of housing. However, some of these phenomena can be seen from another perspective and in light of other research findings. T. Hareven and J. Modell maintain that the widespread system of lodgers among immigrant groups which in urban areas of Massachusetts prevailed well into this century, can be due to economic considerations but primarily to social factors. In particular, relatives and others of the same ethnic group (kinship) may simply have preferred to live together in the new environment.[18]

Swedish immigration to *Worcester* began late in comparison with Chicago and did not accelerate until 1880. It therefore represents the later phase of Swedish immigration, which was largely oriented to the Eastern industrial cities. Worcester had a sizable industrial sector, and two of its branches played a particularly significant role for settlement by Swedes. One was the iron industry, dominated by the Washburn and Moen Company; the other the ceramics industry, headed by the Norton Pottery Works.

Thus, Swedish immigration to Worcester consisted of two principal occupational categories. The first group began arriving in the area in 1868, when a number of potterers from Höganäs in Skåne found employment with the Norton Pottery Works. This stimulated continued immigration to Worcester from Höganäs. The Skåne immigrants seem to have been an attractive source of manpower in the ceramics industry, where Swedes after a few years dominated the working force. The second occupational category largely consisted of foundry workers from the Swedish iron districts. Philip Moen, a co-owner of the Washburn and Moen Wire Works, had visited iron foundries in Sweden and personally encouraged workers to immigrate to the Worcester company. The result was a steady stream of immigrant labor from foundries in Central Sweden, primarily from Örebro and Värmlands län but also from Gävleborgs and Kopparbergs län (cf. the map in Figure 9: 3c). In other words, the early immigration to Worcester was dominated by male iron industry workers. In 1880, for example, as much as 80 per cent of this immigrant manpower was employed in the Worcester metal industry.

In 1876 the Swedish colony in Worcester numbered about 200 persons. In 1880 it was roughly 1 000 according to the U.S. Census. By the turn of the century first and second generation Swedes totalled over 10 000 persons and represented one-tenth of the city's entire population.

Studies of various Swedish settlements in America have shown a concentrated recruitment of immigrants from certain regions in Sweden. One of the reasons for this has already been mentioned. When emigrants from a certain region in Sweden more or less happened to settle in one particular area of America, they often established a tradition of emigration in their home districts which paved the way for subsequent immigration to the same settlement. U. Beijbom has found that such a pattern actually

[18] T. Hareven and J. Modell (1972), *passim.*

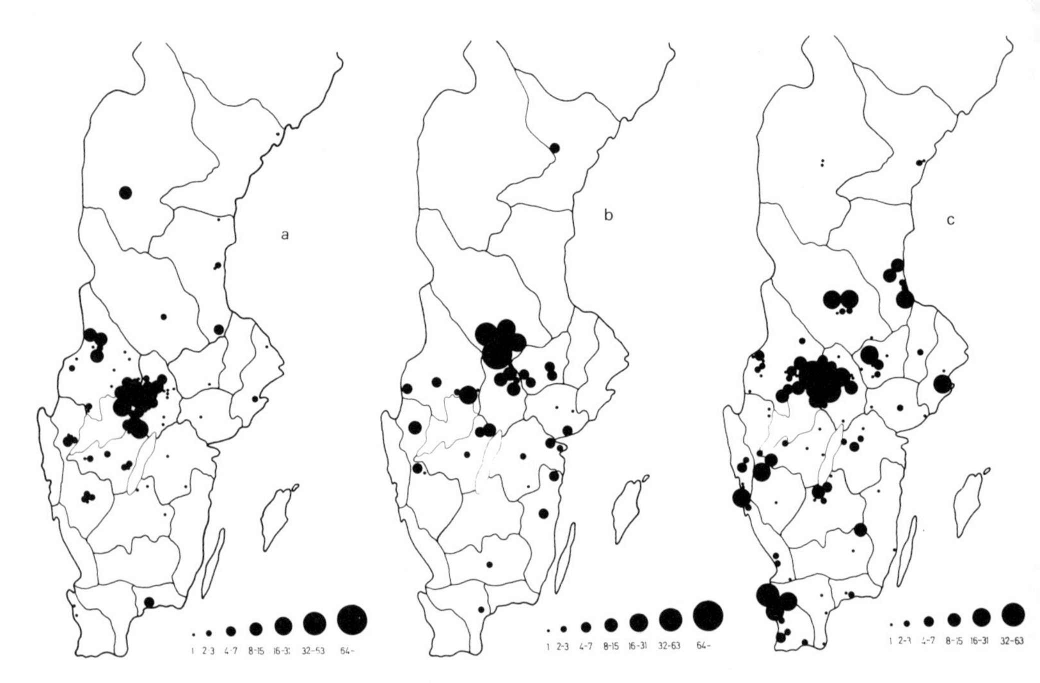

9: 3. Areas of Recruitment for Swedish Immigrants; *a* = Pepin County, Wisconsin, *b* = Burnett County, Wisconsin, *c* = Worcester, Massachusetts, as Based on Notations on Parishes of Birth or Emigration.

Sources Membership Records, Sabylund Lutheran Church (Stockholm) and Zion Lutheran Church (Trade Lake); *Kalender över Svenskarna i Worcester 1883;* H. Norman (1974), p. 242.

emerges among Swedes in Chicago, despite the fact that the city was a transit station for westward movement for most Swedish immigrants. Emigrants from Jönköping and Kalmar län, for example, were prominently overrepresented among members of the Augustana Lutheran Church in Chicago as compared with their share of the total Swedish population in America. The Swedish immigration to Worcester shows a similar recruitment pattern. Thus, two main regions in Sweden stand out as areas of recruitment, namely the Höganäs district in northern Skåne and, even more prominently, the Bergslagen in Central Sweden.

Rural Settlement

Similar patterns of emigrant recruitment are exemplified by two areas of rural settlement in Wisconsin, the Stockholm colony in Pepin County and the Trade Lake colony in Burnett County. Immigrants to Pepin County largely originated from the Karlskoga mining districts in Örebro and Värmlands län (Figure 9: 3 a), whereas Burnett County drew most of its Swedes from Ljusnarsberg in northern Örebro län and the southern parishes of Kopparbergs län (Figure 9: 3 b). These findings fall well in line with the results of an American study of Chisago County, Minnesota, where members of Lutheran congregations in various settlements came from different but highly concentrated emigrant districts in Sweden.[19]

The Stockholm and Trade Lake colonies have several features in common. In both cases settlement occurred first by groups of individuals led by an earlier emigrant and resulted in a large concentration of Swedes.[20]

The first to be colonized was the Stockholm area. Its founding dates from the same period as other Swedish colonies in southern Minnesota and western Wisconsin, which were a part of a scattered belt of settlements along the north-western frontier in the early 1850s. Some of the more famous Swedish settlements of this period are Vasa, in Goodhue County, and Chisago Lake, in Chisago County, farther north in Minnesota. Once the more accessible territory between the prairies and the forests had been colonized, the immigrant pioneers began to filter into the northern sections of these states. The Trade Lake colony, founded in the late 1860s, belongs to this period.

Swedes continued to migrate into the Stockholm area up until the mid 1880s, and the settlement spread not only into Pepin and Frankfort Townships but also to the neighboring Maiden Rock Township to the north, in Pierce County (see map Figure 9: 4).

The largest influx of settlers to the Stockholm colony came during the Swedish emigration of 1868–1869. In-migration continued on a smaller scale after that point but almost entirely stopped prior to 1900. It is striking that the 1880s, which marked the most intensive waves of emigration from Sweden, did not lead to any substantial degree of in-migration to this area. This is probably due to the fact that this section of the United States was already settled and colonized by 1880. In Pepin County, for example, population growth stagnated after 1880. On the other hand, in

[19] R. Ostergren (1972), *passim.*

[20] This account is based on H. Norman (1974), pp. 232–249. The history of these Swedish settlements is also treated in a number of unpublished papers presented to the Uppsala Migration Research Project: Stockholm, by B. Dovelius (1969) and M. Eriksson (1972); Trade Lake, by R. Pedro (1970), A. Jonsson (1973), and G. Lyck (1973).

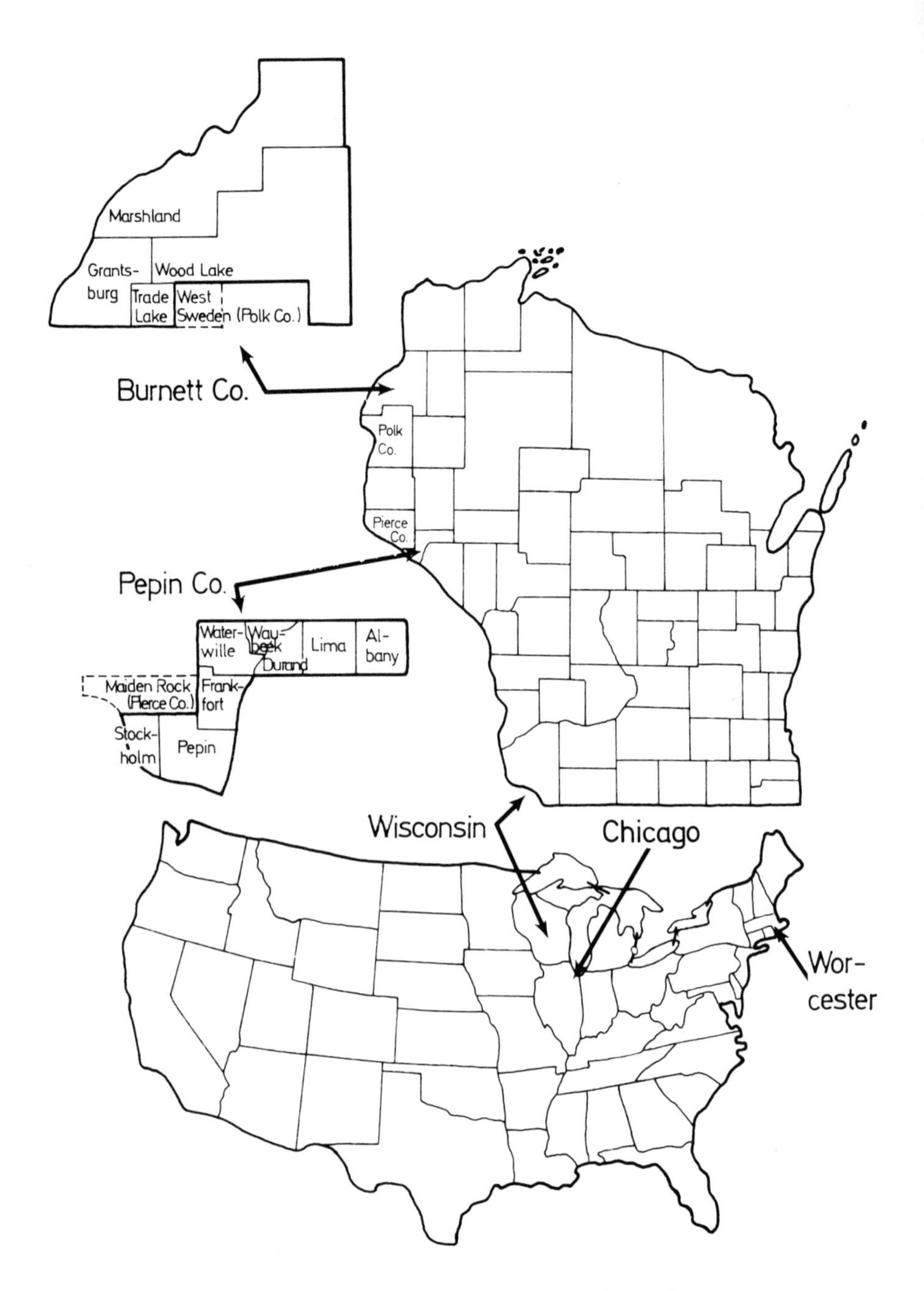

9:4. Map of Study Areas in the U.S. with Emigrants from Örebro län: Pepin and Burnett Counties, Wisconsin, and Worcester, Massachusetts.

Trade Lake Township and in all Burnett County, where colonization started later, the population grew strongly past the turn of the century.

The Swedish population (i.e. native-born Swedes or Americans born of Swedish parentage) in Pepin County totalled 1 335 in 1880 and 1 576 in 1905. Corresponding figures for Burnett County, however, show a pronounced population increase from 1 366 persons in 1880 to 4 098 in 1905. The Trade Lake population increased partially as a result of several new group emigrations from Ljusnarsberg parish. Swedish settlements here were spread over several townships notably Wood Lake and Grantsburg, but also extended to West Sweden in Polk County, immediately south of Burnett (cf. the map in Figure 9:4).

These agrarian settlements in Trade Lake and Stockholm were part of a relatively compact area of Swedish immigrant districts along the upper stretches of the Mississippi River. The most concentrated Swedish colonization took place in Minnesota, but other pioneer settlements were scattered throughout neighboring states. Both Stockholm and Trade Lake face the Minnesota side, where the cities of Minneapolis and St. Paul assumed the role of an urban center for these two settlements.

The populations of Stockholm and Trade Lake contained strong concentrations of Swedes. In Pepin County as a whole Swedes accounted for 21 per cent of the total population in 1880 and 1905. In Burnett County their percentage share was as high as 44 per cent in both census years. This county is one example of areas in the United States where the Swedish population had its strongest concentration. In comparison, the three counties in Minnesota with the largest percentage of Swedes in 1910 were Isanti (66 %), Chisago (60 %), and Kanabec (46 %). Certain townships in Pepin and Burnett Counties registered still higher percentages of Swedes in relationship to their total populations. Stockholm Township in Pepin County, for example, had a Swedish population of 82 per cent in 1880 and 86 per cent in 1905. Trade Lake Township in Burnett County recorded figures of 82 and 92 per cent these same census years.

In other words, Swedes not only had a strong concentration in these settlement areas but frequently showed a highly compact pattern of geographical recruitment in Sweden. As mentioned above, several factors help to explain this development. Moreover, the ways in which many Swedish women came to the United States reinforced this pattern. Many of them emigrated a short time after men from the same home district. In some cases they were "America widows" who followed with their children in order to join husbands who, at times, together with one of the eldest sons, had already begun settling in America. In other cases they were younger women who followed the departure of an intended husband. Emigration for the purpose of marriage is a phenomenon which accentuated an initially localized concentration of emigration. In other words, it constitutes one of the factors which enhanced the self-generating process of emigration resulting from close contacts between American areas of settlement and Swedish areas of emigrant recruitment.

Summary

The Middle West was the prime area of settlement for Swedish immigrants during the earlier phase of mass emigration. A comparison with other Scandinavian immigrant groups shows that the Norwegians were most concentrated to this part of the United States. Studies of emigrant destinations in America have consistently disclosed that their settlement preferences reflected the economic and occupational structures of home districts in Sweden. This was equally true of immigration to agrarian, industrial, and urban areas in America. The emigration from Västernorrland provides illustrative examples of this pattern: farmers and farmers' sons left for farming areas in the Middle West, whereas saw-mill workers left for industrial and forest regions in the northern United States and Canada. These connections also emerge among iron industry workers from Karlskoga, who emigrated to the industrial city of Worcester, and among mine workers from Ljusnarsberg, who emigrated to the mining ranges of northern Michigan.

Another factor which led to a concentration of immigrants from certain definite areas in Sweden was the so-called stock effect, i.e. the significance which prior settlement in America by persons from a specific district had on successive emigration from the area. An obvious example of this phenomenon is immigration to Stockholm and Trade Lake in western Wisconsin. In other words, the first areas in which immigrant settlements more or less happened to occur assumed major significance for the subsequent geographical spread of Swedish emigration in America.

c. Ethnic and Social Conditions

Prior research has only given a small amount of attention to the social situation of the Swedish population in America. However, some recent studies have dealt with the social and ethnic conditions of Swedish immigrants. They discuss occupational structure, marriage patterns, persistence level, the rise of religious and secular institutions, and political activity—i.e. phenomena related to the strength and concentration of the Swedish group in various areas of settlement. Attention has also been given to the Americanization process and the transition from Swedish to English. U. Beijbom has studied these developments among Swedes in Chicago, and H. Norman has resarched similar problems in two rural areas of Wisconsin—Stockholm and Trade Lake—and in the city of Worcester, Massachusetts. Both of these studies cover the earlier phase of emigration and the peak years of mass emigration from Sweden. S. Lindmark has concentrated on efforts by Swedish immigrants in Illinois and Minnesota between 1914 and 1932 to retain their ethnicity in various spheres of activity.

Occupational Structure and Social Status

What were the living conditions among Swedish emigrants in the new country? What occupations did they have? What was the social differentiation among Swedish immigrants, and how did they stand socially in comparison with other ethnic groups?

The analysis of these issues primarily deals with conditions in the two settlements in Pepin and Burnett Counties, Wisconsin, and with the urban situation in Chicago and Worcester.

It comes as no surprise that farming assumed a prominent share of occupations among Swedes in the Wisconsin settlements. According to the Federal Census of 1880, 60 per cent of the Swedes in Pepin County were farmers. In Burnett County the figures was as high as 67 per cent. In addition there was a significant share of immigrant farm workers. The situation was largely similar in 1905, although a certain shift had emerged toward a more differentiated sphere of occupations. The stabilization of pioneer societies spurred the growth of groups employed in various service sectors—i.e. small business owners and the corps of lower salaried civil servants. However, in 1905 over 70 per cent of the Swedes in Burnett County were still engaged in farming: this figure includes both farmers and farm workers. In Pepin County these same categories accounted for more than three-fourths of the Swedish population.[1]

[1] H. Norman (1974), pp. 252 ff.

A comparison between the social patterns among Swedes in Pepin and Burnett Counties discloses essential differences. The entire population in these two areas was ranged on a five-point social scale[2] according to occupational designations in the Census and were broken down into the specific ethnic groups represented in each county. It was found that the social position of Swedish immigrants clearly diverged from one another in these two areas. Their share of the highest skilled occupations (Groups I and II) was greatest in Burnett County.

Among all ethnic groups in Pepin County, native-born Americans heavily dominated occupational categories I and II, both in 1880 and in 1905. However, in Burnett County their representation was less extreme and stood in proportion to their share of the total population. These findings raise the following question: what possible factors were responsible for this disparate pattern of development in two, relatively neighboring Swedish settlements?

In Pepin County the Swedes came to an area where colonization had already begun and where several other ethnic groups were already established. In 1860 native-born Americans totalled 65 per cent of the population, whereas Swedes accounted for only 6 per cent. Moreover, a number of English-speaking groups, such as the Irish, British, and Canadians, were represented in the area. The largest immigrant group at that time were the Germans, who had settled during an earlier wave of immigration.

Although the number of Swedes increased in 1880 to one-fifth of the population, the other groups continued to dominate the settlement. Faced with this competition, Swedes had difficulties in gaining skilled employment and official posts in the county administration.

The situation was entirely different in Burnett County. Although groups of Norwegians were the first to settle the area, the Swedes rapidly became the largest ethnic group with 44 per cent both in 1880 and in 1905. This Scandinavian population also included some Danes. On the whole, Scandinavians comprised between 60 and 65 per cent of the population, whereas native-born Americans only accounted for roughly one-fourth. This meant that from the start Scandinavian immigrants managed to

[2] These social groups had the following order of ranking: I High White Collar; II Low White Collar; III Farmers; IV Skilled (Blue Collar); V Unskilled (Blue Collar). For a more detailed presentation of this social scale, see H. Norman (1974), pp. 171 ff., 310 f., 325 ff.

acquire positions of authority in the county administration and assert themselves in other qualified fields.[3]

The study of the ethnic distribution of elected administrative posts in both counties sheds further light on this development.[4] In Pepin County, where the Swedes comprised 21 per cent of the population in 1880, they were represented by only 6 per cent of the elected officials. Burnett County posed a different picture. In relationship to their share (44 %) of the population in 1880, Swedes fared far better here with 33 per cent of the elected body of officials. The situation was even more favorable for other Scandinavians. Norwegians accounted for an equally large share of county officials, despite the fact that their numerical share of the county population was less than half that of Swedes. It is also worth noting that native-born Americans were not overrepresented in Burnett County. Their share of elected county posts stood in proportion to their percentage of the population. In all, Scandinavians accounted for nearly three-fourths of these posts, a figure which exceeds their numerical share of the population. In other words, Burnett County can in several respects be regarded as a distinctly Scandinavian area.

These statistics reflect the concentration of particular ethnic groups in both counties. In an area like Pepin County, where they were initially a minority, Swedes found their opportunities limited. Here native-born Americans and early immigrant groups had a clear advantage.

In Burnett County, on the other hand, where they were the largest ethnic group almost from the beginning, Swedes asserted themselves much better. This was even more the case with Norwegians, who were the first to settle the area. On the whole, Scandinavian immigrants gained control of leading posts and responsibilities in this county from the start of colonization. Many of them lived in Grantsburg, the county seat, and thereby represented a significant share of the commercial and industrial sectors. Even in this respect Burnett County poses a contrast to conditions in Pepin County. In 1905 the town of Durand, Pepin's county seat, had a total population of 1 367, of which only 19 were Swedes and 25 Norwegians. This same year Pepin Village, the county's second largest town, had a population of 348, of which 27 were Swedes and 4 Norwegians. In Grantsburg, on the other hand, with a population of 711, Swedes

[3] H. Norman (1974), pp. 256 f.

[4] These posts were Sheriff, Register of Deeds, County Treasurer, District Attorney, Clerk of County Board of Supervisors, Clerk of Circuit Court, County Surveyor, and Coroner.

accounted for 324 persons and Norwegians 223—i.e. a combined percentage share of 77.

Two factors apparently played a significant role in enhancing the possibilities of ethnic groups to assert themselves in newly settled areas and in accelerating the influence of these groups. The first was an early arrival in an area; the second a dominant numerical share of the population in relationship to other ethnic groups.[5]

These findings can be compared with those by E. Hamberg, who conducted a comparative study of farms owned by persons of Swedish and American origin in Chisago and Isanti Counties, Minnesota, in 1880. Although both counties had very large Swedish populations, native-born Americans were economically privileged, since large numbers of them were the first to settle in the area. It is possible that the first settlers had more farmland to choose from and, therefore, greater possibilities of locating fertile and easily cultivated land. In many cases they may also have had access to greater starting capital. Hamberg's study shows, for example, that Swedish-owned farms had less total acreage and less cultivated acreage than farms owned by Americans. In turn, the proportion of forest land in relationship to total acreage was greater on Swedish farms. Swedish farmers used draught-oxen in large measure, whereas American farmers could afford to keep greater numbers of horses.

However, in summarizing her results Hamberg assumes that social differences conditioned by economic factors were relatively small. Both the value of production per acreage unit of cultivated land and the value of production in relationship to the total value of farms were higher among Swedes. Similarly, Swedish-owned farmsteads had a higher value when estimated in relationship to respective acreage and with respect to livestock and machinery.[6]

In some respects the occupational situation of Swedes in *Chicago* resembles conditions in the rural areas of the Middle West. Those who arrived in the city during the earlier phase of immigration represented a very small share of skilled occupations. Comparisons with native-born Americans and somewhat earlier immigrant groups illustrate this very clearly. Americans accounted for three to four times as many tradesmen and also dominated the general service occupations and liberal professions. These occupational sectors, along with the transport and communication sectors, em-

[5] H. Norman (1974), pp. 257 ff.
[6] E. Hamberg (1969), *passim.*

ployed greater numbers of earlier immigrant groups—such as Irish and Germans—than Swedes. This observation also holds to a certain extent for Norwegians, whose immigration to Chicago predates that of Swedes. Generally speaking, Norwegians had a somewhat higher occupational status than Swedes during the period 1850–1860.[7]

There was one specific occupation in Chicago where Swedish immigrants had a proportionately large representation. A substantial inmigration by young, unmarried Swedish women led to a situation where they comprised the dominant element in domestic service. They also accounted for a large share of occupations in the textile industry. On the whole, this industry employed a substantial number of Swedish immigrant workers, both men and women. Proportionately twice as many Swedes as Germans worked in the textile industry during the 1870s. The construction industry also became an equally important occupational field for Swedes during this period. In the same respect, Swedes gained a major foothold in the metal industry from the very start. However, they did not establish any occupational tradition in Chicago's well-known food processing industry. The city's highly differentiated economy had no key industry comparable to the iron works in Worcester, Massachusetts, which attracted a selective transatlantic manpower—primarily from Swedish mining districts in the Bergslagen.

In the beginning Swedish immigrant manpower in Chicago was dominated by unskilled workers. In time, growing numbers of skilled workers and lower grade civil servants entered into the picture. Few Swedes were yet in 1880 active as building contractors or other leading *entrepreneurs*. On the other hand, there are numerous examples of Swedish-born business owners, many of whom functioned as subcontractors to large industries and wholesalers. They were especially prominent in the textile, wood processing, metal, and mechanical industries which employed growing numbers of their immigrant countrymen.[8]

The strong position of Swedish immigrants in the *Worcester* iron industry also provided prerequisites favorable for their social status in that city. A comparatively large share of skilled workers settled in Worcester during a very early phase of immigration. Around 1900, when the Swedish immigrant population totalled over 10 000 persons, the occupational composition reflected a differentiated sphere of activity. Judged in terms of the

[7] U. Beijbom (1971), pp. 223 f., 340 f.

[8] U. Beijbom (1971), pp. 224 ff., 340 f.

five-point scale outlined above, the social composition of Swedes in Worcester at this time largely resembled that of a medium-sized Swedish industrial city—such as Örebro. However, Worcester had a somewhat larger group of Swedish industrial workers and proportionately greater numbers of craftsmen and skilled workers.[9]

On the whole, Scandinavians appear to have been well represented among skilled workers in the industrial cities of Massachusetts. This has also been observed in a study of Boston by S. Thernstrom, who found that in 1890 Scandinavians held the greatest share of skilled occupations among all ethnic groups in that city, including native-born Americans.[10]

Many of the Swedes in the Worcester iron industry reached foreman status, and most of them had experience from iron foundries in Sweden. Large numbers found their way to the lower middle class, and quite a few reached higher social status. Many opened their own businesses after an initial period of employment in trade or industry. Contributing factors to this social development were undoubtedly the diversified range of practical experiences and, in some cases, a substantial theoretical education which many immigrants brought from Sweden.[11]

Persistence

Studies of Chicago and the pioneer settlements of western Wisconsin have disclosed a locally strong concentration of Swedes. It is therefore of interest to evaluate the permanence of these rather homogeneous Swedish settlements—i.e. their persistence level.

Chicago's position as a through-station of westward immigrant traffic ought to have distinguished it in terms of low persistence. It must be presumed that many Swedish immigrants who came to Chicago only stayed there for short periods of time. However, it appears that the immigrants stayed in the city longer than one would expect. A study based on the U.S. Census of 1860 and 1870 revealed that around 10 per cent of the Swedes remained in Chicago more than 10 years. Those who did stay constituted a rather permanent core of the population; this is demonstrated by the fact that 50 per cent of those listed in both the Censuses of 1860 and 1870 stayed at least an additional 30 years. A connection also

[9] H. Norman (1974), pp. 262 ff.
[10] S. Thernstrom (1973), p. 131.
[11] H. Norman (1974), pp. 268 f.

existed between occupational categories and persistence. Business men, higher grade employees and craftsmen had a particularly high level of persistence. Around 40 per cent of those listed in the 1860 Census were traced in the 1870 Census. This picture of a relative stability among the Chicago Swedish enclave is reinforced by the demographic composition, where formation of families resembled that of normal conditions in Sweden.[12]

A study of Swedes in Pepin County reveals a surprisingly high level of persistence: 54 per cent of the family heads could be identified from the Census of 1860 to the Census of 1870 and 43 per cent from 1870 to 1880. The persistence of Swedes in Burnett County from 1870 to 1880 was 49 per cent.[13]

An evaluation of the significance of these persistence figures can only be made by way of comparisons with other regions. S. Thernstrom's study contains a list of rural areas in America, where estimates have been made of population persistence. The following figures represent the per cent of persistence in some regions:[14]

1860–1870	Trempeleau County, Wisconsin	25
	Eastern Kansas	26
	East Central Kansas	31
	Central Kansas	42
1870–1880	Trempeleau County, Wisconsin	29
	Roseburg, Oregon	34
	Eastern Kansas	44
	East Central Kansas	46

These figures indicate a low level of persistence, especially during the 1860–1870 decade. Population mobility seems to have been even higher from these rural areas than from the large American cities analyzed in Thernstrom's study. According to Thernstrom, an extremely high level of population mobility existed during the early years of frontier settlement. In his opinion the high mobility in urban as well as rural areas constitutes a specifically American phenomenon. However, several Swedish studies

[12] U. Beijbom (1971), pp. 131 ff.

[13] H. Norman (1974), pp. 249 f. See also M. Eriksson (1972), pp. 29 ff. Men and single women over 15 years of age are considered as family heads; widows are also included.

[14] S. Thernstrom (1973), Table 9: 2. Deceased persons are not covered in these estimates nor in those by M. Curti with reference to Trempeleau County (M. Curti 1959, p. 67) nor in those from Pepin and Burnett Counties.

have disproved this: for example, the persistence in Upsala-Näs, Uppland, was only 46.5 per cent during the five-year period 1881–1885.[15]

It must be emphasized that comparisons of mobility rates which are compiled from different research studies are necessarily uncertain. The results depend heavily upon the size of the regions. Moreover, the exact locality of population concentration in these regions also plays a certain role. The region which offers the closest comparison in this instance is Trempeleau County. However, since it is substantially larger than Pepin County its low persistence rate appears particularly striking here.[16]

Furthermore, persistence is dependent upon such factors as civil status, age, and social position. As shown by M. Curti, married persons were less inclined to migrate than unmarried persons. Persons between 40 and 50 years of age largely had the highest persistance rate. Finally, the study of Trempeleau County clearly showed that mobility declined in proportion to rising property ownership.[17]

It is therefore necessary to observe a great deal of caution when comparing calculated statistics of persistence. However, there are indications that the measurements obtained from study areas in Pepin and Burnett Counties reflect a population mobility which was actually low in relationship to comparable areas.

An important factor deserves mention here: whereas one ethnic group was selected from the population in Pepin and Burnett Counties, the entire population was examined in the areas of comparison—i.e. both immigrants and native-born Americans. The general results reached by H. Eldridge and D. S. Thomas in a nation-wide study have relevance in this case. Immigrants aged 40 years and above were found to have a substantially lower inclination to migrate than native-born Americans in the same age.[18]

A second factor of consideration is the occupational orientation of Swedes in these areas of the Middle West. Great numbers of Swedes were farmowners. As is well-known property ownership in connection with an occupation usually reduces the inclination to migrate. Moreover, the actual system governing land ownership ought to have had the same effect. The Homestead Act of 1862 offered interested persons the possibility of ac-

[15] S. Thernstrom (1973), pp. 220 ff.; I. Eriksson and J. Rogers (1973), pp. 64 ff.

[16] Cf. Chapter 6, above.

[17] M. Curti (1959), pp. 65 ff.

[18] H. Eldridge and D. S. Thomas (1964), pp. 133 ff.

quiring land nearly free of charge, and this opportunity was open to an individual on a one-time basis.[19]

Furthermore, the area of immigrant recruitment in Sweden to both the Stockholm and Trade Lake colonies was geographically highly compact. This falls well in line with the pattern found by R. Ostergren in Chisago County, Minnesota, where a positive correlation existed between a high persistence rate and a high degree of cultural homogeneity.[20]

Finally, strong ethnic concentration in these Swedish settlements, coupled with the fact that Swedes represented the largest immigrant group in both regions, can have had an impact on rates of persistence. Reference can be made to J. Rice's observations regarding Kandiyohi County, Minnesota; the concentration of an ethnic group in a certain area was directly correlated with its inclination to remain on the land acquired during the process of settlement.[21]

Intermarriage

The proportion of intermarriage is customarily cited as one measurement of an ethnic group's assimilation capacity. Sociologists, for example, interpret the inclination to intermarry as a group's capacity for "structural assimilation".

The following three studies of Swedish immigrant marriage patterns show two features in common: a) the preference in selecting marriage partners from other ethnic groups and b) the extent of intermarriage among Swedes.

Up until 1880 intermarriage was relatively unusual in the Swedish pioneer settlements in Pepin and Burnett Counties. When intermarriage did occur it was almost exclusively with other Scandinavians. Among married men in Pepin County there were 8 of 244 (3.3 %) who intermarried: 7 of the wives were from Norway. Among women in the same county 6 of 237 (2.5 %) intermarried: five of the husbands were born in Norway and one in Denmark. In Burnett County the corresponding figures for

[19] The Homestead Act stipulated that every American citizen of legal age or every immigrant who expressed a desire to become an American citizen was entitled on a one-time basis to receive 160 acres of land free of charge. Once an individual had worked the land and lived on it for five years he was entitled to full ownership. (The Homestead Act, 1862.)

[20] R. Ostergren (1972), pp. 61 ff.

[21] J. Rice (1973), pp. 64 ff. Rice has also shown that at a later stage, when an area became fully colonized, a high degree of in-transit migration took place. However, the strong ethnic concentration in that area remained intact.

men were 8 of 264 (3.0 %), where all of the wives were born in Norway, and for women 13 of 261 (5.0 %), where 10 of the husbands were from Norway and one from Denmark.[22]

These results can be compared with others obtained by M. Curti for Trempeleau County, Wisconsin, where colonization began at the same time as in Pepin County. Curti observes a very low proportion of marriages between persons of European descent and native-born Americans: this applies especially to persons from non-English-speaking countries. The dominant ethnic group in this county were Norwegians, who married almost exclusively within ethnic boundaries. In summarizing his findings, Curti maintains that if intermarriage is to be used as a measurement of assimilation, according to the theory of the American "melting pot", it had a slow effect in Trempeleau County.[23]

It might be theoretically assumed that large urban areas represented an environment which encouraged assimilation among immigrant groups in the form of a great deal of intermarriage. The urban environment should have operated as a breeding ground for an ethnic melting pot, which is generally considered typical of the demographic development in the United States. However, in his Chicago study U. Beijbom has found that few Swedes married across ethnic boundaries. His analysis of four census-takings has revealed that only 6–10 per cent of the Chicago Swedes married persons of other nationalities. Norwegians' inclination for intermarriage was even less: 3 per cent in 1850 and 6 per cent in 1860. Moreover, Beijbom has found that intermarriage was most unusual in sections of Chicago where Swedes were highly concentrated. It was more common in areas where they lived side by side with other ethnic groups. He has also observed a connection between intermarriage and social structure. Workers had the lowest inclination for intermarriage, whereas businessmen, office and shop employees intermarried on a much wider scale. In other words, the tendency to intermarry was greatest among occupational groups where a knowledge of English was necessary.[24]

[22] H. Norman (1974), pp. 274 f. Even the results presented in a seminar paper regarding Wyoming Township in Chisago County, Minnesota, for the period 1860–1885 show a low proportion of intermarriage among Swedes. The Swedes were a comparatively large ethnic group in Wyoming Township: consequently, marriage partners could easily be found within ethnic ranks. Moreover, this township was located in a belt of regions with heavy proportions of Swedish immigrants (A. Holmström 1974, pp. 15 ff.).

[23] M. Curti (1959), pp. 104 ff.

[24] U. Beijbom (1971), pp. 136 ff.

These findings fall well in line with the results of a third study dealing with intermarriage, namely S. Lindmark's *Swedish America 1914–1932*. He has found that Norwegians were most preferred by Swedes in intermarriage. Moreover, the stronger the concentration of an ethnic group the less the intermarriage. Lindmark also found that marriage patterns were bound by religious barriers. When intermarriage occurred partners were mostly sought within the Protestant, Catholic, and Jewish faiths. The proportionately high degree of intramarriage among Finnish immigrants represents an example of how the language barrier effectively stifled close contacts between ethnic groups.[25]

Naturalization as American Citizens

Another factor which usually assumes importance for the assimilation of ethnic groups in American society are their efforts to become American citizens. An immigrant was entitled to citizenship after five years' residence in the country. Moreover, two years after his arrival he could declare his intention to seek citizenship by filing a so-called first paper. However, the majority of immigrants postponed the process of naturalization, often as long as 20 years or more. Despite the fact that it was highly advantageous to secure citizenship—for example, with regard to labor market requirements—many immigrants never bothered to do so.[26]

Of all male Swedish residents in Chicago over 21 years of age, only 16 per cent were citizens in 1870. Swedish-language newspapers constantly encouraged their readers to become citizens and registered voters. However, individual interest in naturalization seems to have fluctuated on the basis of social status and economic success. Businessmen and professional groups had the highest rates, lower grade civil employees and skilled workers had lower rates, while unskilled workers had the lowest of all. A connection also existed between efforts made by different social groups to secure citizenship and the various periods of residence in America.[27] Differences also appear to have emerged between rural and urban areas; lesser numbers of urban residents became citizens. In his study of Swedish America Lindmark registers the existence of a clear connection between lengths of residence for various ethnic groups and the attainment of

[25] S. Lindmark (1971), pp. 50 ff. See also G. Jonasson (1972), p. 270.
[26] S. Lindmark (1971), pp. 41 ff.; S. Åkerman (1970), p. 40.
[27] U. Beijbom (1971), pp. 135 f., 335.

citizenship status. Swedes belonged to the so-called "older immigrant groups". Therefore, their relatively high figures for naturalized citizens in 1910, 1920, and 1930 create no surprise, and they do not in any way substantiate the traditional assertion that Swedes were especially eager to become American citizens. On the whole, the statistics on naturalized citizens make it difficult to conclude that one nationality distinguished itself from others by achieving citizenship at an early stage.[28]

Swedish-American Institutions. Ethnic Solidarity

One consistent pattern in the settlement of Swedish immigrants—whether they lived on the American frontier or as enclaves in urban areas—was the establishment of churches and congregations, often within a relatively short time after their arrival.

The first settlers of Stockholm, Wisconsin, arrived in two emigrant contingents in 1854. Two years later a Lutheran, initially Scandinavian congregation, was founded in the colony with the help of the well-known Swedish-American, Erik Norelius, who was a pastor in Vasa, Minnesota, for a long period of time. The two main groups of immigrants, which founded the Trade Lake colony, left Sweden during the famine years and arrived in Wisconsin in 1868 and 1869. The Baptists founded their first congregation as early as 1869, and the Lutherans followed with a congregation in 1871. In subsequent years both settlements saw the rise of several new churches as well as divisions of older congregations. Lutherans and Covenantalists were predominant in the Stockholm colony; Lutherans and Baptists in Trade Lake. Church life appears to have played a major role in these pioneer societies, especially during the early formative years, and served as the central focus of cultural activities. However, church life was periodically characterized by bitter rivalries between different congregations, as for example among Baptists and Lutherans in Trade Lake. The so-called *gatsynoden* in Stockholm and the Seventh Day Adventists in Trade Lake caused a great deal of inner dissension and conflict in the areas.[29]

The first Swedish congregation in Chicago, led by Gustaf Unonius, was founded in 1849, when Swedes only numbered a few hundred souls. Unonius failed in his attempt to give the infant Swedish Episcopal Church

[28] S. Lindmark (1971), pp. 41 ff.
[29] H. Norman (1974), pp. 232 ff., 337; L. J. Ahlström (1924), *passim;* E. H. Johnson (1900), *passim.*

the character of a Swedish "folk church". The status of his St. Ansgarius congregation was partly due to a program of benevolent aid to newly-arrived immigrants and to the lack of competition from other immigrant churches. However, it lost its prominence as a result of increased immigration from Sweden, and during the 1850s Baptists, Methodists, and Lutherans established their own congregations in the Swedish colony.[30]

As church functions were divided among growing numbers of congregations, more and more Swedes gradually refrained from becoming involved in church life. The churches' role as social aid societies and sources of support for new immigrants subsequently diminished in importance, as for example during the 1870s, when conditions became much more stable compared to the pioneer period. Instead, a large number of clubs and secularized societies came into being, arond 40 in all. These included different types of benevolent aid programs for members, such as funds for health insurance and funeral expenses. Yet their primary orientation was in the area of cultural and secular activities. Clubs such as the Svea Society and Svithiod largely became the alternative of church membership for the well-established sector of the immigrant population.[31]

On the whole, the Swedish immigrant population in American cities seems to have been engaged in a wide range of activities both in terms of church life and secular orders and associations. In Worcester, Massachusetts, for example, at the turn of the century, there were no less than eight Swedish churches representing a large number of denominations—Lutherans, Methodists, Baptists, Congregationalists, and Episcopalians. Secular organizations included temperance lodges, choral societies, gymnastic clubs, engineer's and women's associations, etc. Fraternal orders also flourished, such as the Svea Gille and "The Viking Society Independent Order of Mystic Brothers".

Swedish immigrants who settled in cities like Chicago and Worcester evidently took great interest in various forms of organized activities. Their behavior in this respect falls well in line with observations made by R. Braun regarding in-migrants in Switzerland. Persons who move from rural surroundings to an industrial environment—i.e. depart from their natural patterns of social and political contact—experience a strong need for associating in different ways. This explains why a large variety of different associations and societies often spring up in such environments.[32]

[30] U. Beijbom (1971), pp. 228 ff.
[31] U. Beijbom (1971), pp. 266 ff.
[32] H. Norman (1974), p. 270; R. Braun (1960), pp. 137 ff.

The development among Swedes in Chicago reveals a profound dualism in immigrant institutions and cultural strains. There was, on the one hand, the broad mass of immigrants, representing the lower and middle classes of society, who often came from agrarian environments in Sweden. On the other hand, there was a smaller group of upper class immigrants who often had an intellectual and urban background. The first category in particular served as a natural source of membership for the Augustana Lutheran Church, which generally had a broad, popular base. The more exclusive churches, meanwhile, attracted members from the second immigrant category. This dualism is also clearly reflected in attitudes to social and cultural activities. While the churches devoted great attention to benevolent aid programs, schools, and hospitals, secular organizations emphasized a wide variety of artistic and entertainment programs—concerts, evening social gatherings, theatrical productions, and the like. Compared with the churches these organizations based their activities more upon the well-established immigrants and the more diversified strain in the Swedish enclave. The average Chicago immigrant, who probably lacked both the time and money to indulge his interest, must have regarded the activities of fraternal orders and societies as an extension of Swedish *bourgeoisie* exclusivities on the American scene. On the other hand, upperclass immigrants who claimed a liberal outlook on things must have often considered the Augustana Church as the inheritor of religious intolerance in Sweden.

The fact that Chicago acquired the greatest concentration of Swedish immigrants in America meant that a large share of the Swedish-American press set up headquarters there. Many of America's leading Swedish journalists also made Chicago their base of operations. Seen as a whole the Swedish-American press assumed imposing dimensions; more than a thousand different newspapers appeared in circulation over the course of time. The press played a prominent role in the immigrant community both as a news-service, advertising agency, disseminator of information on social, cultural, and political activities, and as a bulwark of national identity and self-consciousness.[33]

The dualistic attitude noted above also emerges in the viewpoints expressed by the Swedish-American press. Two representative examples of this phenomenon are, on the one hand, *Hemlandet*, which opposed the activities of secularized immigrant associations (theaters, dances, and

[33] U. Beijbom (1971), p. 301.

clubs), and, on the other, *Svenska Amerikanaren,* which considered *Hemlandet* as representative of narrow-minded opinions. These two newspapers were also distinguished by their respective attitudes to the process of Americanization. *Hemlandet* represented the cause of Swedish nationalism with the conviction that the Swedish language and cultural traditions could be kept alive in the American environment. *Svenska Amerikanaren,* meanwhile, showed greater understanding for the process of assimilation. *Hemlandet,* in other words, defended the system of church-sponsored parochial schools, where instruction was held in Swedish. However, voices were raised in *Svenska Amerikanaren* to the effect that uneducated pastors thereby prohibited immigrants from learning English and subsequently reduced their chances in American society.[34]

N. Hasselmo analyzes the process of language adjustment among Swedish immigrants in American society. During the late 1800s the Swedish-American speech communities can be said to have comprised a nucleus of persons who spoke only Swedish and a periphery of those who spoke both Swedish and English or merely English. The Swedish language was constantly exposed to gradual influence from English-speaking persons. The language of the public school was English. Although Swedish was spoken by local authorities and institutions, English was still necessary for contact with higher officials. The same was generally true of business contacts outside the neighborhood community. In speaking, then, the Swedish American found himself caught in a sphere of tension, where his choice of language was determined by specific language situations—i.e., by role relationships, areas of activity, and surroundings. As a rule he had to use both languages, but he portioned them out within the framework of a so-called speech economy. Swedish was ordinarily used at home, among neighbors, in church and social gatherings, and in the immigrant press. English, on the other hand, was used in contacts with business circles, public officials, and in school. This speech economy was not stable, but rather stratified along generational lines. While younger persons were generally bilingual after seven years of age, older persons retained unilingual, and this led to tension between generations.[35]

The efforts to preserve Swedish ethnicity and the Swedish language during the progressive course of Americanization is one of the main themes of S. Lindmark's study. He has questioned the notion of rapid

[34] U. Beijbom (1971), pp. 298 ff.
[35] N. Hasselmo (1974), pp. 109 ff.

assimilation among Swedish immigrants and instead tried to capture maintenance phenomena. In conformity with U. Beijbom's observations of Swedes in Chicago, Lindmark maintains that group consciousness and the feeling of solidarity were strongest among Swedes during times of crisis.

During World War I the Swedish-American press expressed outright symphaties for the German cause and persistently requested the American government to follow Sweden's example and remain neutral in the conflict. After the American entrance into the war Swedish-American newspapers did affirm their loyalty, but immigrant groups were now heavily pressured to demonstrate support for their new country. One way of showing patriotism was to buy Liberty Bonds, and in this context there are several factors which indicate a rising solidarity among Swedish immigrants. The Swedish-American press constantly appealed to its readers to purchase Liberty Bonds. Characteristically enough, primary emphasis was given to the reputation and good standing which Swedes would win for their own ethnic group and not to the economic support which their bonds purchases would give the war effort.[36]

There were other phenomena which increased solidarity among Swedish Americans. One was immigrant quota legislation, where every limitation of Swedish immigration was interpreted as an insult to "the best of citizens". Another was the American Depression of the early 1930s. The immigrants' sense of solidarity clearly emerged in their efforts to organize independent forms of relief services to needy countrymen. The language issue also played a central role in efforts to preserve the Swedish heritage. As long as relatively large numbers of Swedes immigrated to America, there was a continual need to retain Swedish as the language of religious worship and immigrant gatherings. However, the second generation frequently made demands for the adoption of English as the language of church worship. Those who advocated the retention of Swedish argued, for example, that the language was necessary for a correct understanding of Swedish culture and history.

Despite efforts to preserve the Swedish language, the transition to English was both a natural and inevitable process. The publication of Swedish literature, magazines, and journals culminated between the turn of the century and the outbreak of World War I, after which it abruptly declined. The ebb flow of immigration during the 1920s generated a profound impact on the Swedish langugage in America. Churches which had long

[36] S. Lindmark (1971), pp. 64 ff.

sought to retain the mother tongue gradually adopted English as the major language of worship. Church records began to be written in English, and the word "Swedish" was deleted from the official names of congregations.[37]

d. Demographic Conditions in New Settlements

Introductory Perspective

Several demographic studies of newly settled regions found a high level of fertility among immigrants. Immigrants ordinarily had higher fertility rates than the original population in an area. One conceivable explanation is that immigrants frequently came from countries with a high level of fertility and that they subsequently retained this pattern among themselves in the new country.[1]

Other studies have disclosed that immigrants to newly colonized areas even had a higher rate of reproduction than was the case in their areas of origin. In line with his thesis on food shortage as a regulator of population growth, Malthus maintained that emigration led to heightened fertility in the delivering country as a result of lower marrying ages. This level of fertility lasted as long as resources allowed, whereafter it diminished and adjusted itself to the supply of food. In other words, the release of population pressure through emigration was only temporary. Malthus also interpreted the high inherent population growth among immigrants as a consequence of the scattered population and larger supplies of foodstuffs in the new country.[2]

F. Isaac has advanced another theoretical explanation for the high fertility among immigrant populations. In many cases immigrants constituted a very select group of their native population which was equipped with the greatest reproductive capacity. In effect, this would lead to diminished population growth in their home country and an equally strong population increase among immigrants themselves.[3]

A Russian researcher, V.-K. Iatsounski, has shown that between 1861 and 1913 the newly colonized areas of southwestern Russia, the so-called

[37] S. Lindmark (1971), pp. 137 ff., 179 ff., 191 ff.
[1] F. Isaac (1947), p. 185.
[2] R. Malthus (1872), *passim.*
[3] F. Isaac (1947), pp. 172 ff.

New Russia, had nearly twice the population growth of older, more central and industrialized areas in western Russia. He has also found that most of this increase cannot be credited to in-migration but rather must be the result of unusally strong, inherent population growth.[4]

Moreover, studies of population conditions in New England during the earliest period of colonization have shown that colonists in the area had a strong, inherent population growth. In his study of four generations in Andover, Massachusetts, P. Greven has discovered that the first generation in particular must have had a high rate of inherent population growth. He bases his conclusions mainly on the early marrying age of women, the large number of children in these families, as well as the low mortality rate.[5]

A study by J. Henripin and Y. Perón has also disclosed a very high level of fertility among the French population of Quebec Province, Canada. Two explanations are cited for this development. First, these French-Canadian families presumably lacked sufficient information on family planning. Second, the Catholic Church probably played an important role in discouraging families from implementing birth control measures. Nationalistic propaganda also advocated the desirability of large families. A high fertility rate among French Canadians enabled them to counterbalance the influx of English-speaking immigrants. According to Henripin and Perón, this was probably a necessity for the survival of the French-Canadian population in Canada.[6]

Published studies dealing with the demographic conditions of Swedish immigrants in America include Chicago Swedes and a study of rural areas in western Wisconsin. The following discussion is essentially based on the latter study.

A central issue in this context is whether a high inherent population increase can be considered a general phenomenon of newly colonized regions and, if so, on what grounds? Does this mean that the population in this new environment had a different demographic structure and, subsequently, a higher level of fertility? In a study of Pepin and Burnett Counties the composition of the immigrant populations was discussed with a view to their sexual distribution, age spread, civil status, and their

[4] V.-K. Iatsounski (1970), pp. 302 ff.

[5] P. Greven (1970), pp. 21 ff. Similar observations of high fertility have also been made by other researchers of the early Colonial era in America. Cf. J. Demos (1970), p. 180 and tabulatory material; K. A. Lockridge (1966), pp. 329 ff.

[6] J. Henripin and Y. Perón (1972), pp. 213 ff. It can be mentioned that the French share of the population retained a surprisingly high level of stability (30 %) up to 1951.

reproductive capacity.[7] This research is based on the U.S. Federal Census of 1880 and thereby focuses on an early phase of immigrant settlement in these areas. The statistics on Swedish immigration to Worcester, Massachusetts, have also been included in the tables. This provides comparative material from an area where Swedes immigrated at a later point in time.[8]

Since a substantial share of immigrants to these study areas came from Örebro län, a comparison has been made between the demographic structure in areas of emigration and immigration. Areas of comparison in Sweden include the Karlskoga Bergslag and Grythytte and Hällefors härad; Nya Kopparbergs and Fellingsbro härad; Kumla härad; Sköllersta härad; cities in Örebro län in 1880, i.e. Örebro, Askersund, Lindesberg, and Nora.

Sex and Age Distribution

Figure 9:5 shows the composition of the Swedish population in Pepin and Burnett Counties and Worcester, Massachusetts, together with the distribution of ages and sexes.[9] The age pyramid for the Swedish population in 1880 has been included for the purpose of comparison. There was a comparatively equal number of Swedes in these three areas of America, but the age distribution varied sharply from one area to the next.

The age pyramids reflect the earlier course of in-migration. A great many Swedes in the pioneer settlements of western Wisconsin had lived there for almost 10 years. Moreover, some persons had resided in Pepin County for up to 25 years. However, at this time Swedes had only just begun to settle in Worcester on a large scale.[10]

The age distribution of Pepin County shows the least divergence from the situation in Sweden. In Burnett County the 30–39 year age span is predominant, especially for males. This reflects the concentrated stream of in-migration to the Trade Lake area nearly 10 years earlier by persons in the most common immigrant age categories (20–30 years). Worcester's age pyramid is heavily dominated by men in the age groups 20–34 years and is

[7] Unless otherwise indicated, this section is based on H. Norman (1974), pp. 271–287.
[8] A source-critical study was made of the U.S. Census in relationship to individual data contained in membership records of Swedish-American Lutheran congregations. See Chapter 9: a, above.
[9] In cases of intermarriage all family members have been classified in the father's ethnic group.
[10] Cf. p. 255.

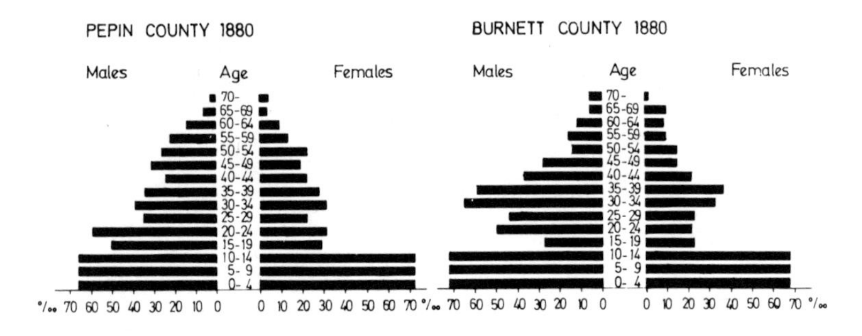

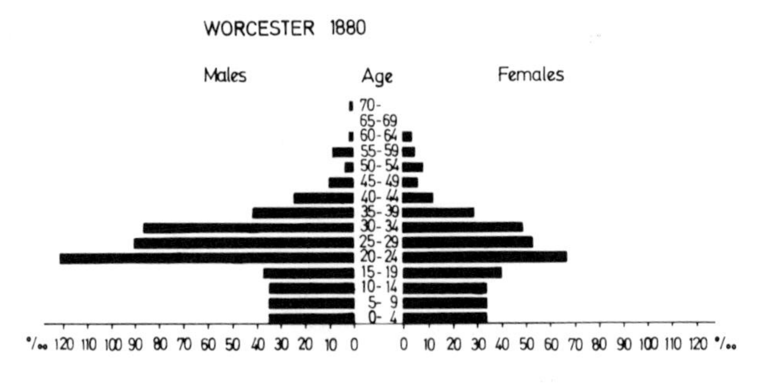

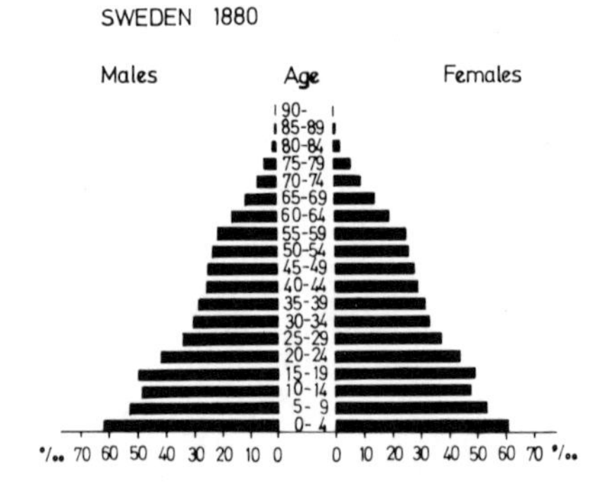

9: 5. Sex and Age Distribution in 1880 of the Swedish Population in Pepin and Burnett Counties, Wisconsin; in Worcester, Massachusetts, and in Sweden. The Horizontal Scale in Per Mille of the Entire Population.

Sources U.S. Census of 1880, The National Archives, Washington, D.C.; *Historisk statistik för Sverige;* H. Norman (1974), p. 274.

an example of the age and sex distribution of an immigrant group at the start of in-migration. The first to in-migrate were often men, particularly during the initial phase of major emigration, whereas female immigrants tended to settle later on. The selective factor is also of significance here: the industrial labor market in Worcester was dominated by the iron

Table 9:6. *The Percentual and Absolute Number of Children, Aged 0–14 Years, in Relationship to the Remaining Population, Aged 15 Years and above, in Swedish-American Settlements and in Areas in Sweden, in the Year 1880*

	Pepin County	Burnett County	Worcester	Karlskoga; Grythytte and Hällefors härad	Nya Kopparbergs härad and Fellingsbro härad	Kumla härad	Sköllersta härad	Cities in Örebro län	Sweden
Children 0–14 years	533	566	321	7 206	6 361	5 198	4 972	4 898	1 488 312
Adults, 15–*w* years	782	800	693	11 856	12 412	9 689	10 138	11 633	3 077 356
Number of children per 100 Adults	70.7	70.8	46.3	60.8	51.2	53.6	49.0	42.1	48.4

Sources U.S. Census of 1880, The National Archives, Washington, D.C.; *Folkräkningen 1880, prickningslistor,* The Central Bureau of Statistics, Stockholm; *Bidrag till Sveriges officiella statistik, Serie A. 3,* Table 1:26.

industry. The small proportion of children aged 0–14 years in Worcester's age pyramid represents another clear divergence from the situation in a normal population.[11] On the other hand, the age distribution in Pepin and Burnett Counties indicates the presence of a large number of children. As a comparison, the Swedish population in Chicago reveals a different pattern, since the most common immigrant ages (20–39 years) dominate. This is not surprising, considering the city's character of a transit station. Yet, on the whole, there are great similarities with the features of a stationary population. The sex structure, age distribution, and marriage rate of the Chicago Swedes have much in common with conditions in Sweden.[12]

[11] Cf. E. A. Wrigley (1969), pp. 24 ff.
[12] U. Beijbom (1971), pp. 110 ff.

Table 9:7. *The Population of Swedish-American Settlements and Areas in Sweden in 1880, Distributed in Per Mille on the Basis of Various Age Spans*

	Pepin County	Burnett County	Worcester	Karlskoga; Grythytte and Hällefors härad	Nya Kopparbergs härad and Fellingsbro härad	Kumla härad	Sköllersta härad	Cities in Örebro län	Sweden
0–14 years	414	415	317	378	339	349	329	296	326
15–49 years	459	485	656	469	472	472	463	533	486
50–*w* years	127	100	27	153	189	179	208	171	188
	1 000	1 000	1 000	1 000	1 000	1 000	1 000	1 000	1 000

Sources *U.S. Census of 1880,* The National Archives, Washington, D.C.; *Folkräkningen 1880, prickningslistor,* The Central Bureau of Statistics, Stockholm; *Bidrag till Sveriges officiella statistik, Serie A. 3,* Table 1:26.

Fertility

The large scores of children in Pepin and Burnett Counties are also observed when estimating the proportion of individuals aged 0–14 years in relationship to the adult population (15-*w* years) and in comparison with selected areas in Sweden. The proportion of children in the immigrant settlements of western Wisconsin is substantially higher than the Swedish national average, and it also exceeds the figures for the other areas (Table 9:6). However, a more detailed age structure analysis must be made in order to evaluate the demographic structure of these settlements. There are also immediate grounds for analyzing the population with a view to the age distribution of adults, i.e. 15 years and above. This can serve as a basis for evaluating the potential capacity for reproduction. How, then, did these pioneer populations stand in comparison with a normal population? Under normal conditions the age span 15–49 years represents half of the entire population in nearly all countries.

The Swedish statistician, G. Sundbärg, head of the Swedish Commission on Emigration from 1908 to 1913, presented three theoretical types of age composition: (1) a progressive type, with strong inherent population growth; (2) a stationary type, where inherent growth is largely non-existent; and (3) a regressive type, where inherent population growth is subsiding. The proportional sizes of these three categories, expressed in per mille, are scaled as follows:[13]

	Progressive	Stationary	Regressive
0–14 years	400	265	200
15–49 years	500	505	500
50–*w* years	100	230	300

Table 9:7 shows the corresponding figures for Swedish-American settlements and comparison areas in Sweden. The proportion of children in the Wisconsin pioneer settlements exceeds that of populations designated by Sundbärg as progressive, despite the fact that the age group 50-*w* years does not fall below the level in the progressive type of population. Instead, this group has considerably higher values in Pepin County (127 compared to 100). Moreover, the 15–49 year age span in these settlements is lower than the level in the progressive population model. On the other hand, it occupies approximately the same level as that of comparable areas in Sweden. However, these populations differ with respect to the numerical shares of children. The varying proportions of children in selected areas of Sweden lie substantially under the levels in Swedish-American settlements and occupy nearly a middle position between Sundbärg's progressive and stationary population categories.[14]

[13] G. Sundbärg (1907), p. 4.
[14] These observations on the age composition of immigrant populations in Pepin and Burnett Counties fall well in line with others regarding Wyoming Township, Chisago County, Minnesota. An analysis of the three dominant ethnic groups in this township in 1880 reveals the following composition:

	Swedes	Germans	Americans	Total population
0–14 years	411	400	250	365
15–49 years	550	455	520	530
50–*w* years	39	145	230	105
Total	1 000	1 000	1 000	1 000

The Swedes, who arrived later than the Germans and Americans, have the most progressive age composition. The Germans have a strikingly large share of children relative to the

Furthermore, the proportion of children in rural areas of Sweden, which sent emigrants to the American settlements, exceeded the national average. This is particularly true of certain mining districts, such as Karlskoga. These features might help to explain the relatively high share of children among immigrants in these settlements . However, the sharp contrast between these settlements and districts in Sweden raises a specific question: is there something special about the demographic composition of these settlements which might explain this situation?

At this point it is essential to gain some understanding of the sex distribution in these study areas. Theoretically the proportion of fertile women in a population is decisive for the inherent population growth.[15]

Table 9:8 shows the age distribution of the various age groups. All three Swedish-American settlements have a large surplus of men. As was expected, women are a majority in the Swedish areas: Örebro as well as the other cities in the same län have a strong surplus of women. The shortage of women in the Swedish-American populations takes nearly the same proportions in all three areas. There were between 7 and 8 women per 10 men in 1880. If one considers the adult population alone (15 years and above) this proportion stands at 6–7 women per 10 men. The shortage is even greater in ages above 20 years and is most apparent in Burnett County. In the 15–29 year age span women account for only about half the number of men in these ages. In Worcester their proportion is even less than half the number of men. I other words, this material shows that the large scores of children born in the Swedish settlements of the Middle West cannot be explained by any abnormally large proportion of fertile women.

The reason for the large shortage of women among Swedes in Worcester during this phase of immigration has been discussed above. Mass immigration had just begun, and the iron industry mainly recruited male workers. Otherwise, it was common that female immigrants moved

number of fertile women. The Americans represent a stationary age composition. (A. Holmström 1974, p. 10 f.)

Examples can also be taken from areas in Sweden with pronounced in-migration, where the population resembled the progressive model outlined by Sundbärg. In 1890 Sköns Parish in Västernorrlands län had the following age composition, as expressed in per mille: 422 (0–14 years); 487 (15–49 years); and 91 (50–*w* years). [Preliminary results from a forthcoming research paper on Sköns Parish by L.-G. Tedebrand.]

[15] The ages of reproductivity used in these estimates cover the age span 15–44 years, during which more than 98 % of all births normally occur. Cf. G. Sundbärg (1907), p. 21.

Table 9: 8. *Sex Distribution. Number of Women Per 1 000 Men in Swedish-American Settlements and in Areas in Sweden in 1880*

	Pepin County		Burnett County		Worcester		Karlskoga, Grythytte and Hällefors härad	Nya Kopparbergs härad and Fellingsbro härad	Kumla härad	Sköllersta härad	Örebro, Askersund, Nora, Lindesberg	Sweden
	M	W	M	W	M	W						
0–14 yrs	265	288	289	277	159	162						
W/1 000 M		1 087		958		1 019	955	960	932	976	1 021	978
15–29 yrs	193	110	166	92	349	158						
W/1 000 M		570		554		453	1 022	1 018	979	1 004	1 297	1 026
30–44 yrs	133	110	219	125	153	90						
W/1 000 M		827		571		588	1 014	1 058	1 042	1 189	1 323	1 082
45–59 yrs	107	73	80	56	21	17						
W/1 000 M		682		700		810	997	1 116	967	1 062	1 299	1 087
60–*w* yrs	35	21	33	29	2	3						
W/1 000 M		600		879		(1 500)	1 493	1 167	1 180	1 245	1 866	1209
Total	733	602	787	579	584	430						
W/1 000 M		821		736		736	1 017	1 032	1 007	1 056	1 256	1 061
15–*w* yrs	468	314	498	302	425	268						
W/1 000 M		671		606		631	1 056	1 071	1 049	1 097	1 372	1 116
20–*w* yrs	401	275	461	271	390	232						
W/1 000 M		686		588		595	1 078	1 082	1 066	1 189	1 424	1 131

Sources *U.S. Census of 1880,* The National Archives, Washington, D.C.; *Folkräkningen 1880, pricknings-listor;* The Central Bureau of Statistics, Stockholm; *Bidrag till Sveriges Officiella Statistik, Serie A. 3,* Table 1: 26.

primarily to large cities and less to agrarian areas. Many of them found employment as maid-servants in urban households. The U.S. Censuses of 1860, 1870, and 1880 show a large surplus of women, especially under 30, among Swedish immigrants in Chicago.[16]

[16] In Chicago the proportion of women per 100 men in the age group 15–49 years was as follows: (note continued on next page).

In order to estimate the actual magnitude of reproductivity it is necessary to compare the number of children with the number of fertile women (15–44 years), as shown in Table 9: 9.[17]

These estimates yield obvious results. The number of children per fertile woman is substantially higher in the Swedish pioneer settlements in western Wisconsin than in the Swedish areas. The proportion in the Swedish-American population is more than $^1/_3$ larger.

However, before these results are accepted it is necessary to view the situation from another perspective and estimate the proportion of children born to married women of the same age.

Few widows and no divorced women were observed in the American material. The calculations include married, widowed, and divorced women

Ages	1860	1870	1880
15–19	117	225	136
20–29	140	133	117
30–39	94	70	73
40–49	92	77	74

The surplus of women was greatest among those aged 15–19 years. In effect, the Chicago Swedes even had a certain overall surplus of women as opposed to the normal pattern among immigrant populations. (U. Beijbom 1971, pp. 19 ff. and Table 14.)

Conditions among the three dominating ethnic groups in Wyoming Township, Chisago County, Minnesota, illustrate that a shortage of women was a normal phenomenon of the population as a whole in rural settlement areas. In this township the percentage share of females (including children) during different years was as follows:

	Swedes	Germans	Americans	Total population
1860	40	43	44	43
1865	39	–	–	46
1870	45	43	49	47
1875	45	52	50	47
1880	43	45	39	38
1885	50	38	41	42

Source A. Holmström (1974), p. 9.

[17] The most correct method of estimating magnitude of reproductivity is to extrapolate on the basis of the number of childbirths. However, such statistics are not extant from the American study areas. Therefore, the estimates are based on the number of living children (0–14 years) at the time of the 1880 Census.

Table 9: 9. *Number of Children (Aged 0–14 Years) in Proportion to the Number of Women in Ages of Reproductivity (15–44 Years) in Swedish-American Settlements and in Areas in Sweden in the Year 1880*

	Pepin County	Burnett County	Worcester	Karlskoga; Grythytte and Hällefors härad	Nya Kopparbergs härad and Fellingsbro härad	Kumla härad	Sköllersta härad	Cities in Örebro län	Sweden
Number of women 15–44 years	220	217	248	4 058	4 042	3 223	3 228	4 345	1 016 645
Number of children 0–14 years	553	566	321	7 206	6 367	5 198	4 972	4 898	1 488 244
Number of children per woman	2.51	2.61	1.29	1.78	1.58	1.61	1.54	1.13	1.46

Sources *U.S. Census of 1880,* The National Archives, Washington, D.C.; *Folkräkningen 1880, prickningslistor,* The Central Bureau of Statistics, Stockholm; *Bidrag till Sveriges officiella statistik, Serie A. 3,* Table 1: 26.

aged 15–44 years in both the American and Swedish sources. The U.S. Census does not specify illegitimate children. All of the estimates cover both legitimate and illegitimate births.

Table 9: 10 shows surprisingly that there was no higher rate of reproductivity per married woman in the Swedish-American settlements than in the areas in Sweden. In Pepin County these rates are equal to those of rural areas in Sweden, and in Burnett County they are even substantially lower.[18] These findings indicate that the factors responsible for this development must be related to the marriage freqency. The marriage frequency among different age groups is shown in Figure 9: 6, which explains a number of demographic and social features in the study areas. The difference in marriage frequency between women in the American settlements and in the Swedish areas must be due to the distorted sex distribu-

[18] By way of comparison, it can be mentioned that conditions were nearly the same in Wyoming Township, Chisago County, Minnesota, where the number of children per married woman among different ethnic groups in 1880 was as follows: Swedes 3.19; Germans 5.00; Americans 2.17; Total Population 3.21. (A. Holmström 1974, p. 14.)

Table 9: 10. *Number of children (0–14 Years) Related to Number of Married and Formerly Married Women (15–44 Years) in Swedish-American Settlements and in Areas in Sweden in 1880*

	Pepin County	Burnett County	Worcester	Karlskoga; Grythytte and Hällefors härad	Nya Kopparbergs härad and Fellingsbro härad	Kumla härad	Sköllersta härad	Cities in Örebro län	Sweden
Number of married and formerly married women 15–44 years	146	181	169	1 693	1 728	1 391	1 318	1 488	435 068
Number of children 0–14 years	553	566	321	7 206	6 367	5 198	4 972	4 898	1 488 244
Number of children per married and formerly married woman	3.79	3.13	1.90	4.26	3.68	3.74	3.77	3.29	3.42

Sources U.S. Census of 1880, The National Archives, Washington, D.C.; *Folkräkningen 1880, prickningslistor,* The Central Bureau of Statistics, Stockholm; *Bidrag till Sveriges officiella statistik, Serie A. 3,* Table 1: 26.

tion among the Swedish-American population, i.e. a shortage of women as opposed to a rather sizable surplus of women in Sweden.[19]

Strikingly enough men in these pioneer settlements were still able to marry to the same degree as men in Sweden, despite the large shortage of women.[20] One factor which might have led to a high inclination for mar-

[19] The proportion of umarried women over 15 years was only 25 per cent in Pepin County and as low as 14 per cent in Burnett County in 1880, whereas in Sweden it was 41 per cent. In Chicago the corresponding figure was 44 per cent: there the total number of men and women was nearly equal, but at the same time there was a large surplus of women in the age span 15–29 years. In other words, this situation was favorable to marriage frequency. As a result, marriage patterns and birth rates among Swedes in Chicago rapidly assumed the same proportions as conditions in Sweden. (U. Beijbom 1971, pp. 121 ff.)

[20] Cf. Fig. 9: 6. In Pepin and Burnett Counties the respective proportions of unmarried men aged 20–49 years were 46.7 and 48.7 per cent in 1880. The corresponding figures for areas of comparison in Örebro län—in order of their standing in Table 9: 10—were 44.2 per cent, 44.4 per cent, 46.2 per cent, 44.6 per cent, and 44.5 per cent. (H. Norman 1974, p. 285.)

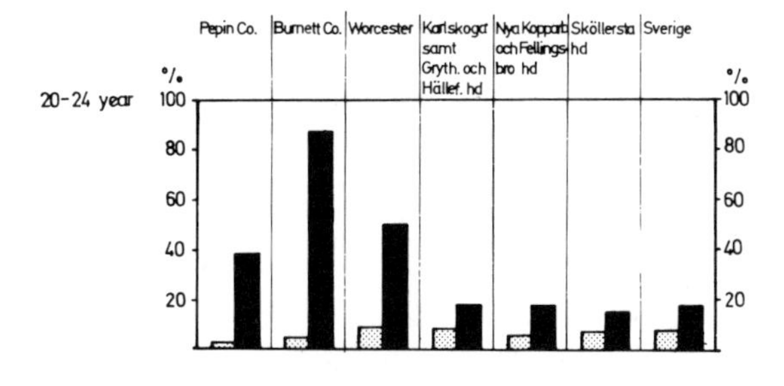

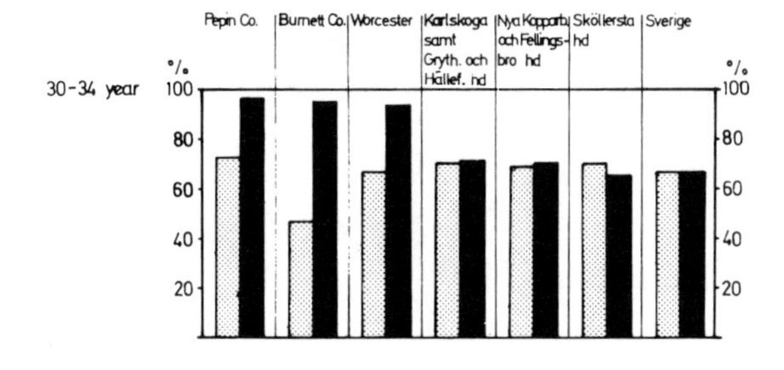

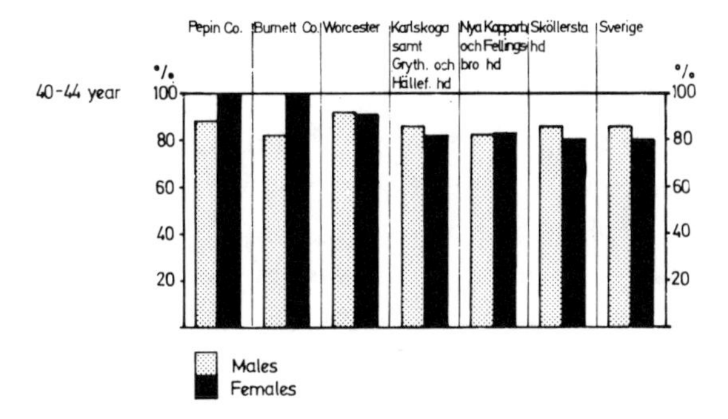

9:6. Percentage Shares of Married Men and Women in Certain Ages in Swedish–American Settlements and in Swedish Areas in 1880.

Sources U.S. Census of 1880, The National Archives, Washington, D.C.; *Folkräkningen 1880, prickningslistor,* The Central Bureau of Statistics, Stockholm; *Bidrag till Sveriges Officiella Statistik, Serie A. 3,* Table 1:26; H. Norman (1974), p. 284.

riage among men in these settlements was the agrarian character of the immediate environment. It might have been difficult for an unmarried man to take on seasonal work, such as railroad construction, to acquire sufficient capital and at the same time manage a farm. Such conditions were, in fact, normal during the first years of immigrant settlement.[21]

[21] L. J. Ahlström (1924), p. 110; E. H. Johnson (1912), p. 97.

Women in these settlements had a particularly high marriage frequency, and many of them married quite young. In certain age spans 100 per cent of the women were married. In Pepin and Burnett Counties as well as in Worcester, Massachusetts, around 95 per cent of the women between 30 and 35 were married. Burnett County, which had the greatest shortage of women, also recorded the highest frequency of early marriages among women. Over 20 per cent of the women aged 15–19 years and 87 per cent of those aged 20–24 years were married in 1880. The number of children per married woman was not particularly high. However, the pattern of early marriages and the prominent marriage frequency among women resulted in fertility rates which, based on the total population and the number of fertile women, were remarkably high in comparison to conditions in the Swedish areas.[22]

Concluding aspects

The shortage of women in these Swedish-American settlements had no effect on the marriage frequency of men, which generally corresponds to the frequency in selected areas of Sweden. On the other hand, this shortage resulted in a very high frequency of marriage among women, and a lower age for women at first marriage. Both factors led to high general birth rates as well as a large number of children in relationship to the number of fertile women. This explains the larger number of children in these immigrant settlements than in home areas in Sweden. However, the number of children per married women was not high but rather matched the normal number in Sweden.

In the opening paragraphs other research findings on the reproductive capacity of immigrant populations were mentioned. It is probable that the factors cited in this study may also have been responsible for some of their findings. As a rule, these results have applied to conditions in newly settled areas, where historians have observed strong, inherent population growths during the initial phase. Might a shortage of women combined with a high marital frequency for women explain some of the noted high reproductive capacity also in these areas?

[22] A parallel development has been observed in the German Ruhr district where in-migration to industrialized areas created a bias sex distribution. The shortage of women caused even here a lower marriage age among women and a higher fertility rate than was seen in agrarian comparable areas. (Wrigley 1961, pp. 133 ff., Tab. 34, 40, 141.)

e. Swedes in Politics

By Sten Carlsson

When a poor immigrant settles in a foreign country to start a new life he has initially much more to think about than his role on the political scene. The physically pressing problems of assimilation and the daily struggle for survival usually claim all of his powers. Moreover, even in a country like the United States, which has shown such generosity toward strangers, legislation sets certain formal restrictions on the newcomer. For example, a certain period of residence in the country and each state is normally required before he is eligible to vote.

The Swedes who came to the United States during the 1850s and 1860s did not participate in politics to any great extent. However, the Civil War did lead to a certain political and military activity on their part, and with few exceptions they supported the Union cause. In subsequent decades the majority of Swedes who were at all involved in politics were rather staunch supporters of the Republican Party. At the same time they did not aspire to any leading political offices. In Chicago for example, where despite large numbers Swedes only accounted for a small share of the total population Swedish political candidates found it rather difficult to win even low-ranking posts in the county and ward administrations. However, sporadic results were reached in some cases, as for example in 1874, when two Chicago Swedes gained seats in the Illinois State Legislature.[1]

Swedes had by far their greatest political opportunities in Minnesota, where they accounted for about 15 per cent of the total population at a rather early stage. Together with the Norwegians and smaller groups of Danes and Finns they comprised a sizable Scandinavian element (around 30% of the total) which was somewhat larger than the second major immigrant group, the Germans. In certain counties the Scandinavians were in the majority. In three counties north of Minneapolis—Chisago, Isanti, and Kanabec—most of the inhabitants were Swedes, and in Minneapolis itself Swedes comprised a substantial minority.[2]

However, some time elapsed before Swedes attained share of the political power proportional to their share of the population. The leading Republicans, most of them Yankees who had migrated from New York or New England, looked down on the Swedes and other Scandinavians as

[1] U. Beijbom (1971), pp. 315 f.
[2] S. Carlsson (1970), pp. 10 ff.

"voting cattle" who could always be relied upon for support, regardless of whether the party did anything for them as an ethnic group. Yet such attitudes could not last. As early as the 1880s the Democratic Party, then a minority in Minnesota supported by the Germans and the Irish, discovered that it could win marginal voters introducing and supporting Scandinavian candidates. For the time being most of these candidates were Norwegians. This gradually forced the Republicans to counteract with their own Scandinavian candidates.[3]

The Norwegians were more political active than the Swedes. First, they outnumbered Swedes in Minnesota then, second, and with the exception of the Swedish concentration in the Chisago–Isanti–Kanabec region, they had a far greater representation in the rural areas of the state. In contrast to both Germans and Norwegians, Swedes settled more often in large urban areas, where it was easier to melt in with the broad masses of the population. The first Scandinavian to make a genuine political breakthrough was the Republican and Norwegian-born Knute Nelson, who for three terms (1883–1889) represented northern Minnesota in the U.S. Congress and later served a short term as the first immigrant governor of Minnesota (1893–1895). He subsequently sat in the U.S. Senate between 1895 and 1923.[4] In state elections Nelson received a great deal of support from Swedish newspapers and organizations. However, Swedes soon began to look for possible candidates of their own.[5]

As early as 1857 a Swede served as a member of the territorial convention which was encharged with the task of preparing for Minnesota statehood. Moreover, several Swedes were appointed to the new State Legislature, the first one in 1865. Although their numbers grew in time they hardly corresponded to the share of Swedish voters in Minnesota. Hans Mattson, an immigrant from Skåne, proved to be of great importance for Swedish representation in Minnesota political circles. Following service as a colonel in the American Civil War and activities as an immigrant recruiter, Mattson served two terms (1870–1872 and 1889–1891) as Minnesota Secretary of State. During the period 1870–1955 this post was largely held by Scandinavians, most of them Swedes.[6]

The real breakthrough for Swedes came in 1886 when the Republican and former Småland immigrant, John Lind, was elected to the U.S. House

[3] S. Carlsson (1970), pp. 22 ff.
[4] M. W. Odland (1926).
[5] S. Carlsson (1970), pp. 17 ff., 41 ff.
[6] S. Carlsson (1970), pp. 31 ff. Cf. H. Mattson (1891), *passim.*

of Representatives. In reality, Lind represented as electoral district in southern Minnesota which contained relatively few Scandinavians. The first Swede to sit in the U.S. Congress, he was re-elected in 1888 and 1890 but declined nomination in 1892.[7] Four years later he ran for governor of Minnesota, no longer as a representative of the Republican Party but as the leader of an opposing coalition of Democrats, Populists, and "Silver Republicans". Though defeated in 1896 Lind won the governorship in 1898. In both elections he received support from Scandinavians, especially from marginal Swedish voters who otherwise voted as faithful Republicans. That Lind became the first Democratic governor of a state controlled by Republicans for nearly 40 years came as some surprise. His election showed the significance of the ethnic factor.[8]

Lind ran for re-election in 1900 but was defeated by a scant margin. The defeat can be attributed both to a technical misfortune and to a lack of support from some sectors of the Swedish population which objected his family's leaving the Lutheran Church to become Methodists. But in 1904 the Democrat John Albert Johnson—born in Minnesota of Swedish parentage—was elected governor while the rest of the state administration stayed in the hands of the Republicans. As in 1898 marginal Scandinavian voters played a decisive role in the election. Johnson proved to be a strong and popular governor. He was re-elected in 1906 and, by a slightly smaller margin of votes, in 1908, when he lost some Norwegian support when the Republicans ran a Norwegian candidate. By 1908 he was already mentioned as a possible presidential candidate, and had he not died the following year he might very well have been chosen to head the Democratic Party ticket in the national elections of 1912.[9]

In the Minnesota elections of 1906 Swedes captured the top two executive offices. The post of Lieutenant Governor was filled by the Republican Adolph Olson Eberhart, an immigrant from Värmland, who was particularly interested in education issues. With the death of John Albert Johnson in 1909, Eberhart succeeded as governor and was elected in 1910 and 1912.[10] Except in 1915, the governorship of the State of Minnesota has been represented by persons of direct or indirect Scandinavian heritage ever since 1905. The present governor, Wendell Anderson (elected 1970,

[7] G. M. Stephenson (1935). See also S. Carlsson (1970), pp. 28 ff.

[8] S. Carlsson (1970), pp. 45 ff.

[9] S. Carlsson (1970), pp. 45 ff. S. Carlsson (1971), pp. 254 ff. See also W. G. Helmes (1949), *passim*.

[10] S. Carlsson (1971), pp. 258 ff. Cf. A. Widén (1954).

re-elected 1974), a Swedish descendant on both sides of his family, is the tenth Swedish American to hold that office.[11]

The Scandinavian dominance in Minnesota has exceeded their numerical share of the population, while the Germans have been clearly underrepresented among leading political offices. This contrast was already apparent prior to World War I. The war itself created special problems for German Americans and, in some measure, also for Scandinavians. It is possible that the political traditions of Sweden and Norway, continued by immigrants in Minnesota, played a certain role. However, the religious divisions among Germans and their lack of succinct constitutional traditions were definitely more important. Despite periodic rivalries Swedish and Norwegian political collaboration has usally been good. Even the rupture of the Swedish-Norwegian Union in 1905 failed to mar Scandinavian relations in Minnesota.[12] Although clubs, newspapers, and churches evidently contributed to this political success among Scandinavians, a great deal of credit must be assigned to personal propaganda on the local level. In theory it has often been held that no one should be elected to public office on the basis of ethnic origin. In practice, however, ethnic considerations have frequently entered into the picture alongside of factors related to party politics which, in the long run, carried a far greater weight.

On the whole, Swedish politicians have shown greater interest in state affairs than national policies. In 1902, however, John Lind was again elected to the House of Representatives, which he left in 1905. In 1907 Charles August Lindbergh first made his appearance in Washington as a member of Congress. Born in Sweden, Lindbergh spent his early childhood in the United States. His father, Ola Månsson, once a well-known representative of the Peasants' Estate in the Swedish *riksdag*, emigrated to America in order to escape a series of personal and legal problems. Lindbergh was a Republican, but in Congress he joined the oppositional wing of the party which took an aggressive attitude on such issues as national finance. To some extent Lindbergh represented the Populist traditions of the Middle West: he was particularly opposed to big business and trust companies. He appealed to the rural and small-town vote as against big city constituencies. His own electoral district in central Minnesota consisted of large numbers of Germans as well as some Scandinavians. Though not a

[11] Cf. A. Naftalin (1969), pp. 12f. Included in this list of governors is Elmer Anderson, who served from 1951–1955. Both of his parents came from the Swedish-speaking section of Österbotten in Finland. A. Myhrman (1972), p. 269.
[12] P. E. Storing (1968), pp. 160 f.; S. Carlsson (1971), p. 258.

typically ethnic politician, he attracted the independent voters among Swedes. Besides Lindbergh several other Scandinavians joined the oppositional wing of the Republican Party in Congress. Most of them were Norwegians, but one was a prominent American-born Swede from the state of Wisconsin, Irvine Lenroot, who was elected to the House of Representatives in 1908. Another Swedish American (of Swedish and Norwegian parentage) was added to the Congress in 1910, when the oppositional Republican, Sidney Anderson from Minnesota, in the Republican primaries surprisingly defeated a leader for the party majority.[13]

World War I created a number of problems for Swedes in America. Traditionally, large sectors of the Swedish immigrant population felt strong ties with Germany, especially with fellow Lutherans. However, after American entrance into the war the majority of Swedish Americans loyally sided with their government.[14] In the House of Representatives the American declaration of war was supported by Lenroot of Wisconsin, Sidney Anderson of Minnesota, and Charles O. Lobeck of Nebraska—a Democrat elected in 1910. Lobeck was born in America of mixed parentage: his mother was Swedish, and his father a German who had lived in Sweden and held Swedish citizenship. Despite his position on the war issue, Lenroot was severely criticized by President Wilson during the senatorial elections of 1918. Though loyal to the American cause, Lenroot was accused of seeking support from traitors, pro-German sympathizers, rebels, and pacifists. However, he won election to the Senate with a scarce majority of votes, thereby becoming the first Swedish American to sit in the Senate. In 1920 he was mentioned as a possible Vice-Presidential candidate. Lenroot's position on the war issue was also held by ex-Governor John Lind, then the special Presidential Emissary to Mexico, and by J. A. A. Burnquist, Governor of Minnesota (1915–1921), who was born in Iowa of Swedish parentage. Despite his ethnic origin Burnquist went to such lengths in his patriotic fervor that he advocated a ban on foreign language instruction in American schools. He felt that all immigrants should either adopt the English language or run the risk of deportation.[15]

However, a rather large number of Scandinavians belonged to the minority which openly criticized President Wilson's war policy. Among the 50 Congressional Representatives who voted against the American decla-

[13] R. B. Lucas (1974), *passim*. Cf. J. Wefald (1971); regarding Wisconsin see J. Weibull (1965).

[14] F. H. Capps (1966), pp. 31 ff., and cited references.

[15] F. Ander (1938), p. 333; S. Lindmark (1971), pp. 90 ff., 131 f.

ration of war were two Norwegians (from North Dakota and Minnesota). A third Norwegian (also from North Dakota) took the same position but was unable to cast his vote due to illness.[16] A Swedish spokesman on the war issue was the Republican Ernest Lundeen of Minnesota, who was elected in 1916. Born in South Dakota of Swedish parents, Lundeen felt he had the support of broad popular opinion, especially among Swedish Americans. In his opinion, both Great Britain and Germany had violated American shipping rights, and he exemplified the Scandinavian countries' policy of neutrality as a pattern worthy of imitation. Lundeen was severely criticized for his statements. Ex-President Theodore Roosevelt called him "a shadow Hun" but admitted, after further explanations from Lundeen that his loyalty could not be questioned, even though Roosevelt could not agree with him.[17] Lundeen lost a bid for re-election in 1918. He joined the Farmer Labor Party (see below) and returned to the House of Representatives in 1933, still an isolationist but at the same time a warm supporter of The New Deal. During the last years of his life he sat in the U.S. Senate (1937–1940).[18]

The strongest Swedish-American criticism of Wilson came from Charles Lindbergh, an outspoken isolationist. Even during the early war years Lindbergh opposed any intervention by the United States which, in his opinion, would be detrimental to the American people but would serve the interests of plutocratic profit-seekers. During the House session of 1916 Lindbergh made very distinct statements in this direction. In elections that year he left his seat and tried instead to reach the Senate. However, in the Republican primaries he was defeated by future Secretary of State Frank B. Kellogg. After American entrance into World War I Lindbergh published a book criticizing official U.S. foreign policy. At this point he sought radical support from the Nonpartisan League. However, he remained a member of the Republican Party and ran for governor of Minnesota against Burnquist. Despite bitter accusations of deficient loyalty and patriotism, Lindbergh received a total of 150 600 votes in the primary elections, but he was unable to prevent Burnquist's re-nomination by 199 300 votes.[19] Burnquist and Lindbergh represented two poles of opinion both among Swedish Americans and Midwestern voters in general.

After his defeat in 1918 Lindbergh tried to distance himself from the

[16] S. Lindmark (1971), pp. 91, 98.
[17] S. Lindmark (1971), pp. 90 ff.
[18] *The National Cyclopaedia of American Bibliography,* Vol. 40 (1955), p. 299.
[19] S. Lindmark (1971), pp. 94 ff.

Republican Party and instead joined the Farmer Labor Party. Though relatively new on the political scene, this party was expanding in membership and came to express the unrest which had then seized farmers and workers in Minnesota, including many Scandinavians. Lindbergh ran in his old home district as the Farmer Labor Party candidate to the House of Representatives but was defeated by the incumbent Harold Knutson (born in Norway). In 1923 he campaigned for the U.S. Senate to fill a vacancy left by the death of Knute Nelson, but in the Farmer Labor Party primaries he was forced to yield to another Swede, Magnus Johnson. At the time of his death in 1924 Lindbergh was preparing a new campaign for the governorship of Minnesota.[20]

Magnus Johnson was another remarkable figure. Born in Värmland, he worked in his youth as a glass-blower. Before emigrating to the United States in 1891 he was influenced by early socialist activities in Sweden. Upon arrival in America he established himself as a farmer in Minnesota and participated in the farm co-operative movement. He joined the Farmer Labor Party and became its gubernatorial candidate in 1922, when he was defeated by the incumbent Republican J. A. O. Preus of Norwegian descent. However, he successfully ran for the Senate in 1923 by defeating Lindbergh in the primaries and Preus in the final elections. This unexpected election result caused major surprise across the nation. During his short term as senator Johnson attracted substantial attention for his Swedish accent, his demands for socialization, his extreme viewpoints on farming, and his call for American recognition of the Soviet Union. He failed in his bid for re-election in 1924 and also lost the gubernatorial election in 1926, but in 1932 he won a seat in the House of Representatives. On that occasion the entire state of Minnesota was technically organized as one electoral district with nine Congressional seats. The three largest parties, the Republican, Democratic, and Farmer Labor nominated 9 candidates each. Of the 27 candidates 13 were Scandinavians. Six of them were elected, including Magnus Johnson who received the greatest share of votes. Despite his popularity Johnson was defeated in 1934 by Harold Knutson, and in the gubernatorial primaries in 1936 he lost to the Norwegian American Elmer Benson. Johnson subsequently planned to run for office as an independent but died shortly before the final elections.[21]

[20] R. Lucas (1974), p. 20.

[21] *The National Cyclopaedia of American Biography*, Vol. 35 (1949), p. 207 f.; S. Carlsson (1973), p. 236 f.

However, the Farmer Labor Party remained a vital political factor in Minnesota political life. One of its members, Floyd Björnstjerne Olson, became one of the best-known and most celebrated politicians in the state's history. He was born in Minneapolis of a Norwegian father and Swedish mother. Though initially a Democrat, he later joined the Farmer Labor Party and became its gubernatorial candidate in 1924. He lost the election but campaigned again six years later and served as governor from 1931 until his death in 1936. Prior to the 1936 elections, which he never lived to see, Olson set his sights on a seat in the U.S. Senate. Many people considered him a strong and radical rival to Franklin D. Roosevelt for Presidency. However, Olson himself chose to support Roosevelt and his New Deal. Judged according to American standards, Floyd Olson was very radical. He had clear socialistic leanings and was sometimes accused of being a communist, although such accusations were false. He supported the workers' cause in general strikes but did not go to extremes. As governor he worked for the introduction of unemployment compensation benefits, general pension programs, price regulations for farm products, as well as interest and mortgage allowances for indebted farmers. In many respects Olson resembles his Swedish contemporary, Per Albin Hansson, leader of the Social-Democratic Party, who also based his administration policy on solidarity between farmers and workers. Like Hansson, Olson had more sympathies with the working class than with farmers, and it appears that toward the end of his career he lost votes among Minnesota farmers, especially in the southern sections of the state. It may be possible that on certain points Floyd Olson was directly influenced by Swedish politics: the issue is interesting but as yet unresearched.[22]

It is rather strange that so many of the leading Swedish-American politicians of this period—men such as Charles Lindbergh, Magnus Johnson, and Floyd Olson—had strong radical tendencies. It would be incorrect to regard them as representative of the majority of Swedish Americans, who were generally more conservative but not as ultra-conservative as many Swedes apparently imagine them to be. On the other hand, there are examples of Swedish Americans who were far more radical than the prominent figures sketched above. The celebrated Joe Hill (originally Joel Hägglund) stands as a prototype for this category. In 1902 he left his native town of Gävle for the United States and joined the syndicalist organization Industrial Workers of the World. His political actions led to his tragic

[22] G. H. Mayer (1951), *passim*; S. Carlsson (1973), pp. 234 f.

end. He was executed in Salt Lake City, Utah, in 1915 as a condemned murderer on the basis of unclear testimony and indistinct evidence, despite his own negation of guilt and after futile protests from Swedish diplomatic quarters.[23] Although a number of socialists and communists of Swedish descent followed Hill's footsteps, they represented only a small minority of the Swedish-American population.[24]

Most of the Swedish-American politicians presented above came from Minnesota: here, as in no other state in the country, Swedes have had the greatest oppotunities for political involvement. Whereas 10 Swedish-Americans have served as governors in Minnesota, only 16 have done so in all other states combined. It is perhaps a coincidence that not less than 3 Swedish Americans served as governors in Montana, where relatively few Swedes settled. Colorado and Nebraska have had two governors of Swedish descent; South Dakota, Oregon, California, Washington, Kansas, Vermont, Idaho, Delaware, and Michigan have each had one.[25] The most celebrated of them all was Earl Warren, born in America of a Norwegian father and Swedish mother and himself married to a Swede. He served as governor of California from 1943–1953 and as Chief Justice of the Supreme Court from 1953–1969. In 1948 he won nomination as the Republican Party's candidate for Vice-President.[26] Both as a politician and Chief Justice Warren can be characterized as a liberal. On the other hand, William H. Renquist, the current Justice of Swedish descent on the Supreme Court, is regarded as a conservative.

It appears that state governorships, with their substantial administrative and representative responsibilities, held a greater attraction for Swedish Americans than the U.S. Congress. In terms of percentage figures, fewer Swedes were probably involved in representative capacities on the national level than on the state level. The total number of Swedish-American senators has been 12, of which Minnesota had 3, Washington 2, and Wisconsin, South Dakota, Montana, Colorado, New Mexico, Kansas, and Nebraska 1 each.[27] The number of Swedish Americans in the House of Represen-

[23] I. Söderström (1970), *passim.*

[24] H. Bengston (1955), *passim.*

[25] This list is reproduced in the chronological order in which respective governors assumed office. Individual data has been compiled from F. Ander (1938), pp. 321 ff.; A. B. Benson and N. Hedin (1950), pp. 257 ff.; A. Kastrup (1975), esp. p. 840.

[26] A. B. Benson and N. Hedin (1950), p. 265; *The National Cyclopaedia of American Biography*, Vol. 3 (1960), pp. 24 ff.

[27] A. Kastrup (1975), p. 839. Here is included A. E. Nelson, who filled a vacancy in Minnesota in 1942–43.

tatives is more difficult to determine, but it must have been many times the number of senators. Considering the absolute size of the Swedish population in the state, it is striking that Illinois has not had one governor or senator of Swedish descent. However, relatively large numbers of Swedes have served in somewhat lower administrative posts in this state, and a greater proportion have been Republicans in contrast to the situation in Minnesota.[28] The most prominent Swedish-American politician of the post-war era is the Democrat Warren Magnuson who since 1944 has represented the state of Washington in the U.S. Senate. Born in Minnesota, Magnuson is one of the scores of Swedish Americans who have moved from the Middle West and settled on the West Coast.[29] At the present time the state of Washington is probably the one state in the country, second to Minnesota, which offers the best opportunities for political involvement by persons with Swedish background.

Considering that around 2 per cent of the American population can probably be classified as Swedish Americans, it can be said that this small ethnic group has been well represented in American political life. Yet, with the exception of Minnesota state government, it has not been substantially overrepresented. It is impossible to detect any particular political orientation among Swedish Americans. They have represented all sectors of the political spectrum, from the ultra-conservative to the most radical. Their ethnic background played an obvious role around the turn of the century when they made their political breakthrough, and even today it is probably considered a merit in districts with substantial numbers of Swedish voters. On the whole, however, Swedish-American politicians must be regarded as having been totally Americanized decades ago. As far as it is known, they have not played any prominent role in the debate on political relations between America and Sweden, which in recent years have often been strained. Nevertheless, it is worth noting that one of Minnesota's senators, former Vice-President Hubert Humphrey—himself of Norwegian descent on his mother's side—has criticized the Nixon administration's hardened attitude toward Sweden. It is conceivable that his feelings have been shared by at least some politicians of Swedish descent. However, in its relations with Sweden the American government is not obliged to take any appreciable consideration to Swedish Americans on the whole or to Swedish-American politicians.

[28] F. Ander (1938), pp. 332 f.; Benson and Hedin (1950), pp. 265 f.

[29] *The National Cyclopaedia of American Biography,* G (1946), p. 552.

10. Swedish Emigration to Latin America

By Harald Runblom

One basic pattern in the transatlantic migration between Europe and America during the 1800s was that Northern and Eastern Europeans chiefly emigrated to North America, whereas Southern Europeans largely dominated the stream of emigrants to South and Central America. Emigration from Sweden fits well into this pattern. Of the roughly 1.2 million people who emigrated from Sweden between 1850 and 1930, only around 5 000 left for destinations in Latin America.

Though limited in size, Swedish emigration to Latin America has not been neglected by research. There are many features which make this phase of Swedish emigration particularly interesting. The active Brazilian immigration propaganda influenced Swedish emigration to South America. Moreover, the social background and group structure of these emigrants were entirely different from that of Swedish emigrants to North America.

Before the middle of the 19th century Swedish emigration to Latin America consisted of unaccompanied migrants. Prior to the first organized emigration at the end of the 1860s only a few Swedes settled in Latin American areas. These included shipwrecked sailors, some businessmen, several exiled officers with financial difficulties, and other persons.[1] The Swedish possession of a colony in the West Indies, Saint Barthélemy (1784–1878), did not lead to any organized Swedish emigration. The island was mainly useful to Sweden as a base for Swedish trade with the American continent.

Swedish emigration to Latin America during the mass emigration period occurred mainly in small waves, which only partially coincided with the general pattern of economically-motivated emigration characterized by fluctuations from year to year.

[1] A. Paulin (1951), *passim*.

The bulk of Swedish emigration to Latin America was made up of four contingents:

a. 1868–1869 emigration to Brazil, the main part originating from the Stockholm area.

b. 1885–1889 emigration, to a large extent from the southern parts of Sweden.

c. 1890–1891 emigration, mainly to Brazil. More than 500 of the approximately 2 000 emigrants came from the Sundsvall area and about 700 from Stockholm.

d. 1909–1911 emigration to Brazil, mainly from Kiruna in the northernmost part of Sweden.

There was no continuous stream of migrants from Sweden to Latin America, and a quantitative analysis of the total emigration consequently yields little. Of interest here is its group character and the circumstances surrounding the emigration of the various contingents.

Group Emigrations

The main work on Swedish mass emigration to Latin America is a thesis by Karin Stenbeck, who has analyzed the group emigrations to Brazil up to the year 1891 (contingents a, b, c above). By combining sources from parish archives with passenger lists she has managed to show the composition of each of the three contingents.[2]

The 1868–1869 emigration to Brazil coincides with a series of severe set-backs for Swedish agriculture, the so-called "famine" years. There was a general rise in external Swedish migration during these years. The driving force behind the emigration to Brazil was a Swedish publicist, Johan Damm, an active emigrant agent. During the years 1868 and 1869 108 persons emigrated from Sweden to Brazil. Only a minority of them (36 individuals) have been completely identified, but nevertheless some conclusions about the group can be drawn. Although the total Swedish emigration during the 1860s was dominated by families, the emigration to Brazil largely consisted of men, most of them between the ages of 20 and 30. The majority of the emigrants were residents of Stockholm.[3]

European emigration to Brazil intensified during the latter half of the 1880s and reached its peak in 1891. Swedish emigration figures conform

[2] K. Stenbeck (1973).

[3] K. Stenbeck (1973), pp. 47–56.

to this general European picture. A great deal of the Swedish emigration in the 1880s originated from the southern part of the country and was attributable to the strong concentration of agency activity in the Malmö area. Swedish emigration to South America was mainly an urban phenomenon during these years. Thus, of 57 emigrants from Malmöhus län, 42 came from urban areas.

Swedish emigration to South America reached its full peak during 1890 and 1891, when about 2 000 persons emigrated. A group emigration in 1891 from a limited area, the Sundsvall district in Västernorrland, is worth special interest. The parishes surrounding the city of Sundsvall formed a center in the sawmill industry in Northern Sweden. The years around 1890 brought a receding demand for timber products, falling prices and over-production. Emigration to South America was strongest in Alnö, a parish with many small sawmills which were particularly sensitive to market fluctuations. Trade unions developed earlier in the sawmill areas of the Sundsvall district than in the rest of the country.[4]

Contemporary sources referred to a "Brazil fever" among the Sundsvall district workers.[5] About twenty public meetings, so-called Brazilian meetings, were organized by a special "Brazilian committee". All the members of this committee were laborers. Preliminary emigrant lists were drawn up, and the Brazilian office in Malmö recruited emigrants by way of frequent advertising in the local newspapers.

This emigration from the Sundsvall district to Brazil in 1891 has been compared with the emigration to North America in the same year. There were obvious differences. The migration to Brazil was strongly concentrated to certain industrial parishes; the North American emigration had a more agrarian character. Emigrants to Brazil had few possibilities of departing on their own. They exhibited great solidarity even at the outset of their journey. While the North American emigration was distinguished by individual emigration, the proportion of families was larger among the passengers to Brazil. The emigrants to Brazil were recruited from the lowest social groups among the working classes; there were few skilled workers. The Brazilian government partially subsidized the transatlantic voyage which explains why these poor emigrants were able to travel with their families. Furthermore, the departure from Sweden was more

[4] For the economic, social and demographic conditions in this area, see L.-G. Tedebrand (1972).

[5] The account of emigration to Brazil from the Sundsvall area is entirely based upon K. Stenbeck (1973), pp. 119–190.

permanent for emigrants bound for Brazil whereas a great deal of the emigrants to North America returned after a year or two.

The Brazilian emigrants from the Sundsvall area expected to settle as new, permanent residents of a country where equality and possibilities for social advancement were within reach. These expectations are obvious from the resolutions adopted in the Brazilian meetings.

The social recruitment of the Brazilian emigrants in the Sundsvall area corresponds with what is also known of the emigrants from Stockholm to Brazil during the years 1890 and 1891. According to calculations, these individuals amounted to 698 persons, most of whom came from the poorest sections of the capital and had a pronounced proletarian origin.[6]

During 1909–1911 the number of Swedish emigrants to Brazil increased markedly. In several respects this upswing is reminiscent of the 1890–1891 emigration to Brazil. Recruitment was concentrated to one area, in this case the mining district of Kiruna in Lappland, and the social composition of this flow of emigrants differed from those who simultaneously left for North America. Furthermore, there was a definite connection between the local labor market situation and the emigration directed to Brazil.[7]

A study of this Kiruna–Brazil emigration gives, among other things, clear insight into the role of the local press in influencing emigration. During the years 1909, 1910 and 1911 two regional daily newspapers (*Norrbottenskuriren* and *Norrskensflamman*) published no less than 1744 advertisements by shipping companies and emigrant agents. Of these 1744 announcements, 41 dealt with emigration to Brazil, while the remaining 1703 advertisements concerned North America. The advertisements concerning emigration to Brazil appeared only in *Norrskensflamman,* a Social Democratic newspaper, which supported the trade union movement and the cause of the working class. Through editorials and published letters from earlier emigrants, this paper encouraged workers to leave Sweden and migrate to Brazil. The workers' own propaganda effort for emigration to Brazil must be seen in the light of the troubles on the labor market, which culminated in the General Strike of 1909 (originally a factory owner lock-out which was extended to include the entire country through a nationwide workers' strike). The other paper, *Norrbottenskuriren,* propagated against emigration to Brazil by publishing letters which described the conditions of previous emigrants in an unfavorable light and through editorials discrediting the emigrant agents.

[6] F. Nilsson (1970), pp. 46–49, 299.
[7] All information about the Kiruna emigration is taken from D. Eriksson and M. Falk (1971).

Table 10: 1. *Family and Individual Emigration to Brazil and North America from Kiruna 1909–1911*

fam. = family, pers. = individual person

	1909		1910		1911	
	Brazil	North America	Brazil	North America	Brazil	North America
Married couples with children	6 fam.	5 fam.	34 fam.	21 fam.	27 fam.	4 fam.
Unmarried couples with children	1 fam.	–	2 fam.	1 fam.	–	–
Single parent (married or unmarried with children)	–	4 fam.	8 fam.	14 fam.	8 fam.	10 fam.
Individual migrants (married or unmarried)	1 pers.	52 pers.	7 pers.	79 pers.	4 pers.	28 pers.
Married and unmarried couples without children	1 fam.	3 fam.	–	3 fam.	–	2 fam.
Total	8 fam. 1 pers.	12 fam. 52 pers.	44 fam. 7 pers.	39 fam. 79 pers.	35 fam. 4 pers.	16 fam. 28 pers.

Source D. Eriksson and M. Falk (1971), p. 13.

As in the 1891 emigration from Sundsvall, this emigration to Brazil was characterized by family groups, as can be seen in Table 10: 1.

Emigrant Agency Activities and Immigration Information

Propaganda for Swedish emigration to Brazil was closely supported by the Brazilian immigration authorities, who worked through emigrant agents in Germany and sub-agents in Sweden. It has been possible to trace and, to some degree, define their activities concerning the group emigrations.[8] The emigrant propaganda in connection with the 1868–1869 emigration stemmed from the above-mentioned Johan Damm, who was the editor of *Sveriges Tidning.* He published emigration advertisements and news-

[8] K. Stenbeck (1973), pp. 15–46; D. Eriksson and M. Falk (1971).

paper articles as well as a booklet with facts for prospective emigrants to Brazil. Damm is mentioned as "general agent for Sweden" in advertisements from the Hamburg shipping company of Heydorn & Lobedanz. Damm's emigration agency was located at the office of *Sveriges Tidning* in Stockholm. He also had local agents in other towns (Malmö, Eskilstuna). His propaganda to prospective emigrants gave unrealistic promises of good wages in Brazil. His booklet, which is largely a translation of German emigrant agency material, incorrectly stated that the Brazilian climate was especially suitable for Swedes. Included are some equally baseless facts about earlier Swedish emigrants to Brazil.

Swedish emigration during the latter half of the 19th century chiefly originated from Southern Sweden partly because the agencies concentrating on Brazil were located there. In Malmö there were three agents (Tufve Mathiasson, Bentham Nelson, Theodor Tufveson) one of which was active from 1885. The Brazilian agency office was registered in Malmö in 1890. This office and its branch in Gothenburg were subordinated to the Brazilian emigration center in Hamburg.

The propaganda issued by the Swedish agents transporting travelers to Brazil was designed to present Brazilian conditions in general and to feature Brazil as an alternative to emigration to North America. The agents spread their information partly through newspapers and advertisements and partly through brochures which were addressed to prospective emigrants. In some cases these brochures had an official or semi-official origin.

Damm's rather suspect activities can be contrasted with an emigrant agency of the 1880s, which has been presented by Berit Brattne in her study of the Larsson Brothers. The information spread by this agency through newspaper advertisements was almost totally devoted to the technical aspects of the voyage and was intended to place the agency in letter contact with interested persons. Another of Brattne's findings, which sharply differs from the emigration to Brazil, is that the information from the agents had almost no importance for the emigrants' choices of destination. One of Brattne's general conclusions is that the transport companies could not increase the volume of emigration, even when their advertisement activity was on a high level. Rather they adjusted their transport capacity to the actual demand.[9]

[9] B. Brattne (1973). See also Chapter 7, above.

Political Dissent and Emigration to Brazil

Swedish emigration to Brazil in the early 1890s and around 1910 contains elements of political dissent.[10]

The emigration from the Sundsvall area in 1891 was a well-organized campaign. At meetings held by prospective emigrants resolutions were adopted which voiced political dissent and had a clearly socialistic tone. The newspaper *Socialdemokraten* stressed the political nature of the gatherings: "These meetings are excellent campaign rallies".[11] In 1890 and 1891 union organizations and trade union leaders in Stockholm played a prominent role in the preparations for emigration to Brazil. In the Swedish capital, as elsewhere in Sweden, emigration to Brazil was strongly characterized by group movements.[12]

In Kiruna the issue of emigration to Brazil was first discussed during a strike meeting in 1909. On that occasion the workers formed an emigration association which was primarily oriented in terms of emigration to Brazil.[13]

The emigration to Brazil from Sundsvall, Stockholm, and Kiruna—which comprised a major share of the total Swedish emigration to Latin America—was politically inspired and largely organized by local trade unions. In this respect Swedish emigration to Latin America clearly differs from the rest of emigration from Sweden.[14]

Swedish Settlement in Latin America

Since the Swedish emigration to Brazil was largely stimulated by the immigration authorities in the receiving country, it was only natural that many Swedes were assigned places of settlement.

The circumstances concerning the emigrants in 1868–1869 are best

[10] In 1930 J. S. Lindberg advocated the theory that the Swedish trade unions were not only hostile to emigration but also attempted to halt its progress. This has been rejected by F. Nilsson (1970) who, on the basis of his Stockholm study, has shown that occupational groups which formed trade unions at an early date (for example, iron industry workers) had a higher tendency to emigrate than other groups on the labor market. Nilsson also found that many prominent trade union leaders in Stockholm emigrated to America (p. 230 f.). On several occasions industrial workers demanded basic school education in the English language as a service to persons inclined to emigrate (p. 232).

[11] K. Stenbeck (1973), p. 147.

[12] F. Nilsson (1970), pp. 99–101.

[13] D. Eriksson and M. Falk (1971), p. 46.

[14] See, however, B. Rondahl (1972), pp. 154–193, regarding mass emigration from Ljusne in 1906.

known through reports from the Swedish and Norwegian Consul in Rio, Leonard Åkerblom. The emigrants of 1868 settled in the Dona Francisca colony in the State of Catharina, but they soon dispersed. Disappointed by the lack of possibilities for acquiring land and work some of them returned destitute to Rio. As time went by many of the 1868–1869 emigrants resorted to the coffee plantations in the State of Sao Paulo. Åkerblom's consular reports about the fate of the emigrants caused some indignation in Sweden.[15]

In a thesis on missionary history Sven Arne Flodell discusses the settlements, societies, social organizations, as well as religious and cultural conditions among settlers from the emigrant contingents of 1890–1891 and 1909–1911. He stresses that the official Brazilian propaganda spread in Sweden with regard to promises of high wages and favorable settlement conditions did not accurately portray the realities of the situation.[16]

The Brazilian authorities directed the emigrants of 1890–1891 to distant places in the State of Rio Grande do Sul, where they were isolated from each other so that it was almost impossible to maintain any ethnic traditions. The living conditions were severe, and many emigrants succumbed to disease, hunger, and poverty. "The settlers' harsh living conditions often led to drunkenness and apathy."[17] The settlers' life in Rio Grande do Sul was characterized by cultural isolation, and the children of the second generation received a deficient education. Knowledge of the Swedish language among these children was weakly developed. Superstition and primitivism were widespread in their living habits and customs.[18]

Around 1910 many Swedes from Brazil crossed the Argentinean border and made their way to the former Jesuit area called Misiones, where immigrants of different nationalities were then settling. Misiones was the destination for the great waves of Swedish migrants who had left their homes in the area west of Porto Alegre. Emigrants from the Kiruna contingent, who quickly found life in Brazil unattractive also settled in Misiones. For many of them emigration was such a failure that they appealed to the Swedish government for support. In 1912 about 500 Swedes were collectively repatriated through actions taken by the Swedish Embassy in Buenos Aires.[19]

[15] K. Stenbeck (1973), pp. 57–62.
[16] S. A. Flodell (1974), pp. 39, 55. Many of Flodell's results have been critically examined by H. Runblom (1975*a*).
[17] S. A. Flodell (1974), p. 45. There are no statistical verifications for these statements.
[18] S. A. Flodell (1974), p. 102.
[19] S. A. Flodell (1974), pp. 36–40.

In Misiones the Swedish settlement became so concentrated that a basis for ethnic solidarity was established. A census undertaken in the mid-1930s by Swedish ecclesiastical officials reported 927 Swedes in the area around Oberá, the heart of Swedish colonization.[20] Swedes living in Misiones retained a greater knowledge of Swedish than the average Swedish American. The number of religious ceremonies conducted in Spanish in the Swedish Oberá parish continuously increased, but until the 1960s Swedish was used as the language of worship. However, there was no total isolation of the Swedish ethnic group comparable to that of certain groups of Japanese immigrants in Brazil. A clear majority of second and third generation Swedes married outside their own ethnic group, and Swedish associations opened their doors to people of other nationalities.[21]

Swedish immigrants in South America tended to form associations and societies aimed at preserving patriotic traditions. The socialistic and anti-nationalistic attitude held by many of the Swedish emigrants prior to their departure did not prohibit their eagerness to maintain cultural bonds with Sweden. Attempts to transplant the Swedish Temperance Movement to South America failed presumably because of different drinking habits in the new country. There was an inclination to religious syncretism during the first decades after emigration. Many of the Swedes had no contact with any evangelical church, and features from foreign church services and occultism found their way into the religious customs, such as those pertaining to death and burial.

Contacts with the Swedish congregation in Buenos Aires and the missionary organ of the Swedish Lutheran Church subsequently represented a turning point in the immigrants' religious situation. Through initiatives from Sweden, the Swedes in Misiones received church services and gradually formed a parish of their own. Like many immigrant churches in the area, the Swedish congregation became a conservative element defending cultural solidarity with the mother country. The church encouraged efforts to maintain a Swedish school and the use of Swedish as the every-day language: this, however, received strong competition from Spanish, especially in the families of intermarried couples.[22]

[20] S. A. Flodell (1974), p. 102.

[21] S. A. Flodell's study on the Swedes' marriages (p. 154) is not convincing and is even contradicted by the author himself (p. 97). For comparative data on inter-marriage among Swedish immigrants in North America, see S. Lindmark (1971), pp. 50–63, and U. Beijbom (1971), pp. 136–140 and Chapter 9*c*, above.

[22] S. A. Flodell (1974), pp. 104–160, 177–185.

Concluding Remarks

Brazilian immigration policy had a decisive influence on mass Swedish emigration to Latin America. It is not merely a coincidence that this emigration culminated in 1890 and 1891. Shortly after Brazil abolished slavery in 1888, the number of coffee plantations in the country increased. The expansion of export-oriented, Brazilian farming was most favored by a free and mobile labor force. Immigration from Europe was encouraged, and the flow of immigrants reached its greatest strength in 1891. Emigrant recruitment was carried on as far north as Scandinavia. Emigration by families was considered most desirable. The family element was also very apparent from the end of the 1880s in the Sweden–Brazil emigration, while Swedish emigration on the whole was gradually characterized by individual movements. Since the emigrants' travel expenses were partially subsidized by the Brazilian authorities it was easier for whole families to emigrate. This policy also affected the social structure of the emigrant groups. Unskilled laborers were more widely represented among these emigrants than among those bound for North America.

For many of the Swedish emigrants to Brazil the whole experience turned out to be a personal failure: among other things, this is demonstrated by the collective repatriation of about 500 Swedes in 1912. The Swedish ethnic group in South America has mainly left traces in the Misiones immigrant territory, where during the course of several generations Swedes have maintained a strong ethnic cohesion.

11. Concluding Remarks

The theme of this volume is the Swedish emigration to America during the nineteenth and twentieth centuries. A comparative orientation has, however, characterized our research and this is mirrored in the text. Hence, we hope that our results may provide insights into migrational phenomena in general and external migration in particular in past and present time. The foregoing chapters, summing up the work of our research group, try to present a wide range of aspects on mass emigration: the chronology and structure of Swedish emigration, causes of emigration, the functioning and the organization of the transport sector, settlement patterns of the receiving areas, demographic characteristics of the immigrant population, and the assimilation process in North America. Systematic research has also been devoted to three topics, which have not been studied very much by international scholars: remigration, emigrant agencies, and emigration policy.

Migration research is situated at the cross-roads of social science studies. Therefore it is natural that we should relate our empirical findings to the theoretical discussions carried on in other disciplines. Our research group has also tried to adopt and evaluate results and techniques from other disciplines such as demography, geography, economics, social anthropology, sociology, and psychology. We have not, however, acted only as passive receivers of information and ideas. To some extent we have been able to develop our own theoretical framework using new techniques and methods. In the following the authors themselves summarize the main results in their respective contributions to this book.

Theories and Methods of Migration Research

The building of theories in the field of migrational studies has had as a starting-point an extensive research work within demography and economy, mainly performed on a highly aggregated level. The interest has been focused on net changes of the population distribution due to the labor market situation and the composition of the population. Demographic and economic conditions have been separately analysed but they have also been combined with each other. A tacit assumption has often been that the individual normally tries to make benefit calculations.

This line of research has gradually developed to allow more interdisciplinary points of view. Spatial aspects have been systematically considered since map analyses are of great importance for all types of migration studies. The geographers, however, have not been content with the study of demographic, economic, and spatial variables. They have also touched upon more sociological aspects and thereby observed the great importance of direct contacts between individuals to create and develop a migrational behavior.

Labor economists have also worked within this research tradition. They have long since left the crude labor market analysis behind and to a certain degree have focused interest on the individual in his search for job and migration alternatives. The perception and knowledge of the opportunity structure due to the information that reaches the individual form a basis for their interpretations. Barriers to certain behavioral alternatives have been noticed as well as the strong fluctuations in the inclination to change work position.

It is, however, within psychological research that we find the real emphasis on the individual. To psychologists migration is not just a matter of labor market problems. They have discerned different motivations decisive for the migration behavior and the effects upon the individuals. The complexity of most decisions to migrate has been strongly emphasized.

But the decision-making will be most effectively treated within a sociopsychological context. Various explanation models have been tried in order to illustrate how a migrational process develops from the state of latent inclination which often can be registered within a population. It is a most revealing thought that we are dealing with a so-called value-added process where certain structural preconditions must be combined to trigger off a migrational behavior.

An even stronger stress on the contextual side of our subject of study leads to a more sociological approach. Thereby the acting of the individual will be related to a social net-work, which seldom will be broken down in connection with migrational departures. Instead these net-works may partly explain the timing and structure of the streams of migration. It must be remarked that this notion of how individuals react and behave is very different from the one dominant among economists and geographers.

Special attention is paid to the main stream of migration research as presented above. The discussion moves from pure economic interpretations to combined efforts (economy, demography, etc.) over to more complicated interdisciplinary approaches like the one presented by B. Thomas. Central place theory and econometric model building are analysed in this context, especially the results reached by T. Moe. It is natural for historians to dwell within this very strong research tradition because the poor supply of data often hinders more detailed analyses.

But the real challenge we may find within the second research tradition using individuals as the research entity. It seems as if the huge body of knowledge, that we now face, will be used more effectively if we change our theoretical starting-point to the second research tradition. The many socio-psychological observations can thereby be integrated and combined to create a more over-arching interpretation. Some attempts in that direction are presented in this survey. Special interest is attached to the tentative model which has been elaborated by J. J. Mangalam et alii. This model stresses the strong interactive character of migrational behavior. Mangalam and his co-workers have, however, stopped at a middle-range level. The question still remains to be answered whether we can construct a more general explanatory model capable of combining the two research traditions. Such an attempt is finally suggested in Chapter 2. This approach works with four types of components:

A. Basic Factors and Conditions
B. Changes in the Basic Structure
C. Stimulators
D. Psychological-Sociological Multiplier Effects

The idea is that we basically are dealing with a so-called value-added process. When basic factors, relevant structural changes, and a set of stimulators interact favorably *multiplier effects* will reinforce a growth in the volume of emigration and vice versa.

It seems as if we are able to treat and explain the dramatic fluctuations of most emigration curves in a satisfactory way, whereby the reactions of the individuals and their latent inclination to move are combined with structural and situational conditions. It must be emphasized that the traditional business cycle analysis now can be incorporated into a broader theoretical framework.

Sources for the History of Swedish Emigration

The empirical orientation of the Uppsala Group and its efforts in testing theories require an adequate source material. On an aggregate level this is amply provided for by the extensive Swedish population statistics. On an individual level uniformly kept yearly listings of all emigrants together with the passenger lists from the shipping companies are the main sources. The presentation and source criticism of the latter can also be seen as a contribution to an international discussion.[1] Valuable supplementary information is to be found in the excellent Swedish population registration system.

Swedish Emigration Policy in an International Perspective

Freedom to emigrate was a main prerequisite for the mass emigration from Europe in the 19th century. Emigration policy in Sweden during the 19th century turns out to be a reflection of a remarkably uniform European development. Mercantilist policies, marked by a great interest in increasing the population and consequently in restricting emigration were replaced with a nearly total freedom of emigration during the first half of the 19th century. The causes of this change are twofold: a rapid population increase and demands from both economic and political liberalism. In Sweden the change from restrictive to liberal emigration policy occurred between 1840 and 1860.

There were, however, different ways of dealing with emigration within a liberal context. Many countries saw so-called assisted emigration as a convenient and cheap way of getting rid of such undesirable population elements as criminals, paupers, orphans, and invalids.

Sweden has also been accused of this type of emigration. On the other hand, some sections of the population were considered especially valuable and as such were prohibited from emigrating, even during periods of free emigration. Most important were the military conscripts, recruited soldiers, etc.

In Sweden, concern over the emigration of conscripts and efforts to stop this emigration increased until the turn of the century, when efforts to stop these emigrants culminated in attempts to stop all emigration. A reaction against emigration ensued and considerable efforts were made to achieve more restrictive legislation. Powerful interest groups can be found

[1] Other sources as census material, citizenship papers etc. are mentioned on p. 322.

behind this reaction, among others those who backed a strong national defense and those engaged in agriculture, who saw emigration as a menace to their labor force. The demands for restrictions resulted in an extensive official investigation of Swedish emigration, but did not, in the end, produce any restrictions on emigration.

The Swedish reaction against emigration has counterparts in other European countries. Nationalism and increasing political and economic competition in Europe may be seen as principal factors behind the renewed interest in restrictions on emigration. An important difference is to be noted, however, between countries with and without colonies. Countries with colonies manifested a growing interest in stopping emigration to, for instance, the US. They attempted instead to direct it to their own provinces overseas. In countries without colonies, such as Sweden, demands were instead raised to stop or restrict emigration.

Chronology and Structure of Swedish Emigration to America

A number of the features of transatlantic emigration from Europe during the 1800s have long been known. The initial phase, characterized by strong emigration from the British Isles and Germany was followed after 1850 by an acceleration of movement from most of the Northern European countries. This, in turn, was succeeded by a major wave of emigration from Central and Southern Europe. The maps included in Chapter 5, showing the emigration from all five of the Nordic countries, clearly demonstrate the necessity of a comparative study of national, regional, and local variations in emigration. They reveal that the early phase of emigration had its greatest strength in relatively limited areas later spreading over larger areas. However, the regional differences in the inclination to emigrate show a high degree of consistency over longer periods.

The Nordic countries display obvious differences in the extent and course of the emigration. As a mass movement it first affected Norway which also had the highest emigration relative to the size of its population during the whole period. The Finnish emigration, which did not start until the late 1880s, should be assigned to the East European wave of transoceanic migration. Denmark with a lower emigration and a less dramatic emigration course than the other Nordic countries shows similarities with other continental Western European countries. The Icelandic emigration had a late start but seems to have reached levels comparable to the Norwegian ones pretty soon.

Swedish source materials generally allow the determination of the specific social classes from which emigrants were recruited. It is therefore possible to pinpoint different stages or phases in the social composition of the emigrant population. There is a certain amount of substantiation for the general conclusion that the first migrants in a migration stream represent a strong positive selection and belong to a comparatively high social class.

Thus, the limited emigration of the 1820s and 1830s can be seen as an elite form of movement with a high degree of economically independent, middle-class persons. The start of actual mass emigration during the 1840s and 1850s saw movement of rather large numbers of agrarian landowners. After that time their share of the emigrant stream successively diminished. The years prior to 1870 were characterized by emigration resulting from crop failures, the so-called "Famine Emigration". The 1880s marked the culmination of rural emigration from Sweden. Although urban emigration comprised an evergrowing share of this movement, rural emigration continued to maintain its dominant position. Emigration during the 1920s consisted of many male farm workers. There was also a change in family structure over time. In the 1840s, 1850s, and 1860s many emigrants traveled in families and groups, but later the overwhelming majority were unmarried people traveling alone. This also coincided with an increase of remigration. A common feature of all periods is that very poor groups were markedly underrepresented among the emigrants. It was not primarily a complete destitution that forced many Swedes, especially many unmarried young men and women, out west but rather a general feeling of insecurity, a lack of steady job opportunities, and an absence of opportunities for social advancement.

Overseas emigration from Sweden shows considerable differences as to regional recruitment. These differences often coincide with old provincial borders. A continuous area of emigration is thus discernible in Southern and Western Sweden. The causes of these regional variations are, of course, difficult to establish. An important factor is the so-called urban influence field, which means that expanding larger towns and cities attracted the population in their surrounding rural areas and thereby curbed the amount of emigration. A typical example of this is Stockholm and its immediate hinterland.

An additional factor is that Swedish towns often are surrounded by fertile farming areas with a population consisting mostly of landless laborers, often with large families, who could hardly afford to emigrate.

The influence of expanding cities was thus important. An intriguing circumstance is, however, that the urban and industrial centers themselves show high frequencies of emigration, sometimes even higher than the rural areas. Industrialization *per se* was thus not an obstacle to emigration. Rapid economic fluctuations played an important role for urban emigration. Moreover many urban emigrants were originally in-migrants from areas of high emigration in the countryside.

This points to the considerable influence from the *tradition to emigrate* (see below) and to the so-called *stock effect,* that is, contacts and influence from relatives or neighbors who had already emigrated. This forms a necessary part among the explanations of Swedish emigration to America.

Causes of Emigration

a. An Attempt at a Multivariate Analysis.

A strong interest has been focused on the traditional type of economic and demographic analysis, as was mentioned above, where only a few variables have been treated to explain the migration pattern. This approach has taken the form of a labor market analysis. Much attention has been paid to fluctuations of business cycles and their correlation with the swings of migrational curves. There is no doubt that the fluctuation of emigration must be connected with changing economic patterns in America and in the emigrants' home countries (the so-called "push and pull" discussion). Using this angle of approach it has not, so far, been possible, however, to reach a generally accepted explanation for the strong short-term oscillations of the emigration curve.

It has been observed, that the fluctuation pattern of emigration has had the same tendency, regardless of the size of the administrative units (the whole country, the *län* or the parishes), due to the business cycles. In one respect, however, there are great differences. Adjacent areas with similar agricultural and industrial structures may very well show quite different patterns of emigration. There might be heavy emigration from one of these areas, and a low emigration from another.

For three *län* in central Sweden an investigation with Automatic Interaction Detector (AID) analysis of twelve different factors was undertaken parish by parish preceded by a so-called stage analysis on Örebro *län.* The results showed that explanations of a cultural and geographical nature had to be added to the economic explanations. A common feature of most migrational movements is a strong consistency over time and space. Most important is *the tradition to emigrate,* whereas *the urban field of influence* offers an additional explanation for certain areas.

In districts where emigration started early, often in the form of group movements, an emigration tradition was created and important contacts with areas in America were established. There are many examples showing that emigration from such areas often remained high during the entire emigration period. Urban influence, on the other hand, worked where the central commercial dominance of a city served as a common and viable alternative to emigration. As a rule such areas show a low transatlantic emigration. The possibility and tradition of moving to the city replaced the alternative of emigration to America.

b. Fear of Military Service—A Cause of Emigration?

In certain situations and for certain individuals the causes of emigration were of a more specific kind, the most prominent being religious and political in nature. Fear of military service has been ascribed importance as a significant cause of emigration, especially in contemporary sources. To investigate the relationship between military service and emigration, the emigration of twenty-year-olds and conscripts has been related to changes in the regulations of military service in Sweden. Prolongation of service and the introduction of a restrictive practice of granting permits to emigrate are occasions which could be expected to cause an increase in emigration. Different ways of correlating these factors have been tested and all give similar results. There is no evidence of a strong causal relationship between fear of military service and emigration. The emigration of these groups co-variate closely with total emigration trends. Even for those about to perform military service, economic conditions were without doubt the most influential causes of emigration. Military service might, however, at least in some cases, have acted as an additional impetus to emigrate, especially if good economic conditions in America made emigration an attractive alternative.

The Importance of the Transport Sector for Mass Emigration

The influence of the transport system on emigration was great according to contemporary opinions. Judging from a close scrutiny of the activities of a Swedish emigrant agency, the new transport organization and its extensive propaganda, does not seem, however, to have had more than a marginal effect on emigration. At least concerning the mass emigration to

North America, a series of investigations seems to show that the activities of the agencies and their method of operation were dictated by the strong fluctuations in the number of emigrants. These fluctuations were caused by other factors.

The price policy of the transoceanic steamship companies did not play a very active role either. Through cartel agreements between the shipping companies ticket prices were raised substantially during the peak years of emigration, while several times attempts were made to stimulate emigration during the trough years. This policy was hardly successful in stimulating transatlantic emigration. On the other hand, the well developed cartel organization which had its counterpart within the coal and steel industries was remarkably successful. This meant that the strong capital interests which were engaged in the North Atlantic shipping industry on a large scale managed to take out more excessive ticket prices than would have been possible in a more open competition.

These results run contrary to the prevailing assumptions within econometric emigration research. They also question recent interpretation attempts suggesting that the transport sector *per se* played a very active role within the whole system of transoceanic mass emigration.

Remigration from America to Sweden

Counterbalanced streams of movement always appear in connection with internal and external migration. What distinguishes Swedish emigration to North America in this context is the relatively weak countermovement and the highly substantial net population loss. Due to the excellent Swedish church book material it is possible to document the remigration to Sweden in detail.

The interpretation of remigration to Sweden from North America presented in this work has stressed the often overlooked fact that this special form of migration must be seen against the background of the extensive international labor movements distinguishable in Europe before World War I. The stream of returning Swedish-Americans becomes, in this way, a natural part of what Brinley Thomas has called "the Atlantic economy". Not entirely unexpected then, it is possible to relate long-term trends in remigration with changes in the level of the degree of expansion of the Swedish and American economies.

The remigration to Sweden begins as a counterflow, partly independent of the development of the economic conditions in America. Increased emigration led to an automatic increase of remigration because prominent years of emigration recruited large numbers of transatlantic labor migrants. Thus, the remigration fits rather well into Ravenstein's scheme of the origin of corresponding counter-flows. The rising oscillations in the course of the remigration graph may, on the other hand, be directly connected with the expulsive effects of the American depressions.

Remigration as a whole did not show any positive covariation with industrialization and urbanization. There was considerable urban remigration primarily in the initial phase of remigration. During the period of mass remigration the towns' share of remigration was only slightly greater than their share of emigration and was not increasing, in spite of the urbanization that was in progress. The rather pronounced remigration to agrarian areas was interpreted in two ways: (1) that the amount of remigration was positively correlated to the amount of individual emigration, and (2) that emigrants who were relatives of agricultural landowners (sons of farmers) preferred to spend some time in America rather than face the prospect of proletarization in the towns and industrial centers of Sweden. This interpretation provides a natural explanation for the male dominance among remigrants and the fact that remigration in most cases occurred only one or two years after emigration.

This leads to the important question of whether the returning migrants' stay in America was a stage in the process of urbanization or industrialization. The answer must be negative. About 80% of the investigated remigrants moved in a constant direction towards the parishes from which they had emigrated. Cities and industrial parishes did not make sizeable population gains at the expense of agricultural parishes in connection with return migration. The "conservative" pattern of return migration is of substantial interest from the standpoint of migration psychology and symbolizes the resistance of numerous agrarian groups to a permanent change in the social and physical environment brought about by the process of industrialization.

Swedes in North America

It is motivated to talk about an axis between certain areas in Sweden and certain areas in America. The whole *transition* process can be illustrated by means of both Swedish and American sources. Letters between earlier emigrants and people in their former home country often caused that colonization districts in America to a great extent were settled by persons from remarkably concentrated areas in Sweden. Various factors contributed to this phenomenon, which is called the self-generating effect or stock effect. Thus the economic structure of the emigrants' home parishes has influenced the choice of area for immigration. Emigrants from rural areas moved to a great extent to the American farming states. People from Swedish sawmill districts moved to lumber and industrial regions in the Middle West. In the same way emigration from iron industries in Sweden to the iron industry in Worcester, Massachusetts, can be mentioned as well as the stream of emigrants from the mining districts in Sweden to the mines in northern Michigan. Emigration for reasons of marriage intensified the initial locally concentrated pattern of emigration. Many women joined an earlier emigrated fiancé in America. Another factor was a common form of family emigration where the husband or some other family member moved in advance and the rest joined them later.

This settlement pattern often led to a strong ethnic and cultural homogeneity, which in turn contributed to a high persistence rate during the early phase of colonization for the Swedish population. This concentration of nationalities was important for the ethnic groups' social possibilities in new settlement areas. Thus a strong ethnic homogeneity and an early arrival to an area have proved to be of importance for an immigrant group to maintain its share of both qualified professions and administrative positions within a county.

Studies on Chicago and Worcester, Massachusetts, show that the Swedish population in American cities seems to have been engaged in a wide range of activities both in terms of church life and secular orders and associations. Among the Swedes in Chicago *a dualism* is to be found in immigrant institutions. This development is similar to e.g. the Italian experience, and it naturally caused cultural strains. On the one hand there was the broad mass of immigrants, representing the lower and the middle classes of society, which often had an agrarian background. On the other hand there was a smaller group, often of an urban and intellectual background.

The first category provided the broad popular base for the Augustana Lutheran Church, while the more exclusive denominations, like the Episcopalian Church attracted the other group of more well-established immigrants. This dualism was also reflected in attitudes toward social and cultural activities. While churches supported aid programs, schools, and hospitals, the secular organizations were more interested in theaters, concerts, and social gatherings. This dualism can also be noticed in the attitude expressed by the big Swedish newspapers. *Hemlandet* ("The Home Country") represented Swedish nationalism and opposed theaters, dances, and clubs, while *Svenska Amerikanaren* ("The Swedish American"), with its greater understanding for the assimilation process, considered *Hemlandet* a representative of narrow-minded opinions.

We also have to remember that a substantial part of the immigrant population never belonged to ethnic organizations. To trace these more anonymous immigrants in detail is a common problem for all historical studies of immigrants.

Publication of Swedish literature in America culminated between the turn of the century and World War I. With the ebb of immigration during the second half of the 1920s, the young American-born generation more and more frequently made demands for the English language in church worship and in literature. Group consciousness and a feeling of solidarity seems to have been strongest among the Swedes during times of crises, for example during World War I and the American depression in the early 1930s.

A majority of the Swedish immigrants waited to apply for citizenship often for as long as 20 years or more. Their interest to naturalize seems to have been correlated to social status and economic success. In general immigrants in urban areas applied for citizenship earlier than the rural immigrants. The statistics on naturalization are difficult to interpret. It is thus rather difficult to find out if the Swedes, who belonged to the "old immigration", distinguished themselves from other nationalities by achieving citizenship at an early stage. Recent research shows, that especially rural English immigrants delayed their applications for citizenship.

The transoceanic emigration was dominated by men. The result was an uneven sex ratio. At the same time more women than men moved into the cities. In a big city like Chicago, there was thus a large surplus of women aged 15–29 years among the Swedish population. This was due to a strong in-migration of maids. In the agrarian areas in the Middle West there was on the other hand, a considerable shortage of women.

There is a traditional opinion that inhabitants in new colonized areas have many children and high reproduction rates. This has been confirmed in a comparative study of fertility where two settlements in the Middle West (Pepin and Burnett Counties, Wisconsin) were correlated to areas of out-migration in Sweden. The reliability of American federal census material for such a study was first tested against Swedish church material.

Paradoxically the high reproduction rate can be explained by the shortage of women. The large surplus of men seems to have caused an exceptionally high marriage frequency among the women. In certain age groups 100 per cent of the women were married with many of them marrying very young. In spite of this sex disproportion Swedish men married to the same extent as in the areas of investigation in Sweden. This was not due to a high frequency of intermarriage, which was relatively uncommon during the early phase of colonization. Several investigations reveal that the stronger the ethnic concentration, the lower the frequency of intermarriage.

Swedes in Politics

Another important part of settlement and assimilation is political participation and the possibilities for an ethnic group to gain political influence. The case of Minnesota, where Swedes and Norwegians together with Germans and Irish formed substantial minorities, shows that Scandinavians especially after the immigration wave in the 1880s became a vital factor in the state's political life. The Republicans regarded the Scandinavians as "voting cattle". The Democrats, however, saw an opportunity to gain more influence by appealing to the ethnic feelings of the immigrants. Political participation also lead to political influence and a high proportion of the government officials were Scandinavian. In this respect, the Swedes played a more important role than, for instance, the German immigrants in Minnesota.

The possibilities to assert oneself in politics have been dependent on the size and geographical distribution of different nationalities in the United States and Canada. But we can also find that the ethnic groups have differed in terms of political engagement. On the American Congress level the Scandinavians have been represented to a rather high degree, especially the Norwegians, when compared to their share of the total population of the United States.

Swedish Emigration to Latin America

Contrary to the Nordic emigration to the United States emigration to Brazil, Australia, New Zealand and in the early years Canada, was directly promoted by agents who were often steered by authorities in the immigration countries. This is especially true concerning the Swedish emigration to Latin America, which reached its peak during the years immediately after the abolition of slavery in Brazil. During the transformation of the agricultural sector in these years, Brazil felt a shortage of labor and hence stimulated family immigration from Europe. The emigration to Brazil was limited to a few areas in Sweden (like in Denmark), which were urban or recently industrialized, like Stockholm, the sawmill district of Sundsvall and the mines in Kiruna close to the Polar circle.

The interest in emigrating to Brazil seems to have been connected with special problems of adjustment and a strong discontent with political and trade union questions. Family emigration to Brazil from Sweden was not the type of labor migration which characterized Southern European emigration to Latin America (birds of passage or the *golondrinas*) and later on also part of the Swedish emigration to America. The high rate of Swedish remigration from Latin America can be explained by the emigrants' inability to adjust to an environment with an unfamiliar climate and culture.

The mass emigration to America from Europe and other continents belongs to those research fields which never seem to lose their relevance. This is natural because external migrations have also characterized the period after the Second World War. In the case of Europe the strong movement from the Mediterranean region to the western and northwestern parts of the continent is especially remarkable. This relocation of people has partly replaced the earlier transoceanic emigration and seasonal movements.

Sweden has also been involved in this new migratory pattern. By a coincidence several old mass emigration regions now have been transformed to immigration districts where people from Greece, Turkey, Yugoslavia etc. work and live. These immigrants have adjustment problems rather similar to those experienced by the Swedish emigrants to North America generations ago. This means that the wheel has come full circle reminding us of the complex pattern of movements of capital, labor and know-how in the modern world. It is apparent, however, that this huge new labor market has its roots in an older dynamic society. This clearly indicates the importance of historical migration research. Therefore we hope that our research will be considered as a general contribution to the developing field of comparative population mobility studies.

Appendix 1. Documentation and Literature Concerning Swedish Emigration to America. An Annotated Bibliography

By Harald Runblom

Swedish emigration to America has been studied from several different perspectives. Historians, economists, church historians, literary historians, ethnologists, and other scholars have contributed to our knowledge. It is impossible to refer to all or even to most of their works, and it must be emphasized that this annotated bibliography is far from complete.

Emphasis is laid on scholarly research published during the last decades. Apart from theoretical works on migration and general works on migration history, studies on Swedish emigration during the mass emigration period (1840–1930) are included. Thus, the scant literature on Swedish emigration during the 1600s and the 1700s is omitted. Interest is concentrated on literature dealing with emigration itself and with political, economic, and socio-historical aspects thereof. With respect to other related areas of research such as literary history and linguistics, we only refer to some basic works which in turn contain extensive bibliographies.

Bibliographies

The Cultural Heritage of the Swedish Immigrant. Selected References by *O. F. Ander* (1956) has a broad format and gives valuable references for anyone studying Swedish emigration to America. This bibliography lists printed source materials and scholarly works from both sides of the Atlantic. There is no corresponding guide to unpublished material, but Ander gives some guidance to such material. Comprehensive references to scholarly and journalistic contributions on Scandinavians in the United States are to be found in *A Report on World Population Migrations* (1956). A list of works on Swedish Americans in the State of Washington is presented by *Robert D. Bingham* (1974). Of direct value also for studies of Swedish emigration is *Ragnar Mannil's* bibliography of Finnish emigration (1972). *Svensk historisk bibliografi* is published annually and provides a systematic list of historical literature, essays and newspaper articles about Swedes abroad.

Documentation

Important documentary sources on Swedish emigration are the Swedish *Parish Archives* (församlingsarkiv), which contain abundant data on individuals. Material up to 1895 is generally deposited in the *Provincial Archives* (landsarkiv). Condensed population reports sent from parishes and deaneries have been deposited in the *Central Bureau of Statistics* (Statistiska Centralbyrån), Stockholm. The main part of the Swedish church book material until 1895 has been microfilmed and is available in the Swedish county libraries (länsbibliotek) and is also kept by the Genealogical Association, Salt Lake City, Utah.

Two institutions formed in Sweden during the 1960s collect material on Swedish emigration. The *Emigrant Institute* (Emigrantinstitutet i Växjö) is the largest of the two and has conducted an inventory and microfilm record of church books in Swedish-American congregations (Lutherans, Covenantalists, Baptists, and Methodists). In 1975 the microfilming will be expanded to cover Canada as well. The collections of the Emigrant Institute also contain newspapers, journals, and other periodicals connected to Swedish-American history including books, brochures, maps and photographs. The Swedish-American church book material microfilmed by the Emigrant Institute, is also available at the *University of Chicago.* Swedish-American churchbooks from the Pacific Northwest are available at the *University of Washington,* Seattle. Situated in Karlstad, the *Emigrant Register* primarily collects documentation on emigration from Värmland. Taped interviews with Swedes in America collected by the *Institute for Dialect and Folklore Research* (Dialekt- och Folkminnesarkivet) in Uppsala are primarily suitable for linguistic studies.

The most comprehensive collection of Swedish-American newspapers can be found at the *Royal Swedish Library* (Kungliga Biblioteket) in Stockholm.

Alphabetically arranged lists of emigrants from Swedish ports are in the *Provincial Archives of Gothenburg* (Landsarkivet i Göteborg). They are adaptations of so-called passenger lists (passagerarlistor, skeppslistor).

The *Vasa Order* in the United States has established its archives in Bishop Hill, Ill. Certain collections pertaining to Swedish-American history are to be found at the *American-Swedish Institute* in Minneapolis, Minn. A guide to source material on Swedish immigration collected at the *National Archives* in Washington, D.C., is written by *Nils William Olsson* (1961).

Printed Sources

An invaluable source for those investigating the history of Swedish emigration is the *Emigrationsutredningen: Betänkande och bilagor.* This material was the result of a large investigating commission appointed by the Swedish Government in 1907. The background was increasing concern about the negative consequences of emigration on Swedish society. The commission's main report was published in 1913. The twenty supplements were published in 1908–1913 and contain detailed demographic and social statistics and reports on Swedish agriculture. Furthermore, there are descriptions of every parish in Sweden. The organization of the Emigrationsutredningen is researched by *Ann-Sofie Kälvemark* (1972).

A collection and recalculation of Swedish population statistics from the 1700s and the 1800s has been made by *Gustav Sundbärg* (1907, reprint 1970). Comprehensive population statistics for the period 1851–1910 were annually published in *Bidrag till Sveriges officiella statistik, serie A.* For the period after 1910 one should consult *Sveriges officiella statistik, serie A.* Swedish population data from 1750 are collected in a condensed version in *Historisk statistik för Sverige. Historical Statistics of Sweden, I: Befolkning, Population 1720–1950* (first edition 1955, second edition 1969).

Special collections of documents suitable for students of Swedish emigration are scarce. *Nils William Olsson's* book *Swedish Passenger Arrivals in New York 1820–1850* (1967) is an important work: aside from a list of Swedish arrivals it also contains biographies and information about the emigrants' Swedish background. A sequel to this work for Swedish passenger arrivals in Boston, Philadelphia, Baltimore and New Orleans is under preparation.

Church book material from the Swedish Lutheran Congregation in Chisago Lake, Minn., has been published by *Karl Olin* (1973), who supplemented the Swedish-American material with information from Swedish church records. Material of great documentary value regarding the heavy waves of emigration from Långasjö Parish in Småland is to be found in the book *En smålandssocken emigrerar* by *John Johansson, Jan Redin* and others (1967).

Several contributions of documentary character are printed in various volumes of the journal *The Swedish Pioneer Historical Quarterly.*

Source Critics

A guide to historical statistics on the Scandinavian countries is published by *Birgitta Odén* (Swedish version in *B. Odén* and *B. Schiller* 1970, English version 1972). *Gösta Lext* (1968) has made source analyses of Swedish poll-tax registers. The presence of systematical errors in Swedish church records during the mass emigration period is analyzed by *Anders Norberg* (1972). A critical study of Stockholm's population records is authored by *Fred Nilsson* (1965). The extent of unregistered emigration is discussed by *Gustav Sundbärg* (1907), *Lars-Göran Tedebrand* (1972) and *Enrique Bernin* (1972), while *Ann-Sofie Kälvemark* (1972) has dealt with the unregistered emigration of military conscripts.

Systematic observations on passenger lists from Swedish ports are made by *Ingrid Eriksson* (1970), *Lars Ljungmark* (1971), *Lars-Göran Tedebrand* (1972) and *Hans Norman* (1974). In conjunction with structural studies of Swedish emigration in 1923 *Torsten Augrell* (1975) has shown that large numbers of emigrants are registered in passenger lists from more than one port.

Information on immigrant Swedes in American statistics is comparatively analyzed by *Adolph Jensen* in *W. F. Willcox* (1929–1931). The incongruity between European emigration statistics and American immigration statistics is discussed by *Kristian Hvidt* (1971).

Critical observations on Swedish-American church book material are made by *Ulf Beijbom* (1971) and *Hans Norman* (1974), both of whom also present systematic examinations of the U.S. Federal Census.

Summarized Presentation

In a lecture given at the World History Conference in Stockholm *Frank Thistlethwaite* (1960) presented some important tasks concerning research on transatlantic mass emigration. He maintained that this stream of emigration could not be regarded as a homogeneous mass and he encouraged European historians to concentrate their efforts on this field of research. Up to that time the most significant contributions had been made by social scientists. *Sune Åkerman* (1975) takes Thistlethwaite's proposals as a starting-point for a survey of external migration research up to 1975. In an often cited presentation on urgent tasks for Scandinavian emigration researchers *Birgitta Odén* (1963) emphasizes the significance of the urban aspects of emigration. In a major essay *Birgitta Odén* (1971) has presented economic emigration models and discussed their explaining value for historical emigration research. The weaknesses of certain econometric models in explaining the structure and fluctuation of emigration are discussed by *Sune Åkerman* (1973), who strongly emphasizes the importance of an interdisciplinary approach. He maintains that observations in demographic, economic, sociological, psychological, and historical research must be combined in order to understand the mechanisms of emigration.

A comparative report on mass emigration from the Nordic countries (Denmark, Finland, Norway, and Sweden) is written by *A. Svalestuen* (1971). A research status report on Scandinavian emigration is published by *Ingrid Semmingsen* (1972). A survey of current problems of Scandinavian emigration research is presented in a volume entitled *Nordic Emigration* (1970), which summarizes a research conference held in Uppsala in 1969. As a result of Scandinavian co-operation in the area of emigration research a commentated cartographical publication entitled *Nordic Emigration Atlas* is presently being prepared. Emigration intensity in the five Scandinavian countries, including Iceland, is described in ten maps covering five year segments of the period 1865–1914.

The standard work on Danish emigration is a dissertation by *Kristian Hvidt* (1971, abbreviated English edition 1975), who makes several comparisons with Swedish conditions. In the same way *Reino Kero* (1974) systematically correlates his research on Finnish emigration with results in Swedish emigration research. Norwegian migration to America is reported in two scholarly surveys, one of them written by *Theodore Blegen* (1931, 1940, two volumes), the other by *Ingrid Semmingsen* (1941, 1950, two volumes). Our knowledge of the waves of emigration from Iceland between 1870 and 1900 is still unsignificant, but a brief survey can be found in an article by *Bjarni Vilhjálmsson* (1971).

Major overall studies of Swedish emigration to America are relatively old. Still worth reading are *Florence Jansson's* (1931) book on the background of Swedish emigration and *John S. Lindberg's* (1930) sociological study. An accessible survey is written by *Lars Ljungmark* (1965).

Regional and Local Studies

Several Swedish emigration researchers have presented studies which formally are of a local or regional nature. A province, län, härad, parish or a district is chosen for analysis of certain aspects of population turnover and emigration.

The major extensive study of Swedish urban emigration is that by *Fred Nilsson* (1970), who has dealt with Stockholm during the period of peak emigration in the 1880s. Provinces with weak emigration such as Uppland and Södermanland, have not attracted concentrated interest, despite the fact that the lack of emigration which characterizes these provinces is a very intriguing phenomenon. Some basic data on emigration from the foundry town of Eskilstuna are presented by *Bo Öhngren* (1974). Risinge Parish in Östergötland and the Finspång foundry district, which was strongly dependent on arms purchase orders from the Swedish armed forces, is the geographical starting-point for emigration studies by *Ulf Ebbeson* (1968). Two southern Swedish provinces, Småland and Öland, which had a high rate of emigration at a very early stage, are the topic of an essay by *Sten Carlsson* (1966–1967). A short survey on emigration from Jönköpings län has been made by *Birgitta Odén* (1966), who also has published emigration studies on Blekinge (1965). A thorough study of emigration from Öland is being prepared by *Margot Höjfors,* a member of the Uppsala Group. A study on Blekinge, concentrated to the initial phase of mass emigration has been made by *Agnes Wirén* (1975).

The structure of emigration from Halmstad, town of residence for Hallands län, is analyzed in a broad migration study by *Bo Kronborg* and *Thomas Nilsson* (1975). An area in Dalsland with an intense frequency of emigration, Sundals härad, has been studied by *Paul Noreen* (1967). Örebro län is the geographical basis for the versatile migration research published by *Hans Norman* (1974). In the same way, *Lars-Göran Tedebrand* (1972) relates his studies on emigration and return migration to Västernorrlands län. *Björn Rondahl's* (1972) dissertation on Söderala Parish in southern Hälsingland concentrates on a strongly industrialized area with pronounced emigration traditions. There are no in-depth studies to date dealing with emigration from Upper Norrland. Åland was long an area of political and migrational tension: its emigration history is researched in an unpublished licentiate thesis by *Frank Blomfelt* (1968). Phase shifts in emigration from Vasa län (Finland) to Russia, Sweden, and America have been studied by *Erik De Geer* and *Holger Wester* (1975).

The history departments of Swedish universities hold a vast number of unpublished papers on emigration, internal migration and demography produced by students on a lower academic level. These papers, which often contain studies of a local character, cannot be listed here.

Internal and External Migration

The selective mechanisms of migration are analyzed in a classic work by *Dorothy Swaine Thomas* (1938). The same author has in a pioneering work (1941) also treated Swedish external and internal migration against changes in economic trends. *Population Movements and Industrialization* (1941) is concerned with local variations in internal migration related to the economic structure of the community. Theoretical frameworks and measurement techniques of migration research are presented in *Migration in Sweden* (1957), which summarizes results gained by Swedish geographers during the 1940s and 1950s.

Emigration must be studied in relation to other forms of migration such as internal migration and seasonal labor migration. The relationship between internal and external migration is illuminated in a theoretical study by *Sune Åkerman* (1971). Our knowledge of internal migration in Sweden before industrialization is very meagre. Recent investigations from Sweden and Finland show, however, that earlier assumptions of low mobility during the pre-industrial phase must be revised. *Sten Carlsson* (1973) has shown in a study of the period 1816–1820 that migration in most parts of Sweden was more intense during that time than in the 1860s and 1870s. Pioneering results concerning internal mobility during the initial phase of industrialization are presented by *Sture Martinius* (1967), who also gives data on intraparish migration. Extremely high population mobility in a rural parish in the Lake Mälar Valley, characterized by large farms with *statare,* is revealed by *Ingrid Eriksson* and *John Rogers* (1973). The connection between seasonal labor migration, internal migration and emigration is illustrated by *Björn Rondahl* (1972) and *Ulla-Britt Lithell* (1971). The urban influence fields and their effect on emigration from surrounding areas were originally mapped by *Eric De Geer* (1959). His results prove to be valid for many Swedish cities. The role of migrational tradition as an explanation of the varying intensity of emigration from various areas is especially emphasized by *Hans Norman* (1974).

The extent of emigration by stages is investigated by *Fred Nilsson* (1970), who has established the fact that the great majority of emigrants from Stockholm were influenced by an urban environment at the time of emigration. In line with Nilsson's results, *Bo Kronborg* and *Thomas Nilsson* (1975) show that the city of Halmstad did not represent a temporary stay for emigrants from rural areas.

Swedish Emigration Policy

Swedish emigration policy during the era of mass emigration is treated by *Ann-Sofie Kälvemark* (1972). The investigation focuses on the restrictive tendencies towards emigration, which in Sweden as elsewhere in Europe emerged around the turn of the century. Legislation on emigration, especially that dealing with emigrant agencies and transport companies, is also presented by *Berit Brattne* (1973).

Sweden and America

The image of America in Swedish literature between 1750 and 1820 has been analyzed by *Harald Elovson* (1930) who has stressed that the strong admiration for America, significantly arising from 1775 on, was a characteristic of the Swedish Enlightenment. A continuation of Elovson's book is, in a way, a dissertation by *Nils Runeby* (1969) about the Swedish opinion on America and the prevailing conception of emigration during the period 1820–1860. Runeby, who gives a full account of the contemporary reaction to the first Swedish religiously motivated group emigrations in the 1840s, draws a dividing line between a conservative view of criticism and a liberal view of enthusiasm towards America. Commentaries about America during the Civil War have been scrutinized by *Kjell Bondestad* (1967, 1968), who has shown that the Swedish public opinion did not swing as wildly as the British. By the victory of the North, America secured the sympathies of her Swedish friends, i.e. the liberals. Emigration as an issue in Swedish political debate at the turn of the century has been analyzed by *Ann-Sofie Kälvemark* (1972). The impact of America in Sweden and the process of Americanization during the 20th century has not yet been thoroughly investigated.

Agencies and Transportation

Atlantic transportation is discussed by *Berit Brattne* (1973), who has focused her attention on a Swedish emigrant agency, Bröderna Larsson. In opposition to *Kristian Hvidt* (1971), who has maintained that emigration was stimulated by the competing shipping lines, Brattne stresses that they only adjusted their capacity to the actual demand for transport.

The Swedish Element in the United States

On the basis of American census material *R. K. Vedder* and *L. E. Gallaway* (1970) have shed light on Scandinavians' choice of immigration areas in the U.S. Their estimations, based on aggregated American statistics, apply to the entire Swedish immigrant stock. *Lars-Göran Tedebrand* (1972) and *Hans Norman* (1974) have reached more diversified results by isolating emigrant categories in Swedish passenger lists according to varying social and geographical background.

Minnesota's propaganda and activities to attract Swedish immigrants are described in detail by *Lars Ljungmark* (1971), who also analyzes the role of railway companies in immigrant traffic.

A mass of data on Swedes in the United States are presented in a voluminous book by *Allan Kastrup* (1975), who also provides an extensive bibliography.

A geographer, *Helge Nelson* (1943), has written the classic and basic work on the regional distribution and settlement of Swedes in the U.S. and Canada. The sociological background of the Swedes in Chicago, their demographic structure and mobility during the period up to 1880 is treated by *Ulf Beijbom* (1971). He emphasizes the role of Chicago as a temporary residence for Swedes on their way west. Theoretically important results on the demographic structure of an immigrant population are reached by *Hans Norman* (1974), who has given particular attention to certain areas in Wisconsin. The settlement of Swedish pioneers in Kansas is discussed by *J. S. Dowie* (1959).

Settlement, assimilation and political activities of Scandinavians in the Western states are almost neglected by research. There are, however, some exceptions. An over-all study on Scandinavians in the West is written by *Kenneth Bjork* (1958). In a study on Scandinavian immigration to the state of Washington during the decades around 1900, *Jørgen Dahlie* (1967) maintains that the Scandinavians insistently presented themselves as good Americans and that they did not behave as an ethnic minority in politics. The gradual integration of Swedish immigrants into American cultural patterns in two settlements in San Joaquin Valley, California, has been studied by *Phebe Fjellström* (1970). *Carl-Erik Måwe* (1971) has plotted the settlement in America of emigrants from Östmark Parish in Värmland and reported data on their adaptation to the new environment.

The Americanization of Swedes during two decades of political disturbances and pressing economic circumstances (1914–1932) is studied by *Sture Lindmark* (1971). By analyzing settlement concentrations and the level of persistance *John Rice* (1973) has measured the tendency toward segregation among various immigrant groups in a farming area of Minnesota. In line with these results *Robert Ostergren* (1971) has observed a strong connection between cultural homogeneity and high persistence rate. By way of statistical analysis of the agriculture and population censuses in two

Minnesota counties *Eva Hamberg* (1969) has demonstrated differences between the size and use of Swedish immigrant farms and American farms.

The majority of the 30 000 Scandinavian Mormons who migrated to Utah between 1850 and 1905 came from Denmark. This group is studied by *William Mulder* (1957), who has also analyzed the Swedish and Norwegian Mormons.

Religious aspects of Swedish immigration to America are dealt with by *George M. Stephenson* (1932), whose study forms a broad sociological and cultural description of Swedish-American church history. Various aspects of the establishment and organization of the Swedish Augustana Church are treated in several works published by *Augustana Historical Society,* Rock Island, Illinois. The history of the Evangelical Covenant Church of America is written by Karl A. Olsson (1962).

The Swedish-American element among foreign students at Uppsala University is discussed by *Jan Sundin* (1973).

As far as known, no systematic studies have been made on the role played by Swedes in shaping local political culture and political institutions or their participation in the educational process. Scandinavian immigrants originated from countries where local government was emerging, and it ought to be of great interest to find out whether this background left its mark on immigrant districts. Concerning the political activities of Swedes on a state level, our knowledge is most extensive for Minnesota, where the Swedes had their greatest numerical concentration. Their political awareness and the role of the ethnic factor among Germans, Norwegians and Swedes in Minnesota elections is discussed by *Sten Carlsson* (1971, 1973*a,* 1973*b*), who has also reported on the role played by Swedes in the political life of Minnesota.

Some Swedes gained seats in the U.S. Congress: among them was Charles Lindbergh, Sr., a representative of Minnesota. *Bruce Larson* (1971) portrays him as a person and politician, while *Richard Lucas* (1974) draws on Lindbergh's early political background to analyze his career as congressman up to 1912 and his political activity in connection with congressional insurgency in the House of Representatives.

A study of the Swedish-American press from the start of World War I to the end of World War II has been presented by *F. C. Capps* (1966), who stresses the inclination for isolationism and conservatism of the Swedish ethnic press.

No comprehensive work exists on the fictional literature of Swedish immigrants. With a combined method of historical analysis and conventional literary criticism *Dorothy Burton Skårdal* (1974) has used fiction and poetry from Danish-American, Norwegian-American and Swedish-American authors to depict the social history of Scandinavian immigrant groups. The development of the Swedish language in America is analyzed by *Nils Hasselmo* (1974) from the standpoint of transformational gramoner and sociolinguistics. An introduction to research on Swedish place-names in the U.S. is an article by *Folke Hedblom* (1972).

Swedes in Canada

Scandinavian immigration to Canada is a so far neglected field of research. However, there is a great deal of documentation and research performed concerning the concentrated immigration of Icelanders to the Prairie Provinces. *F.*

J. Kristjanson's (1965) book on Icelanders in Manitoba can be mentioned as a primary study in this context.

Many circumstances can help to explain the lack of knowledge about the history of Swedes in Canada. Immigration to Canada started at a late phase, when Swedish emigration generally had a large element of labor migration. Large-scale migration by Swedes to Canada did not occur until the turn of the century. Many of the early arrivals were employed by the Canadian railway companies, which willingly recruited labor from Scandinavian countries.[1] Geographical mobility was probably very high among Swedish immigrants. Compared to many districts in the U.S., Swedish settlements in Canada were few. Moreover, Swedish institutions (churches and societies) evidently lacked the cohesiveness which prevailed in many Swedish areas of the U.S. Observations made up to this point indicate that the Scandinavians show a low level of ethnic segregation as compared to other immigrant groups in Canada.[2] The interest among Swedes to collect documentation and knowledge about their own ethnic group has so far been rather weak.

From a research standpoint it is regrettable that essential sources such as the Canadian Manuscript Census are only available for the pre-1871 period.

The best survey on the Swedes' distribution in Canada is that by *Helge Nelson* (1943), who has mapped Swedish settlements on the basis of the Canadian Census of 1931. Certain basic data on Swedes in Canada are to be found in *The Canadian Family Tree* (1967). Other starting-points are provided by *Norman Macdonald*'s (1966) standard work on Canadian immigration and colonization. Scandinavian immigrants in Canada have mainly settled in the Prairie Provinces (Manitoba, Saskatchewan, Alberta) and in British Columbia. The Canadian Pacific Railway Company played a decisive role in the colonization of these provinces. This is the topic of a study by *James B. Hedges* (1939), who also touches upon the activities of Scandinavians as immigrants and settlers. Many of the Scandinavians who settled in the Prairie Provinces came from the American Middle West. The recruiting of Swedish farmers from Minnesota to Canada is described by *Karel Denis Bicha* (1968). An ingenious report of Swedish settlement in New Stockholm, Saskatchewan, which makes no pretentions of being a scholarly work, is that by *Gladys M. Halliwell* and *M. Zetta D. Persson* (1959). Certain aspects of Scandinavian settlement in Camrose, Alberta, are studied by *David Wood* (1967), who stresses the movement by Scandinavians from poor and average farm land to areas with good and excellent acreage.

In a broad context *Howard Palmer* (1972) has provided an inventive historical account of numerous ethnic groups in southern Alberta. He also discusses Scandinavian immigrants, but the lack of previous investigations on Scandinavians has obviously handicapped him. In a sociological study of the religious situation in Alberta, which was largely characterized by non-conformist denominations, *William E. Mann* (1955) makes several references to the churches of Swedish immigrants, primarily the Swedish Evangelical Mission Covenant. Some glimpses of Swedish activities in Vancouver are given by *Irene Howard* (1970).

[1] Payroll sheets, CPR (Canadian Pacific Railway) Archives, Montreal.

[2] H. Palmer (1972), pp. 220ff.

An extensive material on Canadian efforts to recruit Scandinavian immigrants has been collected by *Sten Aminoff* and is now deposited at the Department of American History at Uppsala University.

Sweden and Latin America

Detailed information on Latin American sources in Swedish archives, both official and private, are to be found in *Guía Fuentes para la Historia de Ibero-America en Escandinavia* (1968). The Swedish section of this valuable reference work was prepared by *Magnus Mörner,* who also contributed an introductory survey of Swedish relations with Latin America.

A survey of immigration to Latin America, which includes perspectives on Swedish emigration, is to be found in an essay by *Magnus Mörner* (1960). Swedish mass emigration to Brazil during the late 19th century is studied by *Karin Stenbeck* (1973), who has analyzed the geographical and social structure of the emigrant groups. The emigration from Västernorrland is also related by *Lars-Göran Tedebrand* (1972). Some information on emigrants from Stockholm to Brazil is given by *Fred Nilsson* (1970). Group emigration from Kiruna to Brazil in 1909–1911 is analyzed by *Disa Eriksson* and *Margaretha Falk* (1971).

On the basis of extensive case-study research in Europe and Latin America, *Axel Paulin* (1951) describes the living conditions of Swedish immigrants and temporary visitors in South America from the colonial period up to the end of the 19th century. A shorter account, which also describes Swedish activities in the 20th century, is that by *Martin Rogberg* (1954). Biographical information on Swedes in Brazil is found in a book by *Gualberto de Oliveira* (1952). Information on emigrant Swedish businessmen and their activities connected with Swedish business establishments in Latin America is provided by *Harald Runblom* (1971).

Swedish settlement in southern Brazil and in Misiones, Argentina, is covered by *Sven-Arne Flodell* (1974), who directs special attention to the immigrant's religious situation. Many of Flodell's arguments and conclusions are called into question by *Harald Runblom* (1975).

Appendix 2. Bibliography

Abler, R.; Adams, J. S.; and Gould, P.

1971 *Spatial Organization: the Geographer's View of the World.* Englewood Cliffs: Prentice-Hall 1971.

Abramovitz, M.

1961 "The Nature and Significance of Kuznets Cycles." *Economic Development and Cultural Change.* Chicago IX (3), April 1961, pp. 225–48.

Adamson, R.

1976 *Teori och metod för social och ekonomisk historia.* [Theory and Method in Social and Economic History.] (Forthcoming 1976.)

Adelman, Irma

1965 "Long Cycles—Fact or Artifact?" *American Economic Review,* June 1965, pp. 444–63.

Ahlström, L. J.

1924 *Femtiofem år i vestra Wisconsin.* [Fifty-Five Years in Western Wisconsin.] Minneapolis 1924.

Åkerman, Sune

1971 "Intern befolkningsomflyttning och emigration." [Internal Migration and Emigration.] In *Emigrationen fra Norden indtil 1. Verdenskrig. Rapporter til det Nordiske historikermøde i København 1971.* Copenhagen 1971.

1972*a* "The Psychology of Migration." *American Studies in Scandinavia,* No. 8, 1972, pp. 46–52.

1972*b* "Rural and Urban Immigration." *The Scandinavian Economic History Review* 1972: 1, pp. 95–101.

1973 "Migrationen—ett tvärvetenskapligt forskningsområde." [Migration—an Interdisciplinary Research Field.] In *Kälvemark* (1973), pp. 15–52.

1975 "From Stockholm to San Francisco." In *Annales Academiæ Regiæ Scientiarum Upsaliensis* 19, 1975. Uppsala 1975. (Presented as a Report to the XIV International Congress of Historical Sciences, San Francisco, August 22–29, 1975.)

1976 *Swedish and Scandinavian Population Mobility.* (Manuscript 1976, forthcoming.)

(SPHQ=Swedish Pioneer Historical Quarterly.)

Åkerman, Sune; Cassel, Per Gunnar; and Johansson, Egil
1974 "Background Variables of Population Mobility: An Attempt at Automatic Interaction Detector Analysis. A Preliminary Research Report." *The Scandinavian Economic History Review* 1974: 1, pp. 32–60.

Åkerman, Sune, and Johansson, Egil
1973 "Faktaunderlag för forskning. Planering av en demografisk databas." [Basic Data for Research. The Planning of a Demographic Data Base.] *Historisk tidskrift* 1973: 3, pp. 406–414.

Ander, O. Fritjof
1938 "Public Officials" in Benson, Adolph, and Hedin, Naboth (eds.), *Swedes in America 1638–1938*. New Haven 1938.
1956 *The Cultural Heritage of the Swedish Immigrant. Selected References.* (Augustana Historical Society, Publication No. 27.) Rock Island, Ill., 1956.
1960 "Lincoln and the Founders of Augustana College." *SPHQ* XI: 2, 1960, pp. 45–72.

Augrell, Torsten
1975 "1923 års utvandring. Destinations- och ursprungsuppgifter." [Emigration from Sweden in 1923. Data on Destinations and Geographical Background.] (Unpublished Paper, Dept. of History, University of Uppsala, 1975.)

Barton, H. Arnold
1975 *Letters from the Promised Land. Swedes in America, 1840–1914.* University of Minnesota Press, Minneapolis, 1975.

Beck, Robert N.
1959 "Brief History of the Swedes of Worcester." *SPHQ* X: 3, 1959, pp. 105–117.

Beijbom, Ulf
1969 Review of *N. W. Olsson* (1967). *Historisk tidskrift* 1969: 2, pp. 251–256.
1971 *Swedes in Chicago. A Demographic and Social Study of the 1846–1880 Immigration.* (Studia Historica Upsaliensia, 38.) Växjö 1971.
1972 "The Societies—a Wordly Alternative in the Swedish Chicago Colony." *SPHQ* XXIII: 3, 1972, pp. 135–150.
1973 "En studie i de svenskamerikanska kyrkoböckernas användbarhet för emigrations- och släktforskaren med särskild hänsyn till förhållanden i Chicago." [A Study of the Applicability of the Swedish-American Church Records for Research on Emigration and Genealogy with Particular Attention to Conditions in Chicago.] In Olin, Karl, *Chisago Lake-församlingen i Minnesota,* pp. 3–21. Lund 1973.

Bengston, Henry
1955 *Skandinaver på vänsterflygeln i USA.* [Scandinavians on the Left-Wing in U.S. Politics.] Stockholm 1955.

Benson, Adolph B., and Hedin, Naboth
1950 *Americans from Sweden.* Philadelphia and New York 1950.

Beretning
1971 *Beretning. Foredrag og forhandlinger ved det Nordiske Historikermøde i København 1971, 9–12 August.* [Speeches and Discussions at the Conference of Nordic Historians in Copenhagen 1971.] Copenhagen.

Bergendoff, Conrad
1968 "The Role of Augustana in the Transplanting of a Culture across the Atlantic." In *The Immigration of Ideas. Studies in the North Atlantic Community. Essays to Fritjof Ander.* (Augustana Historical Society, Publication No. 21.) Rock Island, Ill., 1968.
1969 *Augustana. A Profession of Faith. A History of Augustana College 1860–1935.* (Augustana Historical Society, Publication No. 33.) Rock Island, Ill., 1969.

Berger, Vilhelm
1934 "President Roosevelt's Swedish Ancestry." *The American Swedish Monthly,* April 1934, p. 112 f.

Berggren, Håkan
1966 *Förenta Staternas historia.* [A History of the United States.] Stockholm 1966.

Bernin, Enrique
1971 "En studie av nettomigrationen i Sverige 1750–1965 medelst differensmetoden." [A Study of Net Migration in Sweden 1750–1965 on the Basis of the Difference Method.] (Unpublished Paper, Dept. of Demography, University of Gothenburg, 1971.)

Bicha, Karel Denis
1968 *The American Farmer and the Canadian West, 1896–1914.* New York 1968.

Bingham, Robert D.
1974 "Swedish-Americans in Washington State: A Bibliography of Publications." *SPHQ* XXXV: 2, 1974, pp. 133–140.

Bjork, Kenneth O.
1958 *West of the Great Divide. Norwegian Migration to the Pacific Coast, 1847–1893.* Northfield, Minn., 1958.

The Biography of a People.
1974 *The Biography of a People. Past and Future Population Changes in Sweden. Conditions and Consequences.* (Royal Ministry of Foreign Affairs.) Stockholm 1974.

Blalock, H. M., jr. (ed.)
1971 *Causal Models in the Social Sciences.* Chicago 1971.

Blegen, Theodore C.
1931 *Norwegian Migration to America. 1825–1860.* Northfield, Minn., 1931.
1940 *Norwegian Migration to America. The American Transition.* Northfield, Minn., 1940.

Blomfelt, Frank
1968 "Emigrationen från ett skärgårdslandskap. Emigrationen från Åland 1856–1918 med särskild hänsyn till Finström och Föglö socknar." [Emigration from the Åland Islands 1856–1918, with Special Emphasis on Finström and Föglö Parishes.] (Unpublished Licentiate Thesis, Dept. of History, University of Uppsala, 1968.)

Boëthius, Bertil
"Carlsson, Erland." In *Svenskt Biografiskt Lexikon,* Vol. 7, pp. 569–575.

Bondestad, Kjell
1967 *Det amerikanska inbördeskriget i svensk opinion.* [The American Civil War and Swedish Public Opinion.] (Unpublished Licentiate Thesis, Dept. of History, University of Uppsala, 1967.)
1968 "The American Civil War and Swedish Public Opinion." *SPHQ* XIX: 2, 1968, pp. 95–115.

Bonsor, Noel R. P.
1955 *North Atlantic Seaway. An Illustrated History of the Passenger Service Linking the Old World and the New.* Prescot 1955.

Brattne, Berit
1973 *Bröderna Larsson. En studie i svensk emigrantagentverksamhet under 1880-talet.* [The Larsson Brothers. The Activity of Swedish Emigrant Agents During the 1880s.] (Studia Historica Upsaliensia, 50.) Uppsala 1973.

Braun, R.
1960 *Industrialisierung und Volksleben. Veränderungen der Lebensformen unter Einwirkung der verlagsindustriellen Heimarbeit in einem ländlichen Industriegebiet. Züricher Oberland vor 1800.* Winterthur 1960.

Cairncross, Alexander K.
1953 *Home and Foreign Investment 1870–1913. Studies in Capital Accumulation.* Cambridge 1953.

The Canadian Family Tree
1967 *The Canadian Family Tree.* (Prepared by Canadian Citizenship Branch Department of the Secretary of State and Published in Co-Operation with the Centennial Commission.) Ottawa 1967.

Capps, Finis Herbert
1966 *From Isolationism to Involvement. The Swedish Immigrant Press in America, 1914–1945.* Chicago 1966.
1969 "The Views of the Swedish-American Press Toward United States–Japanese Relations 1914–1945." *SPHQ* XX: 3, 1969, pp. 133–146.

Carlsson, Gösta
1969 *Social Mobility and Class Structure.* Lund 1969.

Carlsson, Sten
1966 "Den sociala omgrupperingen efter 1866." [The Social Regrouping after 1866.] In *Samhälle och riksdag. Historisk och statsvetenskaplig framställning utg. i anledning av tvåkammarriksdagens 100-åriga tillvaro.* Stockholm 1966.
1966–67 "Emigrationen från Småland och Öland 1861–1930. Social och regional fördelning." [Emigration from Småland and Öland. Social and Regional Distribution.] *Historielärarnas förenings årsskrift* 1966–1967, pp. 41–63.
1967 "Frikyrklighet och emigration. Ett bidrag." [Emigration and the Free Church Movement. A Contribution.] In *Kyrka, folk, stat. Festskrift till Sven Kjöllerström,* pp. 118–131. Lund 1967.
1968 "Från familjeutvandring till ensamutvandring. En utvecklingslinje i den svenska emigrationens historia." [From Family Emigration to Individual Emigration. A Line of Development in the History of Swedish Emigration.] In *Emigrationer. En bok till Vilhelm Moberg 20.8.1968,* pp. 101–122. Stockholm 1968.
1969 "Some Aspects of the Swedish Emigration to the United States." *SPHQ* XX: 4, 1969, pp. 192–203.
1970 *Skandinaviska politiker i Minnesota 1882–1900. En studie rörande den etniska faktorns roll vid politiska val i en immigrantstat.* [Scandinavian Politicians in Minnesota 1882–1900. A Study of the Role of Ethnic Factors in the Elections of an Immigrant State.] (Acta Universitatis Upsaliensis. Folia Historica Upsaliensia. 1.) Uppsala 1970.
1971 "Scandinavian Politicians in Minnesota Around the Turn of the Century. A Study of the Role of the Ethnic Factor in an Immigrant State." In *Americana Norvegica,* Vol. III. Oslo 1971.
1973 "Flyttningsintensiteten i det svenska agrarsamhället." [Migration Intensity in Swedish Agrarian Society.] *Eripainos. Turun Historiallinen Arkisto* 28/1973.
1973 "Skandinaviska politiker i Minnesota." [Scandinavian Politicians in Minnesota.] In *Kälvemark* (1973), pp. 212–243.

Carlsson, Sten, and Rosén, Jerker
1970 *Svensk historia.* [History of Sweden.] Vol. II. Third ed. Stockholm 1970.

Carrothers, G. A.
1956 "A Historical Review of the Gravity and Potential Concepts of Human

Interaction." *Journal of the American Institute of Planners.* Vol. 22, 1956, pp. 94–102.

Carrothers, W. A.
1929 *Emigration from the British Isles. With Special Reference to the Development of the Overseas Dominions.* London 1929.

Cerase, F. P.
1967 "A Study of Italian Migrants Returning from the USA." *The International Migration Review* 1967: 3, pp. 67–74.

Christaller, Walter
1972 "How I Discovered the Theory of Central Places: A Report About the Origin of Central Places." In English, P. W., and Mayfield, R. C. (eds.) *Man, Space, and Environment,* pp. 601–610. New York/Toronto 1972.

Coleman, J.
1962 "Restless Grant County. Americans on the Move." *Wisconsin Magazine of History, LXVI,* 1962.

Conze, Werner
1948–51 "Die Wirkungen der liberalen Agrarreformen auf die Volksordnung in Mitteleuropa im 19. Jahrhundert." *Vierteljahrschrift für Sozial- und Wirtschaftsgeschichte,* 38, 1948–1951.

Curti, Merle E.
1959 *The Making of an American Community. A Case Study of Democracy in a Frontier County.* Stanford, Cal., 1959.

Dahlie, Jørgen
"A Social History of Scandinavian Immigration, Washington State, 1895–1910." (Unpublished Ph. D. Thesis. Washington State University, 1967.)

Danielsson, Åke; Kronborg, Bo; and Nilsson, Thomas
1969 "Studier i 1923 års emigration." [Studies on Swedish Emigration in 1923.] (Unpublished Paper, Dept. of History, University of Uppsala, 1969.)

Davidsson, Rune
1969 "Den tidiga emigrationen från Kisa socken 1845–1860." [The Early Emigration from Kisa Parish 1845–1860.] In *Svensk 1800-talsemigration.* (... Meddelanden från Historiska institutionen i Göteborg nr 1.) Uppsala 1969.

Dedijer, Steven, and Semmingsen, Ingrid
1967 *Brain Drain and Brain Gain. A Bibliography on the Migration of Scientists, Engineers, Doctors and Students.* Lund Research Policy Program, 1967.

Demos, John
1970 *A Little Commonwealth. Family Life in Plymouth Colony.* New York 1970.

Dore, Grazia
1964 *La democrazia Italiana e l'emigrazione in America.* (Biblioteca di storia contemporanea. Sez. 2: 3.) Brescia 1964.

Dovelius, Bertil
1969 "Sabylunds församling i Stockholm 1856–1920. En studie i etnisk organisation." [Sabylund Congregation in Stockholm, Wisconsin, 1856–1920. A Study in Ethnic Organization.] (Unpublished Paper, Dept. of History, University of Uppsala, 1969.)

Dowie, James I.
1959 *Prairie Grass Dividing.* (Augustana Historical Society, Publication No. 18.) Rock Island, Ill., 1959.

Dowie, James I., and Espelie, Ernest M. (eds.)
1963 *The Swedish Immigrant Community in Transition.* (Augustana Historical Society, Publication No. 20.) Rock Island, Ill., 1963.

Duhac, René
1974 *La Sociologie des Migrations aux États-Unis.* Mouton 1974.

Dupeux, George
1975 "Les Migrations." (Report presented to the XIV International Congress of Historical Sciences, San Francisco, August 22–29, 1975.)

Easterlin, Richard A.
1968 *Population, Labor Force, and Long Swings in Economic Growth. The American Experience.* National Bureau of Economic Research, New York 1968.

Ebbeson, Ulf
1968 "Emigrationen från en bruksbygd i Östergötland. Utvandringen till Amerika åren 1868–1893 från Risinge socken med Finspångs styckebruk." [Emigration from a Foundry District in Östergötland. Emigration from Risinge Parish, Östergötland, with Special Emphasis on the Finspång Iron Works.] (Unpublished Licentiate Thesis, Dept. of History, University of Uppsala, 1968.)

Edin, K. A., and Hutchinson, E. P.
1935 *Studies of Differential Fertility in Sweden.* (Stockholm Economic Studies, No. 4.) Stockholm 1935.

Ehn, Erik
1968 "Emigrationen från en bruksbygd i Östergötland. Utvandringen till Amerika åren 1868–1893 från Risinge socken med Finspångs styckebruk." 129.

Eldridge, Hope T., and Thomas, Dorothy S.
1964 *Population Redistribution and Economic Growth. United States 1870–1950.* Vol. III: Demographic Analyses and Interrelations. Philadelphia 1964.

Ellemers, J. E.
1964 "The Determinants of Emigration. An Analysis of Dutch Studies in Migration." *Sociologica Neerlandica,* II, No. 1 (Summer 1964), pp. 41–52.

Elovson, Harald
1930 *Amerika i svensk litteratur 1750–1820. En studie i komparativ litteraturhistoria.* [America in Swedish Literature 1750–1820.] Lund 1930.

Emigration and Immigration Legislation and Treaties.
1922 *Emigration and Immigration Legislation and Treaties.* International Labour Organisation. Génève 1922.

Emigrationsutredningen
1913 *Emigrationsutredningen. Betänkande och bilagor (I–XX).* [Commission on Emigration. Report and Supplements.] Stockholm 1908–1913.

English, P. W., and Mayfield, F. C.
1972 *Man, Space, and Environment.* New York/Toronto 1972.

Erickson, Charlotte
1957 *American Industry and the European Immigrant 1860–1885.* Cambridge, Mass., 1957.
1972 *Invisible Immigrants. The Adaptation of English and Scottish Immigrants in Nineteenth-Century America.* University of Miami Press 1972.
1975 "Models in Migration and Migration Research." (Paper Presented at a Conference on Scandinavian Emigration to the United States, Oslo, May 1975.)

Eriksson, Disa, and Falk, Margaretha
1971 "Emigrationen till Brasilien från Kiruna stad åren 1909–1911. En jämförelse med den nordamerikanska utvandringen beträffande struktur, propaganda och tidningsdebatt." [The Emigration to Brazil from the City of Kiruna 1909–1911. A Comparison with Emigration to North America with Respect to Structure, Propaganda, and Newspaper Debate.] (Unpublished Paper, Dept. of History, University of Uppsala, 1971.)

Eriksson, Ingrid
1970 "Passenger Lists and the Annual Parish Reports on Emigrants as Sources for the Study of Emigration from Sweden." In *Nordic Emigration.* 1970.

Eriksson, Ingrid, and Rogers, John
1973 "Mobility in an Agrarian Community. Practical and Methodological Con-

siderations." In *Aristocrats, Farmers, Proletarians. Essays in Swedish Demographic History.* (Studia Historica Upsaliensia, 47.) Uppsala 1973.

Eriksson, Margaretha
1971 "Emigrationen från Örebro län 1879–1882 till Nordamerika med utgångspunkt från skeppslistorna i Göteborg." [Emigration from Örebro län 1879–1882 to North America on the basis of Gothenburg Passenger Lists.] (Unpublished Paper, Dept. of History, University of Uppsala, 1971.)
1972 "Ett kolonisationsområde i Wisconsin 1854–1880. En studie av källmaterial och etnisk sammansättning." [An Area of Pioneer Settlement in Wisconsin 1854–1880: Study of Source Material and Ethnic Composition.] (Unpublished Paper, Dept. of History, University of Uppsala, 1972.)

Eriksson, Margaretha, and Åkerman, Sune
1974 "Geografisk och social rörlighet. Resultat från Trestads-studien." [Geographical and Social Mobility. Results from the Three City Study.] *Scandia* 1974: 2, pp. 260–310.

Estey, J. A.
1956 *Business Cycles. Their Nature, Cause, and Control.* Third ed. New Jersey 1956.

Fauchille, F.
1922 *Traité de droit international publique.* Paris 1922.

Ferenczi, Imre
1929 "An Historical Study of Migration Statistics." *International Labour Review,* Vol. XX, 1929.

Fischer, David Hackett
1971 *Historians' Fallacies Toward a Logic of Historical Thought.* London 1971.

Fjellström, Phebe
1970 *Swedish-American Colonization in the San Joaquin Valley in California.* A Study of the Acculturation and Assimilation of an Immigrant Group. (Studia Ethnographica Upsaliensia, XXXIII.) Uppsala 1970.

Flodell, Sven Arne
1974 *Tierra Nueva. Svensk grupputvandring till Latinamerika. Integration och församlingsbildning.* [Tierra Nueva. Swedish Emigration to Latin America. Integration and Church Growth.] (Studia Missionalia Upsaliensia, XXV.) Stockholm 1974.

Foerster, R. F.
1919 *Italian Emigration of Our Times.* 1919.

Friberg, Nils
1954 *Dalarnas befolkning på 1600-talet. Geografiska studier på grundval av kyrkoböckerna med särskild hänsyn till folkmängdsförhållandena.* [The Population of Dalarna in the 1600s. Geographical Studies Based on Church Records with Special Emphasis on Population Conditions.] Stockholm 1954.

Friberg, Nils and Inga
1971 "Sveriges äldsta husförhörslängd." [The Oldest Parish Register of Catechetical Examinations in Sweden.] (Unpublished Manuscript, 1971.)

Friman, Axel
1974 "Svensk utvandring till Nordamerika 1820–1850." [Swedish Emigration to North America 1820–1850.] *Personhistorisk tidskrift* 1974, pp. 18–35. 1974.

Gahn, H.
1916 "Primäruppgifterna i vår svenska befolkningsstatistik 1749–1915." [The Primary Data in the Swedish Population Statistics 1749–1915.] *Statsvetenskaplig tidskrift* 1916, pp. 16–30.

De Geer, Eric
1959 "Emigrationen i Västsverige i slutet av 1800-talet." [Emigration from Western Sweden at the End of the 1800s.] *Ymer* 1959, pp. 194–223.

De Geer, Eric, and Wester, Holger
1975 "Utrikes resor, arbetsvandringar och flyttningar i Finland och Vasa län 1861–90." [Travels Abroad, Migrant Labor Movements and Migration in Finland and Vasa län 1861–90.] In *Österbotten 1975.* (Skrifter utg. av Svensk-Österbottniska Samfundet.) Vasa 1975.

Gibbs, Vernon
1963 *British Passenger Liners of the Five Oceans.* London 1963.

Gilkey, G. R.
1968 "The United States and Italy. Migration and Repatriation." In F. D. Scott (ed.), *World Migration in Modern Times.* New Jersey 1968.

Glass, David V.
1967 *Population Policies and Movements in Europe.* New Ed. London 1967.

Goldlust, John, and Richmond, Anthony H.
1974 "A Multivariate Model of Immigrant Adaptation." *International Migration Review,* No. 26, 1974, pp. 193–225.

Gould, Peter R.
1972 "On Mental Maps." In English, P. W., and Mayfield, R. C. (eds.) *Man, Space, and Environment,* pp. 260–282. New York/Toronto 1972.

Greely, Andrew M.
1974 *Ethnicity in the United States. A Preliminary Reconnaissance.* (The Wiley Series in Urban Research.) 1974.

Gregory, J. W.
1928 *Human Migration and the Future. A Study of the Causes, Effects and Control of Emigration.* London 1928.

Greven, Philip J., Jr.
1970 *Four Generations. Population, Land and Family in Colonial Andover, Massachusetts.* Ithaca, N.Y., 1970.

Grodinsky, Julius
1962 *Transcontinental Railway Strategy 1869–1893. A Study of Businessmen.* Philadelphia 1962.

Gualberto de Oliveira, João
1952 *Suecos no Brasil.* São Paulo 1952.

Guía Fuentes
1968 *Guía Fuentes para la Historia de Ibero-Amèrica Escandinavia.* Obra publicada bajo los auspicios de la UNESCO del Consejo International de Archivos de Investigaciones Humanisticas (Suecia). Estocolmo 1968.

Habakkuk, H. J.
1962 "Fluctuations in House-Building in Britain and the United States in the Nineteenth Century." *The Journal of Economic History,* XXII (2), 1962.

Hägerstrand, Torsten
1957 "Migration and Area. Survey of a Sample of Swedish Migration Fields and Hypothetical Considerations on their Genesis." In *Migration in Sweden. A Symposium.* Lund 1957.
1972 "Aspects of the Spatial Structure of Social Communications and the Diffusion of Information." In English, P. W., and Mayfield, R. C. (eds.) *Man, Space, and Environment,* pp. 328–340. New York/Toronto 1972.

Halliwell, Gladys M., and Persson, M. Zetta D.
1959 *Three Score and Ten 1886–1956. A Story of the Swedish Settlement of Stockholm and District.* Yorktown, Sask., 1959.

Hamberg, Eva
1969 "En jämförande undersökning av jordbruk." [A Comparative Study of Agriculture in Chisago and Isanti Counties, Minnesota.] *Statistisk tidskrift* 1969: 6, pp. 456–477.

Handlin, Oscar
1969 *Boston's Immigrants 1790–1880.* New York 1969.

Hannerberg, David
1940 "Mantalsskriven befolkning och total folkmängd." [Population in the Poll-Tax Registers and Total Population.] In *Gothia,* 5. Göteborg 1940.

Hanssen, Börje
1952 *Österlen. En studie över socialantropologiska sammanhang under 1600- och 1700-talen i sydöstra Skåne.* [A Study on Social-Anthropology During the 1600s and the 1700s in Southeastern Skåne.] Stockholm 1952.

Hareven, Tamara, and Modell, John
1972 "Urbanization and the Malleable Houshold: an Examination of Boarding and Lodging in American Families." (Unpublished Paper, Dept. of History, Clark University, Worcester, Mass., 1972.)

Hasselmo, Nils
1974 *Amerikasvenska. En bok om språkutvecklingen i Svensk-Amerika.* [American Swedish. A Book on Language Development in Swedish America.] Lund 1974.

Heberle, R.
1955 "Theorie der Wanderungen Soziologische Betrachtungen." *Schmollers Jahrbuch für Gesetzgebung, Verwaltung und Volkwirtschaft.* 75. Jahrgang. Erstes Heft. Berlin 1955.

Heckscher, Eli F.
1935 *Mercantilism.* Vols. I–II. London 1935.

Hedblom, Folke
1963 "Om svenska folkmål i Amerika. Från landsmåls- och folkminnesarkivets bandinspelningsexpedition 1962." [Swedish Language in America. From a Tape Recording Expedition of the Institute for Dialect and Folklore Research.] In *Svenska Landsmål och Svenskt Folkliv* 1962.
1965 "Bandinspelningsexpeditionen till Svensk-Amerika 1964. En reserapport." [The Tape Recording Expedition to Swedish America 1964.] In *Svenska Landsmål och Svenskt Folkliv* 1965.
1966 "Den tredje inspelningsexpeditionen till Svensk-Amerika." [The Third Recording Expedition to Swedish America.] In *Svenska Landsmål och Svenskt Folkliv* 1966.
1967 "Research of Swedish Speech and Popular Traditions in America 1966." *SPHQ* XVIII: 2, 1967, pp. 76–92.
1972 "Place-Names in Immigrant Communities. Concerning the Giving of Swedish Place-Names in America." *SPHQ* XXIII: 4, 1972, pp. 246–260.

Hedges, James B.
1939 *Building the Canadian West. The Land and Colonization Policies of the Canadian Pacific Railway.* New York 1939.

Hedman, Inga, and Tjernström, Gunnel
1970 "Migration och äktenskapsmarknad—befolkningsrörelsen i Timrå socken 1865–1899." [Migration and Marriage Market—Population Movement in Timrå Parish 1865–1899.] (Unpublished Paper, Dept. of History, University of Uppsala, 1970.)

Hellström, Olle
"Jansson, Erik." In *Svenskt biografiskt lexikon,* Vol. 20, pp. 121–125.

Helmes, Winifred G.
1949 *John A. Johnson, the People's Governor. A Political Biography.* Minneapolis and London 1949.

Henriksson, Rolf
1969 "An Interpretation of the Significance of Emigration for the Growth of Economic Welfare in Sweden, 1860–1910." (Unpublished Ph.D. Thesis. Evanston 1969.)

Henripin, Jacques, and Perón, Yves
1972 "The Demographic Transition of the Province of Quebec." In Glass, D.V., and Revelle, R. (eds.), *Population and Social Change,* pp. 213–229. London 1972.

Henry, N. W.; McGinnis, R.; and Tegtmeyer, H. W.
1971 "A Finite Model of Mobility." *Journal of Mathematical Sociology,* 1971.

Hierta, Lars Johan
Riksdagsmotioner och anföranden. [Motions and Speeches Given in the *Riksdag.*] Published by Aldén, G., Vol. I. Stockholm 1913.

Hirschman, A.
1958 *The Strategy of Economic Development.* New Haven 1958.

Historisk statistik för Sverige
1955 *Historisk statistik för Sverige. Historical Statistics of Sweden.* Part I: Population.
1969 Stockholm, First ed. 1955, Second ed. 1969.

Hjelt, A.
1899 *De första officiella relationerna om Svenska tabellverket åren 1749–1757. Några bidrag till den svensk-finska befolkningsstatistikens historia.* [The First Official Descriptions of the Swedish National Bureau of Statistics. Some Contributions to the History of Swedish and Finnish Population Statistics.] Helsingfors 1899.
1900 *Det svenska tabellverkets uppkomst, organisation och tidigare verksamhet. Några minnesblad ur den svensk-finska befolkningsstatistikens historia.* [The Swedish National Bureau of Statistics. Its Establishment, Organization and Early Operations.] Helsingfors 1900.

Höjfors, Margot
1971 "Emigrationen över Kalmar 1880–1893. En studie i Johan Magnus Fogelbergs agenturverksamhet." [The Emigration via Kalmar 1880–1893. A Study of J. M. Fogelberg's Emigrant Agency.] (Unpublished Paper, Dept. of History, University of Uppsala, 1971.)

Holmström, Arne
1974 "Befolkningsförhållanden i Wyoming township, Minnesota, åren 1860–1885." [Population Conditions in Wyoming Township, Minnesota, 1860–1885.] (Unpublished Paper, Dept. of History, University of Uppsala, 1974.)

Howard, Irene
1970 *Vancouver's Svenskar. A History of the Swedish Community in Vancouver.* Vancouver 1970.

Hutchinson, E. P.
1967 *The Population Debate. The Development of Conflicting Theories up to 1900.* Boston 1967.

Hvidt, Kristian
1971*a* *Flugten til Amerika eller Drivekræfter i massutvandringen fra Danmark 1868–1914.* [The Flight to America or Push Factors in Mass Emigration from Denmark.] Odense 1971.
1971*b* "Informationsspredning og emigration med særligt henblik på det atlantiske transportsystem." [Spread of Information and Emigration with Special Emphasis on the Atlantic Transport System.] In *Emigrationen fra Norden indtil 1. Verdenskrig. Rapporter til det Nordiske historikermøde i København 1971.* Copenhagen 1971.
1972 "Mass Emigration from Denmark to the United States 1868–1914." *American Studies in Scandinavia,* No. 9, 1972.
1974 "Scandinavian Discord on Emigration." *SPHQ* XXV: 3–4, 1974, pp. 254–263.
1975 *Flight to America. The Social Background of 300 000 Danish Emigrants.* Academic Press, New York 1975.

Iatsounski, V.-K.
1970 "Le rôle des migrations et de l'accroissement naturel dans la colonisation des nouvelles régions de la Russie." *Annales de Démographie Historique* 1970, pp. 302–308.

International Labour Office
1947 *First Report of the International Labour Organization to the United Nations.* (Reports, Vol. I.) Geneva 1947.

Isaac, Julius
1947 *Economics of Migration.* London 1947.

Isaksson, Olov, and Hallgren, Sören
1969 *Bishop Hill. A Utopia on the Prairie.* Stockholm 1969.

Jackson, J. A. (ed.)
1969 *Migration.* (Sociological Studies 2.) Cambridge University Press, 1969.

Janson, Florence E.
1931 *The Background of Swedish Emigration 1840–1930.* Chicago, Ill., 1931.

Johansson, Egil
1972 "En studie med kvantitativa metoder av folkundervisningen i Bygdeå socken 1845–1873." [A Quantitative Study of Popular Education in Bygdeå Parish 1845–1873.] (Unpublished Ph.D. Dissertation, Dept. of Education, University of Umeå, 1972.)
1973 *Literacy and Society in a Historical Perspective—Conference Report.* Edited by Egil Johansson. (Educational Reports, 2.) Umeå 1973.

Johnson, Amandus
1911 *The Swedish Settlements on the Delaware, their History and Relation to the Indians, Dutch and English 1638–1644 with an Account of the South, the New Sweden, and the American Companies, and the Efforts of Sweden to Regain the Colony.* Vols. 1, 2. University of Pennsylvania 1911.

Johnson, E. H.
1900 "Barndomsminnen från nybyggaretiden i norra Wisconsin." [Childhood Memories from the Pioneer Period in Northern Wisconsin.] In *Valkyrian* 1900.
1912 "Så var det i början." [The Way it was in the Beginning.] In *Prärieblomman* 1912.

Johnson, Gustav E.
1952 "Some Swedish Travelogues and Records of Experiences in America." *SPHQ* III:4, 1952, pp. 104–112.
1964 "A Selected Bibliography of Bishop Hill Literature." *SPHQ* XV:3, 1964, pp. 109–122.

Johnson, Stanley C.
1966 *A History of Emigration from the United Kingdom to North America 1763–1912.* Second ed. London 1966.

Johnston, H. J. M.
1972 *British Emigration Policy 1815–1830. "Shovelling Out Paupers."* Oxford 1972.

Jöhr, Walter Adolf
1952 *Theoretische Grundlagen der Wirtschaftspolitik,* Band II: Die Konjunkturschwankungen. Tübingen/Zürich 1952.

Jonasson, Gustaf
1973 "Svenskhetens bevarande i USA." [Preservation of Swedish Ethnicity in the U.S.] Review of *Lindmark* (1971). *Historisk tidskrift* 1973: 2, pp. 267–275.

Jonsson, Anita
1973 "Bosättningen i Trade Lake, Wisconsin 1880. En prövning av censusmaterial och lutherska kyrkoböcker som källa för studier av befolkningens migration och struktur." [The Settlement in Trade Lake, Wisconsin, 1880. An Examination of Census Material and Swedish Lutheran Church Records as Sources for Studies of Demographic Structure and Migration.] (Unpublished Paper, Dept. of History, University of Uppsala, 1973.)

Jörberg, Lennart
1966 "Några tillväxtfaktorer i 1800-talets svenska industriella utveckling." [Some Factors of Growth in 19th Century Swedish Industrial Development.] In Ragnhild Lundström, *Kring industrialismens genombrott i Sverige,* pp. 13–47; Stockholm 1966.
1972 *A History of Prices in Sweden 1732–1914.* Vols. I, II. Lund 1972.

Kälvemark, Ann-Sofie
1972 *Reaktionen mot utvandringen. Emigrationsfrågan i svensk debatt och politik 1901–1904.* [The Swedish Reaction Against Emigration. The Issue of Emigration in Swedish Debate and Politics 1901–1904.] (Studia Historica Upsaliensia, 41.) Uppsala 1972.
1973 *Utvandring. Den svenska emigrationen till Amerika i historiskt perspektiv. En antologi.* [Emigration. Swedish Emigration to America in an Historical Perspective. An Anthology.] Edited by Ann-Sofie Kälvemark. Malmö 1973.

Kastrup, Allan
1975 *The Swedish Heritage in America. The Swedish Elements in America in Their Historical Perspective.* (Swedish Council of America.) St. Paul, Minn., 1975.

Kero, Reino
1971 "Ekonomiska faktorer som förklaringsgrund i emigrationsforskningen." [Economic Factors as a Basis of Explanation in Emigration Research.] In *Emigrationen fra Norden indtil 1. Verdenskrig. Rapporter til det Nordiske historikermøde i København 1971.* Copenhagen 1971.
1974 *Migration from Finland to North America in the Years Between the United States Civil War and the First World War.* Turku 1974.

Kindleberger, C. P.
1967 *Europe's Postwar Growth: The Role of Labor Supply.* Cambridge, Mass., 1967.

Knights, Peter
1969 "City Directories as Aides to Ante-Bellum Urban Studies." *Historical Methods Newsletter,* II, 1969.

1974 *Internal Migration: Native-Born Bostonians in the Later 19th Century.* (Unpublished Report, Presented at the Convention of the Organization of the American Historians in Denver, Col., 1974.)

Knights, Peter, and Thernstrom, Stephan
1970 "Men in Motion." *Journal of Interdisciplinary History,* I, 1970.

Köbbin, André J.
1968 "The Logic of Cross-Cultural Analysis: why Exceptions?" In Rokkan, S. (ed.) *Comparative Research across Cultures and Nations.* Paris/The Hague 1968.

Koivukangas, Olavi
1974 *Scandinavian Immigration and Settlement in Australia before World War II.* Kokkola 1974.

Köllmann, W., and Marschalck, P.
1974 "German Emigration to the United States." In *Dislocation and Emigration.* (Perspectives in American History VII, 1973.) Cambridge, Mass., 1974, pp. 499 ff.

Kristjanson, F. J.
1965 *The Icelandic People in Manitoba.* Winnipeg 1965.

Kronborg, Bo, and Nilsson, Thomas
1975 *Stadsflyttare. Industrialisering, migration och social mobilitet med utgångspunkt från Halmstad, 1870–1910.* [Urban Migrants. Industrialization, Migration and Social Mobility on the Basis of Halmstad, 1870–1910.] (Studia Historica Upsaliensia, 65.) Uppsala 1975.

Kuenne, Robert E. (ed.)
1967 *Monopolistic Competition Theory. Studies in Impact. Essays in Honor of Edward H. Chamberlin.* New York 1967.

Kuznets, Simon
1930 *Secular Movements in Production and Prices.* 1930.
1956 "Quantitative Aspects of the Economic Growth of Nations: I. Levels and Variability of Rates of Growth." *Economic Development* and *Cultural Change, V, 1,* (Oct. 1956) p. 10.
1965 *Economic Growth and Structure.* London 1965.

Kuznetz, Simon, and Rubin, E.
1954 "Immigration and the Foreign Born." National Bureau of Economic Research, Occasional Paper 46, 1954. New York.

Langholm, Sivert
1971 "On the Concepts of Center and Periphery." *Journal of Peace Research* 1971, pp. 273–278.

Larsson, Bruce L.
1971 "Charles A. Lindbergh Sr. of Minnesota." (Unpublished Ph.D. Dissertation, University of Kansas, 1971.)
1973 "The Early Life of Charles A. Lindbergh, Sr., 1859–1883." *SPHQ* XXIV: 4, 1973, pp. 203–222.

Larson, Esther E.
1963 *Swedish Commentators on America 1638–1865. An Annotated List of Selected Manuscript and Printed Materials.* New York and Chicago 1963.

Larsson, Lars-Olof
1972 *Kolonisation och befolkningsutveckling i det svenska agrarsamhället 1500–1640.* [Colonization and Population Growth in Swedish Agrarian Society 1500–1640.] (Bibliotheca Historica Lundensis, 27.) Lund 1972.

Laurie, Bruce; Hershberg, Theodore; and Alter, George
1973 "Immigrants and Industry: The Philadelphia Experience 1850–1880."
1974 (Prepared for a Conference, "Immigrants in Industrial America, 1850–1920." Unpublished, second revision, July 1974.)

Lazarsfield, Paul F., and Stanton, Frank N. (eds.)
1949 *Communication Research 1948–49.* New York 1949.

Lee, Everett S.
1969 "A Theory of Migration." *Demography,* 1966: 3, pp. 47–57.

Lehmann, Sylvia
1949 *Grundzüge der schweizerischen Auswanderungspolitik.* Bern 1949.

Lext, Gösta
1968 *Mantalsskrivningen i Sverige före 1860.* [Poll-Tax Registration in Sweden before 1860.] (Meddelanden från Ekonomiskhistoriska institutionen vid Göteborgs universitet, 13.) Göteborg 1968.

Lianos, Theodore P.
1975 "Flows of Greek Out-Migration and Return Migration." *International Migration.* Vol. XIII, No. 3, 1975.

Lijfering, J. H. W.
1968 *Selectieve migratie.* (With a summary in English: Selective Effects of Rural Migration in the Netherlands). Wageningen 1968.

Lindberg, John S.
1930 *The Background of Swedish Emigration to the United States. An Economic and Sociological Study in the Dynamics of Migration.* University of Minnesota Press, Minneapolis, 1930.

Linde, H.
1959 "Generative Strukturen." *Studium Generale,* 12. Jahrg. Heft 6, 1959.

Lindén, Ingemar
1971 *Biblicism, apokalyptik, utopi. Adventismens historiska utformning i USA samt dess svenska utveckling till omkring 1939.* [Biblicism, Apocalyptic, Utopia. The Historical Development of Adventism in the United States and in Sweden to About 1939.] Uppsala 1971.

Lindmark, Sture
1971 *Swedish America 1914–1932. Studies in Ethnicity with Emphasis on Illinois and Minnesota.* (Studia Historica Upsaliensia, 37.) Uppsala 1971.

Lindquist, Emory
1958 "A Proposed Scandinavian Colony in Kansas Prior to the Civil War." *SPHQ* IX: 2, 1958, pp. 48–60.
1965 "The Swedish-Born Population and the Swedish Stock: The United States Census of 1960 and Comparative Data with Some Concluding Observations." *SPHQ* XVI: 2, 1965, pp. 76–90.
1970 *Vision for a Valley. Olof Olsson and the Early History of Lindsborg.* (Augustana Historical Society, Publication No. 22.) Rock Island, Ill., 1970.

Lithell, Ulla-Britt
1971 "Arbetsvandringar och befolkningsrörelser från Lekvattnets församling 1861–1914." [Migrant Labor Movements and Migration in Lekvattnet Parish 1861–1914.] (Unpublished Paper, Dept. of History, University of Uppsala, 1971.)

Littmarck, R.
1930 *Mälardalens nomader.* [The Nomads of the Lake Mälar Valley.] Uppsala 1930.

Ljungmark, Lars
1965 *Den stora utvandringen. Svensk emigration till USA 1840–1925.* [The Great Emigration. Swedish Emigration to the U.S. 1840–1925.] Stockholm 1965.
1971 *For Sale–Minnesota. Organized Promotion of Scandinavian Immigration 1866–1873.* (Studia Historica Gothoburgensia, XIII.) Stockholm 1971.

Lockridge, Kenneth A.
1966 "The Population of Dedham, Massachusetts, 1636–1736." *The Economic History Review* 1966, pp. 329 ff.

Lucas, Richard
1974 *Charles August Lindbergh, Sr. A Case Study of Congressional Insurgency, 1906–1912.* (Studia Historica Upsaliensia, 61.) Uppsala 1974.

Lundkvist, Sven

1974 "Rörlighet och social struktur i 1610-talets Sverige." [Mobility and Social Structure in Sweden during the 1610s.] *Historisk tidskrift* 1974:2, pp. 192–258.

Lundström, Hans

1975 "Metoder att korrigera brister i den befintliga migrationsstatistiken." [Methods of Correcting Irregularities in the Existing Migration Statistics.] (Manuscript, 1975.)

Lyck, Gunilla

1973 "Ett svenskt kolonisationsområde i Wisconsin 1870–1880. En studie över etnisk och social struktur i Burnett County." [A Swedish Settlement Area in Wisconsin, 1870–1880. A Study of Ethnic and Social Structure in Burnett County.] (Unpublished Paper, Dept. of History, University of Uppsala, 1973.)

Mabogunje, Akin L.

1972 "Systems Approach to a Theory of Rural-Urban Migration." In English, P. W., and Mayfield, R. C. (eds.) *Man, Space, and Environment,* pp. 193–206. New York/Toronto 1972.

Macdonald, Norman

1966 *Canada. Immigration and Colonization. 1841–1903.* Aberdeen University Press 1966.

Mackenroth, G.

1955 "Die Generative Strukture von Bevölkerungen und Sozialschichten." *Weltwirtschaftliches Archiv.* Vol. 75, 1. 1955, pp. 1 ff.

Maginnis, Arthur J.

1892 *The Atlantic Ferry. Its Ships, Men and Working.* London 1892.

Majava, A.

1975 "Migrations Between Finland and Sweden from 1946–1974." (Unpublished Paper, Ministry of Labour Planning Division, Helsinki, 1975).

Malin, J. C.

1935 "The Turnover of Farm Population in Kansas." *Kansas Historical Quarterly,* IV, 1935.

Malthus, Thomas Robert

1872 *An Essay on the Principle of Population.* Seventh Ed. London 1872.

Mangalam, J. J.

1968 *Human Migration.—A Guide to Migration. Literature in English 1955–62.* Lexington 1968.

Mann, William E.
1955 *Sect, Cult and Church in Alberta.* University of Toronto Press 1955.

Mannil, Ragnar
1972 "Emigration—bibliografisk översikt." [Short Bibliography of Finnish Emigration.] In *Emigrationen och dess bakgrund,* pp. 123–148. (Svenska kulturfondens skrifter, V.) Ekenäs 1972.

March, J. G., and Simon, H. A.
1958 *Organizations.* New York 1958.

Marschalck, Peter
1973 *Deutsche Überseewanderung in 19. Jahrhundert.* Ein Beitrag zur soziologischen Theorie der Bevölkerung. Stuttgart 1973.

Martinius, Sture
1967 *Befolkningsrörlighet under industrialismens inledningsskede i Sverige.* [Population Mobility in Sweden during the Initial Phase of Industrialism.] (Meddelanden från Ekonomisk-historiska institutionen vid Göteborgs universitet, 8.) Göteborg 1967.

Mattson, Hans
1891 *Minnen.* [Memoirs.] Second ed. Lund 1891.

Måwe, Carl-Erik
1971 *Värmlänningar i Nordamerika. Sociologiska studier i en anpassningsprocess. Med särskild hänsyn till emigrationen från Östmark.* [Immigrants from Värmland in North America. Sociological Studies of the Assimilation Process. With Special Emphasis on the Emigration from Östmark Parish.] Säffle 1971.

Mayer, George H.
1951 *The Political Career of Floyd B. Olsson.* Minneapolis 1951.

Meadows, Dennis L.; Meadows, Donella H.; Randers, Jørgen; and Behrens III, William W.
1973 *The Limits to Growth. A Report for the Club of Rome's Project on the Predicament of Mankind.* London 1973.

Meier, Heinz
1963 *The United States and Switzerland in the Nineteenth Century.* (Studies in American History. I.) The Hague 1963.

Merton, Robert
1957 "Manifest and Latent Functions." In *Social Theory and Social Structure.* Glencoe, Ill., 1957.

Mikkola, Kimmo
1973 "Migration in Finland in 1970." *Migration Research in Scandinavia.* Proceedings of the Nordic seminar on migration research held at Siikaranta, Finland on January 3–5, 1973. Migration reports 4.

Minnesskrift
1949 *Minnesskrift med anledning av den Svenska Befolkningsstatistikens 200-åriga bestånd.* [Memorial Publication on the Occasion of the Bicentenary of the Swedish Population Statistics.] Stockholm 1949.

Moe, Thorvald
1970 *Demographic Developments and Economic Growth in Norway 1740–1940: An Econometric Study.* (Unpublished dissertation, Stanford University, Cal., 1970.)

Montgomery, Arthur
1921 *Svensk tullpolitik 1816–1911.* [Swedish Tariff Policy 1816–1911.] Stockholm 1921.

Moore, Jane
1938 *Cityward Migration.* University of Chicago Press. Chicago 1938.

Mörner, Magnus
1960 "Invandringen och det moderna Latinamerikas tillblivelse." [Immigration and the Rise of Modern Latin America.] *Ymer* 1960, pp. 260–274.

Morrill, Richard L., and Pitts, Forest R.
1972 "Marriage, Migration and the Mean Information Field: A Study in Uniqueness and Generality." In English, P. W., and Mayfield, R. C. (eds.) *Man, Space, and Environment,* pp. 359–384. New York/Toronto 1972.

Mulder, William
1957 *Homeward to Zion. The Mormon Migration from Scandinavia.* University of Minnesota Press, Minneapolis 1957.

Myhrman, Anders
1972 *Finlandssvenskar i Amerika.* [Finland-Swedes in America.] Helsingfors 1972.

Myrdal, Gunnar
1958 *Economic Theory and Under-Developed Countries.* London 1957.
1968 *An Asian Drama. An Inquiry in Poverty of the Nations.* Vols. 1–3. London 1968.

Naftalin, A.
1969 "Address of greeting." *SPHQ* XX: 1, 1969, pp. 10–14.

Nagel, E.
1961 *The Structure of Science.* London 1961.

The National Cyclopaedia
The National Cyclopaedia of American Biography. New York 1898 ff.

Nelson, Helge
1943 *The Swedes and the Swedish Settlements in North America*. Vol. I: Text. Vol. II: Atlas. Lund 1943.

Nelson, Herman G.
1952 "Swedish Settlers in Rockford." *SPHQ* III: 4, 1952, pp. 91–103.

Nerander, Margareta
1969 "Mitt bröd Du gav så ringa ... Från 1800-talets Köla." [Narratives from Köla Parish during the 19th Century.] *Emigranten* 1969.

Neymark, E.
1961 *Selektiv rörlighet. Flyttningstendenser och yrkesval i relation till utbildning, begåvning och härkomst. Uppföljning av en åldersklass.* [Selective Mobility. Migration Tendencies and Occupational Choices in Relation to Education, Aptitude, and Origin. A Follow-up Study of an Age-Cohort.] Stockholm 1961.

Nilsson, Fred
1965 "Folkbokföringsmaterialet i Stockholm med särskild hänsyn till rotemansarkivet." [The Population Registers in Stockholm with Special Regard to *Rotemansarkivet*.] In *Berättelse över Arkivnämndens förvaltning och verksamhet under år 1965*.
1970 *Emigrationen från Stockholm till Nordamerika 1880–1893. En studie i urban utvandring*. [Emigration from Stockholm to North America 1880–1893. A Study in Urban Emigration.] (Studia Historica Upsaliensia, 31.) Stockholm 1970.

Norberg, Anders
1972 "Tankar om den svenska kyrkobokföringen." [Viewpoints on the Swedish Church Records.] (Unpublished Paper, Dept. of History, University of Uppsala, 1972.)

Norberg, Anders, and Åkerman, Sune
1973 "Migration and the Building of Families. Studies on the Rise of the Lumber Industry in Sweden." In *Aristocrats, Farmers, Proletarians. Essays in Swedish Demographic History*. (Studia Historica Upsaliensia, 47.) Uppsala 1973.

Nordic Emigration
1970 *Nordic Emigration. Research Conference in Uppsala Sept. 1969*. Uppsala 1970.

Nordic Emigration Atlas
1976 *Nordic Emigration Atlas*. Report from a Nordic Study Group. (Forthcoming.)

Nordström, Elsa
1973 "Journaler över utrikesresenärer 1735–1851 i Krigsarkivet." [Lists of Foreign Travelers 1735–1851 in the Military Record Office.] *Meddelanden från Kungl. Krigsarkivet*, VI, 1973.

Noreen, Paul
1967 "Emigrationen från Sundals härad i Dalsland 1860–1895. Emigrationens orsaker och förlopp." [Emigration from Sundals härad, Dalsland, 1860–1895. Its Causes and Course of Development.] (Unpublished Licentiate Thesis, Dept. of History, University of Uppsala, 1967.)

Norman, Hans
1967 "Emigration från bygder med uppväxande industrier i Örebro län 1861–1905. Med särskild hänsyn till Karlskoga och Kumla socknar." [Emigration from Rising Industrial Districts in Örebro län 1861–1905, with Special Emphasis on Karlskoga and Kumla Parishes.] (Unpublished Licentiate Thesis, Dept. of History, University of Uppsala, 1967.)
1974 *Från Bergslagen till Nordamerika. Studier i migrationsmönster, social rörlighet och demografisk struktur med utgångspunkt från Örebro län 1851–1915.* [From Bergslagen to North America. Studies in Migration Pattern, Social Mobility and Demographic Structure on the Basis of Örebro County, 1851–1915.] (Studia Historica Upsaliensia, 62.) Uppsala 1974.

Odén, Birgitta
1963 "Emigrationen från Norden till Nordamerika under 1800-talet. Aktuella forskningsuppgifter." [Emigration from Scandinavia to North America During the 1800s. Current Tasks of Research.] *Historisk tidskrift* 1963: 2, pp. 261–277.
1965 "Emigrationsstudier i Blekinge." [Studies of Emigration from Blekinge.] *Ale* 1965: 3, pp. 14–21.
1966 "Emigrationen från Jönköpings län." [Emigration from Jönköpings län.] *Småländska kulturbilder* 1966, pp. 20–32.
1971 "Ekonomiska emigrationsmodeller och historisk forskning. Ett diskussionsinlägg." [Economic Models of Emigration and Historical Research. A Contribution to the Present Discussion.] *Scandia* 1971: 1, pp. 1–70.
1972 "Historical Statistics in the Nordic Countries." In Lorwin, Val R., and Price, Jacob M. (eds.) *The Dimensions of the Past. Materials, Problems, and Opportunities for Quantitative Work in History.* New Haven and London 1972.

Odland, M. W.
1926 *The Life of Knute Nelson.* Minneapolis 1926.

Öhngren, Bo
1974 *Folk i rörelse. Samhällsutveckling, flyttningsmönster och folkrörelser i Eskilstuna 1870–1900.* [People on the Move. Social Development, Migration Patterns and Popular Movements in Eskilstuna 1870–1900.] (Studia Historica Upsaliensia, 55.) Uppsala 1974.

O'Leary, P. J., and Lewis, W. Arthur
1955 "Secular Swings in Production and Trade, 1870–1913." *The Manchester School of Economic and Social Studies* XXIII (2), May 1955, pp. 113–252.

Olsson, Gunnar
1962 "Utflyttningen från centrala Värmland under 1880-talet." [Out-Migration from Central Värmland During the 1880s.] *Värmland vår hembygd,* V. Karlstad 1962.

Olsson, Karl A.
1962 *By one Spirit. A History of the Evangelical Covenant Church of America.* Chicago 1962. Second Printing 1972.

Olsson, Nils William
1961 "Source Materials on Emigration in the United States National Archives, With Particular Emphasis on Swedish Emigration to the United States." *SPHQ* XII: 1, 1961, pp. 17–34.
1967 *Swedish Passenger Arrivals in New York 1820–1850.* Stockholm 1967.
1974 "The Swedish Brothers: An Experiment in Immigrant Mutual Aid." *SPHQ* XXV: 3–4, 1974, pp. 220–229.

Ostergren, Robert C.
1972 "Cultural Homogeneity and Population Stability in Swedish Immigrant Communities." (Unpublished Paper, University of Minnesota, Minneapolis, 1972.)

Overbeek, J.
1974 *History of Population Theories.* Rotterdam 1974.

Palmer, Howard
1972 *Land of the Second Chance. A History of Ethnic Groups in Southern Alberta.* Lethbridge 1972.

Parnes, H. S.
1968 "Labor Force Market and Mobility." In *International Encyclopedia of the Social Sciences,* Vol. 8. New York 1968.

Paulin, Axel
1951 *Svenska öden i Sydamerika.* [The Situation of Swedes in South America.] Stockholm 1951.

Pedro, Rolf
1970 "Den evangelisk-lutherska församlingen i Trade Lake, Wisconsin, USA, 1870–1946. En studie i religiös organisation med lokalhistorisk anknytning." [The Evangelical Lutheran Congregation in Trade Lake, Wisconsin, U.S.A., 1870–1946. A Study in Religious Organization as Related to Local History.] (Unpublished Paper, Dept. of History, University of Uppsala, 1970.)

Petersen, William
1964 *The Politics of Population.* London 1964.
1969 *Population.* Second ed. London 1969.

Population Movements and Industrialization
1941 *Population Movements and Industrialization. Swedish Counties 1895–1930.* By the Staff of the Institute for Social Sciences, Stockholm University. (Stockholm Economic Studies 10: 2.) London 1941.

Poussou, Jean-Pierre
1970 "Les mouvements migratoires en France et à partir de la France de la fin du XVe siècle au début du XIXe siècle: approche pour une synthèse." *Annales de Démographie Historique 1970.* Paris 1970.

Price, Charles A.
1963*a* *Southern Europeans in Australia.* Melbourne 1963.
1963*b* *The Method and Statistics of "Southern Europeans in Australia."* Canberra 1963.

Prins Wilhelm
1948 *Röda Jordens svenskar.* [Swedes of the Red Soil.] Stockholm 1948.

Puskas, Julianna
1975 "Emigration from Hungary to the United States before 1914." (*Studia Historica Academiae Scientiarum Hungaricae.*) Budapest 1975.

Pyle, Gerald F.
1972 "The Diffusion of Cholera in the United States in the Nineteenth Century." In English, P. W., and Mayfield, R. C. (eds.) *Man, Space, and Environment,* pp. 410–421. New York/Toronto 1972.

Qualey, Carlton C.
1938 *Norwegian Settlements in the United States.* Northfield, Minn., 1938.

Ravenstein, E. G.
1885 "The Laws of Migration." *Journal of the Royal Statistical Society* 48, Part 2,
1889 June 1885, and 52, June 1889.

Reinhard, M.; Armengaud, A.; and Dupaquier, J.
1968 *Histoire générale de la population mondiale.* Paris 1968.

Rice, John G.
1973 *Patterns of Ethnicity in a Minnesota County 1880–1905.* (Geographical Reports, No. 4, Dept. of Geography, University of Umeå.) Umeå 1973.

Rogberg, Martin
1954 *Svenskar i Latinamerika.* [Swedes in Latin America.] Örebro 1954.

Rogers, Everett M.
1971 *Diffusions of Innovations.* New York 1971.

Rondahl, Björn
1972 *Emigration, folkomflyttning och säsongarbete i ett sågverksdistrikt i södra Hälsingland 1865–1910. Söderala kommun med särskild hänsyn till Ljusne industrisamhälle.* [Emigration, Internal Migration and Migrant Labor Movements in a Sawmill District in Southern Hälsingland 1865–1910.] (Studia Historica Upsaliensia, 40.) Uppsala 1972.

Rönnegård, Sam
1961 *Utvandrarnas kyrka. En bok om Augustana.* [The Emigrants' Church. A Book on Augustana.] Stockholm 1961.

Rosenberg, Antti
1966 "Mobility of Population in the Finnish County of Uusimaa (Nyland) 1821–1880." *Scandinavian Economic History Review* 1966: 1, pp. 39–59.

Rundblad, Bengt
1964 *Arbetskraftens rörlighet.* [The Mobility of Manpower.] Uppsala 1964.

Runblom, Harald
1971 *Svenska företag i Latinamerika. Etableringsmönster och förhandlingstaktik 1900–1940.* [Swedish Enterprises in Latin America Before the Second World War. The Course of Their Establishment and Their Tactics in Negotiations.] (Studia Historica Upsaliensia, 35.) Uppsala 1971.
1975 "Svenskar i Tierra Nueva." [Swedes in Tierra Nueva.] Review of *A. Flodell 1974. Kyrkohistorisk Årsskrift,* 1975.

Runeby, Nils
1962 "Amerika i Sverige. Herman Lagercrantz, emigrationen och den nationella väckelsen." [America in Sweden. Herman Lagercrantz, Emigration and the National Revival Movement.] *Arkivvetenskapliga studier, 3.* Lund 1962.
1969 *Den nya världen och den gamla. Amerikabild och emigrationsuppfattning i Sverige 1820–1860.* [The New World and the Old. The Picture of America and Concept of Emigration.] (Studia Historica Upsaliensia, 30.) Uppsala 1969.

Saloutos, Th.
1956 *They Remember America. The Story of the Repatriated Greek-Americans.* Berkeley and Los Angeles 1956.

Samson, Leopold
1975 "Internal and External Migration in the Netherlands 1880–1910. A Study in the Geographical Mobility of Wisch." (Manuscript, Dept. of History, University of Uppsala, 1975.)

Sandberg, Arnold

1948 *Linköpings stifts kyrkoarkivalier till och med år 1800.* [The Records in Linköping Diocese up to 1800.] Lund 1948.

Sanger, Margaret (ed.)

1927 *Proceedings of the World Population Conference.* London 1927.

Saul, S. B.

1962 "House Building in England 1890–1914." *The Economic History Review,* Second Series, XV (1) August 1962, pp. 119–37.

Schiller, Bernt, and Odén, Birgitta

1970 *Statistik för historiker.* [Statistics for Historians.] Stockholm 1970.

Schnore, Leo F. (ed.)

1975 *The New Urban History. Quantitative Explorations by American Historians.* Princeton University Press 1975.

Schrier, Arnold

1958 *Ireland and the American Emigration 1850–1900.* Minneapolis 1958.

Schumpeter, Joseph A.

1939 *Business Cycles. A Theoretical, Historical, and Statistical Analysis of the Capitalist Process.* Vols. 1–2. New York and London 1939.

Schwarzweller, Harry K.; Brown, James S.; and Mangalam, J. J.

1971 *Mountain Families in Transition. A Case Study of Appalachian Migration.* The Pennsylvania State University Press, 1971.

Scott, Franklin D.

1960 "The Study of the Effects of Emigration." *The Scandinavian Economic History Review* 1960: 2, pp. 161–174.

1965 "Literature in Periodicals of Protest of Swedish-America." *SPHQ* XVI: 4, 1965, pp. 193–215.

1965 "Sweden's Constructive Opposition to Emigration." *Journal of Modern History,* Vol. 37, 1965: 3, pp. 307–335.

Semmingsen, Ingrid

1941 *Veien mot Vest. Utvandringen fra Norge til Amerika, 1825–1865.* [The Way West. Emigration from Norway to America.] Oslo 1941.

1950 *Veien mot Vest. Utvandringen fra Norge til Amerika, 1865–1915.* [The Way West. Emigration from Norway to America.] Vol. 2. Oslo 1950.

1960 "Norwegian Emigration in the Nineteenth Century." *Scandinavian Economic History Review* 1960: 2, pp. 150–160.

1972 "Emigration from Scandinavia." *The Scandinavian Economic History Review* 1972, pp. 45–60.

Severin, E.
1919 *Svenskarna i Texas i ord och bild 1838–1918*. [The Texas Swedes in Words and Pictures, 1838–1918.] 1919.

Skårdal, Dorothy Burton
1974 *The Divided Heart. Scandinavian Immigrant Experience through Literary Sources*. Oslo 1974.

Smith, C. H.
1931 "Notes on the Distribution of the Foreignborn Scandinavian in Wisconsin in 1905." *Wisconsin Magazine of History*, Vol. XIV, 1931.

En Smålandssocken emigrerar
1967 *En Smålandssocken emigrerar. En bok om emigrationen till Amerika från Långasjö socken i Kronobergs län*. [A Book About Emigration to America from Långasjö Parish in Kronobergs län.] Växjö 1967.

Söderberg, Kjell
1974 "Alfta Sockens Befolkningsrörlighet 1881–1885. Introduktion, Källmaterial, Metod, Undersökningsområde." [Population Mobility in Alfta Socken 1881–1885. Introduction, Source Material, Method, Investigation Area.] (Unpublished Paper, Dept. of History, University of Umeå, 1974.)

Söderström, Ingvar
1970 *Joe Hill, diktare och agitator. En biografi*. [Joe Hill, Poet and Agitator. A Biography.] Stockholm 1970.

Sonnenfeld, Joseph
1972 "Geography, Perception, and the Behavioral Environment." In English, P. W., and Mayfield, R. C. (eds.) *Man, Space, and Environment*, pp. 244–251. New York/Toronto 1972.

Sonquist, J. A.
1970 *Multivariate Model Building. The Validation of a Search Strategy*. Ann Arbor, Mich., 1970.

Sonquist, J. A.; Baker, E. L.; and Morgan, J. N.
1973 *Searching for Structure*. Ann Arbor, Mich., 1973.

Special Consular Reports
1890 *Special Consular Reports. European Emigration. Studies in Europe of Emigration Moving out of Europe, Especially that Flowing to the United States*. (Made under the Authority of the Department of State During the Year Ending October 1, 1890. By F. L. Dingley. Issued from the Bureau of Statistics, Department of State.) Washington 1890.

1903 *Special Consular Reports. XXVII. Markets for Agricultural Implements and Vehicles in Foreign Countries.* (Bureau of Statistics, Department of Commerce and Labor.) Washington 1903.

1904 *Special Consular Reports. XXX. Emigration to the United States.* (Bureau of Statistics, Department of Commerce and Labor.) Washington 1904.

Stenbeck, Karin

1973 "Utvandringen från Sverige till Brasilien 1868–1891." [Emigration from Sweden to Brazil 1868–1891.] (Unpublished Licentiate Thesis, Dept. of History, University of Uppsala, 1973.)

Stephenson, Charles

"Determinants of American Migration: Methods and Models in Mobility Research." (Forthcoming in the *Journal of American Studies.*)

Stephenson, George M.

1929 "Documents Relating to Peter Cassel and the Settlement at New Sweden." *Swedish-American Historical Bulletin II: 1,* 1929.

1932 *The Religious Aspects of Swedish Immigrations. A Study of Immigrant Churches.* Minneapolis, Univ. of Minnesota Press, 1932.

1935 *John Lind of Minnesota.* Minneapolis 1935.

Storing, P. E.

1968 "United States' Recognition of Norway in 1905." In *Americana Norvegica,* Vol. II, pp. 160 ff. Oslo 1968.

Stouffer, S. A.

1940 "Intervening Opportunities: A Theory Relating Mobility and Distance." *American Sociological Review,* Vol. 5. New York 1940.

Sundbärg, Gustav

1885–86 "Bidrag till utvandringsfrågan från befolkningsstatistisk synpunkt." [Contributions to the Issue of Emigration from the Standpoint of Population Statistics.] *Uppsala Universitets Årsskrift,* 1885 and 1886.

1907 *Bevölkerungsstatistik Schwedens 1750–1900.* Stockholm 1907. (Reprint in *Urval.* Skriftserie utgiven av Statistiska Centralbyrån, nr. 3, 1970.)

Sundin, Jan

1973 *Främmande studenter vid Uppsala Universitet före andra världskriget. En studie i studentmigration.* [Foreign Students at Uppsala University 1595–1939. A Study in Student Migration.] (Studia Historica Upsaliensia, 45.) Uppsala 1973.

Sundt, Eilert

1855 *Om giftermaal i Norge: bidrag til kundskab om folkets kaar og sæder.* [Marriage in Norway. Contributions to the Knowledge of the Circumstances and Habits of the People.] Christiania 1855.

Svalestuen, Andres A.
1971 "Nordisk emigrasjon—en komparativ oversikt." [Nordic Emigration. A Comparative Survey.] In *Emigrationen fra Norden indtil 1. Verdenskrig. Rapporter til det Nordiske historikermøde i København 1971.* Copenhagen 1971.

The Swedish Immigrant Community in Transition
1963 *The Swedish Immigrant Community in Transition. Essays in Honor of Dr Conrad Bergendoff.* (Augustana Historical Society, No. 20.) Rock Island, Ill., 1963.

Taylor, A. J.
1968 *The Coal Industry.* (The Development of British Industry and Foreign Competition 1875–1914. Studies in Industrial Enterprise. Ed. by Derek H. Aldcroft.) London 1968.

Taylor, Philip
1971 *The Distant Magnet. European Emigration to the U.S.A.* London 1971.

Taylor, R. C.
1971 "Migration and Motivation: a Study of Determinants and Types." In *J. A. Jackson* (1971).

Tedebrand, Lars-Göran
1972 *Västernorrland och Nordamerika 1875–1913. Utvandring och återinvandring.* [Emigration from Västernorrland County to North America and Re-immigration to Västernorrland County.] (Studia Historica Upsaliensia, 42.) Uppsala 1972.

Tetzschner, Helge; Gundelach, Peter; Hillestrøm, Karsten; and Brogaard, Henning
1974 *Arbejdskraftens Mobilitet 1.* [A Study of Literature on Labour Mobility.] (Socialforskningsinstituttet. The Danish National Institute of Social Research. Studie 30.) Copenhagen 1974.

Thernstrom, Stephan
1969 *Poverty and Progress. Social Mobility in a Nineteenth Century City.* New York 1969.
1973 *The Other Bostonians. Poverty and Progress in the American Metropolis, 1880–1970.* Harvard University Press, Cambridge, Mass., 1973.

Thistlethwaite, Frank
1960 "Migration from Europe Overseas in the Nineteenth and Twentieth Centuries." (*Rapports. Vol. V, XI:e Congrès International des Sciences Historiques.*) Uppsala 1960.

Thomas, Brinley
1954 *Migration and Economic Growth. A Study of Great Britain and the Atlantic Economy.* Cambridge University Press 1954.

1972 *Migration and Urban Development. A Reappraisal of British and American Long Cycles.* London 1972.

Thomas, Dorothy Swaine
1936 "Internal Migrations in Sweden: A Note on Their Extensiveness as Compared with Net Migration Gain or Loss." *The American Journal of Sociology* XXXVI, 1936, pp. 345–357.
1938 *Research Memorandum on Migration Differentials.* New York 1938.
1941 *Social and Economic Aspects of Swedish Population Movements 1750–1933.* New York 1941.

Thörn, Olof
1959*a* "Glimpses from the Activities of a Swedish Emigrant Agent." *SPHQ* X: 1, 1959, pp. 3–24.
1959*b* "Glimpses from the Activities of a Swedish Emigrant Agent." *SPHQ* X: 2, 1959, pp. 52–66.

Todaro, M. P.
1973 "Rural-Urban Migration, Unemployment, and Job Probabilities: Recent Theoretical and Empirical Research." (Unpublished Paper for the Annual Meeting of Social Scentists. Valescure, France 1973.)

Tuma, E.
1961 "Theories of Economic Change." In *European Economic History,* pp. 18–43. New York 1961.

Wallander, Jan
1948 *Flykten från skogsbygden. En undersökning i Klarälvsdalen.* [The Flight from the Forest Districts. A Study of the Klarälven Valley.] Stockholm 1948.

Walker, Mack
1964 *Germany and the Emigration, 1816–1885.* (Harvard Historical Monographs, 56.) Cambridge, Mass., 1964.

Wargentin, P. W.
1780 *Undersökning om folkutflyttningen så väl utur hela riket som utur hvart höfdingedöme särskilt, i anledning af Tabell-verket för åren 1750, til och med 1773.* [A Study of the External and Internal Migration in Sweden 1750–1773.] Vetenskapsakademiens handlingar 1780.

Vecoli, Rudolph J.
"European Americans: From Immigrants to Ethnics." *International Migration Review,* Vol. 6, 1972, pp. 403–434.

Vedder, R. K., and Gallaway, L. E.
1970 "The Settlement Preferences of Scandinavian Emigrants to the United

States, 1850–1960." In *The Scandinavian History Economic Review 1970,* pp. 159–176.

Wefald, Jon
1971 *A Voice of Protest. Norwegians in American Politics, 1890–1917.* Northfield, Minn., 1971.

Weibull, Jörgen
1965 "The Wisconsin Progressives, 1900–1914." *Mid-America,* Vol. 47, 1965, pp. 213 ff.

Wester, Holger
1969 "Finska Ångfartygs Aktiebolagets passagerarlistor." [The Passenger Lists of The Finnish Steamboat Company.] (Unpublished Paper, Dept. of History, University of Uppsala, 1969.)
1970 "Den finländska emigrationen över Sverige och andra länder." [The Finnish Emigration via Sweden and other Countries.] (Unpublished paper, Dept. of History, University of Uppsala, 1970.)

Westerberg, Wesley M.
1961 "Swedish Methodists in Chicago in the 1850's." *SPHQ* XII: 4, 1961, pp. 146–156.

Westin, Gunnar
1957 "Emigration and Scandinavian Church Life." *SPHQ* VIII: 2, 1957, pp. 35–48.

Wheeler, Wayne Leland
1959 "An Analysis of Social Change in a Swedish-Immigrant Community: The Case of Lindsborg, Kansas." (Unpublished dissertation, Columbia, Mo., 1959.)

Widén, Albin
1954 *Emigrantpojken som blev guvernör.* [The Emigrant Boy Who Became a Governor.] Stockholm 1954.
1966. *Amerikaemigrationen i dokument.* [Emigration to America in Documents.] Falköping 1966.
1971 *När Svensk-Amerika grundades.* [When Swedish America was Founded.] Borås 1971.

Wiebe, Robert H.
1967 *The Search for Order, 1877–1920.* (The Making of America, Vol. 5.) New York 1967.

Vilhjálmsson, Bjarni
1971 "Udvandringen fra Island. En oversikt." [Emigration from Iceland. A Sur-

vey.] In *Emigrationen fra Norden indtil 1. Verdenskrig. Rapporter til det Nordiske historikermøde i København 1971*. Copenhagen 1971.

Wilkinson, M.
1967 "Evidences of Long Swings in the Growth of Swedish Population and Related Economic Variables, 1860–1965." *Journal of Economic History*, XXVII, 1967.

Willcox, W. F. (ed.)
1931 *International Migrations*. Vols. I, II. New York 1929, 1931.

Winberg, Christer
1969 "Emigrationen från de västsvenska socknarna Askim och Släp 1881–1895." [The Emigration from Askim and Släp Parishes in Western Sweden, 1881–1895.] In *Svensk 1800-talsemigration*. (Meddelanden från Historiska institutionen i Göteborg, nr 1.) Uppsala 1969.

Wirén, Agnes
1975 *Uppbrott från örtagård. Utvandring från Blekinge under begynnelseskedet till och med år 1870*. [The Initial Phase of Emigration from Blekinge län up to 1870.] (Bibliotheca Historica Lundensis, XXXIV.) Lund 1975.

Wood, David
1967 "Scandinavian Settlers in Canada Revised." *Geografiska Annaler* 1967, 49 B.

Wright, C. D.
1900 *The History and Growth of the United States Census. Prepared for the Senate Committee on the Census*. Washington, D.C., 1900.

Wrigley, E. A.
1961 *Industrial Growth and Population Change*. Cambridge 1961.
1969 *Population and History*. London 1969.
1973 (ed.) *Identifying People in the Past*. London 1973.

Young, E. C.
1924 *The Movement of Farm Population*. (Cornell University, Agricultural Experiment Station, Bulletin 426.) Ithaca, N.Y., 1924.

Appendix 3. Members of the Research Project "Sweden and America after 1860"

Sune Åkerman, research leader 1966–1973
Christer Andersson
Torsten Augrell
Ulf Beijbom
Håkan Berggren, research leader 1962–1966
Frank Blomfelt
Kjell Bondestad
Berit Brattne
Sten Carlsson, head of the project
Eric De Geer
Ulf Ebbeson
Ingrid Eriksson
Margaretha Eriksson
Viveca Halldin
Kerstin Hallert
Margot Höjfors
Ann-Sofie Kälvemark
Bo Kronborg
Jan Larsson
Sture Lindmark
Ulla-Britt Lithell
Richard Lucas
Bo Malmberg
Fred Nilsson
Thomas Nilsson
Anders Norberg
Paul Noreen
Hans Norman
Tua Öhvall
John Rogers
Mats Rolén
Björn Rondahl
Harald Runblom, research leader 1973–
Leopold Samson
Olle Sjöberg
Gösta Söderberg
Karin Stenbeck
Jan Sundin
Lars-Göran Tedebrand
Holger Wester

24–752439

List of Names*

* The names of the project members are here omitted. They are listed in Appendix 3.

List of Places

Index

List of Tables

List of Figures

The Uppsala Migration Research Project

Historians during the post-war period have given the field of social history a more prominent place in their research and have placed strong emphasis on an interdisciplinary outlook. The need for a systematic collection and processing of large quantities of data has created new organizational problems. Team work within the frame of long-term planning and frequent contacts between scholars have proved to be a satisfactory solution. This book is the result of such activities.

Within the context of an extensive international exchange among migration scholars a special project entitled Nordic Emigration has been created. The achievements of the internordic cooperation with members from Denmark, Finland, Iceland and Norway have proved to be of great value in this volume.

During a ten year period some 30 scholars have been connected with this project. Most of the results have been presented in doctoral dissertations, conference reports and other publications.

Sten Carlsson took the initiative in creating the project and has been responsible for its functioning ever since. Sune Åkerman has been the project leader during most of its existence. He has mainly been engaged in the planning and development of the research strategy. After him Harald Runblom has been project leader and he has planned and together with Hans Norman edited this book. Furthermore Håkan Berggren, Ann-Sofie Kälvemark, Hans Norman and Lars-Göran Tedebrand have during different periods been in charge of the work and participated as instructors of the doctoral candidates.

About the Authors

Sune Åkerman started with a study on financial history. He has also treated political history and migrational and demographic history in general with a strong emphasis on methodological problems. He is now working with an evaluation of the family reconstitution technique.

Berit Brattne has done a study of emigration and the transport system focusing on the agencies. Special attention is given to an investigation of the latent inclination to emigrate within the Swedish population.

Sten Carlsson's dissertation treats the political turbulence in Sweden around 1800. His extensive research deals with political and social history focusing on social structure, social mobility, and the political changes related to agrarian Sweden and the era of industrialization.

Ann-Sofie Kälvemark's main work is a study of Swedish emigration policy at the turn of the century. She has also done research on marriage patterns in the 19th century and is now working on Swedish population policy in the 1930s.

Hans Norman's Ph.D. thesis deals with migrational movements in general and their causes. He has also treated social mobility, colonization settlements, and the demographic patterns of emigrant populations.

Harald Runblom has published a study of Swedish enterprises in Latin America, concentrating on their course of establishment and tactics in negotiations. He is now doing research on Scandinavian settlements in Canada.

Lars-Göran Tedebrand's main study is dealing with the industrialization of lumber areas and general population turnover. He has especially treated the remigration problem and recently presented a study in the field of urban history.

Acta Universitatis Upsaliensis
STUDIA HISTORICA UPSALIENSIA

After having been an independent series, this series is from vol 53 included in the publication group *Acta Universitatis Upsaliensis.*

Copies of vols. 1–52 may be ordered through your local bookseller. Distributor: *Esselte Studium, S-112 85 Stockholm (Sweden).*

Vols. 53 and following may be ordered from your local bookseller or directly from the distributor: *Almqvist & Wiksell International, Box 62, S-101 20 Stockholm (Sweden).*

The listed volumes, with some exception, contain summaries in either German, English or French. The letters following the titles stand for the language of summary. G=German, E=English, F=French.

1. *Gustav Jonasson:* Karl XII och hans rådgivare. Den utrikespolitiska maktkampen i Sverige 1697–1702. (Charles XII and his Advisors. The Power Struggle over Foreign Policy in Sweden 1697–1702.) G. Uppsala 1960.
2. *Sven Lundkvist:* Gustav Vasa och Europa. Svensk handels- och utrikespolitik 1534–1557. (Gustavus Vasa and Europe. Swedish Trade and Foreign Policy 1534–1557.) G. Uppsala 1960.
3. *Tage Linder:* Biskop Olof Wallquists politiska verksamhet till och med riksdagen 1789. (Bishop Olof Wallquist's Political Activity up to the Riksdag of 1789.) E. Uppsala 1960.
4. *Carl Göran Andræ:* Kyrka och frälse i Sverige under äldre medeltid. (The Swedish Church and its Land during the Early Middle Ages.) G. Uppsala 1960.
5. *Bengt Henningsson:* Geijer som historiker. (Erik Gustaf Geijer as Historian.) G. Uppsala 1961.
6. *Nils Runeby:* Monarchia mixta. Maktfördelningsdebatt i Sverige under stormaktstiden. (Monarchia Mixta. The Division of Power Debate in Great Power Sweden.) G. Uppsala 1962.
7. *Åke Hermansson:* Karl IX och ständerna. Tronfrågan och författningsutvecklingen 1598–1611. (Charles IX and the Estates. The Succession Issue and Constitutional Developments 1598–1611.) G. Uppsala 1962.
8. Hundra års historisk diskussion. Historiska föreningen i Uppsala 1862–1962. (A Hundred Years of History. The Uppsala Historical Association 1862–1962.) Uppsala 1962.
9. *Sten Carlsson:* Byråkrati och borgarstånd under frihetstiden. (The Bureaucracy and the Estate of Burghers in Sweden during the Age of Freedom [1718–72].) E. Stockholm 1963.
10. *Gunnar Christie Wasberg:* Forsvarstanke og suverenitetsprinsipp. Kretsen om Aftenposten i den unionspolitiske debatt 1890–mars 1905. (The Editorial Circle around Aftenposten, and the Debate in Swedish-Norwegian Union Politics, from 1890 to March 1905.) E. Oslo 1963.
11. *Kurt Ågren:* Adelns bönder och kronans. Skatter och besvär i Uppland 1650–1680. (Crown and Noble Peasants. Taxes and Dues in Uppland 1650–1680.) G. Uppsala 1964.
12. *Michael Nordberg:* Les ducs et la royauté. Etudes sur la rivalité des ducs d'Orléans et de Bourgogne 1392–1407. Uppsala 1964.

13. *Stig Hadenius:* Fosterländsk unionspolitik. Majoritetspartiet, regeringen och unionsfrågan 1888–1899. (Patriotic Union Policy. The Majority Party, the Government, and the Issue of the Swedish-Norwegian Union 1888–1899.) E. Uppsala 1964.
14. *Stellan Dahlgren:* Karl X Gustav och reduktionen. (Charles X Gustavus and the Reduction of Crown Lands.) G. Uppsala 1964.
15. *Rolf Torstendahl:* Källkritik och vetenskapssyn i svensk historisk forskning 1820–1920. (Source Analysis and Rules for Scholarly History in Swedish Historical Research 1820–1920.) E. Uppsala 1964.
16. *Stefan Björklund:* Oppositionen vid 1823 års riksdag. Jordbrukskris och borgerlig liberalism. (Governmental Opposition at the 1823 Riksdag. Agrarian Crisis and Bourgeois Liberalism.) E. Uppsala 1964.
17. *Håkan Berggren & Göran B. Nilsson:* Liberal socialpolitik 1853–1884. Två studier. (Swedish Social Politics 1853–1884. I. For Justice and Security. II. Swedish Poor Relief Legislation 1853–71.) E. Uppsala 1965.
18. *Torsten Burgman:* Svensk opinion och diplomati under rysk-japanska kriget 1904–1905. (Swedish Opinion and Diplomacy during the Russo-Japanese War of 1904–1905.) E. Uppsala 1965.
19. *Eric Wärenstam:* Sveriges Nationella Ungdomsförbund och högern 1928–1934. (Sweden's National Youth League and the Conservative Party 1928–1934.) E. Stockholm 1965.
20. *Torgny Nevéus:* Ett betryggande försvar. Värnplikten och arméorganisationen i svensk politik 1880–1885. (The Issue of Defence in Swedish Politics between 1880 and 1885.) E. Uppsala 1965.
21. *Staffan Runestam:* Förstakammarhögern och rösträttsfrågan 1900–1907. (The Right Wing in the First Chamber and the Suffrage Issue 1900–1907.) F. Uppsala 1966.
22. *Stig Ekman:* Slutstriden om representationsreformen. (The Final Debate Leading to the Representation Reform of 1866.) E. Uppsala 1966.
23. *Gunnar Herrström:* 1927 års skolreform. En studie i svensk skolpolitik 1918–1927. (The School Reform of 1927. A Study of Swedish Educational Policy 1918–1927.) E. Stockholm 1966.
24. *Sune Åkerman:* Skattereformen 1810. Ett experiment med progressiv inkomstskatt. (The Swedish Taxation Reform 1810—An Experiment with Progressive Income Tax.) E. Stockholm 1967.
25. *Göran B. Nilsson:* Självstyrelsens problematik. Undersökningar i svensk landstingshistoria 1839–1928. (The Problem of Regional Government. Investigations in the History of the Swedish County Councils 1839–1928.) E. Stockholm 1967.
26. *Klaus-Richard Böhme:* Bremisch-verdische Staatsfinanzen 1645–1676. Die schwedische Krone als deutsche Landesherrin. Stockholm 1967.
27. *Gustaf Jonasson:* Karl XII:s polska politik 1702–1703. (Charles XII and his Policy 1702–1703.) G. Stockholm 1968.
28. *Hans Landberg:* Statsfinans och kungamakt. Karl X Gustav inför polska kriget. (State Finances and Royal Power. Charles X Gustavus Prepares for the Polish War.) G. Stockholm 1969.
29. *Rolf Torstendahl:* Mellan nykonservatism och liberalism. Idébrytningar inom högern och bondepartierna 1918–1934. (Between New Conservatism and Liberalism. The Ideological Discussions within the Party of the Right and the Farmers' Parties.) E. Stockholm 1969.
30. *Nils Runeby:* Den nya världen och den gamla. Amerikabild och emigrationsuppfattning i Sverige 1820–1860. (The New World and the Old. Opinion on America and Emigration in Sweden 1820–1860.) E. Stockholm 1969.
31. *Fred Nilsson:* Emigrationen från Stockholm till Nordamerika 1880–1893. En studie i urban utvandring. (Emigration from Stockholm to North America 1880–1893. A Study in Urban Emigration.) E. Stockholm 1970.
32. *Curt Johanson:* Lantarbetarna i Uppland 1918–1930. En studie i facklig taktik och organisation. (Agricultural Workers in Uppland 1918–1930. A Study of Trade Union Organization and Strategy.) E. Stockholm 1970.
33. *Arndt Öberg:* De yngre mössorna och deras utländska bundsförvanter 1765–1769. Med särskild hänsyn till de kommersiella och politiska förbindelserna med Storbritannien, Danmark och Preussen. (The Young Caps and their Foreign Allies 1765–69.) E. Stockholm 1970.
34. *Torgny Börjeson:* Metall 20 – fackför-

eningen och människan. (Metall 20–Trade Union and the Individual.) E. Stockholm 1971.

35. *Harald Runblom:* Svenska företag i Latinamerika. Etableringsmönster och förhandlingstaktik 1900–1940. (Swedish Enterprises in Latin America before the Second World War. The Course of their Establishment and their Tactics in Negotiations.) E. Stockholm 1971.
36. *Hans Landberg, Lars Ekholm, Roland Nordlund & Sven A. Nilsson:* Det kontinentala krigets ekonomi. Studier i krigsfinansiering under svensk stormaktstid. (The Economy of the Continental War. Studies of Swedish Military Finances during the Great Power Period.) G. Stockholm 1971.
37. *Sture Lindmark:* Swedish America 1914–1932. Studies in Ethnicity with Emphasis on Illinois and Minnesota. Stockholm 1971.
38. *Ulf Beijbom:* Swedes in Chicago. A Demographic and Social Study of the 1846–1880 Immigration. Växjö 1971.
39. *Staffan Smedberg:* Frälsebonderörelser i Halland och Skåne 1772–76. (The Peasant-Farmer Movements in Halland and Skåne in the Period 1772–76.) E. Stockholm 1972.
40. *Björn Rondahl:* Emigration, folkomflyttning och säsongarbete i ett sågverksdistrikt i södra Hälsingland 1865–1910. Söderala kommun med särskild hänsyn till Ljusne industrisamhälle. (Emigration, Internal Migration and Migratory Labour Movements in a Saw-Mill District in Southern Hälsingland 1865–1910.) E. Stockholm 1972.
41. *Ann-Sofie Kälvemark:* Reaktionen mot utvandringen. Emigrationsfrågan i svensk debatt och politik 1901–1904. (The Swedish Reaction against Emigration 1901–1904.) E. Stockholm 1972.
42. *Lars-Göran Tedebrand:* Västernorrland och Nordamerika 1875–1913. Utvandring och återinvandring. (Emigration from Västernorrland County to North America and Re-immigration to Västernorrland County.) E. Stockholm 1972.
43. *Ann-Marie Petersson:* Nyköping under frihetstiden. Borgare och byråkrater i den lokala politiken. (The Burghers and the Bureaucrats in Nyköping in the period 1719–1772.) E. Uppsala 1972.
44. *Göran Andolf:* Historien på gymnasiet. Undervisning och läroböcker 1820–1965. (The Teaching of History in Swedish Secondary Schools between 1820 and 1965.) E. Uppsala 1972.
45. *Jan Sundin:* Främmande studenter vid Uppsala universitet före andra världskriget. En studie i studentmigration. (Foreign Students at Uppsala University 1595–1939.) E. Uppsala 1973.
46. *Christer Öhman:* Nyköping och hertigdömet 1568–1622. (The Town of Nyköping and the Duchy of Södermanland, 1568–1622.) E. Uppsala 1973.
47. *Sune Åkerman, Ingrid Eriksson, David Gaunt, Anders Norberg, John Rogers & Kurt Ågren.* Aristocrats, Farmers and Proletarians. Essays in Swedish Demographic History. Stockholm 1973.
48. *Uno Westerlund:* Borgarsamhällets upplösning och självstyrelsens utveckling i Nyköping 1810–1880. (The Dissolution of the Burgess Society and the Growth of Self-Government in Nyköping, 1810–80.) E. Uppsala 1973.
49. *Sven Hedenskog:* Folkrörelserna i Nyköping 1880–1915. Uppkomst, social struktur och politisk aktivitet. (The Popular Movements in Nyköping 1880–1915. Rise, Social Structure and Political Activity.) E. Uppsala 1973.
50. *Berit Brattne:* Bröderna Larsson. En studie i svensk emigrantagentverksamhet under 1880-talet. (The Larsson Brothers. A Study of the Activity of Swedish Emigrant Agencies during the 1880's.) E. Stockholm 1973.
51. *Anders Kullberg:* Johan Gabriel Stenbock och reduktionen. Godspolitik och ekonomiförvaltning 1675–1705. (Johan Gabriel Stenbock and the Reduction of Crown Lands. Estate Management and Economic Administration 1675–1705.) G. Stockholm 1973.
52. *Gunilla Ingmar:* Monopol på nyheter. Ekonomiska och politiska aspekter på svenska och internationella nyhetsbyråers verksamhet 1870–1919. (Monopoly and News. Economic and Political Aspects of Swedish and International News Bureaus 1870–1919.) G. Stockholm 1973.
53. *Sven Lundkvist:* Politik, nykterhet och reformer. En studie i folkrörelsernas politiska verksamhet 1900–1920. (Politics, Temperance, and Reforms. A Study in the Political Activity of the Popular Movements 1900–1920.) E. Uppsala 1974.
54. *Kari Tarkiainen:* "Vår gamble Arffiende

Ryssen." Synen på Ryssland i Sverige 1595–1621 och andra studier kring den svenska Rysslandsbilden från tidigare stormaktstid. ("Our Old Arch-Enemy Russia." Views of Russia in Sweden 1595–1621.) G. Uppsala 1974.

55. *Bo Öhngren:* Folk i rörelse. Samhällsutveckling, flyttningsmönster och folkrörelser i Eskilstuna 1870–1900. (People on the Move. Social Development, Migration Patterns and Popular Movements in Eskilstuna 1870–1900.) E. Uppsala 1974.

56. *Lars Ekholm:* Svensk krigsfinansiering 1630–1631. (Swedish War Finances 1630–1631.) E. Uppsala 1974.

57. *Roland Nordlund:* Krig på avveckling. Sverige och tyska kriget 1633. (Disengaging from War. Sweden and the Germanic War 1633.) E. Uppsala 1974.

58. *Clara Nevéus:* Trälarna i landskapslagarnas samhälle. Danmark och Sverige. (Thralldom in Early Medieval Danish and Swedish Society.) G. Uppsala 1974.

59. *Bertil Johansson:* Social differentiering och kommunalpolitik. Enköping 1863–1919. (Social Structure and Local Politics in Enköping 1863–1919.) G. Uppsala 1974.

60. *Jan Lindroth:* Idrottens väg till folkrörelse. Studier i svensk idrottsrörelse till 1915. (Athletics Becomes a Popular Movement. Studies in the Swedish Athletics Movement up until 1915.) E. Uppsala 1974.

61. *Richard B. Lucas:* Charles August Lindbergh, Sr. A Case Study of Congressional Insurgency, 1906–1912. Uppsala 1974.

62. *Hans Norman:* Från Bergslagen till Nordamerika. Studier i emigrationsmönster, social rörlighet och demografisk struktur med utgångspunkt från Örebro län 1851–1915. (From Bergslagen to North America. Studies in Migration Pattern, Social Mobility and Demographic Structure on the Basis of Örebro County, 1851–1915.) E. Uppsala 1974.

63. *David Gaunt:* Utbildning till statens tjänst. En kollektivbiografi av stormaktstidens hovrättsauskultanter. (The Education and Social Position of Officials in Early Modern Sweden.) E. Uppsala 1974.

64. *Eibert Ernby:* Adeln och bondejorden. En studie rörande skattefrälset i Oppunda härad under 1600-talet. (The Nobility and Peasant Land. A Study of Peasant Land under Noble Control in 17th Century Oppunda.) G. Uppsala 1975.

65. *Bo Kronborg & Thomas Nilsson:* Stadsflyttare. Industrialisering, migration och social mobilitet med utgångspunkt från Halmstad, 1870–1910. (Urban Migrants. Industrialization, Migration and Social Mobility on the Basis of Halmstad, 1870–1910.) E. Uppsala 1975.

66. *Rolf Torstendahl:* Teknologins nytta. Motiveringar för det svenska tekniska utbildningsväsendets framväxt framförda av riksdagsmän och utbildningsadministratörer 1810–1870. (The Value of Technology. Reasons in Favor of Technological Education Given by Swedish Parliamentarians and Administrators 1810–1870.) E. Uppsala 1975.

67. *Allan Ranehök:* Centralmakt och Domsmakt. Studier kring den högsta rättskipningen i kung Magnus Erikssons länder 1319–1355. (State Power and Jurisdiction. Studies in High Jurisdiction in King Magnus Eriksson's Realm 1319–1355.) E. Uppsala 1975.

68. *James Cavallie:* Från fred till krig. De finansiella problemen kring krigsutbrottet år 1700. (From Peace to War. The Financial Problems in Sweden at the Beginning of the Great Northern War.) G. Uppsala 1975.

69. *Ingrid Åberg:* Förening och politik. Folkrörelsernas politiska aktivitet i Gävle under 1880-talet. (Associations and Politics. The Political Activity of Popular Movements in Gävle in the 1880s.) E. Uppsala 1975.

70. *Margareta Revera:* Gods och gård 1650–1680. Magnus Gabriel De la Gardies godsbildning och godsdrift i Västergötland. I. (A Magnate's Estate 1650–1680. M. G. De la Gardies Landprocurement and Estate Management in Västergötland. Part I.) E. Uppsala 1975.

71. *Aleksander Loit:* Kampen om feodalräntan. Reduktionen och domänpolitiken i Estland 1655–1710. I. (Struggle over Feudal rent. The Reduction and Demesne Policy in Estonia 1655–1710. Part I.) G. Uppsala 1975.

72. *Torgny Lindgren:* Banko- och Riksgäldsrevisionerna 1782–1807. »De redliga män, som bevakade ständers rätt». (Political control of the Bank of Sweden and the Swedish National Debt Office, 1782–1807.) E. Uppsala 1975.
73. *Rolf Torstendahl:* Dispersion of Engineers in a Transitional Society. Swedish Technicians 1860–1940. Uppsala 1975.
74. *Harald Runblom & Hans Norman* (eds.): From Sweden to America. A History of the Migration. A Collective Work of The Uppsala Migration Research Project. Uppsala 1976.